Digital Finance and Regulatory Competition

International Banking and Finance Law Series

VOLUME 39

Series Editors

Professor Joseph Norton, Professor Ross Buckley and Professor Douglas Arner.

Subjects

Topical issues in international banking and financial services law, such as regulatory responses to the global financial crisis or regulation of alternative investment funds

Objective & Readership

To provide authoritative analysis of trends and complex subjects for academics, regulators and practitioners involved in international banking and financial services law.

The titles published in this series are listed at the end of this volume.

Digital Finance and Regulatory Competition

Regulating Distributed Ledger Technology-Based Financial Products and Services

Lucien J. van Romburg

Wolters Kluwer

Published by:
Kluwer Law International B.V.
PO Box 316
2400 AH Alphen aan den Rijn
The Netherlands
E-mail: lrs-sales@wolterskluwer.com
Website: www.wolterskluwer.com/en/solutions/kluwerlawinternational

Sold and distributed by:
Wolters Kluwer Legal & Regulatory U.S.
920 Links Avenue
Landisville, PA 17538
United States of America
E-mail: customer.service@wolterskluwer.com

ISBN 978-94-035-4518-9

e-Book: ISBN 978-94-035-4528-8
web-PDF: ISBN 978-94-035-4538-7

To my loving grandmothers, Mary-Anne and Magdalene

About the Author

Lucien J. van Romburg is a Postdoctoral Research Fellow at the Faculty of Law & Justice, University of New South Wales, Sydney under the Australian Research Council Laureate Project 'The Financial Data Revolution: Seizing the Benefits, Controlling the Risks'. His research interests lie at the intersection of law, finance, technology, and development, focusing on the regulation of financial products and services underlined by novel technologies, and their broader impact on society. Prior to completing his PhD at the University of Hong Kong, he read for the Bachelor of Civil Law at the University of Oxford as a UK Commonwealth Scholarship award recipient. He also holds an LLB (*summa laude*), with the Cliffe Dekker Hofmeyr Gold Medal for outstanding academic performance, from the University of the Western Cape. He is an admitted Attorney (South Africa) and has practised financial services regulation and commercial litigation in Cape Town, Johannesburg, and London.

Table of Contents

About the Author	vii
List of Abbreviations	xv
List of Figures	xix
List of Tables	xxi
Acknowledgements	xxiii
CHAPTER 1	
Introduction	1
1.1 The Intersection of Fintech and Regulatory Competition	1
1.2 The Emergence of Fintech	3
1.3 Theory of Regulatory Competition	6
1.4 The Case for International Regulatory Competition	8
1.4.1 The Economic Case	8
1.4.2 The Social Case	10
1.5 International Regulatory Competition: The Dog That Never Barks?	13
1.6 Research Design	14
1.7 Chapter Summaries	16
CHAPTER 2	
DLT: From ICO to Crypto	19
2.1 The Emergence and Impact of DLT	19
2.2 Demystifying DLT	24
2.3 The Core Features of DLT	28
2.3.1 Distributed and Decentralised Ledger	29
2.3.2 P2P Network	31

2.3.3 Consensus Mechanism 32
2.3.3.1 Proof-of-Work 33
2.3.3.2 Proof-of-Stake 34
2.3.3.3 Practical Byzantine Fault Tolerance 35
2.3.4 Cryptography 36
2.4 Types of DLT 37
2.4.1 Blockchain 38
2.4.2 Hashgraph 39
2.4.3 Directed Acyclic Graph 39
2.4.4 Holochain 40
2.4.5 Tempo (Radix) 41
2.5 DLT Applications and Use Cases in Financial Services 42
2.5.1 A Medium of Exchange 44
2.5.2 Funding Mechanism 47
2.5.2.1 Cryptocurrency Exchanges 47
2.5.2.2 Initial Coin Offerings 49
2.5.3 Payment Rail 52

CHAPTER 3
Regulatory Competition: A (De)Construction 55
3.1 Introduction 55
3.2 Defining Regulatory Competition 56
3.3 Framing Regulatory Competition 58
3.3.1 Environmental Context 59
3.3.1.1 Intra-national Regulatory Competition 59
3.3.1.2 International Regulatory Competition 60
3.3.2 Regulatory Competition Direction 61
3.3.2.1 Horizontal 62
3.3.2.2 Vertical 62
3.3.3 System of Government 63
3.3.4 Regulatory Competition Actors 65
3.3.4.1 Primary Actors 66
3.3.4.1.1 Local Governments 66
3.3.4.1.2 Regional Governments 68
3.3.4.1.3 Government Departments 68
3.3.4.1.4 National Governments 69
3.3.4.1.5 Sovereign Nation-States 70
3.3.4.2 Secondary Actors 71
3.3.4.2.1 Firms 72
3.3.4.2.2 Voters 74
3.3.4.3 Tertiary Actors 75
3.3.4.3.1 Non-governmental Organisations 75
3.3.4.3.2 Interest Groups 77
3.3.5 Regulatory Competition Means 78

3.3.6 Regulatory Competition Drivers 81
3.3.6.1 Capital Investment 82
3.3.6.2 Human Capital 84
3.4 Regulatory Competition Outcomes 85
3.4.1 Tiebout Equilibrium 85
3.4.2 Race to the Bottom 87
3.4.3 Race to the Top 92

CHAPTER 4
Regulating DLT Financial Products and Services: The SAR of Hong Kong 99
4.1 Introduction 99
4.1.1 Input: 2008-2017 102
4.1.1.1 Competition Policy and the Role of Fintech 102
4.1.1.2 Discussion 107
4.1.1.2.1 Competition Policy 107
4.1.1.2.2 Significant Policy Themes 108
4.1.2 Process: 2015-2018 109
4.1.2.1 Developing a Regulatory Approach to DLT 109
4.1.2.2 Discussion 115
4.1.2.2.1 Regulatory Approach 115
4.1.2.2.2 Underlying Principles 115
4.1.3 Output: 2017-2019 117
4.1.3.1 Regulatory Rules 117
4.1.3.1.1 Initial Coin and STOs 117
4.1.3.1.2 Fund Distribution 118
4.1.3.1.3 Futures Contracts and Investment Products 119
4.1.3.1.4 Portfolio Management 121
4.1.3.1.5 Trading Platforms 123
4.1.3.2 Discussion 124
4.1.3.2.1 Regulatory Framework 125
4.1.3.2.2 Central Components 125
4.1.3.2.3 Regulatory Approach 126
4.1.4 Feedback 2019-2022 127
4.1.4.1 Trading Platforms 127
4.1.4.2 Virtual Asset Service Providers 128
4.1.4.3 Stablecoins 129
4.1.4.4 Fund Distribution 130
4.1.4.5 Discussion 130
4.1.4.5.1 Updated Regulatory Response 131
4.1.4.5.2 Competition Policy Influence 131

CHAPTER 5
Regulating DLT Financial Products and Services: The City of London, United Kingdom 133
5.1 Introduction 133

5.1.1 Input 136
5.1.1.1 Competition Policy and the Role of Fintech 137
5.1.1.2 Discussion 142
5.1.1.2.1 Competition Policy 143
5.1.1.2.2 Significant Policy Themes 144
5.1.2 Process: 2014-2017 145
5.1.2.1 Developing a Regulatory Approach to DLT 145
5.1.2.2 Discussion 153
5.1.2.2.1 Regulatory Approach 153
5.1.2.2.2 Underlying Principles 153
5.1.3 Output: 2019-2020 155
5.1.3.1 Regulatory Rules 155
5.1.3.1.1 Perimeter Regulatory Guidance on Cryptoassets 155
5.1.3.1.2 Prohibiting the Sale to Retail Clients of Investment Products That Reference Cryptoassets 157
5.1.3.2 Discussion 158
5.1.3.2.1 Regulatory Framework 158
5.1.3.2.2 Central Components 158
5.1.3.2.3 Regulatory Approach 159
5.1.4 Feedback 160
5.1.4.1 Regulatory Rules 160
5.1.4.1.1 Money Laundering and Regulatory Arbitrage 160
5.1.4.1.2 Cryptoasset Promotions 161
5.1.4.1.3 Stablecoins 163
5.1.4.2 Discussion 165
5.1.4.2.1 Updated Regulatory Response 165
5.1.4.2.2 Competition Policy Influence 167

CHAPTER 6
Regulating DLT Financial Products and Services: The State of New York, United States 169
6.1 Introduction 169
6.1.1 Input: 2008-2013 171
6.1.1.1 Competition Policy and the Role of Fintech 171
6.1.1.2 Discussion 174
6.1.1.2.1 Competition Policy 174
6.1.1.2.2 Significant Policy Themes 175
6.1.2 Process: 2013-2014 176
6.1.2.1 Developing a Regulatory Approach to DLT 176
6.1.2.2 Discussion 182
6.1.2.2.1 Regulatory Approach 182
6.1.2.2.2 Underlying Principles 182

6.1.3 Output: 2014-2015 184
6.1.3.1 BitLicense Regulatory Framework 184
6.1.3.2 Discussion 184
6.1.3.2.1 Regulatory Framework 185
6.1.3.2.2 Central Components 185
6.1.3.2.3 Regulatory Approach 186
6.1.4 Feedback 187
6.1.4.1 Market Manipulation and Fraud 187
6.1.4.2 New Virtual Currency Listing Regime 187
6.1.4.3 Conditional BitLicense 189
6.1.4.4 BitLicense Application Procedures 190
6.1.4.5 Stablecoin Guidance 190
6.1.4.6 Discussion 192
6.1.4.6.1 Updated Regulatory Response 192
6.1.4.6.2 Competition Policy Influence 193

CHAPTER 7
The Dog That Never Barks: Regulatory Competition Between International Financial Centres 195
7.1 Introduction 195
7.1.1 Input 196
7.1.1.1 Converging Patterns 197
7.1.1.2 Diverging Patterns 198
7.1.1.3 External Factors 199
7.1.2 Process 199
7.1.2.1 Converging Patterns 200
7.1.2.2 Diverging Patterns 201
7.1.3 Output 203
7.1.3.1 Converging Patterns 203
7.1.3.2 Diverging Patterns 204
7.1.4 Feedback 205
7.1.4.1 Converging Patterns 206
7.1.4.2 Diverging Patterns 208
7.2 Did Hong Kong, London, and New York Engage in Regulatory Competition with Each Other? 209
7.2.1 The Significance of Competition Policy Agenda 210
7.2.2 Analogous Regulatory Treatment of DLT Offerings 212
7.2.3 Setting Themselves Apart: Competitive Advantage 214
7.3 Lessons Distilled: A View to the Future 217
7.3.1 The Role of Competition Policy: Bark Worse than Its Bite 218
7.3.2 Competitive Advantage: The Last Holdout? 220
7.3.3 Quick to React, Slow to Legislate: Technology Neutrality 223

CHAPTER 8
Conclusion 229

Bibliography 233

Index 243

List of Abbreviations

5AMLD	Fifth Anti-money Laundering Directive
AML	Anti-money Laundering
ASTRI	Applied Sciences and Technology Research Institute
BIS	Bank for International Settlements
BoE	Bank of England
BSI	British Standards Institution
CBDC	Central Bank Digital Currency
CIS	Collective Investment Schemes
CLC	City of London Corporation
COBS	Conduct of Business Sourcebook
CPA	Certified Public Accountant
CTF	Counter-Terrorism Financing
DAG	Directed Acyclic Graph
DeFI	Decentralised Finance
DIT	Department for International Trade
DLT	Distributed Ledger Technology
ECB	European Central Bank
ECF	Enhanced Competency Framework
ETN	Exchange-Traded Note
EU	European Union
FATF	Financial Action Task Force
FCA	Financial Conduct Authority
FDI	Foreign Direct Investment
Fintech	Financial Technology
FPC	Financial Policy Committee
FPO	Financial Promotions Order

FRB	Federal Reserve Board
FSB	Financial Stability Board
FSDC	Financial Services Development Council
FSMA	Financial Services and Markets Act 2000
FSTB	Financial Services and Treasury Bureau
GDP	Gross Domestic Product
GFC	Global Financial Crisis
HKMA	Hong Kong Monetary Authority
HOC	House of Commons
HOL	House of Lords
ICO	Initial Coin Offering
IMF	International Monetary Fund
IOSCO	International Organization of Securities Commissions
KYC	Know-Your-Customer
LEP	London Enterprise Panel
NGO	Non-governmental Organisation
NRRS	Non-readily Realisable Securities
NYBD	NY State Banking Department
NYDFS	New York Department of Financial Services
NYESD	NY State Empire State Development Corporation
OECD	Organisation for Economic Co-operation and Development
P2P	Peer-to-Peer
PKI	Public Key Cryptography
POS	Proof-of-Stake
POW	Proof-of-Work
PRA	Prudential Regulation Authority
PSR	Payment Services Regulation
PTPA	Peer-to-Peer Agreements
RAO	Financial Services and Markets Act 2000 (Regulated Activities) Order 2001
RTGS	Real-Time Gross Settlement
SAR	Special Administrative Region
SFC	Securities and Futures Commission of HK
SFC COC	Securities and Futures Commission Code of Conduct
SFO	Securities and Futures Ordinance
SME	Small-to-Medium Enterprises
STO	Security Token Offering
SUNY	State University of NY
UKTI	UK Trade and Investment
UN	United Nations

US	United States
WB	World Bank
WEF	World Economic Forum

List of Figures

Figure 7.1	Input Analyses of Governmental Actions and Behaviours for the Time Period 2008-2017
Figure 7.2	Process Analyses of Governmental Actions and Behaviours for the Time Period 2013-2020
Figure 7.3	Output Analyses of Governmental Actions and Behaviours for the Time Period 2014-2020
Figure 7.4	Feedback Analyses of Governmental Actions and Behaviours for the Time Period 2014-2022

List of Tables

Table 3.1	Summary of the Essential Elements Underlining Regulatory Competition
Table 3.2	Summary of the Regulatory Competition Framework Observed in the Literature
Table 7.1	Regulatory Competition Framework Applied to RC Hypothesis Analysis

Acknowledgements

I would like to express my gratitude to Professor Douglas W Arner and Professor Ross P Buckley for their invaluable guidance and continuous encouragement of my academic pursuits. I would also like to thank the University of New South Wales, Sydney and the University of Hong Kong for their support in the publication of this book and the team at Wolters Kluwer and Newgen for the assistance in polishing this manuscript. Last, and most importantly, I would like to convey my deep appreciation for and gratefulness to my loved ones for their endless cheerleading.

CHAPTER 1

Introduction

This chapter sets the premise for this book by highlighting the importance of the intersection of Fintech and regulatory competition. To this end, it provides a brief exposition of the foundational concepts which are pertinent to the reading of this book. It also provides a description of the research design employed and a summary of the main conclusions drawn from the research which forms the subject-matter of this book. Finally, this chapter provides a brief description of the subsequent chapters of this book.

1.1 THE INTERSECTION OF FINTECH AND REGULATORY COMPETITION

History is scattered with tales of ancient rivalries vying for scarce resources and subduing foes posing threats to the retention of power. While the violent and callous intent with which this competition played out in the past has somewhat led to more refined sensibilities in the modern age, the tussle for limited resources and ultimate power remains a long-standing feature of human behaviour. Governments, like people, compete against each other to obtain foreign investment and human capital, in a bid to successfully meet their myriad economic, political, and social agendas. In rules-based regulatory competition,[1] governments formulate rules with the intention of attracting businesses and people to their domains. During this process, governments direct the limited resources to themselves and thus away from their competitors.

As studied in an array of fields, and popularised by the so-called regulatory races, regulatory competition is a prominent feature of our world.[2]

1. Also referred to as 'RC' interchangeably in this book.
2. Andrew P Morris, 'The Role of Offshore Financial Centers in Regulatory Competition' (2008) University of Illinois Law and Economics Research Paper No. LE07-032, 2.

In the more recent part of the twenty-first Century, regulatory competition has taken on a new dimension in the face of increased fragmentation and the rapid advancement of digital finance, as bolstered by the emergence of novel technologies. Globally, legal and regulatory frameworks governing pertinent sectors and industries are experiencing accelerated fragmentation. Christine Lagarde, President of the ECB, noted in 2023 that the world 'is witnessing a fragmentation of the global economy into competing blocs, with each bloc trying to pull as much of the rest of the world closer to its respective strategic interests and shared values'.[3] This global economy fragmentation naturally filters through to decision-making by government authorities responsible for formulating the rules which underpin their legal and regulatory systems. Bearing in mind this global context, the role of international regulatory competition between sovereign nation-states is now more relevant than ever.

At the same time, the rapid advancement of technology and accelerated digitisation serve as hallmarks of human development over the last few decades. The role of Fintech, in particular, as a tool for achieving a multitude of economic, political, and social aims, cannot be overstated. Since 2016, and in the US alone, the total market capitalisation of digital assets increased from around USD 14 billion to over USD 3 trillion in 2022, before its collapse to less than USD 1 trillion in 2023.[4] Further, in 2022, the global cryptocurrency market alone was valued at USD 4.1 billion, with projections anticipating a compound annual growth rate of 11.4% between 2023 and 2030, and a valuation of USD 9.8 billion by the end of the decade.[5] The monetary system landscape is evolving too, with 130 jurisdictions, representing 98% of the global domestic gross product, exploring a CBDC at the time of the publication of this book.[6] The emergence of DLT, which ultimately spurred the proliferation of digital assets, was a watershed moment for technological advancement and presents a ripe opportunity for governments to defend their competing claims for resources. Enter long-standing global financial centre rivals: Hong Kong (HK), London, and New York (NY).

These traditional global financial hubs have pioneered the development of Fintech and the rules which govern the financial products and services it underlines. HK is considered the de facto commercial gateway to Mainland China and has established itself as a preeminent Fintech hub globally.[7] London has been lauded for pioneering innovative regulatory initiatives, most notably through establishing the

3. Christine Lagarde, 'Central Banks in a Fragmenting World' (Web page, 17 April 2023), https://www.ecb.europa.eu/press/key/date/2023/html/ecb.sp230417~9f8d34fbd6.en.html.
4. James Eyers, 'How Crypto is Forcing Banks, Funds Towards New Digital Asset Markets' (Financial Review, 13 October 2023), https://www.afr.com/companies/financial-services/how-crypto-is-forcing-banks-funds-towards-new-digital-asset-markets-20231013-p5ec0c and The White House, 'Executive Order on Ensuring Responsible Development of Digital Assets' (9 March 2023), https://www.whitehouse.gov/briefing-room/presidential-actions/2022/03/09/executive-order-on-ensuring-responsible-development-of-digital-assets/.
5. Fairfield Market Research, 'Cryptocurrency Market' (November 2023), https://www.fairfieldmarketresearch.com/report/cryptocurrency-market.
6. Atlantic Council, 'Central Bank Digital Currency Challenge', https://www.atlanticcouncil.org/cbdctracker/.
7. *See* FintechHK, 'Fact Sheet: Hong Kong FinTech Landscape' (22 January 2024), https://www.hongkong-fintech.hk/en/insights/news/news-2024/fact-sheet-hong-kong-fintech-landscape/index.html.

first-ever regulatory sandbox.[8] Finally, NY, as the seat of the largest stock exchange, helmed the implementation of the first comprehensive digital currency licensing framework in the form of the 'BitLicense'.[9] The marked effort and resources expended by these governments evidence the significance of Fintech for the achievement of their continued economic expansion, together with ancillary socio-political aims.

Accordingly, the intersection between the regulation of financial products and services underlined by DLT[10] and international regulatory competition is prime for further debate and discussion, particularly as there are very few studies covering this issue. This book provides a comprehensive analysis of the extent to which regulatory competition has influenced the formulation of the rules which govern DLT-based financial products and services in the world's major financial centres. In doing so, a clear and cohesive framework is developed for understanding regulatory competition, utilising a narrative lens based on a comparative study of legal, regulatory and policy instruments. The result is a thought-provoking text which distils unique observations regarding how financial products and services underlined by DLT are regulated, and the potential implications for the future regulation of other novel technologies in the financial services industry.

1.2 THE EMERGENCE OF FINTECH

The mingling of finance and technology is by no means sui generis, but a symbiotic union forged over several decades.[11] In recent years, this union has solidified with accelerated advances in technology, and an increasingly interconnected global economy. This has led to the emergence and popularisation of Fintech, commonly referred to as Fintech.[12] No universally accepted definition has been fashioned for Fintech.[13] However, Fintech generally encompasses financial products and services offered through automated means using a digital online platform.[14] Fintech Offerings are often underlined by burgeoning forms of technology which offer the potential to transform the financial services industry.[15] It may have been easy to dismiss Fintech as

8. Giulio Cornelli et al., 'Regulatory Sandboxes and Fintech Funding: Evidence from the UK' (November 2020) Bank for International Settlements (BIS) Working Papers No. 901, https://www.bis.org/publ/work901.pdf.
9. New York Department of Financial Services (NYDFS), 'NY DFS Releases Proposed Bitlicense Regulatory Framework For Virtual Currency Firms' (17 July 2014), https://www.dfs.ny.gov/reports_and_publications/press_releases/pr1407171.
10. Also referred to as 'DLT Offerings' in this book.
11. Douglas W Arner, Janos N Barberis & Ross P Buckley, 'The Evolution of FinTech: A New Post-Crisis Paradigm?' (2016) 47 Georgetown Journal of International Law 1271 https://doi.org/10.2139/ssrn.2676553.
12. Dirk Zetzsche et al., 'Regulating a Revolution: From Regulatory Sandboxes to Smart Regulation' (2017) University of Luxembourg 7, https://www.researchgate.net/publication/319579261_Regulating_a_Revolution_From_Regulatory_Sandboxes_to_Smart_Regulation.
13. Patrick Schueffel, 'Taming the Beast: A Scientific Definition of Fintech' (2016) 32 Journal of Innovation Management 1 https://doi.org/10.24840/2183-0606_004.004_0004.
14. Also referred to as 'Fintech Offerings' in this book.
15. International Organisation of Securities Commission, 'Research Report on Financial Technologies' (2017) 2, 5, https://www.iosco.org/library/pubdocs/pdf/IOSCOPD554.pdf.

just another technology bubble during the initial days of its popularisation. However, according to Schueffel, Fintech's longevity is evidenced by the wide-spread use of technologies, particularly those relating to online sales and data capture.[16] Fintech Offerings have the potential to advance economic growth and financial inclusion for those currently excluded from the formal banking system through, for example, lowering the cost of financial services.[17] In 2016, 2 billion people and 200 million businesses in emerging economies were reported as having limited access to financial services, including access to credit and savings accounts.[18] Significant progress has been made since then with the WB reporting in 2021 that 1.4 billion around the world remain excluded from the formal economy, through their lack of access to a banking account.[19] Fintech and smartphones, owned by a large majority of those financially excluded, have played a significant role in closing the gap between those financially included and excluded from the formal banking system.[20]

The advancement of financial inclusion as an integral international policy objective has also played a role in bridging this gap. For example, financial inclusion is an enabler of several UN's 2030 Sustainable Development Goals.[21] Research conducted by McKinsey has confirmed that the pervasive use of Fintech Offerings has the potential to increase the GDP of all emerging economies by 6% by 2025. India and Nigeria, for example, could potentially increase their GDP by 10%-12% bearing in mind the large number of its citizens excluded financially, and the increased use of digital payments. In addition, more developing economies, including the People's Republic of China (Mainland China), could potentially increase their GDP by 4%-5%, leading to a significant boost to its economy.[22]

The rapid development and use of Fintech have also been noted in advanced economies. The Global Fintech Rankings 2021 have placed Mainland China, the UK, and the US as 15, 2, and 1, respectively.[23] The UK and the US are also regarded as

16. Patrick Schueffel, 'Taming the Beast: A Scientific Definition of Fintech' (2016) 32 Journal of Innovation Management 50 https://doi.org/10.24840/2183-0606_004.004_0004.
17. *See* Alliance for Financial Inclusion, 'Defining Financial Inclusion', Guidance Note No. 28 (2017).
18. McKinsey Global Institute, 'Digital Finance for All: Powering Inclusive Growth in Emerging Economies' (2016) 8.
19. World Bank, 'Financial Inclusion: Financial Inclusion is a Key Enabler to Reducing Poverty and Boosting Prosperity' (13 September 2022), https://www.worldbank.org/en/topic/financialinclusion/overview#:~:text=Great%20strides%20have%20been%20made,adult%20population%20had%20an%20account.
20. World Bank Group, 'Finance Inclusion on the Rise, But Gap Remains, Global Findex Database Shows' (19 April 2018), https://www.worldbank.org/en/news/press-release/2018/04/19/financial-inclusion-on-the-rise-but-gaps-remain-global-findex-database-shows.
21. UNCDF, 'Financial Inclusion and the SDGs', https://www.uncdf.org/financial-inclusion-and-the-sdgs.
22. McKinsey Global Institute, 'Digital Finance for All: Powering Inclusive Growth in Emerging Economies' (2016) 8, 11 and 20, https://www.mckinsey.com/~/media/McKinsey/Featured%20Insights/Employment%20and%20Growth/How%20digital%20finance%20could%20boost%20growth%20in%20emerging%20economies/MGI-Digital-Finance-For-All-Executive-summary-September-2016.ashx.
23. Global Fintech Rankings Report (*Findexable*, 2021) 21, https://findexable.com/wp-content/uploads/2021/06/Global-Fintech-Rankings-2021-v1-23-June-21.pdf.

having the most advanced ecosystems for Fintech based on their blend of innovative regulation and traditional finance structures, respectively.[24] This is supported by research which has noted that Fintech start-ups are more prone to flourishing in advanced economies based on their stable economies, and more widely accessible venture capital funding.[25] The impact of Fintech on all economies, and the commensurate economic and social benefits, can therefore not be overstated.[26]

The pervasive use of Fintech Offerings underlined by DLT also has the potential to increase efficiencies through the reduction in both time and costs to execute payment transactions. Generally, DLT encompasses a digital database shared by a geographically dispersed network of computers which are used to verify and record transactions.[27] The technology has been developed on the basis of several groundbreaking innovations including: (i) double-entry accounting;[28] (ii) the Internet;[29] (iii) P2P file-sharing networks;[30] and (iv) public-key cryptography.[31] As a general-purpose technology, DLT may be used to develop applications in multiple industries including cyber security, health care, manufacturing, real estate, retail, tourism, and transport.[32] The financial service industry, in particular, has ploughed significant investment into the development of DLT use cases, particularly its use as a payment rail and source of funding. The pervasive adoption of DLT in the financial services industry has also contributed to advancing the international policy goal of financial inclusion.

24. The Global Fintech Hub Report, 'The Future of Finance is Emerging: New Hubs, New Landscapes' (2018) 7, https://www.jbs.cam.ac.uk/wp-content/uploads/2020/08/2018-ccaf-global-fintech-hub-report-eng.pdf.
25. Christian Haddad & Lars Hornuf, 'The Emergence of the Global Fintech Market: Economic and Technological Determinants' (2019) 53 Small Bus Econ 92 https://doi.org/10.1007/s11187-018-9991-x.
26. Ross Buckley & Louise Malady, 'The New Regulatory Frontier: Building Consumer Demand for Digital Financial Services' (2015) 132(1) The Banking Law Journal 35 https://doi.org/10.2139/ssrn.2478482.
27. Julie Maupin, 'Mapping the Global Legal Landscape of Blockchain and other Distributed Ledger Technologies' (2017), https://papers.ssrn.com/sol3/papers.cfm?abstract_id=2930077; Advait Deshpande et al., 'Distributed Ledger Technologies/Blockchain: Challenges, Opportunities and Prospects for Standards' (*BSI*, 2017), https://www.bsigroup.com/LocalFiles/zh-tw/InfoSec-newsletter/No201706/download/BSI_Blockchain_DLT_Web.pdf and D Richard Kuhn, Jeff Voas & Dylan Yaga, 'Rethinking Distributed Ledger Technology' (*IEEE Computer*, February 2019) https://www.researchgate.net/publication/331260506_Rethinking_Distributed_Ledger_Technology.
28. *See* Murphy Smith, 'Luca Pacioli: The Father of Accounting' (SSRN, 2013) https://papers.ssrn.com/sol3/papers.cfm?abstract_id=2320658.
29. *See* Jonathan Hogeback, 'Who Invented the Internet' (*Britannica*), https://www.britannica.com/story/who-invented-the-internet.
30. *See* Paratii, 'A Brief History of P2P Content Distribution, in 10 Major Steps' (*Medium*, 26 October 2017), https://medium.com/paratii/a-brief-history-of-p2p-content-distribution-in-10-major-steps-6d6733d25122.
31. *See* Primavera De Filippi & Aaron Wright, 'Blockchains, Bitcoins and Decentralized Computing Platforms' in Primavera De Filippi & Aaron Wright (eds), *Blockchain and the Law* (Harvard University Press 2018).
32. *See* Calastone, 'White Paper: Distributed Ledger Technology' (2019), https://www.theia.org/sites/default/files/2019-10/DLT%20and%20funds%20white%20paper.pdf.

1.3 THEORY OF REGULATORY COMPETITION

In an increasingly globalised world, jurisdictions, akin to companies, direct many of their development strategies towards the aim of wealth creation. How exactly jurisdictions plan to achieve this objective in the face of globalised competitive pressures has been the subject of much debate academically.[33] Generally, competition is the process in which rival firms aim to expand their financial returns through sales and profit generation and is often described as the driving force behind markets.[34] According to Podobnik et al., levels of productivity, as determined by institutions and policies, can evidence a jurisdiction's level of competitiveness.[35] Even in the face of increased global competitive pressures, some jurisdictions have responded disinterestedly to the role which competition can play in advancing their economies, such as increasing investment and wealth. Competition is also key to developing growth, productivity and innovation which reduces poverty levels and creates wealth.[36] To this end, it has been reported that advanced economies are considered to be more competitive than emerging economies.[37] Despite these studies, there is evidence that emerging economies are becoming more concerned about global competition, and the positive benefits which it may yield. The Commission for Africa, for example, has highlighted the significant role which competition policy may play in developing investment opportunities.[38] The Asian Development Bank has also highlighted the significance of competition policy in creating the fertile business environments required for progressing economic advancement.[39]

Competition policy, and the objectives, actions, and behaviours associated therewith, are often explained with reference to the theory of regulatory competition. This theory generally encompasses the process through which jurisdictions compete against each other for identified resources by using specific means at their disposal to direct such competition Regulatory competition has been lauded for its potential to motivate complacent regulatory authorities to take appropriate action in their

33. *See* Richard HK Vietor, *How Countries Compete: Strategy, Structure, and Government in the Global Economy* (Harvard Business School Press 2007).
34. Nick Godfrey, 'Why Is Competition Important for Growth and Poverty Reduction' (27-28 March 2008) Paper Presented at the OECD Global Forum on International Investment, Session 1.3.: Competition policy, 3.
35. Boris Podobnik, et al., 'The Competitiveness Versus the Wealth of a Country' (2012) 678 Science Reports 1.
36. Nick Godfrey, 'Why Is Competition important for Growth and Poverty Reduction' (27-28 March 2008) Paper Presented at the OECD Global Forum on International Investment, Session 1.3.: Competition policy, 5.
37. Boris Podobnik, et al., 'The Competitiveness Versus the Wealth of a Country' (2012) 678 Science Reports 2.
38. Commission for Africa, 'Our Common Interest: Report of the Commission for Africa' (2005) 43, https://reliefweb.int/report/world/our-common-interest-report-commission-africa.
39. Asian Development Outlook, 'Promoting Competition for Long-term Development' (2005), https://www.adb.org/publications/asian-development-outlook-2005-promoting-competition-long-term-development. *See also* Asian Development Outlook, 'Transcending the Middle-Income Challenge' (2017).

supervisory roles.[40] Further, Macey has argued that regulatory competition can have a chilling effect on special interest group behaviours in their attempts to influence regulatory outcomes, ultimately aimed at transferring wealth to themselves, and away from institutions less mobilised.[41]

However, regulatory competition has been criticised for creating unintended welfare-reducing outcomes, primarily in the form of regulatory arbitrage and regulatory races. For example, in company law, regulatory arbitrage takes place when firms choose or later decide to move their seat of incorporation,[42] often driven by the indirect and direct costs of incorporation.[43] However, according to Fleischer regulatory arbitrage is 'a perfectly legal planning technique used to avoid taxes, accounting rules, securities disclosure, and other regulatory costs'.[44] In this context, Klöhn and Ringe have argued that regulatory arbitrage will result in jurisdictions engaging in defensive regulatory competition, such as by adjusting their company law rules in an effort to avoid losing customers.[45] Regulatory arbitrage is therefore only possible with the existence of a balance of variances, differences and similarities, in laws and regulations, which a complex economy requires.[46]

The theory of regulatory arbitrage therefore assumes that governments are predominantly concerned with increasing local economic growth and employment. In aiming to achieve these objectives, jurisdictions may therefore respond to changes in laws and regulations in other jurisdictions by weakening their own rules and regulations[47] to attract capital investment and highly skilled labour.[48] The downward pressure leading to the weakening of rules and regulations in different jurisdictions for the purposes of outbidding has been coined the 'Race to the Bottom' or the 'Delaware

40. The terms RC Hypothesis and RC are used interchangeably. However, when the context calls for it, 'RC Hypothesis' refers to the specific theory of RC, and 'RC' refers to the RC Hypothesis in operation between jurisdictions.
41. Anna M Dionne & Jonathan R Macey, 'Offshore Finance and Onshore Market: Racing to the Bottom or Moving Toward Efficient?' in Andrew P Morriss et al. (eds), *Offshore Financial Centers and Regulatory Competition* (AEI Press 2010).
42. Lars Hornuf & Julia Linder, 'End of Regulatory Competition in European Company Law' (2014) Andrássy Working Paper Series No. 33, 6.
43. *See* Marco M Becht, Colin Meyer & Hannes Wagner, 'Where Do Firms Incorporate? Deregulation and the Cost of Entry' (2008) 14 Journal of Corporate Finance https://doi.org/10.1016/j.jcorpfin.2008.04.002.
44. Victor Fleischer, 'Regulatory Arbitrage' (2010) 89 Texas Law Review 229 https://doi.org/10.2139/ssrn.1567212.
45. Lars Klöhn, 'Supranationale Rechtsformen im Europäischen Gesellschaftsrecht' (2012) 76 RabelsZ 300 and Wolf-Georg Ringe, 'Corporate Mobility in the European Union: A Flash in the Plan' (2013) 10 European Company and Financial Law Review 230 https://doi.org/10.1515/ecfr-2013-0230.
46. Claudio M Radaelli, 'The Puzzle of Regulatory Competition' (2014) 24 Journal of Public Policy 8 https://doi.org/10.1017/s0143814x04000017 and Frank H Easterbrook, 'The Race for the Bottom in Corporate Governance' (2009) 95 Virginia Law Review 689. *See* Ségolène Barbou des Places, 'Taking Legal Rules into Consideration: EU Asylum Policy and Regulatory Competition' (2004) 24 Journal of Public Policy 75-98 https://doi.org/10.1017/s0143814x04000042.
47. Bruce G Carruthers & Naomi R Lamoreaux, 'Regulatory Races: The Effects of Jurisdictional Competition' (2016) 54(1) Journal of Economic Literature 55 https://doi.org/10.1257/jel.54.1.52.
48. Claudio M Radaelli, 'The Puzzle of Regulatory Competition' (2014) 24 Journal of Public Policy 8 https://doi.org/10.1017/s0143814x04000017.

Effect'.[49] The Race to the Bottom naturally resulted in the development of an alternative school of thought, the 'Race to the Top'. In this race, jurisdictions, instead of relaxing legal and regulatory standards, opt to enforce standards of a stricter and more onerous nature as a result of their interconnected economic relationship with other jurisdictions.[50] In these instances, governments, through their citizens, may feel pressured to enforce legal and regulatory standards similar to those of their neighbouring governments.[51] The clearest expression of the Race to the Top was evidenced when US states emulated California's decision to raise emission standards.[52]

1.4 THE CASE FOR INTERNATIONAL REGULATORY COMPETITION

At the heart of this book, the most crucial point evaluated is to what extent jurisdictions find DLT Offerings valuable enough to be motivated to compete for the benefits which may result from developing appropriate laws and regulations to govern it. Presented below are two cases, economic and social, which highlight the importance of DLT Offerings for the jurisdictions forming the focus of this book, and for other jurisdictions that have made the development of DLT an important domestic policy priority.[53]

1.4.1 The Economic Case

The intersection of DLT Offerings, in particular cryptocurrencies, and the theory of regulatory competition can be viewed through the economic benefits which it may bring about through its wider adoption and use.

First, it has been well evidenced that policymakers use finance as a mechanism to stimulate economic development to support growth in both advanced and emerging countries.[54] In the context of the theory of regulatory competition specifically, Morriss

49. Veerle Heyvaert, 'Regulatory Competition: Accounting for the Transnational Dimension of Environmental Regulation' (2012) 25(1) Journal of Environmental Law 7 https://doi.org/10.1093/jel/eqs019. *See* Guhan Subramanian, 'The Disappearing Delaware Effect' (2004) 20(1) Journal of Law, Economics, and Organization 32-59 https://doi.org/10.1093/jleo/20.1.32 and Joseph McCahery & Erik Vermeulen, 'Does the European Company Prevent the Delaware Effect' (2005) 11 European Law Journal 785 https://doi.org/10.1111/j.1468-0386.2005.00288.x.
50. Cristina A Lucier & Brian J Gareau, 'From Waste to Resources: Interrogating "Race to the Bottom" in the Global Environmental Governance of the Hazardous Waste Trade' (2015) 21(2) Journal of World-Systems Research 500 https://doi.org/10.5195/jwsr.2015.11.
51. Robin Hollander & Louise Thornthwaite, 'Competitive Federalism and Workers' Compensation: Do States Race to the Bottom?' (2018) 53(3) Australian Journal of Political Science 339 https://doi.org/10.1080/10361146.2018.1477115.
52. *See* David Vogel, *Trading Up: Consumer and Environmental Regulation in a Global Economy* (Harvard University Press 1995) and Arthur PJ Mol, 'Ecological Modernization: Industrial Transformations and Environmental Reform' in Michael R Redclift & Graham Woodgate (eds), *The International Handbook of Environmental Sociology* (Elgar Publishing 1997).
53. Douglas W Arner et al., 'Policy and Regulatory Challenges of Distributed Ledger Technologies and Digital Assets in Asia' in Chris Brummer (ed.), *Cryptoassets* (OUP USA 2019) 264.
54. Douglas W Arner, Janos N Barberis & Ross P Buckley, 'Fintech, Regtech and the Reconceptualisation of Financial Technology' (2016) Northwestern Journal of International Law and Business 12. *See* Douglas W Arner, *Financial Stability, Economic Development and the Role of Law* (New York: Cambridge University Press 2017).

has posited that wealth creation is a primary motivating factor for jurisdictions to compete against each other.[55] On this basis, RC operates on the assumption that the actions and behaviours of jurisdictions are directed at achieving the objective of 'maximising national welfare', based on the actions and behaviours of *other* jurisdictions.[56] For example, in Europe in the 1990s, building powerful financial centres was an important legislative goal in Germany, France and the UK.[57] In particular, the UK noted in the White Paper 'Competitiveness: Forging Ahead' that London, while established as the leading financial centre in Europe, continued to face competitive pressures from elsewhere in the EU. The white paper pointed out rival financial centres, such as Europlace for Paris, and Finanzplatz Deutschland for Frankfurt, and the initiatives undertaken at the time to increase their attractiveness.[58]

Second, wealth creation, principally through capital investment, is a significant driver for jurisdictions engaging in regulatory competition. According to CoinDesk, the cryptocurrency industry's market capitalisation has been valued at USD 1.6 trillion at the start of the first quarter of 2022.[59] Bitcoin, Ethereum, and Tether are the largest cryptocurrencies in terms of individual market capitalisation, as of February 2022.[60] The market capitalisation of the cryptocurrency industry, together with capital investment, will only increase with further the adoption and use of DLT. Chainalysis has reported that cryptocurrency use is being driven by increased DeFi transaction volumes in advanced economies.[61] In this regard, HK, the UK, and the US are ranked high as 19, 5, and 1 respectively on Chainalysis' 2021 Global DeFI Adoption Index.[62] In addition, Chainalysis has reported that cryptocurrency use is being driven by P2P platforms in emerging economies.[63] In this regard, Mainland China, the UK, and the US are ranked in the top 25 of the 2021 Global Crypto Adoption Index as 13, 21, and 8, respectively.[64]

Third, the impact of DLT through the market capitalisation of the cryptocurrency industry, and increased adoption and use of DLT Offerings, may have a significant

55. Andrew P Morriss, 'The Role of Offshore Financial Centers in Regulatory Competition' (2008) University of Illinois Law and Economics Research Paper No. LE07-032, 3.
56. *See* Hans Werner Sinn HW, *The New Systems Competition*, Yrjö Jahnsson lectures (Blackwell Publishing Ltd UK 2003) 9.
57. Ehud Kamar, 'Beyond Competition for Incorporations' (2006) 94(6) Georgetown Law Journal 1749 https://doi.org/10.2139/ssrn.720121.
58. Department of the Environment, Transport, and the Regions, 'Competitiveness: Forging Ahead' (1995) 3.3 in Ehud Kamar, 'Beyond Competition for Incorporations' (2006) 94(6) Georgetown Law Journal 1749 https://doi.org/10.2139/ssrn.720121.
59. Tracy Wang, 'Crypto Sell-Off Wipes $700B From Industry Market Cap So Far in 2022' (*CoinDesk*, 25 January 2022), https://www.coindesk.com/markets/2022/01/24/crypto-sell-off-wipes-700b-from-industry-market-cap-so-far-in-2022/#: ~ :text = Cryptocurrencies%20are%20deep%20in%20the,in%20just%20over%20three%20weeks.
60. Kat Tretina & John Schmidt, 'Top 10 Cryptocurrencies in February 2022' (*Forbes*, 1 February 2022), https://www.forbes.com/advisor/investing/top-10-cryptocurrencies/.
61. Chainalysis, 'The 2021 Geography of Cryptocurrency Report' (*Chainalysis*, October 2021) 12, https://go.chainalysis.com/rs/503-FAP-074/images/Geography-of-Cryptocurrency-2021.pdf.
62. Chainalysis, 'The 2021 Geography of Cryptocurrency Report' (*Chainalysis*, October 2021) 17, https://go.chainalysis.com/rs/503-FAP-074/images/Geography-of-Cryptocurrency-2021.pdf.
63. Chainalysis, 'The 2021 Geography of Cryptocurrency Report' (*Chainalysis*, October 2021) 12, https://go.chainalysis.com/rs/503-FAP-074/images/Geography-of-Cryptocurrency-2021.pdf.
64. Chainalysis, 'The 2021 Geography of Cryptocurrency Report' (*Chainalysis*, October 2021) 117, https://go.chainalysis.com/rs/503-FAP-074/images/Geography-of-Cryptocurrency-2021.pdf.

impact on the global economy, and implicitly on RC and competition policy. According to the Future of the Blockchain Market Report, DLT would impact the global economy positively and would provide approximately USD 120 billion internationally between the period 2018-2024.[65] A study conducted by PwC has reported that DLT has the potential to contribute USD 176 trillion to the global economy by 2030.[66] The report has further indicated that the total DLT impact for Mainland China, the UK and the US will be USD 440.4 billion, USD 72.2 billion, and USD 407.2 billion respectively by 2030.[67] The high growth rate predicted for the DLT market has been predicated upon increased venture capital funding and investment in the technology, among other factors.[68] Further, the WEF has reported that by 2027, 10% of the global economy's GDP would be stored using DLT.[69]

The potential economic gains presented by the use of DLT through its wider adoption and usage; together with its increasingly significant impact on the global economy provide ample motivation for jurisdictions to potentially engage in regulatory competition with one another.

1.4.2 The Social Case

The intersection of DLT Offerings, particularly cryptocurrencies, and the theory of regulatory competition can be viewed through the social benefits which DLT may bring about through its wider adoption and usage.

First, from a social welfare perspective, governments have an interest in maintaining the living standards which their populations have become accustomed to, particularly in advanced economies.[70] The adoption and use of new technology is one way in which governments can utilise the efficiencies derived therefrom to maintain and improve the living standards of their populations. As will discussed in Chapter 2, DLT has many use cases and applications, but is most synonymously associated with providing more efficient and cheaper payments and cross-border remittances, and

65. Critical Future, 'The Future of the Blockchain Market Report' (*Critical Future*, 2018) in Burcu Sakız & Ayşen Hiç Gencer, 'Blockchain Technology and Its Impact on the Global Economy' (2019) International Conference on Eurasian Economies 102 (98-105), https://www.avekon.org/papers/2258.pdf.
66. Price Waterhouse Coopers, 'Time for Trust' (October 2020) 3 https://image.uk.info.pwc.com/lib/fe31117075640475701c74/m/2/434c46d2-a889-4fed-a030-c52964c71a64.pdf.
67. Price Waterhouse Coopers, 'Time for Trust' (October 2020) 17 https://image.uk.info.pwc.com/lib/fe31117075640475701c74/m/2/434c46d2-a889-4fed-a030-c52964c71a64.pdf.
68. Markets and Markets, 'Blockchain Market with COVID-19 Impact Analysis' (November 2021) https://www.marketsandmarkets.com/Market-Reports/blockchain-technology-market-90100890.html#:~:text=%5B441%20Pages%20Report%5D%20The%20Blockchain,68.4%25%20during%20the%20forecast%20period.
69. World Economic Forum, 'Deep Shift Technology Tipping Points and Societal Impact' (September 2015) 24, https://www3.weforum.org/docs/WEF_GAC15_Technological_Tipping_Points_report_2015.pdf.
70. Manolo Abella, 'Global Competition for Skilled Workers' in Christiane Kuptsch & Eng Fong Pang (eds) *Competing for Global Talent* (Institute for Labour Studies, ILO, Geneva, 2006).

storage of electronic records safely and securely.[71] It should also be noted, however, that DLT, and the successful development of use cases and applications, are not without their faults. Through public scandals such as 'The Silk Road' and Mt Gox, cryptocurrencies suffer from the general view that it is used to achieve criminal and nefarious ends. In addition, developing DLT use cases and applications is fraught with scaling and interoperability issues, systemic changes in processes and roles, and regulatory and legal uncertainty.[72]

Second, on a policy basis, the use of DLT has been associated with the policy objective of financial inclusion, which has also been referred to as the democratisation of finance.[73] The Alliance for Financial Inclusion has described 'financial inclusion' as involving the delivery of financial services to all segments of society at an affordable cost.[74] The WB has reported that a third of the global population remains unbanked.[75] This is not endemic to emerging economies alone as the US Federal Reserve has reported that 22% of adults in the US are either unbanked or underbanked.[76] Financial inclusion is an important policy objective, whose achievement has received significant support from several international institutions.[77] For example, the Asian Development Bank has highlighted financial inclusion as being integral to the development of the financial services industry, and stated '[w]ithout access to formal financial services, the unserved and underserved segments of society will be excluded from growth and its benefits'.[78] In addition, financial inclusion is an enabler of several UN 2030 Sustainable Development Goals.[79]

71. Christina Lagarde, 'A Regulatory Approach to Fintech' (Straight Talk, 18 June 2018) 9 https://www.elibrary.imf.org/view/journals/022/0055/002/article-A003-en.xml.
72. World Economic Forum, 'Digital Assets, Distributed Ledger Technology and the Future of Capital Markets' (May 2021) 12, https://www3.weforum.org/docs/WEF_Digital_Assets_Distributed_Ledger_Technology_2021.pdf.
73. *See* Stephen Stonberg, 'Cryptocurrencies are Democratizing the Financial World. Here's How' (World Economic Forum, 22 January 2022), https://www.weforum.org/agenda/2021/01/cryptocurrencies-are-democratising-the-financial-world-heres-how and Sarah Grace Manski, 'Building the Blockchain World: Technological Commonwealth or Just More of the Same?' (2017) 25 Strategic Change 511-522 https://doi.org/10.1002/jsc.2151.
74. Alliance for Financial Inclusion, 'Defining Financial Inclusion' Guidance Note No. 28 (2017) 6.
75. World Bank, 'Financial Inclusion' (2 October 2018), https://www.worldbank.org/en/topic/financialinclusion/overview#1.
76. Board of Governors of the Federal Reserve System, 'Report on the Economic Well-Being of U.S. Households in 2018: May 2019' (5 June 2019), https://www.federalreserve.gov/publications/2019-economic-well-being-of-us-households-in-2018-banking-and-credit.htm.
77. Alfred Hannig & Stefan Jansen, 'Financial inclusion and Financial Stability: Current Policy Issues' (2010) ADBI Working Paper 259 [2]. *See* World Bank, 'Financial Inclusion' (2 October 2018), https://www.worldbank.org/en/topic/financialinclusion/overview#1.
78. Asian Development Bank, 'Accelerating Financial Inclusion in South-East Asia with Digital Finance' (2017). *See also* Asian Development Bank, 'Midterm Review of 2020 Strategy: Meeting the Challenges of a Transforming Asian and Pacific' (2004); Asian Development Bank, 'Strategy 2020: The Long-Term Strategic Development of the Asian Development Bank' (2008).
79. UNCDF, 'Financial Inclusion and the SDGs', http://www.uncdf.org/financial-inclusion-and-the-sdgs. *See also* Leora Klapper, Mayada L Zogbhi & Jake Hess, 'Achieving the Sustainable Development Goals: The Role of Financial Inclusion' (2016) Consultative Group to Assist the Poor.

Several initiatives have been proposed to use Fintech to successfully bring more people into the formal financial system.[80] In particular, a large body of literature has been developed regarding using DLT for the purposes of advancing financial inclusion.[81] For example, DLT platforms have been used to effect P2P payments and cross-border remittances, using a smartphone. As such, the WEF has posited that increased financial inclusion is being achieved using cryptocurrency bearing in mind the high adoption rates in emerging economies such as Nigeria, South African and Vietnam.[82] DLT may also be used to overcome the challenges associated with opening banking accounts, account usability, and costs which are incurred by financial intuitions which represent obstacles to increased financial inclusion.[83] It has also been proposed that DLT can be used to increase financial inclusion through accelerating payments, formalising collateral improving identification validation, and reducing compliance costs.[84]

Finally, from a labour market perspective, governments have an interest in maintaining the living standards of their populations through job creation. The adoption and use of DLT could potentially create more jobs throughout the global economy, spurring RC between jurisdictions. In 2019, Gartner reported that the DLT sector could potentially create business opportunities with a value of more than USD 3.1 trillion by 2030.[85] These employment opportunities are expected to be provided in the business, computer science finance, legal, management, and software industries.[86] Most significantly, the adoption and use of DLT could lead to the creation of 40 million employment opportunities by 2030.[87]

The potential social benefits of DLT through bringing more people into the formal financial system and through job creation provide ample motivation for Primary Actors

80. *See* Douglas W Arner et al., 'Sustainability, FinTech and Financial Inclusion' (2019) European Banking Institute Working Paper Series 14, https://papers.ssrn.com/sol3/papers.cfm?abstract_id=3387359#.
81. *See* generally International Telecommunications Union, 'Distributed Ledger Technologies and Financial Inclusion' (March 2017), https://www.itu.int/en/ITU-T/focusgroups/dfs/Documents/201703/ITU_FGDFS_Report-on-DLT-and-Financial-Inclusion.pdf.
82. Stephen Stonberg, 'Cryptocurrencies are Democratizing the Financial World. Here's How' (*World Economic Forum*, 22 January 2022), https://www.weforum.org/agenda/2021/01/cryptocurrencies-are-democratising-the-financial-world-heres-how and Katharina Buchholz, 'These are the Countries where Cryptocurrency use is the Most Common' (*World Economic Forum and Statista*, 18 February 2021), https://www.weforum.org/agenda/2021/02/how-common-is-cryptocurrency.
83. Chamber of Digital Commerce, 'Blockchain and Financial Inclusion' (March 2017) 8-9, https://d3h0qzni6h08fz.cloudfront.net/reports/blockchain-and-financial-inclusion.pdf.
84. Michael S Barr et al., 'Should Central Banks use Distributed Ledger Technology and Digital Currencies to Advance Financial Inclusion' (*Centre on Finance, Law and Policy*, 17 May 2021) 20-21, https://financelawpolicy.umich.edu/sites/cflp/files/2021-07/cbotf-paper-7-should-central-banks-use-dlt-and-digital-currencies-to-advance-financial-inclusion.pdf.
85. *See* Gartner Inc, 'Forecast: Blockchain Business Value, Worldwide, 2017-2030', https://www.gartner.com/en/documents/3627117/forecast-blockchain-business-value-worldwide-2017-2030.
86. *See* Steven Muegge & Gregory Sandstrom, 'Distributed Ledger Technologies for Smart Digital Economies' (2021) 11(6) Technology Management Review 3-5.
87. Price Waterhouse Coopers, 'Time for Trust' (October 2020) 17, https://image.uk.info.pwc.com/lib/fe31117075640475701c74/m/2/434c46d2-a889-4fed-a030-c52964c71a64.pdf.

to engage in RC with one another. Overall, therefore, competition is fundamental to developing productivity, growth, and innovation, which in turn creates wealth and can lead to reduced levels of poverty.[88]

1.5 INTERNATIONAL REGULATORY COMPETITION: THE DOG THAT NEVER BARKS?

The main thesis of this book considers the extent to which HK, London, and NY have engaged in regulatory competition with one another through their regulation of DLT financial products and services in their respective jurisdictions. It thus evaluates the extent to which these jurisdictions have been influenced by regulatory competition or the threat thereof, in their regulation of DLT Offerings. It also identifies how the relevant legislative and regulatory texts and policy instruments in these jurisdictions have been formulated according to the influence of regulatory competition. Accordingly, this book focusses primarily on governmental action and behaviour as they relate primarily to legal, regulatory and policy-making competences, in the context of the regulation of DLT Offerings during the key period of legislative and regulatory development of 2008-2022.

To this end, this book provides a critical review of the theory of regulatory competition through the lens of the rapid development of technology in what has been called the 'Fourth Industrial Revolution'.[89] In doing so, a clear and cohesive framework for regulatory competition is formulated through an identification and classification of the essential elements of which it is composed. This framework is used to determine the extent to which HK, London, and NY have engaged in regulatory competition with each other. On this basis, the analysis set out in this book shows that regulatory competition between HK, London, and NY influenced their regulation of financial products and services underlined by DLT to a limited extent. It shows further that these jurisdictions advanced their own competitiveness through a consideration of competition policy concerns, but largely absent any targeted legislative and regulatory rules directed in response to external competitive pressures. The limited regulatory competition was evidenced on the basis of three underlining thematic observations, as informed by specific patterns which support the view that limited regulatory competition took place between the world's leading financial centres.

First, it was evidenced that HK, London, and NY were influenced by regulatory competition concerns, or the threat thereof, as evidenced primarily through the policy goal of maintaining their respective reputations as leading international financial centres. However, this influence did not extend to the creation of lax or stricter regulatory rules to govern DLT Offerings for the purpose of engaging in regulatory competition. As such, the analysis evidenced that regulatory competition influenced HK, London, and NY's 'competitive appetites' in formulating regulatory responses and developing regulatory rules to govern DLT Offerings, this influence only extended to

88. Nick Godfrey, 'Why Is Competition important for Growth and Poverty Reduction' (2008) Department for International Development, London OECD Global Forum on Investment 5.
89. *See* Klaus Schwab, *The Fourth Industrial Revolution* (Penguin UK 2017).

how they viewed their positions as individual competitors more generally, and not how these positions were harnessed to engage in regulatory competition.

Second, in place of directed rules-based competition in which HK, London, and NY developed regulatory frameworks containing features meant to lure Secondary Actors to their jurisdictions, and thus away from competing jurisdictions, the cities focussed on developing regulatory frameworks characterised by similar regulatory features and underlined by similar foundational regulatory strategies. Finally, while HK, London, and NY did not engage in rules-based competition, in developing their regulatory frameworks to govern financial products and services underlined by DLT they chose instead to promote other regulatory and policy features to attract actors to their jurisdictions (i.e., competitive advantages), but without any direct intention to lure those actors away from each other's locales.

Overall, the analysis provided by this book, by homing in on regulatory competition specifically, sets out unique observations concerning the actions and behaviours of the relevant authorities in formulating rules governing financial products and services underlined by novel technologies. While a large majority of the legal analyses of regulatory competition have been applied in the federal government context, this book considers regulatory competition in an international context by focussing on competition between the globe's leading financial centres. The book is also framed within the context of law and innovation which provides a fresh prism through which to study regulatory competition.

Broadly, it is hoped that this book will assist with drawing deductions regarding the extent to which laws and regulations governing DLT Offerings are being relaxed, undercut or made stricter as a regulatory competition policy response. The approach taken by the three jurisdictions in this regard may have consequences for how DLT Offerings are regulated in other jurisdictions. As top global financial centres are forerunners in the development and creation of financial services regulation, they have a role to play in international rule setting.

1.6 RESEARCH DESIGN

The scope of this book can be viewed through the lens of qualitative research of a doctrinal, comparative, and thematic approach nature. The doctrinal research methodology was used through a two-pronged approach. First, doctrinal analysis was used to systematically select the most significant primary and secondary sources of law which govern DLT Offerings, specifically cryptocurrencies, in the case study jurisdictions of HK, London, and NY. Second, the doctrinal approach was used as part of the analysis to 'validate the authority of the legal doctrine' to determine the status of the primary and secondary sources of law governing DLT Offerings.[90] This two-pronged approach provided the foundation for evaluating any ambiguities, inconsistencies, and criticisms associated with the way in which DLT Offerings are governed by law.

90. Terry Hutchinson, 'Doctrinal Research: Researching the Jury' in Dawn Watkins & Mandy Burton (eds), *Research Methods in Law* (Routledge 2017) 10.

Comparative law as a method of research, in place of employing it as a specific research methodological approach, was used in conducting this study.[91] First, in the context of the RC Framework devised for this study, the comparative method was used to comparatively examine relevant laws, regulations, regulatory authority rules, legislative processes, and policy approaches concerned with DLT. Second, the comparative method was used to discern and unpack themes of convergence and divergence, and existing trends, through an examination of conflicts and similarities apparent from the identified and compared features.

Finally, a thematic approach, through an institutional lens focussing on governmental action and behaviour, was adopted in conducting the regulatory competition analysis. The themes developed for this study span the legal and policy processes concerned with formulating the governance of DLT Offerings and include Input, Process, Output, and Feedback, each discussed in turn below.

In the context of this book, 'Input' refers to the governmental actions and behaviours of the leading international financial centres studied which are directed to formulating and implementing competition policy within the context of the emergence of Fintech and its position of importance on the legal and policy agendas. First, this includes an analysis of the general approach applied to competition policy in each of the cities studied. Second, this includes an analysis of the role of Fintech in directing competition policy in each of the cities. The aim of the Input analysis is to assess the 'competitive appetites' of the cities based on their initial responses to the emergence of Fintech, and whether any actions and behaviours were influenced in part by those levied by the cities studied, as competitors in the operation of regulatory competition.

'Process' refers to the governmental actions and behaviours of the leading international financial centres studied which are directed towards formulating and implementing their regulatory approach to the governance of DLT Offerings. The actions and behaviours considered were those advanced prior to the promulgation of legal and regulatory rules, or the issuance of regulatory guidance based on the pre-existing regulatory framework, which had the effect of formalising the rules governing DLT Offerings (i.e., the 'Output'). The role of competition policy in advancing these directives was also considered. To this end, the focus of the Process analysis was on processes and approach, rather than the content of the legal and regulatory rules, which form the focus of the analysis in the Output section.

'Output' refers to the governmental actions and behaviours of the leading international financial centres studied directed to promulgating legal and regulatory rules, or to the issuance of regulatory guidance based on the pre-existing regulatory framework, which had the effect of formalising the rules governing DLT Offerings. This entailed an analysis of the content of the legal and regulatory rules and guidance, considering the legal and regulatory approaches developed by the cities studied as reflected by the Process analysis. The aim of the Output analysis was to examine the formalised rules governing DLT Offerings to identify salient regulatory features to

91. Matt Henn, Mark Weinstein & Nick Foard, *A Critical Introduction to Social Research* (2nd edn, Sage 2006) 10.

formulate a view on the manner in which the Concerned Jurisdictions regulate DLT Offerings.

'Feedback' refers to the governmental actions and behaviours of the leading international financial centres studied which are directed at modifying the initial regulatory response to governing DLT Offerings. The modification of the initial regulatory responses analysed included: (i) adaptations of the established regulatory approaches, or proposals thereof (i.e., the Process); and (ii) amendments effected to regulatory frameworks, or proposals thereof (i.e., the Output). This entailed an analysis of the amended regulatory frameworks and regulatory approaches for governing DLT Offerings established by the cities studied. The aim of the Feedback analysis was to examine the underlying rationale for any modifications to the initial regulatory response, in particular, whether this was motivated by any regulatory competition or competition policy considerations.

This thematic approach allows for a wider net to be cast for the analysis by not focussing solely on adjustments made to laws, regulations, and regulatory approaches, or newly promulgated legislative texts governing DLT Offerings in the concerned jurisdictions. Instead, it placed these texts in context by systematically considering the policy approaches, parliamentary processes, and regulatory stances applied. The adoption of this systematic approach enabled the examination of dominant legal and policy themes, arguments and evidence supporting the regulatory competition analysis set out in this book. It also enabled the incorporation of a range of forces shaping government action and behaviours.[92] External variables, in the form of legal and policy drivers impacting the governance of DLT Offerings, have therefore been accounted for through their identification and having their significance compared.

1.7 CHAPTER SUMMARIES

This book is organised into eight chapters, including this introductory chapter which sets out the premise of this book.

To this end, Chapter 2 provides an overview of DLT with the primary aim of untangling the well-known complexity attributed to this often misunderstood technology. In doing so, the DLT landscape is examined from its emergence as a burgeoning form of technology to its catapulting to the centre of the public imagination, and status as a mainstay on government agendas world-wide. This narrative tracks the originally intended use cases of the technology up until its most recent, and perhaps unintended, applications, through the guise of the failed and successful attempts of its rollout in the financial services industry. The varying attempts made to define the technology are also critically explored, in tandem with an evaluation of its essential technical core features, and the paradigmatic instances of the technology. The chapter, as far as possible, uses simplified yet robust explanations to avoid the usual technological

92. Katharina Holzinger & Thomas Sommerer, '"Race to the Bottom" or "Race to Brussels"? Environmental competition in Europe' (2011) 49(2) Journal of Common Market Studies 337 https://doi.org/10.1111/j.1468-5965.2010.02135.x.

jargon associated with attempts to provide descriptions of novel and revolutionary technologies.

Chapter 3 provides a critical evaluation of the theory of regulatory competition by considering its definitional treatment and isolating its underlining and essential elements. It thereby formulates a well-defined definitional matrix which provides a clear and comprehensive explanation of the theory of regulatory competition, an endeavour which has received little attention in the discourse. In doing so, the origins of the theory are traced through relevant literature, from the infamous Tieboutian model to the infamous regulatory races, including the 'races to the bottom' in corporate law in the 1980s, triggered by regulation set by the state of Delaware. Overall, this chapter conceives a sound and coherent framework which is applied in subsequent chapters of this book, and which can be applied in future studies turning an eye towards investigating the regulatory competition in practice.

Chapters 4, 5, and 6 provide a comprehensive narrative analysis of the development of the laws and regulations governing DLT financial products and services in the case study jurisdiction. The analysis is conducted over key periods of development and harkens back to the publication of the Bitcoin White Paper in 2008, with the major stablecoin regulation developments in the early 2020s serving as the bookend. A pointed discussion of relevant laws, regulations, and policy approaches is integral to this analysis and is framed within the regulatory competition framework devised in Chapter 3. It is within the confines of these chapters that the intersection of Fintech and regulatory competition is surveyed. This provides impetus to achieving the ultimate aim of evaluating the extent to which regulatory competition may have influenced the formation of the rules governing DLT-based financial products and services in the world's leading financial centres (as set out in the subsequent chapter).

Chapter 7 sets out the analysis regarding the extent to which regulatory competition has influenced the formulation of the rules governing DLT Offerings in HK, London, and NY on the basis of the theoretical framework developed in Chapter 3. It is argued that regulatory competition between the leading global financial centres was evidenced, but only to a limited extent. It is noted, in particular, that the aforementioned cities took account of and were cognisant of regulatory competition concerns and took measures to market themselves as attractive locations to an array of Fintech stakeholders. However, these measures excluded any targeted legislative or regulatory adjustments to the rules governing DLT-based financial products and services in specific response to external competitive pressures. The jurisdictions, however, did make use of competitive advantages to set themselves apart from potential competitors.

Nevertheless, the analysis, by homing in on regulatory competition specifically, reveals several unique observations concerning the actions and behaviours of the relevant authorities in formulating rules governing financial products and services underlined by novel technologies. These observations are grouped together in Chapter 7 culminating in a set of conclusions based on converging and diverging patterns, as evidenced through the conduct of the authorities in the cities concerned. In particular, it is shown that the analysis evidenced a 'step-wise' or parallel movement of the actions and behaviours of the authorities concerned in directing competition policy within the context of the emergence of Fintech and DLT, and its regulation. Overall, this part of Chapter 7 provides the answer to the central thesis of this book and provides a critical view of the timely intersection of Fintech regulation and regulatory competition.

Chapter 7 also sets out lessons drawn from the analysis concerning the role of regulatory competition in shaping the rules which govern financial services and products underlined by novel technologies. These lessons reveal unique insights concerning the actions and behaviours of governmental actors and how authorities may potentially approach the regulation of the financial products and services underlined by different novel technologies in the future. In particular, these lessons assist in understanding the extent and influence of competition policy, how regulatory approaches inform the creation of rules, and how jurisdictions position themselves against perceived threats of competition. As such, this chapter is crucial for lawmakers, policymakers and regulators to deepen their understanding of this topic, and for providing practical insights into the potential impact of regulatory competition in this age of rapid technological advancement.

Chapter 8 provides the conclusion of this book and includes a pointed call for future research.

CHAPTER 2

DLT: From ICO to Crypto

This chapter highlights the importance of regulatory competition for financial products and services underlined by DLT. In doing so, it provides an examination of the emergence of DLT and its impact as a relatively new technology in the age of digital transformation. On this basis, attempts to define DLT are explored, together with an analysis of the essential features which underline this technology. The different types of DLT which have been developed are also discussed briefly. Finally, this chapter sets out the principal applications and use cases which have been developed for DLT.

2.1 THE EMERGENCE AND IMPACT OF DLT

According to Arner et al., the clipped compound 'Fintech' originated in the early 1990s through Citigroup's Financial Services Technology Consortium.[93] The term is used as a general descriptor for technology-driven innovation in the financial services industry. The outcomes of Fintech innovations are ordinarily represented as applications, new business models, or products which materially impact the way the financial services industry operates.[94] Fintech has been classified into different types or activities,[95] each utilising novel technologies or combining pre-existing technologies to create new

93. Douglas W Arner, Janos N Barberis & Ross P Buckley, 'The Evolution of FinTech: A New Post-Crisis Paradigm?' (2015) University of Hong Kong Research Paper No. 2015/047, 3, https://papers.ssrn.com/sol3/papers.cfm?abstract_id=2676553.
94. European Commission, 'Communication from the Commission to the European Parliament, the Council, the European Central Bank, the European Economic and Social Committee and the Committee of the Regions: FinTech Action Plan: For a More Competitive and Innovative European Financial Sector' (Brussels 8.3.2018 COM (2018) 109 Final) 2, https://eur-lex.europa.eu/legal-content/EN/TXT/?uri=CELEX%3A52018DC0109.
95. *See* Financial Stability Board, 'Financial Stability Implications from FinTech' (27 June 2017), https://www.fsb.org/wp-content/uploads/R270617.pdf.

financial products and services. DLT is one such type of Fintech.[96] While DLT is still regarded as a burgeoning form of Fintech,[97] it is not an entirely novel innovation.[98]

The technology was first introduced in 2008 through Satoshi Nakamoto's seminal White Paper 'Bitcoin: A Peer-to-Peer Electronic Cash System' (Bitcoin White Paper).[99] Since then, DLT has received wide-spread attention both as a source of academic study and through the public eye, particularly concerning its perceived questionable nature based on its well-publicised use for illicit activity.[100] However, long before 2008, several pioneering technologies steered the way for the development of what is now referred to without differentiation as 'Blockchain', 'Blockchain Technology' or 'DLT'. Correct etymological-use aside, DLT is built on the foundations of, most notably, accounting-based systems and other old and contemporary innovations.[101] These innovations, among others, include double entry bookkeeping;[102] (ii) the Internet;[103] (iii) P2P file-sharing networks, such as Napster, Gnutella, and BitTorrent;[104] and (iv) cryptography: public-private key cryptography and cryptographic validation.[105]

The philosophical foundation for the emergence of DLT can be viewed through the underpinnings of cyber libertarianism.[106] Proponents of cyber libertarianism espouse individual liberty and self-governance in Internet and related digital media usage through non-interference of governmental and commercial structures.[107] The

96. Financial Stability Board, 'Financial Stability Implications from FinTech' (June 2017) 9, https://www.fsb.org/wp-content/uploads/R270617.pdf.
97. *See* World Bank Group, 'Blockchain and Distributed Ledger technology' (12 April 2018) https://www.worldbank.org/en/topic/financialsector/brief/blockchain-dlt.
98. Saifedean Ammous, 'Blockchain Technology: What Is It Good For?'(2019) 34(2) Banking and Finance Law Review 239 https://doi.org/10.2139/ssrn.2832751 and Primavera De Filippi & Aaron Wright, *Blockchain and the Law* (Harvard University Press 2018) 2.
99. Satoshi Nakamoto, 'Bitcoin: A Peer-to-Peer Electronic Cash System', https://bitcoin.org/bitcoin.pdf.
100. *See* Rainer Böhme et al., 'Bitcoin: Economics, Technology, and Governance' (2015) 29(2) Journal of Economic Perspectives 222 https://doi.org/10.1257/jep.29.2.213.
101. Robleh Ali, 'Innovations in Payments Technologies and the Emergence of Digital Currencies' 2014 Quarterly Bulletin Q3 267, Garrick Hileman & Michel Rauchs, 'Global Cryptocurrency Benchmarking Study' (*Cambridge Centre for Alternative Finance*, 2017), https://www.jbs.cam.ac.uk/wp-content/uploads/2020/08/2017-04-20-global-cryptocurrency-benchmarking-study.pdf; Primavera De Filippi & Aaron Wright, 'Introduction' in Primavera De Filippi & Aaron Wright (eds) *Blockchain and the Law* (Harvard University Press 2018) 2, and Organisation for Economic Co-operation and Development, 'OECD Blockchain Primer' (2018) 3, https://cdn.gihub.org/umbraco/media/2431/oecd-blockchain-primer.pdf.
102. *See* Murphy Smith, 'Luca Pacioli: The Father of Accounting' (*SSRN*, 2013), https://papers.ssrn.com/sol3/papers.cfm?abstract_id=2320658.
103. *See* Jonathan Hogeback, 'Who invented the internet' (Britannica), https://www.britannica.com/story/who-invented-the-internet.
104. *See* Paratii, 'A Brief History of P2P Content Distribution, in 10 Major Steps' (*Medium*, 26 October 2017), https://medium.com/paratii/a-brief-history-of-p2p-content-distribution-in-10-major-steps-6d6733d25122.
105. Rainer Böhme et al., 'Bitcoin: Economics, Technology, and Governance' (2015) 29(2) Journal of Economic Perspectives 216 https://doi.org/10.1257/jep.29.2.213.
106. *See* Primavera De Filippi & Aaron Wright, 'Code as Law' in Primavera De Filippi & Aaron Wright (eds) *Blockchain and the Law* (Harvard University Press 2018) 193 and Kevin Werbach, 'Trust, but Verify' (2018) 33(2) Berkeley Technology Law Journal 492.
107. Lincoln Dahlberg, 'Cyberlibertarian' (*Oxford Research Encyclopedia*, 26 October 2017), https://oxfordre.com/communication/communication/view/10.1093/acrefore/9780190228613.001.0001/acrefore-9780190228613-e-70 and John Perry Barlow, 'Declaration of the Independence

initial conceptualisation of DLT, through Blockchain Technology and Bitcoin, finds favour with cyber libertarianism by 'cutting out the middle-man' for the purposes of effecting payments. Traditionally, these middlemen include trusted central authorities such as banks, credit card companies and other electronic payment messaging services, such as SWIFT.[108] In this paradigm, incumbent trusted central authorities take the functional role of the gatekeepers of the financial system, controlling the processes for effecting and verifying transactions. The pragmatic basis for the emergence of DLT, however, can be viewed through its creation for solving an issue which has long since plagued the effective deployment of cryptocurrencies. This issue was represented in the form of solving the 'double-spending' problem without having to rely on a centralised authority to verify transactions.[109] In the Bitcoin White Paper, Nakamoto described the double-spending problem as encompassing a payee being unable to verify that an owner did not use a coin more than once.[110] This unverifiability stems from cryptocurrencies' innate ability to be easily replicated in the absence of appropriate security measures.[111]

Nakamoto indicated that the conventional solution to the double-spending problem was using a trusted central authority to verify transactions, thereby ensuring that coins were not duplicated for repeated use.[112] This was the case for one of the earliest digital money companies, Digicash, for example, which solved the double-spending problem by using blind signatures and RSA encryption.[113] The defective deployment of DigiCash, however, was strained by its reliance on banks, thereby creating a single point of failure.[114] In Digicash's eCash system, this failure was represented by banks maintaining their traditional gate-keeping role in having the final word on whether eCash deposits could be accepted or not.[115] Overall, this severely impacted the widespread adoption and use of eCash, but it nevertheless provided the impetus for the development of several other solutions. These solutions were primarily concerned with solving the double-spending problem without the need for a trusted central authority to verify

of Cyberspace' (2019) 18 Duke Law & Technology Review 5-7 (originally published in 1996) https://www.eff.org/cyberspace-independence.

108. Rainer Böhme et al., 'Bitcoin: Economics, Technology, and Governance' (2015) 29(2) Journal of Economic Perspectives 213 https://doi.org/10.1257/jep.29.2.213.
109. Primavera De Filippi & Aaron Wright, 'Blockchain and the Law' in Primavera De Filippi & Aaron Wright (eds), *Blockchain and the Law* (Harvard University Press 2018) 19-20.
110. Satoshi Nakamoto, 'Bitcoin: A Peer-to-Peer Electronic Cash System' (2008) 2, https://bitcoin.org/bitcoin.pdf.
111. Cristina Pérez-Solà et al., 'Double-Spending Prevention Fort Bitcoin Zero-Confirmation Transactions' (2019) 18 International Journal of Information Security 451 https://doi.org/10.1007/s10207-018-0422-4.
112. Satoshi Nakamoto, 'Bitcoin: A Peer-to-Peer Electronic Cash System' (2008) 2, https://bitcoin.org/bitcoin.pdf.
113. Primavera De Filippi & Aaron Wright, 'Blockchain and the Law' in Primavera De Filippi & Aaron Wright (eds), *Blockchain and the Law* (Harvard University Press 2018) 19.
114. Primavera De Filippi & Aaron Wright, 'Blockchain and the Law' in Primavera De Filippi & Aaron Wright (eds), *Blockchain and the Law* (Harvard University Press 2018) 19.
115. Julie Pitta, 'Requiem for a Bright Idea' (Forbes, 1999), https://www.forbes.com/forbes/1999/1101/6411390a.html?sh=66976bdf715f.

transactions. Most notably, these solutions included HashCash,[116] B-money,[117] BitGold and Re-usable Proofs of Work.[118] However, as with eCash, these solutions failed to gain wide-spread adoption and use as their attempts to solve the double-spending problem involved significant compromises and other constraints.[119]

DLT, through Blockchain Technology, provided the most efficient solution to the double-spending problem in dispensing with the need for a trusted central authority to verify transactions. This solution was effected by using a decentralised network of computers, called 'nodes', who compete against each other to verify transactions through a process called 'mining'.[120] By cyber libertarianism standards, the architecture of this decentralised system is squarely opposed to the concentration of power which ordinarily embalms trusted central authorities and their roles in the financial system.[121] However, if cyber libertarianism is used as the philosophical underpinning for DLT's emergence, then its aims have been sorely thwarted. At first blush, while there may be merit in assuming that incumbent central parties would fear the introduction of new technology as an existential threat to the success of their businesses, the opposite seems to be the case for DLT. Banks and other financial institutions have devoted vast resources to researching how DLT can be made fit for their own purposes.[122] Further, the increasingly widespread adoption and use of DLT, particularly in the form of cryptocurrencies, has given way to increased regulatory oversight of DLT Offerings.[123] These twin factors have been largely responsible for introducing DLT into the broader public arena impacted in particular by what Schwab calls the 'Fourth Industrial Revolution'.[124]

The specific impact of the introduction of DLT in the age of digital transformation has received significant focus in the literature. While it is widely appreciated that DLT is not entirely a novel invention, the prevailing sentiment appears to be that DLT is a disruptive technology.[125] This sentiment has precipitated more detailed discussions surrounding the precise nature of DLT's impact, as a form of Fintech, and more broadly in the public discourse. In particular, academic dissonance has arisen regarding

116. *See* Adam Back, 'Hashcash: A Denial of Service Counter-Measure' (1 August 2012), http://www.hashcash.org/hashcash.pdf.
117. Wei Dai, 'B-money' (1998), http://www.weidai.com/bmoney.txt.
118. *See* https://nakamotoinstitute.org/finney/rpow/index.html.
119. Delton Rhodes, 'The Double Spending Problem, Explained' (*Komodo*, 11 November 2020), https://komodoplatform.com/en/academy/double-spending-problem/.
120. Saifedean Ammous, 'Blockchain Technology: What Is It Good For?' (2019) 34(2) Banking and Finance Law Review 245 https://doi.org/10.2139/ssrn.2832751.
121. Rainer Böhme et al., 'Bitcoin: Economics, Technology, and Governance' (2015) 29(2) Journal of Economic Perspectives 213 https://doi.org/10.1257/jep.29.2.213.
122. Including central banks. *See* World Economic Forum, 'Central Banks and Distributed Ledger Technologies: How are Central Banks exploring Blockchain Today' (March 2019), https://www3.weforum.org/docs/WEF_Central_Bank_Activity_in_Blockchain_DLT.pdf.
123. Rainer Böhme et al., 'Bitcoin: Economics, Technology, and Governance' (2015) 29(2) Journal of Economic Perspectives 229 https://doi.org/10.1257/jep.29.2.213.
124. Klaus Schwab, *The Fourth Industrial Revolution* (Penguin UK 2017).
125. Betty Jepkemei & Andrew Kipkebut, 'Blockchain: A Disruptive Technology in Financial Assets' (2019) 2(9) IRE Journals 46.

whether DLT's impact on the financial services industry can be categorised as 'revolutionary' or 'evolutionary' in nature.[126]

Witzig, for example, has advanced that Blockchain Technology is 'revolutionary' as it facilitates the transfer of value, avoids the double-spending issue, is impossible to hack and very difficult to shut down.[127] Similar terminology has been used by the UK's Chief Scientific Adviser in describing DLT and the ancillary inventions which it enables.[128] This tone is also echoed by Norberg who has posited that Blockchain Technology may potentially 'revolutionalize, reinvent, or disrupt' the manner in which international trade is conducted.[129] Gupta and Gupta have also posited that Blockchain Technology may even be the catalyst for the Fourth Industrial Revolution worldwide.[130] There have, however, been more nuanced discussions surrounding DLT's impact on the financial services industry. For example, in the context of securities post-trading, the ECB have posited that DLT 'is more likely to cause a gradual change in processes, rather than a revolution in the market'.[131] In relation to ICOs, Town has noted that '[w]hile the ICO as it exists today may be gone tomorrow, the Blockchain brings evolution, not revolution'.[132] From an etymological perspective, Sandstrom has highlighted that 'evolution' is historically associated with Darwin's Theory of Natural Selection and a process which occurs without purpose or vision.[133] DLT considered through an evolutionary paradigm fails to account for the historical developments which have intentionally and purposefully led to DLT in its current form.

126. *See* Mark Buitenhek, 'Understanding and Applying Blockchain Technology in Banking: Evolution or Revolution?' (2016) 1(2) Journal of Digital Banking 111-119 https://doi.org/10.69554/txyn8464; Mark Fenwick, Wulf A Kaal & Erik PM Vermeulen, 'Legal Education in the Blockchain Revolution' (2017) 20 V and J Ent & Tech L 351 https://doi.org/10.2139/ssrn.2939127; Andrea Pinna & Ruttenberg Wiebe, 'Distributed Ledger Technologies in Securities Post-Trading Revolution or Evolution?' (2016) ECB Occasional Paper No. 172, https://www.ecb.europa.eu/pub/pdf/scpops/ecbop172.en.pdf https://doi.org/10.2139/ssrn.2770340 and Kaido Künnapas, 'From Bitcoin to Smart Contracts: Legal Revolution or Evolution from the Perspective of De Lege Ferenda?' in Tanel Kerikmäe & Addi Rull (eds), *The Future of Law and eTechnologies* (Springer 2016).
127. Pascal Witzig & Victoriya Salomon, 'Cutting Out the Middleman: A Study of Blockchain-Induced Reconfigurations in the Swiss Financial Services Industry' (2018) Working Paper 1, 2018/E, 5, https://libra.unine.ch/Publications/37297.
128. UK Government Office for Science, 'Distributed Ledger Technology: Beyond Blockchain' (2015), https://www.gov.uk/government/news/distributed-ledger-technology-beyond-blockchain.
129. Hanna C Norberg, 'Unblocking the Bottlenecks and Making the Global Supply Chain Transparent: How Blockchain Technology can Update Global Trade' (2019) 12(9) Canadian Affairs Global Institute 4.
130. Abishek Gupta & Stuti Gupta, 'Blockchain Technology: Application in Indian Banking Sector' (2019) 19(2) Delhi Business Review 76 https://doi.org/10.51768/dbr.v19i2.192201807.
131. Andrea Pinna & Wiebe Ruttenberg, 'Distributed Ledger Technologies in Securities Post-trading: Revolution or Evolution?'(2016) ECB Occasional Paper Series No. 172, 5, https://www.ecb.europa.eu/pub/pdf/scpops/ecbop172.en.pdf.
132. Sam Town, 'Beyond the ICO Part 3: Evolution Versus Revolution' (*Cryptoslate*, 2018), https://cryptoslate.com/beyond-the-ico-part-3-evolution-versus-revolution/.
133. Gregory Sandstrom, 'Is Blockchain an "Evolutionary" or "Revolutionary" Technology, and So What If It Is?: Digitally Extending Satoshi Nakamoto's Distributed Ledger Innovation' (2019) 8(3) Social Epistemology Review and Reply Collective 37.

Further, Sandstrom has noted defining DLT's impact through the 'revolution' paradigm is misplaced as it is still considered a burgeoning form of Fintech, and the extent to which it will impact the world is still largely unknown. This is particularly apparent when regard is had to the manner in which DLT is to be used in conjunction with other forms of technology, such as the 'Internet of Things' and virtual reality. Overall, Sandstrom has suggested that the terms 'revolution' and 'evolution' should be dispensed with in the context of understanding DLT's impact. Instead, they have posited that the development of Blockchain Technology (and DLT by incorporation) should be viewed as an 'extension of people's choices' in which the technology is being built upon consciously and intentionally through the invention of new applications which shed light on the desires and values of people.[134] This view finds support when regard is had to the manner in which DLT has developed from its first iteration, Blockchain Technology, to the multitude of use cases and applications at present, in and beyond the financial services industry. On a macro level, DLT's introduction into the Fintech foray is having an impact on financial systems, influencing the setting of monetary policy, particularly through catalysing broader discussions about central bank digital currencies.[135]

The preoccupation with whether DLT's impact will be revolutionary or evolutionary may perhaps be misplaced. Instead, as Fintech and new technologies become more pervasive in our daily lives, perhaps it is best to focus on the current societal problems which DLT solves and the manner in which such use should be regulated by law. The discussion above nevertheless sheds light on DLT's potential and provides a good foundation for understanding the core underlying features which makeup the technology.

2.2 DEMYSTIFYING DLT

One of the major obstacles, at least initially, to understanding how new technology operates practically, and its potential application and use cases, is the lack of clarity surrounding the terminology used to describe it.[136] This sentiment applies equally to DLT bearing in mind its foundation in computer science and economics, and the trough of technical jargon which those fields intimate. The BSI reported, for example, that authorities, businesses, and consumers lack an understanding of how DLT operates, and the uses to which the technology may be put.[137] Overtime, the use of DLT has become more

134. Gregory Sandstrom, 'Is Blockchain an "Evolutionary" or "Revolutionary" Technology, and So What If It Is?: Digitally Extending Satoshi Nakamoto's Distributed Ledger Innovation' (2019) 8(3) Social Epistemology Review and Reply Collective 38.
135. World Economic Forum, 'Central Banks and Distributed Ledger Technologies: How are Central Banks exploring Blockchain Today' (March 2019), https://www3.weforum.org/docs/WEF_Central_Bank_Activity_in_Blockchain_DLT.pdf.
136. Advait Deshpande et al., 'Distributed Ledger Technologies/Blockchain: Challenges, Opportunities and Prospects for Standards' (*BSI*, 2017), https://www.bsigroup.com/LocalFiles/zh-tw/InfoSec-newsletter/No201706/download/BSI_Blockchain_DLT_Web.pdf.
137. Advait Deshpande et al., 'Distributed Ledger Technologies/Blockchain: Challenges, Opportunities and Prospects for Standards' (*BSI*, 2017), https://www.bsigroup.com/LocalFiles/zh-tw/InfoSec-newsletter/No201706/download/BSI_Blockchain_DLT_Web.pdf.

pervasive, particularly in the financial services industry. This increased adoption may imply an increased understanding of DLT and its potential application overall. However, there are still several challenges facing widespread DLT use, and its solidification overall as a 'general purpose technology'. However, before these challenges can be addressed accordingly, it is necessary to understand the foundational basis of DLT.

First, there is no universally accepted formal definition of DLT in the literature.[138] This, however, is not surprising as DLT is a relatively new form of technology.[139] Its use is still being tested in a multiplicity of fields and sectors, and the full extent of its functionality and corresponding limitations are still unknown. For example, according to Gartner, as of July 2021, users of DLT, particularly Blockchain Technology, are 'stuck trying to align use cases to the technology'.[140] The absence of a universally accepted formal definition of DLT can also be explained by the heterogeneous nature of the study of DLT through the diverse range of academic disciplines leading ostensibly to definitions of DLT tailored for the specific academic context. This position is, however, not particularly novel and is characteristic of the manner in which subjects are studied when popularised in many fields. As such, the heterogeneous ontological approach to defining DLT is characteristic of its divisive definitional treatment by academic scholars.

This divisive definitional treatment finds expression, most notably, in the incorrect interchangeable use of the terms 'Bitcoin', 'Blockchain', 'DLT'.[141] This misnomer has led to the formulation of DLT definitions which fail to adhere to the inherent distinction between these terms.[142] Understandably, the interchangeable use of the terms is viewed most blaringly through the initial research conducted in the formative years of Bitcoin's popularisation. Nakamoto's conceptualisation of Bitcoin and the system through which Bitcoins are created in the Bitcoin White Paper effectively embodied the first use case of DLT: Blockchain Technology. The interchangeable use of the above-mentioned terms in much of the present-day literature

138. Hossein Kakavind, Nicolette Kost De Sevres & Bart Chilton, 'The Blockchain Revolution: An Analysis of Regulation and Technology Related to Distributed Ledger Technologies' (2017) 4, https://papers.ssrn.com/sol3/papers.cfm?abstract_id=2849251.
139. Hossein Kakavind, Nicolette Kost De Sevres & Bart Chilton, 'The Blockchain Revolution: An Analysis of Regulation and Technology Related to Distributed Ledger Technologies' (2017) 21, https://papers.ssrn.com/sol3/papers.cfm?abstract_id=2849251.
140. *See* Gartner https://blogs.gartner.com/avivah-litan/2021/07/14/hype-cycle-for-blockchain-2021-more-action-than-hype/.
141. Robert M Townsend, 'Distributed Ledgers: Innovation and Regulation in Financial Infrastructure and Payment Systems' (2019) Working Paper 6, https://economics.mit.edu/sites/default/files/2022-09/Distributed%20Ledgers%20-%20Innovation%20and%20Regulation%20in%20Financial%20Infrastructure%20and%20Payment%20Systems.pdf and Hasib Anwar, 'Distributed Ledger Technology: Where Technological Revolution Starts' (101 Blockchains, 30 January 2019), https://101blockchains.com/distributed-ledger-technology-dlt/. *See also* Michael Mainelli & Simon Mills, 'The Missing Links in the Chains? Mutual Distributed Ledger (aka Blockchain) Standards' (*Long Finance*, November 2016), https://www.chainzy.com/media/documents/The_Missing_Links_In_The_Chain_Mutual_Distributed_Ledger_aka_blockchain_Standa_DMN9ulM.pdf.
142. Michel Rauchs et al., 'Distributed Ledger Technology Systems: A Conceptual Framework' (*Cambridge Centre for Alternative Finance*, August 2018) 20, https://www.jbs.cam.ac.uk/fileadmin/user_upload/research/centres/alternative-finance/downloads/2018-10-26-conceptualising-dlt-systems.pdf.

therefore largely ignores that Blockchain Technology is one type of DLT. DLT was therefore conceptualised to serve as a general-purpose technology[143] to be utilised in developing multiple iterations of the technology for bespoke purposes.[144] This is supported by DLT's 'asset-agnostic nature' which permits multiple use case dimensions in the recordkeeping, storage and transfer of virtually any type of asset.[145]

Second, in addition to the incorrect etymological use of 'Bitcoin', 'Blockchain', 'DLT', attempts in the literature to define DLT have been either too broad or too narrow, often characterised by the use of contradictory language.[146] Broadly, for example, Wall and Malm have defined DLT as 'any type of consensus-oriented distributed database that records information on a shared ledger'.[147] On a similar basis, the BSI has defined DLT as 'a type of database which is spread over multiple locations (i.e., a distributed database) and which can be used like a digital ledger to record and manage transactions'.[148] Underlined by the text of the Bitcoin White Paper, but on a similarly broad basis, the OECD has defined DLT as permitting 'transfers of monetary amounts peer-to-peer with transactions authenticated by many computers (of users around the world) without the need for any intermediary'.[149] According to Brogan, DLT can be defined as 'a distributed database, maintained by a consensus protocol run by nodes in a P2P network. This consensus protocol replaces a central administrator since all peers contribute to maintaining the integrity of the database'.[150]

These broad definitions are generally helpful, but they lack the necessary descriptiveness and hence fail to provide a comprehensive explanation of DLT. For example, the absence of a reference to DLT's use of cryptography is particularly noticeable. However, this is apparent in Davidson et al.'s definition of DLT as being a 'distributed, cryptographically secure, and crypto-economically incentivised consensus

143. Examples of other GPTs include electricity, the Internet and the steam engine.
144. International Telecommunication Union, 'Technical Report FG DLT D2.1: Distributed Ledger Technology Use Cases' (1 August 2019), https://www.itu.int/en/ITU-T/focusgroups/dlt/Documents/d21.pdf and Organisation for Economic Co-operation and Development, 'Draft OECD High-Level Guidance Regarding Policy Considerations on Responsible Innovation and Adoption of Distributed Ledger Technology (DLT)' 3, https://www.gleif.org/lei-solutions/regulatory-use-of-the-lei/consultation-responses/draft-oecd-high-level-guidance-regarding-policy-considerations-on-responsible-innovation-and-adoption-of-dlt.pdf.
145. David Mills et al., 'Distributed Ledger Technology in Payments, Clearing, and Settlement' (2016) Finance and Economics Discussion Series 095, 17.
146. Michel Rauchs et al., 'Distributed Ledger Technology Systems: A Conceptual Framework' (*Cambridge Centre for Alternative Finance*, August 2018) 19, https://www.jbs.cam.ac.uk/fileadmin/user_upload/research/centres/alternative-finance/downloads/2018-10-26-conceptualising-dlt-systems.pdf.
147. Eric Wall & Gustaf Malm, 'Using Blockchain Technology and Smart Contracts to Create a Distributed Securities Depository' (*Lund University*, 29 June 2016) 3, https://lup.lub.lu.se/student-papers/search/publication/8885750.
148. Advait Deshpande et al., 'Distributed Ledger Technologies/Blockchain: Challenges, Opportunities and the Prospects for Standards' (*BSI*, 2017) iv, https://www.bsigroup.com/LocalFiles/zh-tw/InfoSec-newsletter/No201706/download/BSI_Blockchain_DLT_Web.pdf.
149. Xavier Vives, 'Digital Disruption in Financial Markets' (*OECD*, 16 May 2019) 5, https://one.oecd.org/document/DAF/COMP(2019)1/en/pdf.
150. James Brogan, Immanuel Baskaran & Navin Ramachandran, 'Authenticating Health Activity using Distributed Ledger Technologies' (2018) 16 Computational and Structural Biotechnology Journal 257 https://doi.org/10.1016/j.csbj.2018.06.004.

engine'.[151] This is similarly echoed by the UK's FCA which has defined DLT as enabling 'a single, sequenced, standardised and cryptographically-secured record of activity to be safely distributed to, and acted upon by, a network of varied participants'.[152] Maupin has posited that DLT can be defined as a shared digital database which is usually dispersed geographically over a number of jurisdictions via a P2P network which is used to manage, verify and record electronic transactions with the use of cryptographic algorithms.[153]

Some suggested definitions appear to be more functional in nature by referencing the purposes for which DLT can be put. For example, the US FRB have defined DLT broadly as being 'essentially asset-agnostic, meaning the technology is potentially capable of providing the storage, recordkeeping, and transfer of any type of asset'.[154] Further, Bott has defined DLT as 'the open and networked basis for proving ownership and transfers of such currencies - dramatically shorten the time it takes to clear transactions, wherever they take place in the world'.[155] Further, it has been posited that DLT's main purpose is to provide a 'trust solution' or a 'trust machine'[156] through which trust is enhanced by multiple disintermediated parties who provide authenticated transactions, disposing with the need for a singular centralised authority who traditionally provides this role.[157] Further, DLT has been characterised as providing legibility and clarity to the recording of transactions (i.e., by providing a particular sequence of recorded transactions including time-stamped information), and consistency and consensus (i.e., established authentication mechanisms which provide a proved factual basis for the recording of information relating to property, identity, and price and value).[158]

151. Sinclair Davidson, Primavera De Filippi & Jason Potts, 'Disrupting Governance: The New Institutional Economics of Distributed Ledger Technologies' (July 2016) 2, https://ssrn.com/abstract=2811995.
152. Financial Conduct Authority, 'Discussion Paper on Distributed Ledger Technology' (April 2017), https://www.fca.org.uk/publication/discussion/dp17-03.pdf.
153. Julie Maupin, 'Mapping the Global Legal Landscape of Blockchain and Other Distributed Ledger Technologies' (2017), https://papers.ssrn.com/sol3/papers.cfm?abstract_id=2930077 https://doi.org/10.2139/ssrn.2930077; Advait Deshpande et al., 'Distributed Ledger Tech nologies/Blockchain: Challenges, opportunities and prospects for standards' (*BSI*, 2017), https://www.bsigroup.com/LocalFiles/zh-tw/InfoSec-newsletter/No201706/download/BSI_Blockchain_DLT_Web.pdf and D Richard Kuhn, Jeff Voas & Dylan Yaga, 'Rethinking Distributed Ledger Technology' (*IEEE Computer*, February 2019), https://www.researchgate.net/publication/331260506_Rethinking_Distributed_Ledger_Technology.
154. David Mills et al., 'Distributed Ledger Technology in Payments, Clearing, and Settlement' (2016) Finance and Economics Discussion Series 095, 17.
155. Jurgen Bott & Udo Milkau, 'Towards a Framework for the Evaluation and Design of Distributed Ledger Technologies in Banking and Payments' (2016) 10(2) Journal of Payments Strategy and Systems 154 https://doi.org/10.69554/dcty1654.
156. The Economist, 'The Promise of the Blockchain: The Trust Machine' (2015), https://www.economist.com/leaders/2015/10/31/the-trust-machine.
157. Dirk Zetzsche, Douglas W Arner & Ross P Buckley, 'The Distributed Liability of Distributed Ledger Technologies: The Legal Risks of Blockchain' (2017) EBI Working Paper Series No. 14, 6, https://papers.ssrn.com/sol3/papers.cfm?abstract_id=3018214.
158. Sinclair Davidson, Primavera De Filippi & Jason Potts, 'Disrupting Governance: The New Institutional Economics of Distributed Ledger Technologies' (July 2016), https://ssrn.com/abstract=2811995.

On an individual basis, there have therefore been multiple attempts to develop a formalised definition of DLT. From an ontological perspective, however, these definitions appear to be tailored mostly to apply within the context of the papers authored, thus losing broad appeal. Given the melee of suggested definitions across a wide variety of disciplines which have been tailored to fit specific contexts, it is prudent to analyse the commonly used descriptive indicators to arrive at a more complete way to define DLT. One method of doing this would be to compare the differences and similarities which exist in the current suggested definitions.

Rauchs et al. at the Cambridge Centre for Alternative Finance have identified similar issues with the attempts to define DLT and have therefore carried out an analysis of existing DLT ontologies in their paper 'Distributed Ledger Technologies: A Conceptual Paper'.[159] The study used a 'systems perspective' approach to deconstruct and reconstruct DLT for the purposes of reaching a consensus on its definitions and taxonomies. This was done by analysing categorisations of DLT systems previously formulated by academic scholars and professionals who have written on the topic. As a result, the following working definition of DLT has been suggested: 'A DLT system is a system of electronic records that enables a network of independent participants to establish consensus around the authoritative ordering of cryptographically validated ("signed") transactions. These records are made persistent by replicating the data across multiple nodes, and tamper-evident by linking them by cryptographic hashes. The shared result of the reconciliation/consensus process – the "ledger" – serves as the authoritative version of these records'.[160] This is by far the most robust definition which has been suggested. It should be noted that the ontology is framed within constructing a definition of DLT systems, rather than specifically providing a formal and more traditionally framed definition of DLT itself.

2.3 THE CORE FEATURES OF DLT

Having reviewed the most notable literature on Fintech, the following terms are used most commonly in descriptions of DLT: storage; record-keeping; transfer; consensus; distributed; ledger; ownership; verification; P2P; transaction; decentralised; cryptography; manage; database; and unalterable. These commonly used indicators accord overall with the working definition of DLT proposed by the Cambridge Centre for Alternative Finance. These indicators include shared multi-party consensus; independent validation; recordkeeping; tamper evident; and tamper resistance. On this basis, the terms record-keeping, consensus, distributed, ledger, verification, P2P,

159. Michel Rauchs et al., 'Distributed Ledger Technology Systems: A Conceptual Framework' (*Cambridge Centre for Alternative Finance*, August 2018) 20, https://www.jbs.cam.ac.uk/fileadmin/user_upload/research/centres/alternative-finance/downloads/2018-10-26-conceptualising-dlt-systems.pdf.
160. Michel Rauchs et al., 'Distributed Ledger Technology Systems: A Conceptual Framework' (*Cambridge Centre for Alternative Finance*, August 2018) 24, https://www.jbs.cam.ac.uk/fileadmin/user_upload/research/centres/alternative-finance/downloads/2018-10-26-conceptualising-dlt-systems.pdf.

decentralised, cryptography, and unalterable, appear to be the core underlining features which denote DLT systems.

It should also be noted that DLT system architecture often depends on who may access a ledger and the extent to which those who have access may make use of it. On this basis, DLT can be further characterised as being: (i) public or permissionless ledgers; and (ii) private or permissioned ledgers.[161] The distinction between these two types of ledgers is informed by the extent to which it is open for view to users. For example, public or permissionless DLT platforms are generally open to anyone to read and view and thus allow to add new transactions to the ledger for record (i.e., to write) and to verify the addition of new transactions to the ledger (i.e., to commit). However, private or permissioned ledgers restrict access and thus place controls on the category of users who may execute actions and functions on the ledger.[162] Each of the identified core features of DLT systems is defined below in turn.

2.3.1 Distributed and Decentralised Ledger

DLT systems are characterised as being both distributed and decentralised.[163] First, DLT systems are distributed by a replicated digital ledger spread across multiple locations or multiple users. This can be contrasted with central ledgers which are centrally stored and maintained in one fixed location.[164] Second, DLT systems have no central coordinating authority which verifies or settles transactions before they are added to the shared digital ledger (the role synonymously associated with banks in the traditional financial system). Instead, a consensus algorithm or protocol, setting out the rules for how nodes come to an agreement in verifying and recording transactions to the digital ledger, is followed by the P2P network who contribute to the maintenance of the ledger's integrity.[165]

161. Hasib Anwar, 'Distributed Ledger Technology: Where Technological Revolution Starts' (101 Blockchains, 30 January 2019), https://101blockchains.com/distributed-ledger-technology-dlt/.
162. Organisation for Economic Co-operation and Development, 'OECD Blockchain Primer' (2018) 5, https://www.oecd.org/finance/OECD-Blockchain-Primer.pdf.
163. Rick Kuhn, Jeff Voas & Dylan Yaga, 'Rethinking Distributed Ledger Technology' (*IEEE Computer*, February 2019) 2, https://www.researchgate.net/publication/331260506_Rethinking_Distributed_Ledger_Technology.
164. Tradeix, 'The Difference between Blockchain and Distributed Ledger Technologies' https://tradeix.com/distributed-ledger-technology/. *See* Julie Maupin, 'Mapping the Global Legal Landscape of Blockchain and other Distributed Ledger Technologies' (2017), https://papers.ssrn.com/sol3/papers.cfm?abstract_id=2930077 https://doi.org/10.2139/ssrn.2930077; Advait Deshpande et al., 'Distributed Ledger Technologies/Blockchain: Challenges, opportunities and prospects for standards' (*BSI*, 2017), https://www.bsigroup.com/LocalFiles/zh-tw/InfoSec-newsletter/No201706/download/BSI_Blockchain_DLT_Web.pdf and D Richard Kuhn, Jeff Voas & Dylan Yaga, 'Rethinking Distributed Ledger Technology' (*IEEE Computer*, February 2019), https://www.researchgate.net/publication/331260506_Rethinking_Distributed_Ledger_Technology.
165. James Brogan, Immanuel Baskaran & Navin Ramachandran, 'Authenticating Health Activity using Distributed Ledger Technologies' (2018) 16 Computational and Structural Biotechnology Journal 257 https://doi.org/10.1016/j.csbj.2018.06.004.

Townsend has correctly noted that distributed ledgers are mistakenly referenced as being synonymous with decentralised systems.[166] This has been further conflated by the repeated and often unexplained use of the schematic diagram made famous by American engineer Paul Baran comparing centralised, decentralised and distributed networks, used to define the 'redundancy level'.[167] Baran's claim to fame came in the early 1960s when they reported being able to transmit pieces of data from one computer to another and have these pieces magically reassemble using packet switching technology. Vitalik Buterin, co-founder of Ethereum, has indicated that decentralisation can be divided into three categories being: (i) architectural de(centralisation), concerned with the number of physical computers which make up the system; (ii) political de(centralisation) concerned with the number of people who control the computers which make up the system; and (iii) logical de(centralisation), concerned with whether the structure of the system is presented as a single entity or an 'amorphous swarm'.[168] As an illustration therefore, Buterin has argued that Blockchains are architecturally decentralised (no central point of failure in its infrastructure) and politically decentralised (no single entity in control) but are logically centralised (system acts as a single computer together with an agreed common state).

DLT therefore operates in contrast to centralised ledger networks as no single entity has control over the network nor is responsible for the overall operation or maintenance thereof.[169] Centralised networks and centralised ledger systems usually entail a single trusted third party overseeing the storage of data and the recording of transactions, such as transfers of assets, upon receiving the relevant approved notifications.[170] These structures are often criticised for not being very secure as they have a single point of failure. However, entities in financial services who utilise centralised ledger systems traditionally include banks and clearing and settlement houses, and utilise this concentration of risk to focus on the management of security.[171] The distributed nature of DLT systems can be distinguished from centralised ledger systems in two respects. First, and as mentioned above, DLT systems can be used to record and

166. Robert M Townsend, 'Distributed Ledgers: Innovation and Regulation in Financial Infrastructure and Payment Systems' (2019) Working Paper 6, http://www.robertmtownsend.net/sites/default/files/files/papers/working_papers/Distributed%20Ledgers-first%20circulation-041819.pdf.
167. Paul Baran, 'On Distributed Communication Networks' (The Rand Corporation, September 1962), https://www.rand.org/content/dam/rand/pubs/papers/2005/P2626.pdf.
168. Vitalik Buterin, 'The Meaning of Decentralisation' (*Medium*, 6 February 2017), https://medium.com/@VitalikButerin/the-meaning-of-decentralization-a0c92b76a274.
169. Primavera De Filippi & Aaron Wright, 'The Characteristics of Blockchains' in Primavera De Filippi & Aaron Wright (eds), *Blockchain and the Law* (Harvard University Press 2018).
170. Douglas W Arner et al., 'Policy and Regulatory Challenges of Distributed Ledger Technologies and Digital Assets in Asia' in Chris Brummer (ed.), *Cryptoassets* (OUP USA 2019) https://doi.org/10.1093/oso/9780190077310.003.0011.
171. Douglas W Arner et al., 'Policy and Regulatory Challenges of Distributed Ledger Technologies and Digital Assets in Asia' in Chris Brummer (ed.), *Cryptoassets* (OUP USA 2019) https://doi.org/10.1093/oso/9780190077310.003.0011.

store data on a network of computers in which changes to the ledger are updated simultaneously across the entire network. Second, the relevant data recorded and stored are authenticated with the use of cryptographic signatures.[172]

2.3.2 P2P Network

DLT systems are also characterised by a distributed P2P network.[173] P2P networks are usually composed of a network of computers that have equal access to data and resources, capable of communicating and sharing information with each other.[174] The individual computers in a P2P network are referred to as 'nodes' or 'peers'.[175] The now-defunct audio file-sharing service provider Napster is widely recognised as one of the first use cases of P2P networks.[176] However, several other earlier technologies such as The ARPANET and later technologies such as Usenet, Gnutella, and BitTorrent have been cited as being fundamental to the development and popularisation of P2P network architectures.[177]

The participants, i.e., nodes in the network of DLT systems, include independent computers, servers, and other storage devices which record, share, store, and synchronise transactions and other related information based on the rules and procedures of the consensus mechanism deployed.[178] Most DLT systems are broadly composed of nodes who perform one of two core functions: (i) validation; and (ii) broadcast and consensus. Nodes who perform the validation function work together to validate every new transaction, and whether these transactions can be added to a ledger. They may validate information such as the identity of the owner of the asset being acquired.[179] However, nodes who perform the broadcast and consensus function work together by broadcasting information about validated transactions. They communicate among

172. Advait Deshpande et al., 'Distributed Ledger Technologies/Blockchain: Challenges, Opportunities and Prospects for Standards' (*BSI*, 2017), https://www.bsigroup.com/LocalFiles/zh-tw/InfoSec-newsletter/No201706/download/BSI_Blockchain_DLT_Web.pdf.
173. Hong Kong Applied Science and Technology Research Institute, 'Whitepaper on Distributed Ledger Technology' (11 November 2016) 18, https://www.hkma.gov.hk/media/eng/doc/key-functions/finanical-infrastructure/Whitepaper_On_Distributed_Ledger_Technology.pdf.
174. Naomi J Alpern & Robert J Shimonski, *Eleventh Hour Security: Exam SY0-201 Study Guide* (Syngress 2010) 4.
175. Hong Kong Applied Science and Technology Research Institute, 'Whitepaper on Distributed Ledger Technology' (11 November 2016) 18, https://www.hkma.gov.hk/media/eng/doc/key-functions/finanical-infrastructure/Whitepaper_On_Distributed_Ledger_Technology.pdf.
176. *See* Zupeng Li et al., 'Research of Peer-to-Peer Network Architecture' (2003) 1 ICCT 2003 International Conference 312 https://doi.org/10.1109/icct.2003.1209091.
177. Delton Rhodes, 'The Double Spending Problem, Explained' (*Komodo*, 11 November 2020), https://komodoplatform.com/en/academy/double-spending-problem/.
178. Delton Rhodes, 'Distributed Ledger Technology: An Overview of DLT Systems' (*Komodo*, 15 May 2020), https://komodoplatform.com/en/academy/distributed-ledger-technology/.
179. Hong Kong Applied Science and Technology Research Institute, 'Whitepaper on Distributed Ledger Technology' (11 November 2016) 10, https://www.hkma.gov.hk/media/eng/doc/key-functions/finanical-infrastructure/Whitepaper_On_Distributed_Ledger_Technology.pdf.

themselves to reach a consensus on the collection of commonly validated transactions to be entered into the ledger.[180]

The specific function and purpose of nodes are, however, largely dependent on the type of DLT system being utilised. For example, in the Blockchain DLT system 'miner' nodes, through a process called 'mining', function to participate in the consensus process by validating transactions and adding blocks, while other nodes only store a precise or nearly precise replica of the list of transactions.[181] In the Hedera Hashgraph DLT system, consensus nodes function to participate in the consensus process, receive transactions and store the ledger's most recent version, while mirror nodes store the ledger's historical data.[182] In the Holochain DLT system, each node functions to maintain and process its own individual ledger. Further, nodes are not required to reach consensus by being synchronised with each other, nor are they required to 'mine' based on the Blockchain consensus mechanism discussed below.[183]

Nodes are therefore crucial to DLT systems as they enforce the rules and procedures governing them, and act as the substitute for the central authority traditionally utilised.[184] They do this principally through being connected with each other and acting as points for communication. They thus function overall to participate in the building and maintenance of DLT systems.[185]

2.3.3 Consensus Mechanism

DLT systems are also characterised by a consensus mechanism consisting of mathematical algorithms which delineate the rules and procedures for how nodes reach a consensus on the current state of a ledger by validating new transactions before they are added to a ledger.[186] These rules and procedures essentially govern how nodes

180. Hong Kong Applied Science and Technology Research Institute, 'Whitepaper on Distributed Ledger Technology' (11 November 2016) 10, https://www.hkma.gov.hk/media/eng/dcc/key-functions/finanical-infrastructure/Whitepaper_On_Distributed_Ledger_Technology.pdf.
181. ITU-T, 'Technical Report FG DLT D1.2: Distributed Ledger Technology Overview, Concepts, Ecosystem' (1 August 2019) 3, https://www.itu.int/en/ITU-T/focusgroups/dlt/Documents/d12.pdf and Organisation for Economic Co-operation and Development, 'OECD Blockchain Primer' (2018) 7, https://www.oecd.org/finance/OECD-Blockchain-Primer.pdf.
182. *See* Hedera Hashgraph, 'Hedera: A Public Hashgraph Network & Governing Council' Whitepaper V.2.1 (15 August 2020), https://hedera.com/hh_whitepaper_v2.1-20200815.pdf.
183. *See* Arthur Brock et al., 'Holo Green Paper' (December 2017), https://files.holo.host/2018/03/Holo-Green-Paper.pdf.
184. Garrick Hileman & Michel Rauchs, 'Global Cryptocurrency Benchmarking Study' (*Cambridge Centre for Alternative Finance*, 2017) 104, https://www.jbs.cam.ac.uk/fileadmin/user_upload/research/centres/alternative-finance/downloads/2017-global-cryptocurrency-benchmarking-study.pdf.
185. Hong Kong Applied Science and Technology Research Institute, 'Whitepaper on Distributed Ledger Technology' (11 November 2016) 10, https://www.hkma.gov.hk/media/eng/dcc/key-functions/finanical-infrastructure/Whitepaper_On_Distributed_Ledger_Technology.pdf.
186. Depository Trust and Clearing Corporation (DTCC), 'Security of DLT Networks: A Distributed Ledger Technology Security Framework for the Financial Services Industry' (February 2020) 4, https://www.dtcc.com/-/media/Files/Downloads/WhitePapers/Security-of-DLT-Networks-Paper.pdf; Christian Catalini, 'Some Simple Economics of the Blockchain', (2018) NBER Working Paper Series No. 22952, https://www.nber.org/papers/w22952; ITU-T, 'Technical Report FG DLT D1.2: Distributed Ledger Technology Overview, Concepts, Ecosystem' (1

record information to a ledger, together with the organised sequencing of such information, without having to rely on a central authority. The most common consensus mechanisms used in public DLT systems include POW; POS; and Delegated POS.[187] The consensus mechanisms Practical Byzantine Fault Tolerance and Proof-of-Elapsed Time have also been developed for private DLT systems. Several other consensus mechanisms have been developed, including Proof of Authority, Proof of Burn and Proof of Value, but these have been proven to be less well-established.[188]

2.3.3.1 Proof-of-Work

The POW consensus mechanism used in Bitcoin, Litecoin and Dogecoin DLT systems, among others, is the most well-established.[189] This consensus mechanism entails miner nodes competing against each other to produce and broadcast 'blocks' for approval by solving a computational puzzle.[190] Blocks record and store transaction data chronologically to Blockchain's continuous linear chain of transactions and must be composed of specific information before being validated and added to a chain.[191] Once a miner node has solved the computational puzzle, the solution provided is the 'proof' of the work performed.[192] The Blockchain DLT system is programmed so that POW is created every 10 minutes.[193]

Where POW is created simultaneously leading to the creation of parallel blocks (in a process known as 'forking'), the proof with the higher score measured by difficulty is accepted, i.e., the longest chain.[194] The likelihood of validating a new block and ensuring that it is added to a ledger is dependent upon the computing ability and

August 2019) 2, https://www.itu.int/en/ITU-T/focusgroups/dlt/Documents/d12.pdf and Organisation for Economic Co-operation and Development, 'OECD Blockchain Primer' (2018) 6, https://www.oecd.org/finance/OECD-Blockchain-Primer.pdf.

187. International Monetary Fund, 'Fintech Note: Blockchain Consensus Mechanisms: A Primer for Supervisors' Note/2022/003 (January 2022) 12.
188. *See* Bahareh Lashkari & Petr Musilek, 'A Comprehensive Review of Blockchain Consensus Mechanisms' (2021) 1 IEEE Access, https://ieeexplore.ieee.org/stamp/stamp.jsp?arnumber=9376868 for a comprehensive review of DLT system consensus mechanisms.
189. International Monetary Fund, 'Fintech Note: Blockchain Consensus Mechanisms: A Primer for Supervisors' Note/2022/003 (January 2022) 8.
190. Organisation for Economic Co-operation and Development, 'OECD Blockchain Primer' 7, https://www.oecd.org/finance/OECD-Blockchain-Primer.pdf.
191. *See* Cryptopedia, 'How a Block in the Bitcoin Blockchain Works' (22 December 2021), https://www.gemini.com/cryptopedia/what-is-block-in-blockchain-bitcoin-block-size.
192. ITU-T, 'Technical Report FG DLT D1.2: Distributed Ledger Technology Overview, Concepts, Ecosystem' (1 August 2019) 2, https://www.itu.int/en/ITU-T/focusgroups/dlt/Documents/d12.pdf and World Bank, 'Distributed Ledger Technology and Blockchain' FinTech Note No. 1 (2017) 6. *See* Phillip Hacker & Chris Thomale, 'Crypto-Securities Regulation: ICOs, Token Sales and Cryptocurrencies under EU Financial Law' (2018) 15(4) European Company and Financial Law Review, De Gruyter 645-696 https://doi.org/10.1515/ecfr-2018-0021.
193. World Bank, 'Distributed Ledger Technology and Blockchain' FinTech Note No. 1 (2017) 6.
194. International Monetary Fund, 'Fintech Note: Blockchain Consensus Mechanisms: A Primer for Supervisors' Note/2022/003 (January 2022) 12 and World Bank Group, 'Distributed Ledger Technology and Blockchain' FinTech Note No. 1 (2017) 6.

processing time at the disposal of the miner node.[195] Once a block has been successfully validated and added to a ledger, miner nodes are rewarded with a specific amount of Bitcoin (3.125 for every block mined as of April 2024),[196] or transaction fees when users send Bitcoins.[197] These rewards serve as a financial incentive which enables the maintenance of the Blockchain DLT system's integrity.[198]

2.3.3.2 Proof-of-Stake

The POS consensus mechanism used in the Polkadot and EO.SIO DLT systems is less well-established.[199] However, it has been used in place of POW to expel the need for the large amounts of energy which nodes require to mine Bitcoin.[200] This consensus mechanism entails consensus being reached based on users' existing stake in the DLT system.[201] Users are selected at random by an algorithm to validate transactions in the same manner that miner nodes validate transactions for Blockchain.[202] However, these users, called 'validators', are not required to solve computational puzzles, but instead stake an amount of stored native cryptoassets held to become eligible for selection.[203] Users who hold the largest amounts of native cryptoassets have a higher likelihood of being selected by the algorithm.[204]

195. ITU-T, 'Technical Report FG DLT D1.2: Distributed Ledger Technology Overview, Concepts, Ecosystem' (1 August 2019) 2, https://www.itu.int/en/ITU-T/focusgroups/dlt/Documents/d12.pdf. *See* Phillip Hacker & Chris Thomale, 'Crypto-Securities Regulation: ICOs, Token Sales and Cryptocurrencies under EU Financial Law' (2018) 15(4) European Company and Financial Law Review, De Gruyter 645-696 https://doi.org/10.1515/ecfr-2018-0021.
196. Omkar Godbole, 'Crypto Miners Still Selling Their Bitcoin as Reward Halving Looms, Blockchain Data Show' (Coindesk, 29 February 2024), https://www.coindesk.com/markets/2024/02/29/crypto-miners-still-selling-their-bitcoin-as-reward-halving-looms-blockchain-data-show/.
197. International Monetary Fund, 'Fintech Note: Blockchain Consensus Mechanisms: A Primer for Supervisors' Note/2022/003 (January 2022) 9.
198. World Bank, 'Distributed Ledger Technology and Blockchain' FinTech Note No. 1 (2017) 6.
199. *See* Gavin Wood, 'Polkadot: Vision for a Heterogenous Multi-Chain Framework Draft 1', https://polkadot.network/PolkaDotPaper.pdf and Daniel Larimer, 'ESO.IO Technical White Paper v2', https://github.com/EOSIO/Documentation/blob/master/TechnicalWhitePaper.md.
200. Bahareh Lashkari & Petr Musilek, 'A Comprehensive Review of Blockchain Consensus Mechanisms' (2021) 1 IEEE Access 43635, https://ieeexplore.ieee.org/stamp/stamp.jsp?arnumber=9376868.
201. World Bank, 'Distributed Ledger Technology and Secured Transactions: Legal, Regulatory and Technological Perspectives: Guidance Notes Series' (May 2020) 17, https://documents1.worldbank.org/curated/en/541741588053800973/pdf/Distributed-Ledger-Technology-and-Secured-Transactions-Framework.pdf.
202. International Monetary Fund, 'Fintech Note: Blockchain Consensus Mechanisms: A Primer for Supervisors' Note/2022/003 (January 2022) 10 and ITU-T, 'Technical Report FG DLT D1.2: Distributed Ledger Technology Overview, Concepts, Ecosystem' (1 August 2019) 2, https://www.itu.int/en/ITU-T/focusgroups/dlt/Documents/d12.pdf.
203. International Monetary Fund, 'Fintech Note: Blockchain Consensus Mechanisms: A Primer for Supervisors' Note/2022/003 (January 2022) 10 and ITU-T, 'Technical Report FG DLT D1.2: Distributed Ledger Technology Overview, Concepts, Ecosystem' (1 August 2019) 2, https://www.itu.int/en/ITU-T/focusgroups/dlt/Documents/d12.pdf.
204. Giulia Fanti, Leonid Kogan & Pramod Viswanath, 'Economics of Proof-of-Stake Payment Systems' 2, http://econ.ruc.edu.cn/docs/2021-05/9f60b7d1e15e4ce2b578d4458bb51643.pdf.

The POS consensus mechanism is therefore built on the idea that users who invest directly into the DLT system by participating in reaching a consensus are less likely to undermine it.[205] For example, the process referred to as 'slashing' ensures that validators who behave incompetently or maliciously are expelled from the DLT system's network, in addition to losing their stake. Validators who participate in reaching consensus are also incentivised by rewards in the form of network transaction fees for each block which they successfully validate.[206] Overall, the POS is concerned with rewarding seniority and proving ownership of assets, in place of the required computing power characteristic of the POW consensus mechanism.[207]

2.3.3.3 Practical Byzantine Fault Tolerance

Practical Byzantine Fault Tolerance (pBFT) is one of the most widely known examples of consensus mechanisms used in private and permissioned DLT systems. In general, the Byzantine Fault problem refers to the failure of components in computer systems, particularly decentralised systems, and the existence of flawed information as to its failure.[208] In DLT systems, the Byzantine Fault problem is presented in the form of nodes who may exhibit unpredictable behaviours.[209] The pBFT consensus mechanism therefore operates under the assumption that nodes in the DLT system may act fraudulently by transmitting malicious messages. Unlike public and permissionless consensus mechanisms, in this consensus mechanism, the identities of all operating nodes are known as they are required to agree on the network participants.[210] To counter the likelihood of nodes acting maliciously, consensus on block validation is reached with the participation of all users by majority consensus, ordinarily consisting of several voting rounds.[211] During the block validation process, nodes exchange messages in four

205. ITU-T, 'Technical Report FG DLT D1.2: Distributed Ledger Technology Overview, Concepts, Ecosystem' (1 August 2019) 2, https://www.itu.int/en/ITU-T/focusgroups/dlt/Documents/d12.pdf.
206. ITU-T, 'Technical Report FG DLT D1.2: Distributed Ledger Technology Overview, Concepts, Ecosystem' (1 August 2019) 2, https://www.itu.int/en/ITU-T/focusgroups/dlt/Documents/d12.pdf.
207. World Bank, 'Distributed Ledger Technology and Blockchain' FinTech Note No. 1 (2017) 8.
208. Sanatan Shrivastava & Ashish Sharma, 'Distributed Ledger Technology and Byzantine Fault Tolerance in Blockchain' No. 7198 (Easy Chair Preprint, 9 December 2021) 4, https://easychair.org/publications/preprint/qcKr.
209. Bahareh Lashkari & Petr Musilek, 'A Comprehensive Review of Blockchain Consensus Mechanisms' (2021) 1 IEEE Access 43627, https://ieeexplore.ieee.org/stamp/stamp.jsp?arnumber=9376868.
210. International Monetary Fund, 'Fintech Note: Blockchain Consensus Mechanisms: A Primer for Supervisors' Note/2022/003 (January 2022) 13 and ITU-T, 'Technical Report FG DLT D1.2: Distributed Ledger Technology Overview, Concepts, Ecosystem' (1 August 2019) 2, https://www.itu.int/en/ITU-T/focusgroups/dlt/Documents/d12.pdf.
211. ITU-T, 'Technical Report FG DLT D1.2: Distributed Ledger Technology Overview, Concepts, Ecosystem' (1 August 2019) 2, https://www.itu.int/en/ITU-T/focusgroups/dlt/Documents/d12.pdf.

rounds called 'views', which overall ensures the accuracy of transaction data. These rounds are initiated by a leader or primary node, who can be replaced after each round.[212] Leader nodes are ordinarily replaced by nodes through a majority vote.

2.3.4 Cryptography

DLT systems are also characterised by their use of cryptographic hashes and PKI (i.e., digital signatures) which ensure that data recorded and stored in a ledger are highly tamper-proof and immutable.[213] However, it is important to bear in mind that cryptographic hashes and public-private key cryptography are not unique to DLT system usage,[214] and have been deployed elsewhere, such as for message integrity authentication.[215]

Hashing occurs when a user inputs transaction data into a cryptographic hashing algorithm consisting of a complicated mathematical formula.[216] The transaction data includes the details of the sender and receiver, in addition to the amount being transferred. Once the transaction data has been inputted, the algorithm (hash function) creates a 'digest' composed of letters and numbers of a determined length unique to each transaction.[217] A timestamp is also applied.[218] Hashes have therefore been compared to digital fingerprints as specific transaction data input will always produce the same precise hash.[219] If the original transaction data is changed, the hash would be altered leading to its incompatibility with the remainder of the linked chain of hashes.[220] This is because the hash of each block contains a reference to the previous block's hash, including its timestamp, ensuring an accurate sequential ordering of transactions.[221] Nodes are therefore able to detect any changes to hashes and respond by declining to accept that specific version of the ledger.[222]

212. International Monetary Fund, 'Fintech Note: Blockchain Consensus Mechanisms: A Primer for Supervisors' Note/2022/003 (January 2022) 13.
213. De Filippi P & Wright A, 'Digital Currencies and Decentralised Payment Platforms' in De Filippi & Wright (eds), *Blockchain and the Law* (Harvard University Press 2018) 2; Anton Badev & Matthew Chen, 'Bitcoin: Technical Background and Data Analysis' (*Federal Reserve Board*, 2014) 7 and Organisation for Economic Co-operation and Development, 'OECD Blockchain Primer' 6, https://www.oecd.org/finance/OECD-Blockchain-Primer.pdf.
214. Anton Badev & Matthew Chen, 'Bitcoin: Technical Background and Data Analysis' (*Federal Reserve Board*, 2014) 7.
215. *See* Tomaso Aste, Paolo Tasca & T Di Matteo, 'Blockchain Technologies: Foreseeable Impact on Industry and Society' (2017) 50(9) Computer 18 https://doi.org/10.1109/mc.2017.3571064.
216. Organisation for Economic Co-operation and Development, 'OECD Blockchain Primer' 7, https://www.oecd.org/finance/OECD-Blockchain-Primer.pdf.
217. World Bank, 'Distributed Ledger Technology and Blockchain' FinTech Note No. 1 (2017) 8 and Organisation for Economic Co-operation and Development, 'OECD Blockchain Primer' 7, https://www.oecd.org/finance/OECD-Blockchain-Primer.pdf.
218. World Bank, 'Distributed Ledger Technology and Blockchain' FinTech Note No. 1 (2017) 8.
219. Organisation for Economic Co-operation and Development, 'OECD Blockchain Primer' 7, https://www.oecd.org/finance/OECD-Blockchain-Primer.pdf.
220. D Richard Kuhn, Jeff Voas & Dylan Yaga, 'Rethinking Distributed Ledger Technology' (*IEEE Computer*, February 2019) 3, https://www.researchgate.net/publication/331260506_Rethinking_Distributed_Ledger_Technology.
221. Kim Kilburn & Taewon Kang, 'Does Technology Against Corruption Always Lead to Benefit? The Potential Risks and Challenges of the Blockchain Technology' (*OECD Anti-corruption*

PKI is deployed in DLT systems for creating digital signatures through asymmetric encryption composed of two sets of keys: public and private.[223] Digital signatures are used to sign transactions, i.e., a block, binding the sender in the same manner traditional ink signatures do.[224] All users in a DLT system network possess a private key, known only to the individual user, used for signing the hash digests of transactions, i.e., digital messages. All users also possess a public key which is publicly known and used to verify the identity of the user when digital messages are received.[225] These two keys operate together so that the private key is used to validate the 'true owner' of the public key through algorithmic encryption which verifies that the two keys are mathematically linked to each other.[226] Practically, this means that PKI is used to verify the authenticity of transactions using a private key to decrypt transaction data, and a public key to encrypt it.[227] Thus, a user who attempts to sign a transaction using a different private key can be detected easily as the public key would not match.

2.4 TYPES OF DLT

Since the publication of the Bitcoin White Paper in 2008 and the emergence of Blockchain technology, several alternative types of DLT systems have been developed. Some of these systems attempt to address the weaknesses presented by Blockchain technology, such as its energy-intensive POW consensus mechanism. Others have been developed to create new forms of cryptocurrencies or are arranged so that nodes perform different functions to achieve different ends. In the main, therefore, these alternative DLT systems propose alternative consensus mechanisms. The discussion below provides a brief overview of the more significant alternative DLT systems (including Blockchain) focussing on the specific consensus mechanisms used, and is not intended to be an exhaustive list.

Forum, 2017) 6, https://blog.kakaocdn.net/dn/TRXUu/btqECv9HbX0/1GQfKMjihCKYJzF7vKunUK/tfile.pdf and Satoshi Nakamoto, 'Bitcoin: A Peer-to-Peer Electronic Cash System' (2008) 2, https://bitcoin.org/bitcoin.pdf.

222. Organisation for Economic Co-operation and Development 'OECD Blockchain Primer' 7, https://www.oecd.org/finance/OECD-Blockchain-Primer.pdf.
223. World Bank Group, 'Distributed Ledger Technology and Blockchain' FinTech Note No. 1 (2017) 8.
224. Global System for Mobile Communications Association, 'Distributed Ledger Technology, Blockchains, and Identity: A Regulatory Overview' (*GSMA*, September 2018) 10, https://www.gsma.com/identity/wp-content/uploads/2018/09/Distributed-Ledger-Technology-Blockchains-and-Identity-20180907ii.pdf.
225. World Bank, 'Distributed Ledger Technology and Blockchain' FinTech Note No. 1 (2017) 9.
226. Global System for Mobile Communications Association, 'Distributed Ledger Technology, Blockchains, and Identity: A Regulatory Overview' (*GSMA*, September 2018)10-11, https://www.gsma.com/identity/wp-content/uploads/2018/09/Distributed-Ledger-Technology-Blockchains-and-Identity-20180907ii.pdf.
227. Hong Kong Applied Science and Technology Research Institute, 'Whitepaper on Distributed Ledger Technology' (11 November 2016) 25-26, https://www.hkma.gov.hk/media/eng/doc/key-functions/finanicalinfrastructure/Whitepaper_On_Distributed_Ledger_Technology.pdf.

2.4.1 Blockchain

Blockchain is a public decentralised digital ledger which facilitates the transfer of value between users and dispenses with the need for third-party intermediation.[228] On a practical level, the Blockchain DLT system permits the recording of transactions which are stored on a ledger as a chain of blocks once transactions have been verified. Each 'block' on a chain includes specific information, such as the date, time, value of the transaction and the sender's information, in the form of a pseudonymous digital signature. Prior to a block being added to the chain, the transaction has to be verified by the distributed network of nodes.[229] As mentioned above, the method used to verify transactions is dependent on the specific consensus mechanism deployed by a DLT system. In the case of Blockchain, the POW consensus mechanism entails solving a mathematical puzzle associated with each block. This process is referred to as 'mining', and generally requires large amounts of computing power.[230] The mining process also determines which miner node is rewarded for the labour expended in mining blocks.[231]

The transaction is stored in a block together with the recipient's digital signature with the majority consensus of all nodes. The value of the transaction is then deducted from the sender's online account, referred to as a wallet.[232] Thereafter, the recipient of the funds receives the value transferred into their own account. Wallets are digital account software programmes used primarily to send, receive and store cryptocurrencies, through the use of both public and private keys.[233] When a new block is added to the chain it is provided with a unique ID, referred to as a hash, which also contains the hash of the recent block to maintain the chain sequence.[234] Once the transaction has been added to the Blockchain it cannot be deleted, reversed or altered in any way.

228. Hossein Kakavand, Nicolette Kost De Sevres & Bart Chilton, 'The Blockchain Revolution: An Analysis of Regulation and Technology Related to Distributed Ledger Technologies' (*Luther Systems*, 2016) 12, https://papers.ssrn.com/sol3/papers.cfm?abstract_id=2849251.
229. Financial Conduct Authority, 'Discussion Paper on Distributed Ledger Technology' (2017) 10, https://www.fca.org.uk/publication/discussion/dp17-03.pdf.
230. Garrick Hileman & Michel Rauchs, 'Global Cryptocurrency Benchmark Study' (*Cambridge Centre for Alternative Finance*, 2017) 19, https://www.jbs.cam.ac.uk/fileadmin/user_upload/research/centres/alternative-finance/downloads/2017-global-cryptocurrency-benchmarking-study.pdf.
231. Garrick Hileman & Michel Rauchs, 'Global Cryptocurrency Benchmark Study' (*Cambridge Centre for Alternative Finance*, 2017) 97, https://www.jbs.cam.ac.uk/fileadmin/user_upload/research/centres/alternative-finance/downloads/2017-global-cryptocurrency-benchmarking-study.pdf.
232. For a discussion on the different types of digital wallets *see* Garrick Hileman & Michel Rauchs, 'Global Cryptocurrency Benchmark Study' (*Cambridge Centre for Alternative Finance*, 2017) 46, https://www.jbs.cam.ac.uk/fileadmin/user_upload/research/centres/alternative-finance/downloads/2017-global-cryptocurrency-benchmarking-study.pdf.
233. Garrick Hileman & Michel Rauchs, 'Global Cryptocurrency Benchmark Study' (*Cambridge Centre for Alternative Finance*, 2017) 106, https://www.jbs.cam.ac.uk/fileadmin/user_upload/research/centres/alternative-finance/downloads/2017-global-cryptocurrency-benchmarking-study.pdf.
234. Financial Conduct Authority, 'Discussion Paper on Distributed Ledger Technology' (2017) 18, https://www.fca.org.uk/publication/discussion/dp17-03.pdf.

Blockchain's most significant feature is its ability to be immutable in providing a permanent record of transactions stored on a ledger or database. Its decentralised system, together with its use of cryptographic encryption, also enhances security and is generally able to provide faster settlement times. The most well-known Blockchain DLT systems include Bitcoin, Ethereum, Hyperledger Fabric and R3 Corda.

2.4.2 Hashgraph

The Hashgraph DLT system is a public distributed ledger developed by Leemon Baird in 2016 as an alternative to the Blockchain DLT system. Hashgraph differs from Blockchain by facilitating multiple transactions called 'Events', which can be recorded and stored in a parallel structure to a ledger using the same timestamp. The users in the Hashgraph DLT system are not able to control the process of Events by altering or postponing them. This is unlike miner nodes in the Blockchain DLT system who decide which transactions are included in a block. Hashgraph uses a 'Gossip Protocol' to transmit information about Events across the entire network. This occurs in the form of nodes randomly sharing information about transactions with neighbouring nodes once an Event has occurred. Nodes then aggregate all the information received about an Event and transmit this aggregated information to other neighbouring nodes. Once this has occurred, all nodes become aware of an Event through *gossiping about gossip* which takes place in a matter of minutes.[235]

The Hashgraph DLT system is thus Byzantine by not permitting a single group or entity to influence the manner in which consensus is reached with respect to the occurrence of Events. The Byzantine agreement is reached through a 'Virtual Voting Protocol' by which transactions are validated with the consensus of two-thirds of the network. Further, Hashgraph uses the POS consensus mechanism in which nodes are required to declare one or more accounts under their control. They must also provide the private cryptographic keys to such accounts before they are able to join the network. Hashgraph has been praised for its unique data structure permitting the orderly validation and recording of transactions onto ledgers using the Gossip Protocol and the Virtual Voting Protocol.[236] The most well-known Hashgraph DLT systems include Hedera Hashgraph, Mingo and NOIA.

2.4.3 Directed Acyclic Graph

The DAG DLT system provides all the benefits of the Blockchain DLT system, but without using its underlying architecture and structure, i.e., the creation of blocks

235. Leemon Baird, Mance Harmon & Paul Madsen, 'Hedera: A Public Hashgraph Network & Governing Council' (19 February 2019) 53, https://hedera.com/hh_whitepaper_v2.1-20200815.pdf.
236. Hasib Anwar, 'Distributed Ledger Technology: Where Technological Revolution Starts' (*101 Blockchains*, 30 January 2019), https://101blockchains.com/distributed-ledger-technology-dlt/.

forming an interlinked transactional chain.[237] DAG is by no means a novel concept but consists of a model which has been researched extensively in the disciplines of computer science and mathematics. In alignment with the Blockchain DLT system, DAG consists of a network of distributed nodes who validate and add new transactions to a ledger by reaching a consensus. Nodes in the DAG DLT system, however, validate new transactions by verifying at least two previous transactions which have been added to the ledger. These previous transactions are selected randomly by an algorithm to ensure that nodes do not validate their own transactions.[238] A sequence of transactions on the DAG ledger is called a 'Branch'. The overall weight accorded to an individual Branch is determined by its length through the number of transactions which have been validated. The DAG DLT system therefore does not use miner nodes to confirm the validity of transactions before they are recorded and stored onto a ledger.[239] As a result, the DAG DLT system is more time efficient in confirming transactions in comparison to the Blockchain DLT system's POW consensus mechanism. This aids greater scalability, a criticism often levied against the Blockchain DLT system.[240] Scalability is also aided through increased growth of the network as nodes are required to validate more transactions. Further, in the absence of miner node fees and mining equipment costs, the DAG DLT system lowers transaction fees, making it suitable for use in nano- or micro-transactions. Overall, the DAG DLT system operates to reduce the amount of hashing power required for previous transactions to be validated.[241] The most well-known DAG DLT systems include Byteball and IOTA.

2.4.4 Holochain

The Holochain DLT system was developed by Arthur Brock and Eric Harris-Braun in 2016 as an agent-centric open-source digital platform enabling the creation of distributed and P2P applications.[242] The Holochain DLT system consists of two important architectural features, which include: (i) Holo, a distributed network for hosting and running applications; and (ii) Holochain, a P2P open-source network for creating

237. Max Thake, 'What Is DAG Distributed Ledger Technology?' (9 November 2018), https://medium.com/nakamo-to/what-is-dag-distributed-ledger-technology-8b182a858e19.
238. 'Breaking the Chain: Directed Acyclic Graph ("DAG") challenges Blockchain's dominance' (*Hassans*), https://www.gibraltarlaw.com/directed-acyclic-graph-vs-blockchain/ and Hasib Anwar, 'Distributed Ledger Technology: Where Technological Revolution Starts' (*101 Blockchains*, 30 January 2019), https://101blockchains.com/distributed-ledger-technology-dlt/.
239. 'Breaking the Chain: Directed Acyclic Graph ("DAG") challenges Blockchain's dominance' (*Hassans*), https://www.gibraltarlaw.com/directed-acyclic-graph-vs-blockchain/.
240. Hasib Anwar, 'Distributed Ledger Technology: Where Technological Revolution Starts' (*101 Blockchains*, 30 January 2019), https://101blockchains.com/distributed-ledger-technology-dlt/.
241. Hasib Anwar, 'Distributed Ledger Technology: Where Technological Revolution Starts' (*101 Blockchains*, 30 January 2019), https://101blockchains.com/distributed-ledger-technology-dlt/.
242. Eric Braun, Nicolas Luck & Arthur Brock, 'Holochain: Scalable Agent-Centric Distributed Computing' (15 February 2008), https://github.com/holochain/holochain-proto/blob/whitepaper/holochain.pdf. *See also* 'What is Holochain?', https://holo.host/faq/what-is-holochain/.

applications.[243] Holochain does not rely on a global consensus mechanism used to validate transactions, but instead operates by each node, called 'agents', possessing an individual ledger which is tied to the Holochain public ledger through the use of cryptographic keys.[244] The Holochain DLT system operates by agents sharing new information with groups of random peers in their network using validation rules called 'DNA'. The agents in the network work to verify whether the information has been correctly shared in alignment with the DNA.[245] Once the information has been verified as such, it is relayed over the network through Gossip.[246] However, if data is not shared correctly in alignment with the DNA, it is rejected by the network of peers. Further, agents who are liable for sharing or validating bad data are removed and blocked from the network through warnings sent to others via Gossiping.[247]

The Holochain DLT system has been developed to be a customisable platform upon which different consensus mechanisms may possibly be built. However, such an approach may undermine its inherent flexibility. Holochain has been praised for its agent-centric approach, which differs from the Blockchain DLT system's overall data-centric focus. This is primarily because agents are provided with their own ledger and are not compelled to validate every transaction available in the queue. The Holochain DLT system has therefore been described as a 'true' distributed ledger as all nodes function as single and separate entities encompassing the whole system. Furthermore, the Holochain DLT system does not utilise the POW consensus mechanism making it more energy-efficient and cost-effective when compared to other types of DLT systems.[248]

2.4.5 Tempo (Radix)

The Tempo (Radix) DLT system is a public ledger developed by Daniel Hughes in 2013.[249] It operates through a consensus mechanism utilising 'logical clocks' and the Gossip Protocol (as present in the Hashgraph DLT system). Nodes in the Tempo (Radix) DLT system are not compelled to save a complete replica of the ledger at all times. Instead, nodes possess only a section of the complete global ledger called

243. Medium, 'What Comes after Blockchain?' (9 November 2019), https://medium.com/superorder/holochain-what-comes-after-blockchain-3650744933e1.
244. Steve Bushko, 'What is Holochain (HOT): A Guide to the Agent-Centric Non-Blockchain' (*Coin Central*, 3 April 2019), https://coincentral.com/holochain-hot-guide/#how-does-holochain-work.
245. 'How Does Holochain Manage Consensus and Data Integrity', https://holo.host/faq/how-does-holochain-manage-consensus-data-integrity/.
246. Hasib Anwar, 'Distributed Ledger Technology: Where Technological Revolution Starts' (*101 Blockchains*, 30 January 2019), https://101blockchains.com/distributed-ledger-technology-dlt/.
247. 'How Does Holochain Manage Consensus and Data Integrity', https://holo.host/faq/how-does-holochain-manage-consensus-data-integrity/.
248. Hasib Anwar, 'Distributed Ledger Technology: Where Technological Revolution Starts' (*101 Blockchains*, 30 January 2019), https://101blockchains.com/distributed-ledger-technology-dlt/.
249. 'Dan Radix's Tech Journey' (Web page, 11 February 2020), https://www.radixdlt.com/blog/dan-and-radixs-tech-journey.

'shards', each equipped with a unique ID. As a result, the network has the ability to possess large amounts of data with Tempo having been sharded to scale to 7 billion people and 30 billion devices simultaneously.[250] Nodes validate transactions using logical clocks, described as a timer incremented by 1 and set off when a new occurrence takes place in the Tempo (Radix) DLT system. This new occurrence takes place when a node communicates information about new events or transactions to another node. These new events or transactions are called 'Atoms'. Each node receives its own time stamp based on network activity which is in turn used to produce a sequence of events. A Gossip Protocol is used to spread information across the network rapidly. This information includes the relevant node's logical clock data.

All nodes are therefore able to view new information, in addition to the logical clock time at which that information was viewed by other nodes in the network. Practically, this means that each node has a logical clock with an integer value which reflects the number of events which the node has viewed, increasing with each new Atom witnessed.[251] Tempo (Radix) has been praised for its innovative sharding structure which supports scalability and the use of logical clocks.

2.5 DLT APPLICATIONS AND USE CASES IN FINANCIAL SERVICES

According to Gartner, as of 2023, world-wide spending on blockchain solutions continues in both private and public sectors.[252] In spite of the rapid pace with which DLT applications have been developed since 2008, it is yet to be adopted fully in the mainstream and classified as a general-purpose technology.[253] Although, as of March 2024, 130 countries and currency unions, representing 98 % of the world's GBP,[254] are exploring a CBDC. On the basis that these digital currencies are structured using DLT as their underlining architecture, this technology may be brought even further into the mainstream. Nevertheless, the most mature use cases for DLT have been conceived for use in the financial services industry.[255] Support has been levied in favour of DLT usage to combat inefficiencies and weaknesses present in the frameworks and processes of financial markets. The International Telecommunication Union, a specialised UN agency, have argued that DLT system functionality could be used for: (i) guarding against cybersecurity threats associated with centralised ledger networks; (ii) establishing trust between different industry players; (iii) reducing expensive and time-intensive

250. 'Radix Platform: How Does Radix Work?', https://docs.radixdlt.com/kb/learn/platform.
251. Hasib Anwar, 'Distributed Ledger Technology: Where Technological Revolution Starts' (*101 Blockchains*, 30 January 2019), https://101blockchains.com/distributed-ledger-technology-dlt/.
252. Gartner, 'Hype Cycle for Blockchain and Web3, 2023' (2 August 2023), https://www.gartner.com/en/documents/4594099.
253. *See Gartner Hype Cycle for Blockchain* (2021).
254. Atlantic Council, 'Central Bank Digital Currency Challenge' (Web page), https://www.atlanticcouncil.org/cbdctracker/.
255. 'Technical Report FG DLT D2.1: Distributed Ledger Technology Use Cases' (*ITU-T*, 1 August 2019) 7, https://www.itu.int/en/ITU-T/focusgroups/dlt/Documents/d21.pdf.

data reconciliation processes; and (iv) equipping processes which require round-the-clock operation.[256]

According to the UK's Office for Science, DLT systems can be applied to the financial services industry to: (i) provide a platform to facilitate the trade and exchange of cryptocurrency; (ii) enable the management and creation of new forms of 'smart' contracts; and (iii) facilitate third parties in the development of new applications.[257] A vast amount of research has been devoted to the use of DLT systems in capital markets, particularly its use in post-trade settlement and clearing processes.[258] In particular, settlement and clearing processes can benefit from DLT system automation to reduce costs and increase efficiency. Further, use cases for DLT systems have also been proposed for the verification of customer information through KYC and AML processes.[259] The OECD has defined smart contracts as 'distributed applications created and run over the blockchain, which consist of self-executing contracts written as code on blockchain ledgers, automatically executed upon reaching pre-defined trigger events written in the code'.[260] For example, smart contracts enable the execution of ICOs and DeFi platforms.[261]

The most advanced deployment of DLT systems in the financial services industry is by far the: (i) digitalisation of financial products, including security and utility tokens;[262] and (ii) most significantly, tokenisation in the form of cryptocurrencies and

256. 'Technical Report FG DLT D2.1: Distributed Ledger Technology Use Cases' (*ITU-T*, 1 August 2019) 7, https://www.itu.int/en/ITU-T/focusgroups/dlt/Documents/d21.pdf. *See also*, Swift, 'Swift and Accenture Outline Path to Distributed Ledger Technology Adoption Within Financial Services' (April 2016) 3, https://www.swift.com/news-events/press-releases/swift-and-accenture-outline-path-distributed-ledger-technology-adoption-within-financial-services.
257. Government Office for Science, 'Distributed Ledger Technology: Beyond Block Chain: A Report by the UK Government Chief Scientific Adviser' (2016) London: Government Office for Science https://www.gov.uk/government/uploads/system/uploads/attachment_data/file/492972/gs-16-1-distributed-ledger-technology.pdf.
258. *See* World Economic Forum, 'Digital Assets, Distributed Ledger Technology and the Future of Capital Markets' (May 2021), https://www3.weforum.org/docs/WEF_Digital_Assets_Distributed_Ledger_Technology_2021.pdf; Randy Priem, 'Distributed Ledger Technology for Securities Clearing and Settlement: Benefits, Risks, and Regulatory Implications' (2020) 6 Financial Innovation 11 https://doi.org/10.1186/s40854-019-0169-6; Bank for International Settlements, 'Distributed Ledger Technology in Payment, Clearing and Settlement' (BIS, February 2017) https://www.bis.org/cpmi/publ/d157.pdf and David Mills, et al., 'Distributed Ledger Technology in Payments, Clearing, and Settlement' (2016) Finance and Economics Discussion Series 095.
259. International Telecommunication Union, 'Technical Report FG DLT D2.1: Distributed Ledger Technology Use Cases' 8 (1 August 2019), https://www.itu.int/en/ITU-T/focusgroups/dlt/Documents/d21.pdf.
260. Organisation for Economic Co-operation and Development, 'Initial Coin Offerings (ICOs) for SME Financing' (2019) 45, https://www.oecd.org/en/publications/initial-coin-offerings-icos-for-sme-financing_ee35cc9a-en.html.
261. Chainalysis, 'The 2021 Geography of Cryptocurrency Report: Analysis of Geographic Trends in Cryptocurrency Adoption and Usage' (October 2021) 14, https://go.chainalysis.com/rs/503-FAP-074/images/Geography-of-Cryptocurrency-2021.pdf.
262. *See* World Economic Forum, 'Digital Assets, Distributed Ledger Technology and the Future of Capital Markets' (May 2021), https://www3.weforum.org/docs/WEF_Digital_Assets_Distributed_Ledger_Technology_2021.pdf.

payment tokens.[263] As such, the discussion below focusses on the use cases which have been developed for DLT systems through the creation of cryptocurrencies. This approach has been taken for two reasons. First, the use of DLT systems to create native cryptocurrencies is the most widely researched and implemented use case of DLT. Second, the regulatory competition analysis which forms the subject of this book focusses squarely on laws and regulations governing cryptocurrencies in HK, London, and NY. It is, however, important to note, that not all DLT systems operate to facilitate and support the creation of a native cryptocurrency. Further, cryptocurrencies may also be used to develop 'non-monetary use cases' harnessing DLT's decentralised and censorship-resistant properties. Nevertheless, the three primary examples of using DLT systems for the creation of cryptocurrencies discussed below focus on monetary use cases for the technology.

2.5.1 A Medium of Exchange

The first iteration of DLT, the Blockchain DLT system, was initially conceived as a platform to facilitate the creation of Bitcoin, the first cryptocurrency to successfully operate without being impeded by the double-spending problem. In the Bitcoin White Paper, Nakamoto described 'electronic coin' as a 'chain of digital signatures'.[264] Nakamoto contemplated that Bitcoin could be used as a P2P version of electronic cash used to transfer value through online payments. With this functionality in mind, Bitcoin, as a cryptocurrency, could be used as digital bearer assets whose ownership is predicated upon the user in possession of its private key.[265] Cryptocurrencies have therefore been likened to money and in particular as a possible alternative medium of exchange to be used in the trade of goods and services.

Cryptocurrencies are a subset of the broader digital currency category, characterised in particular by its use of cryptography which guards against counterfeiting.[266] The FCA has defined cryptocurrency broadly as 'any publicly available *electronic medium of exchange* that features a permissionless distributed ledger and a decentralised system for exchanging value' (my emphasis added).[267] This definition, while helpful, fails to reference the encryption techniques used to protect the value of

263. International Telecommunication Union, 'Technical Report FG DLT D2.1: Distributed Ledger Technology Use Cases' 8 (1 August 2019), https://www.itu.int/en/ITU-T/focusgroups/dlt/Documents/d21.pdf.
264. Satoshi Nakamoto, 'Bitcoin: A Peer-to-Peer Electronic Cash System' (2008) 2, https://bitcoin.org/bitcoin.pdf.
265. Gareth Hileman & Michel Rauchs, 'Global Cryptocurrency Benchmarking Study' (*Cambridge Centre for Alternative Finance*, 2017), https://www.jbs.cam.ac.uk/fileadmin/user_upload/research/centres/alternative-finance/downloads/2017-global-cryptocurrency-benchmarking-study.pdf.
266. Chris Rose, 'The Evolution of Digital Currencies: Bitcoin, A Cryptocurrency Causing A Monetary Revolution' 14(4) International Business and Economics Research 617-622.
267. Financial Conduct Authority, 'Discussion Paper on Distributed Ledger Technology' (2017) 11, https://www.fca.org.uk/publication/discussion/dp17-03.pdf.

cryptocurrencies, such as asymmetric PKI.[268] Thus, according to Hileman and Rauchs, a cryptocurrency may be defined as a *digital token* which exists within a DLT structure consisting of a consensus mechanism, a P2P network and the utilisation of public key cryptographic encryption.[269] This definition is all-encompassing and also highlights the core underlining features of general DLT systems. The Blockchain DLT system, as an open-source software, has been used to develop several alternative cryptocurrencies, referred to as 'altcoins'. In most cases, altcoins do not represent a significant departure from the Blockchain DLT system architecture, having been developing primarily as public and permissionless DLT systems. The most well-known altcoins include Ethereum's Ether, Dogecoin, Ripple, and Polkadot.

There appears to be some doubt in the literature concerning whether cryptocurrencies can in fact be classified as a medium of exchange in the long-term. According to Baur, Hong and Lee, Bitcoin is used mainly for speculative investment, rather than as a medium of exchange, or as an alternative currency, based on an assessment of transaction data.[270] This view has been supported by several other studies.[271] However, Hileman and Rauchs have posited that cryptocurrencies could be considered a medium of exchange.[272] They contend that while cryptocurrencies are being increasingly accepted by merchants globally as a payment method, it is not the primary payment method for daily purchases of goods and services.[273] Further, other studies have focussed on whether cryptocurrencies can fulfil the function of traditional currency. Traditionally, money serves three functions, which include: (i) a medium of

268. Benjamin Geva, 'Cryptocurrencies and the Evolution of Banking, Money and Payments' in Chris Brummer (ed.) *Cryptoassets* (OUP 2019) https://doi.org/10.1093/oso/9780190077310.003.0002 and Roy Lai & David Lee Kuo Chuen, 'Blockchain- From Public to Private' in David Lee Kuo Chuen & Robert Deng (eds), *Handbook of Blockchain, Digital Finance, and Inclusion, Volume 2: ChinaTech, Mobile Security and Distributed Ledger* (Elsevier 2017).
269. Garrick Hileman & Michel Rauchs, 'Global Cryptocurrency Benchmark Study' (*Cambridge Centre for Alternative Finance,* 2017) 104, https://www.jbs.cam.ac.uk/fileadmin/user_upload/research/centres/alternative-finance/downloads/2017-global-cryptocurrency-benchmarking-study.pdf.
270. Dirk Baur, Kihoon Hong & Adrian D Lee, 'Bitcoin: Medium of Exchange or Speculative Assets?' (2017) 54 Journal of International of Financial Markets, Institutions and Money 178 https://doi.org/10.1016/j.intfin.2017.12.004.
271. *See* Pavel Ciaian, Miroslava Rajcaniova & D'Artis Kancs, 'The Digital Agenda of Virtual Currencies: Can BitCoin Become a Global Currency' (2016) 14 Information Systems and E-Business Management 883-919 https://doi.org/10.1007/s10257-016-0304-0 and Dale H Shao et al., 'The Reality of Digital Currency as a Financial Medium of Exchange' (2013) 13(3) Journal of International Finance Studies 45-50 https://doi.org/10.18374/jifs-13-3.5.
272. Garrick Hileman & Michel Rauchs, 'Global Cryptocurrency Benchmark Study' (*Cambridge Centre for Alternative Finance,* 2017) 104, https://www.jbs.cam.ac.uk/fileadmin/user_upload/research/centres/alternative-finance/downloads/2017-global-cryptocurrency-benchmarking-study.pdf.
273. Garrick Hileman & Michel Rauchs, 'Global Cryptocurrency Benchmark Study' (*Cambridge Centre for Alternative Finance,* 2017) 104, https://www.jbs.cam.ac.uk/fileadmin/user_upload/research/centres/alternative-finance/downloads/2017-global-cryptocurrency-benchmarking-study.pdf and Paolo Tasca, Shaowen Liu & Adam Hayes, 'The Evolution of the Bitcoin Economy: Extracting and Analyzing the Network of Payment Relationship' (2016), https://papers.ssrn.com/sol3/papers.cfm?abstract_id=2808762.

exchange; (ii) a store of value; and (iii) a unit of account.[274] According to Ammous, only Bitcoin can convincingly serve the function of money based on its focus on low supply growth, its distributed nature, and the lack of authority in its system with the ability to alter its supply schedule.[275]

Despite this contrasting discourse, in 2021 the acceptance of cryptocurrencies as a medium of exchange appeared to reach its apex when El Salvador adopted the use of Bitcoin as the second legal tender alongside the US dollar.[276] In particular, the proliferation of the adoption of cryptocurrencies has been evidenced widely in developing nations. For example, in 2021 Statista reported that 33 % of Nigerians have reported owning some form of cryptocurrency.[277] Cryptocurrency is used often in Nigeria to effect P2P money transfers and is accepted as a medium of exchange for the purchase of goods and services at stores through smartphones. It has also been reported recently that businesses in Nigeria have begun to instal cryptocurrency plugins into their smartphone payment options. Statista has also reported that Vietnam and the Philippines are the second and third largest adopters of cryptocurrencies. In the Philippines, for example, a Bitcoin ATM has been installed in Manilla, evidencing the more mainstream use of cryptocurrencies in the country. In 2023, Chainalysis ranked India number 1 in its Global Crypto Adoption Index, with central and south Asia dominating the top ranking.[278] Europe, however, has been reported to be the world's second-largest crypto economy in the world, with European investors leading the way to creating an innovative crypto sector in the eurozone.[279] Overall, and despite the 'crypto-winter' of 2022, during which the crypto markets saw valuation drop by USD 2 trillion, the WEF has reported that 'cryptography and blockchains will continue to be integral parts of the modern economic toolkit'.[280]

While it appears that consumers are increasingly recognising and harnessing the benefits of cryptocurrencies, through faster and cheaper payments, several risks are

274. *See* Amaresh Das, 'Money as a Medium of Exchange: Then and Now: Can Technology Be a Faciliatory of Exchange?' (2015) 15(11) Global Journal of Management and Business Research, https://globaljournals.org/GJMBR_Volume15/6-Money-as-a-Medium-of-Exchange.pdf.
275. Saifedan Ammous, 'Can Cryptocurrencies Fulfil the Functions of Money' (2018) 70 The Quarterly Review of Economics and Finance 38-51 https://doi.org/10.1016/j.qref.2018.05.010.
276. Alvaro Trigueros-Argüello & Marjorie Chorro de Trigueros, 'Bitcoin as Legal Tender in El Salvador: The First Fifty Days' (*Georgetown Journal of International Affairs*, 30 November 2021), https://gjia.georgetown.edu/2021/11/30/bitcoin-as-legal-tender-in-el-salvador-the-first-fifty-days/#: ~ :text = On%20June%205%2C%20in%20a,previous%20knowledge%20by%20El%20Salvadorans.
277. Katharina Buchholz, 'These are the Countries Where Cryptocurrency Use is the Most Common' (*World Economic Forum and Statista*, 18 February 2021), https://www.weforum.org/agenda/2021/02/how-common-is-cryptocurrency.
278. Chainalysis, 'The 2023 Global Crypto Adoption Index: Central & Southern Asia Are Leading the Way in Grassroots Crypto Adoption' (12 September 2023), https://www.chainalysis.com/blog/2023-global-crypto-adoption-index/.
279. CME Group, 'Europe's Blossoming Admiration for Crypto' (17 March 2024), https://www.cmegroup.com/articles/2024/europes-blossoming-admiration-for-crypto.html.
280. Dante Disparte, 'This is What the Future Holds for Cryptocurrencies' (World Economic Forum, 2 January 2023), https://www.weforum.org/agenda/2023/01/future-of-cryptocurrencies-davos2023/.

still presented through such usage. Cryptocurrency markets are volatile as cryptocurrencies do not have any intrinsic value and as a result, users may be exposed to liquidity and price volatility risks.[281] Fintech companies, however, have attempted to counter these risks through the creation of stablecoins, whose value is ordinarily pegged to a more stable external fiat currency or other commodity.[282] The stablecoin market has grown rapidly, and as of May 2024, its market capitalisation was valued at USD 160.8 billion.[283] The use and trade of cryptocurrencies also provide opportunities for fraud and scams to be perpetrated, such as those associated with unregulated cryptocurrency exchanges and ICOs made worse by the geographically dispersed character attributed to cryptocurrencies.[284] These factors, among others, have resulted in the proliferation of policy-making, laws and regulations to combat the risks associated with rising cryptocurrency use.

2.5.2 Funding Mechanism

2.5.2.1 Cryptocurrency Exchanges

Cryptocurrencies are primarily purchased through centralised cryptocurrency exchanges that act as 'on- and off-ramps' and operate primarily to facilitate the sale, purchase, and trade of cryptocurrencies for other forms of money or assets. They also provide ancillary services such as custodial digital wallet services. The first cryptocurrency exchange was conceived to provide services to users with no direct access to Blockchain or who wished to trade Bitcoin via an organised trading platform.[285] At present, cryptocurrency exchanges operate to provide a trading platform in addition to brokerage and order-book exchange services (i.e., matching buyers and sellers).[286] Some exchange platforms only exchange cryptocurrencies for other cryptocurrencies, while others provide fiat currency exchange services as well.[287] Cryptocurrency exchanges charge fees for the services levied, roughly 0.5%-5% of the amount of

281. Abhishek Gupta, 'Blockchain Technology: Application in Indian business sector' (2019) 19(2) Delhi Business Review 78.
282. Jennah Huxley, 'Cryptoassets in Asia: Consumer Attitudes, Behaviours and Experiences' (Organisation for Economic Co-operation and Development, December 2019) 12, https://policycommons.net/artifacts/3796455/cryptoassets-in-asia-consumer-attitudes-behaviours-and-experiences/4602283/.
283. Forbes, https://www.forbes.com/digital-assets/categories/stablecoins/?sh=a7ce85e1cd01 (8 May 2024).
284. Organisation for Economic Co-operation and Development, 'Cryptoassets in Asia: Consumer Attitudes, Behaviours and Experiences' (December 2019) 12, https://www.oecd.org/finance/2019-cryptoassets-in-asia.pdf.
285. Asress Adimi Gikay, 'European Consumer Law and Blockchain based Financial Services: A Functional Approach against the Rhetoric of Regulatory Uncertainty' (2019) 24(1) Tilburg Law Review 30 https://doi.org/10.5334/tilr.135.
286. Garrick Hileman & Michel Rauchs, 'Global Cryptocurrency Benchmark Study' (*Cambridge Centre for Alternative Finance*, 2017) 27, https://www.jbs.cam.ac.uk/fileadmin/user_upload/research/centres/alternative-finance/downloads/2017-global-cryptocurrency-benchmarking-study.pdf.
287. Robby Houben & Alexander Snyers, 'Cryptocurrencies and Blockchain: Legal Context and Implications for Financial Crime, Money Laundering and Tax Evasion' (2018) European

transaction, called 'trading fees'.[288] Ordinarily, they also charge 'withdrawal fees' when coins are withdrawn from their platforms. Additional charges may also be levied for the use of credit and debit cards for trading, or through deployment of advanced trading techniques, such as margin trading.

As centralised platforms and providers of digital wallet software, cryptocurrency exchanges are susceptible to both internal and external fraudulent action, including digital hacking and theft.[289] For example, in 2014 the Tokyo-based exchange Mt. Gox filed for bankruptcy after having lost custody of USD 450 million worth of Bitcoin.[290] Other cases of cyber hacking have also been reported, including the cryptocurrency NEM which reported a loss of funds totalling USD 530 million in 2018,[291] and the well-publicised failure of FTX Exchange in 2022.[292]

As a result, cryptocurrency exchanges have been heavily criticised regarding their observance and enforcement of consumer law rights to their customer base. For example, because of its distributed nature and the use of automated support systems, cryptocurrency exchanges lack necessary complaint mechanisms.[293] In addition, unlicensed cryptocurrency exchanges also pose risks to consumers. In 2021, a criminal complaint was filed against Binance by Thailand's Securities and Exchange Commission for operating without a licence.[294] In the same year, the FCA issued a Consumer Warning notice against Binance's UK arm barring it from undertaking regulated activity in the UK.[295] Significantly, in 2023 Binance and its Founder and CEO pled guilty to federal charges including those relating to AML and unlicensed money transmission,

Parliament 15, http://www.europarl.europa.eu/cmsdata/150761/TAX3%20Study%20on%20cryptocurrencies%20and%20blockchain.pdf.

288. World Economic Forum, 'Cryptocurrencies: A Guide to Getting Started – Global Future Council on Cryptocurrencies' (June 2021) 5, https://www3.weforum.org/docs/WEF_Getting_Started_Cryptocurrency_2021.pdf.
289. Asress Adimi Gikay, 'European Consumer Law and Blockchain based Financial Services: A Functional Approach against the Rhetoric of Regulatory Uncertainty' (2019) 24(1) Tilburg Law Review 34 https://doi.org/10.5334/tilr.135.
290. Robert McMillan, 'The Inside Story of Mt. Gox, Bitcoin's $460 Million Disaster' (*Wired*, 3 March 2014), https://www.wired.com/2014/03/bitcoin-exchange/. *See* Ilya Kokor, 'When Bitcoin Meets Insolvency' (*Leiden Law Blog*, 22 March 2018), https://leidenlawblog.nl/articles/when-bitcoin-meets-insolvency.
291. Daniel Shane, '$530 Million Cryptocurrency Heist May Be Biggest Ever' (*CNN* 29 January 2018), https://money.cnn.com/2018/01/29/technology/coincheck-cryptocurrency-exchange-hack-japan/index.html.
292. *See* Kalley Huang, 'Why Did FTX Collapse? Here's What to Know' (New York Times, 18 November 2022), https://www.nytimes.com/2022/11/10/technology/ftx-binance-crypto-explained.html.
293. Asress Adimi Gikay, 'European Consumer Law and Blockchain based Financial Services: A Functional Approach against the Rhetoric of Regulatory Uncertainty' (2019) 24(1) Tilburg Law Review 35 https://doi.org/10.5334/tilr.135.
294. Thailand Securities and Exchange Commission, 'SEC Files a Criminal Complaint against Binance for Operating Digital Asset Business without License' (2 July 2021), https://www.sec.or.th/EN/Pages/News_Detail.aspx?SECID=9017 12 February 2022.
295. Financial Conduct Authority, 'Consumer Warning on Binance Markets Limited and the Binance Group' (26 June 2021), https://www.fca.org.uk/news/news-stories/consumer-warning-binance-markets-limited-and-binance-group.

admitted to prioritising its profits and growth over its compliance with US law, and agreed to pay over USD 4 billion to resolve its violations.[296]

Overall, cryptocurrency exchanges play an essential role in providing liquidity, a trading marketplace and price discovery.[297] Examples of current operational cryptocurrency exchanges include Bitstamp licensed in the UK, Coinbase licensed in California and Bit-Z and OKEx in HK (without a licence). The UK and the US lead the world in terms of the number of exchanges operating in their jurisdictions.[298] As of February 2022, the largest cryptocurrency exchanges by trading volume include Binance (USD 16.07 billion), Zedcex Exchange (USD 11.15 billion), and UEEx (USD 5.82 billion).[299]

2.5.2.2 Initial Coin Offerings

An ICO is a novel way of securing external finance from the public through the issue of digital tokens to funders in exchange for fiat currency or well-established cryptocurrencies, such as Bitcoin.[300] They have been used largely by start-up firms to raise funds from retail and institutional investors,[301] as an alternative to traditional venture capital funding.[302] According to the OEDC, digital tokens issued in an ICO can be defined as 'digitally-represented, cryptographically-secured units of value, whose creation is enabled by DLTs and the blockchain'.[303] Digital tokens are distinguished from ordinary cryptocurrencies. For example, digital tokens are built upon pre-existing DLT systems, in contrast to ordinary cryptocurrencies conceived through their own DLT system.[304] Further, digital tokens have been described as coupons or vouchers of a funding

296. US Department of Justice, 'Binance and CEO Plead Guilty to Federal Charges in $4B Resolution' (21 November 2023), https://www.justice.gov/opa/pr/binance-and-ceo-plead-guilty-federal-charges-4b-resolution.
297. Garrick Hileman & Michel Rauchs, 'Global Cryptocurrency Benchmark Study' (*Cambridge Centre for Alternative Finance*, 2017) 28, https://www.jbs.cam.ac.uk/fileadmin/user_upload/research/centres/alternative-finance/downloads/2017-global-cryptocurrency-benchmarking-study.pdf.
298. Garrick Hileman & Michel Rauchs, 'Global Cryptocurrency Benchmark Study' (*Cambridge Centre for Alternative Finance*, 2017) 28, https://www.jbs.cam.ac.uk/wp-content/uploads/2020/08/2017-04-20-global-cryptocurrency-benchmarking-study.pdf.
299. Statista, 'Largest Cryptocurrency Exchanges Based on 24h Trade Volume in the World on May 6, 2024', https://www.statista.com/statistics/864738/leading-cryptocurrency-exchanges-traders/#:~:text=Top%20100%20crypto%20exchanges%20in,volume%20on%20May%206%2C%202024&text=Crypto%20trader%20Binance%20ranked%20among,high%20as%20Bybit%20or%20OKX.
300. Organisation for Economic Co-operation and Development, 'Initial Coin Offerings (ICOs) for SME Financing' (2019) 7, https://www.oecd.org/finance/ICOs-for-SME-Financing.pdf.
301. Asress Adimi Gikay, 'European Consumer Law and Blockchain based Financial Services: A Functional Approach against the Rhetoric of Regulatory Uncertainty' (2019) 24(1) Tilburg Law Review 41 https://doi.org/10.5334/tilr.135.
302. 'Technical Report FG DLT D2.1: Distributed Ledger Technology Use Cases' (*ITU-T*, 1 August 2019) 25, https://www.itu.int/en/ITU-T/focusgroups/dlt/Documents/d21.pdf.
303. Organisation for Economic Co-operation and Development, 'Initial Coin Offerings (ICOs) for SME Financing' (2019) 45, https://www.oecd.org/finance/ICOs-for-SME-Financing.pdf.
304. Organisation for Economic Co-operation and Development, 'Initial Coin Offerings (ICOs) for SME Financing' (2019) 42, https://www.oecd.org/finance/ICOs-for-SME-Financing.pdf.

mechanism, in contract to ordinary cryptocurrencies conceived as a medium of exchange.[305]

Digital tokens provided to investors for participating in an ICO usually entail the attachment of token rights or entitlements. Broadly, the process by which digital assets are imbued with rights based on assets in the real world is referred to as 'tokenisation'.[306] Three types of ICO-based digital tokens have been broadly identified. First, investment or security tokens include an entitlement to equity in a company with profit sharing and voting rights.[307] Second, pure currency or payment tokens include entitlements to cryptocurrencies such as Bitcoin. Last, utility tokens include rights to receive goods and services at a particular date and time.[308] ICOs also make use of hybrid forms of these digital tokens in their funding strategies. The nature of the rights and entitlements attached to digital tokens are ordinarily dependent on the purpose of the specific digital token issuance, and the strategy of the company initiating the ICO.[309]

The first ICO took place in 2013 through the sale of Mastercoin, now Omni, raising more than USD 5 billion in Bitcoins.[310] The ICO process usually entails a start-up company publishing a whitepaper which sets out the terms and conditions of the intended ICO. A technical paper containing the technical details of the ICO, and its related project, may also be published. If the minimum fund-raising target is achieved, i.e., the 'soft cap', the new digital tokens are created using a DLT system. If the soft cap is not achieved, funds raised are returned to investors. Investors wishing to subscribe to an ICO are required to join a relevant cryptocurrency exchange platform. A digital wallet is then created to effect the purchase and sale of the newly issued digital tokens between the investor and the ICO issuer. Once newly issued digital tokens have been received, investors may trade them on cryptocurrency exchange platforms that act as secondary markets for the sale, purchase, and trade of cryptocurrencies.[311]

ICOs offer an alternative funding mechanism, especially for start-up firms and SMEs who take advantage of the low transaction costs, and the wide pool of investors

305. *See* Albert J Hu, Christine A Parlour & Uday Rajan, 'Cryptocurrencies: Stylized Facts on a New Investible Instrument' (2018), http://webuser.bus.umich.edu/urajan/research/crypto.pdf.
306. Organisation for Economic Co-operation and Development, 'OECD Blockchain Primer' (2018) 8, https://www.oecd.org/finance/OECD-Blockchain-Primer.pdf.
307. Asress Adimi Gikay, 'European Consumer Law and Blockchain based Financial Services: A Functional Approach against the Rhetoric of Regulatory Uncertainty' (2019) 24(1) Tilburg Law Review 40 https://doi.org/10.5334/tilr.135.
308. Asress Adimi Gikay, 'European Consumer Law and Blockchain based Financial Services: A Functional Approach against the Rhetoric of Regulatory Uncertainty' (2019) 24(1) Tilburg Law Review 41. *See* Phillip Hacker & Chris Thomale, 'Crypto-Securities Regulation: ICOs, Token Sales and Cryptocurrencies under EU Financial Law' (2018) 15(4) European Company and Financial Law Review, De Gruyter 645-696 https://doi.org/10.1515/ecfr-2018-0021. *See* Organisation for Economic Co-operation and Development, 'OECD Blockchain Primer' (2018), https://www.oecd.org/finance/OECD-Blockchain-Primer.pdf.
309. Organisation for Economic Co-operation and Development, 'Initial Coin Offerings (ICOs) for SME Financing' (2019) 46, https://www.oecd.org/finance/ICOs-for-SME-Financing.pdf.
310. Michael Mendelson, 'From Initial Coin Offerings to Security Tokens: A U.S. Federal Securities Law Analysis' (2019) 22 Stanford Technology Law Journal 6.
311. Organisation for Economic Co-operation and Development, 'Initial Coin Offerings (ICOs) for SME Financing' (2019) 42-44, https://www.oecd.org/finance/ICOs-for-SME-Financing.pdf.

spread globally.[312] In addition, ICOs provide investors with more flexible exit alternatives based on the liquidity of cryptocurrency exchanges. According to the OECD, ICOs provide innovative and inclusive financing for SMEs by diversifying their funding options, democratising the financing of SMEs through DLT's decentralised and distributed nature, reduced costs, and faster execution (when compared to regular public offerings).[313] At the same time, ICOs also pose significant potential risks for investors through regulatory uncertainty, investor protection, corporate governance and regulatory compliance, and associated operational business risks. The cyber security risks associated with ICOs, including fraud and hacking attacks have been cited as a major obstacle for the mainstream use of ICOs.[314] According to the IMF, the large upsurge in ICO usage spurred financial regulatory authorities to take a stance on the cryptocurrency market, in particular its lack of clear and cohesive legal and regulatory frameworks.[315]

Ethereum, through its native cryptocurrency Ether, remains one of the most well-known and successful ICOs.[316] However, successful ICOs appear to be the exception rather than the rule, as failed ICOs are a regular feature of the digital asset market. For example, Dragon Coin raised USD 320 million through an ICO in 2018, before a string of controversies led to its failure and current low market capitalisation. On trend, the total amount of funding raised from ICOs has drastically plateaued since 2018, which marked an overall funding high of USD 7.5 billion.[317] It was reported in 2019 that ICOs may altogether disappear as an alternative funding mechanism in 2020 bearing in mind the 95% decline in funding.[318] However, as of January 2021, it was reported that ICO projects to date led to an estimated USD 27 billion in fund raising,[319] and may therefore still be viewed as a viable alternative funding mechanism. However, as of 2023, it is still uncertain whether ICOs will be pegged as a sustainable source for raising funds.[320]

---

312. Paul P Momtaz, 'Initial Coin Offerings' (2020) 15(5) PloS One 1 https://journals.plos.org/plosone/article/file?id=10.1371/journal.pone.0233018&type=printable.
313. Organisation for Economic Co-operation and Development, 'Initial Coin Offerings (ICOs) for SME Financing' (2019) 30-31, https://www.oecd.org/finance/ICOs-for-SME-Financing.pdf.
314. Pablo de Andres et al., 'Challenges of the market for initial coin offerings' (2022) 72 International Review of Financial Analysis 6-7 https://doi.org/10.1016/j.irfa.2021.101966.
315. Cristina Cuervo, Anastasiia Morozova & Nobuyasu Sugimoto, 'Regulation of Cryptoassets' (International Monetary Fund, 10 January 2020) 7, https://www.imf.org/en/Publications/fintech-notes/Issues/2020/01/09/Regulation-of-Crypto-Assets-48810.
316. Oksana A Karpenko, Tatiana K Blokhina & Lali V Chebukhanova, 'The Initial Coin Offering (ICO) Process: Regulation and Risks' (2021) 14(12) Journal of Risk and Financial Management 599 https://doi.org/10.3390/jrfm14120599.
317. Pablo de Andres et al., 'Challenges of the Market for Initial Coin Offerings' (2022) 72 International Review of Financial Analysis 3 https://doi.org/10.1016/j.irfa.2021.101966.
318. Anja van Oosterhout, 'ICOS Will Disappear in 2020 as Data Shows 95% Fund Decline' (*Bitcoinist*, 3 October 2019), https://bitcoinist.com/icos-will-disappear-in-2020-as-data-shows-95-funding-decline/.
319. Oksana A Karpenko, Tatiana K Blokhina & Lali V Chebukhanova, 'The Initial Coin Offering (ICO) Process: Regulation and Risks' (2021) 14(12) Journal of Risk and Financial Management 599 https://doi.org/10.3390/jrfm14120599.
320. *See* https://www.coindesk.com/consensus-magazine/2023/01/31/us-senate-cryptocurrency-fraud-ico, Don Phan, 'Initial Coin Offerings Deserve a Rethink' (*Coindesk*, 1 February 2023), https://www.coindesk.com/opinion/2023/01/31/us-senate-cryptocurrency-fraud-ico/.

2.5.3 Payment Rail

Payment rails are the necessary networks which provide the infrastructural backbone required to effect payments digitally from one individual or institution to another. The most well-known payment rails include Automated Clearing House, Mastercard, The Clearing House, and PayPal. Traditionally, payments at a retail customer level, particularly on a cross-border basis, are effected using credit and debit card transfers via existing correspondent banking relationships. These payments often include the levying of multiple fees at various points in the transfer process,[321] which makes payments costly especially when transmitted internationally. In place of these costly traditional payment rails, DLT systems can be used to effect real-time and more cost-effective payments, often denominated in the relevant national fiat currency.[322] It can be used as an alternative payment rail platform to effect payments for businesses[323] or for the purposes of remittances,[324] predominantly on a cross-border basis.[325] In these circumstances, DLT operates to effectively replace the intermediaries required to effect cross-border payments based on its distributed and decentralised nature. In this regard, Hileman and Rauch's Global Cryptocurrency Benchmark Study reported that 86% of the payment companies surveyed used Bitcoin as the primary payment rail to effect cross-border transactions.[326]

DLT through cryptocurrencies can also provide banks with direct access to relevant networks thereby reducing costs and providing more transparent systems.[327] A more transparent cross-border payment system can potentially provide the public with wider access to financial services, such as through smartphones, thereby facilitating financial inclusion.[328] In emerging economies, DLT systems and cryptocurrency infrastructure may be useful in providing alternative means to effect digital payments

321. Bank for International Settlements, 'Correspondent Banking' (Committee on Payment and Market Infrastructures 2016), http://www.bis.org/cpmi/publ/d147.pdf.
322. Garrick Hileman & Michel Rauchs, 'Global Cryptocurrency Benchmark Study' (*Cambridge Centre for Alternative Finance*, 2017) 11, https://www.jbs.cam.ac.uk/wp-content/uploads/2020/08/2017-04-20-global-cryptocurrency-benchmarking-study.pdf.
323. Garrick Hileman & Michel Rauchs, 'Global Cryptocurrency Benchmark Study' (*Cambridge Centre for Alternative Finance*, 2017) 69, https://www.jbs.cam.ac.uk/wp-content/uploads/2020/08/2017-04-20-global-cryptocurrency-benchmarking-study.pdf.
324. International Telecommunication Union, 'Technical Report FG DLT D2.1: Distributed Ledger Technology Use Cases' (1 August 2019) 7, https://www.itu.int/en/ITU-T/focusgroups/dlt/Documents/d21.pdf.
325. David Mills et al., 'Distributed Ledger Technology in Payments, Clearing, and Settlement' (2016) Finance and Economics Discussion Series 095, 18.
326. Garrick Hileman & Michel Rauchs, 'Global Cryptocurrency Benchmark Study' (*Cambridge Centre for Alternative Finance*, 2017) 67, https://www.jbs.cam.ac.uk/wp-content/uploads/2020/08/2017-04-20-global-cryptocurrency-benchmarking-study.pdf.
327. David Mills et al., 'Distributed Ledger Technology in Payments, Clearing, and Settlement' (2016) Finance and Economics Discussion Series 095, 19.
328. David Mills et al., 'Distributed Ledger Technology in Payments, Clearing, and Settlement' (2016) Finance and Economics Discussion Series 095, 19. *See* Robby Houben & Alexander Snyers, 'Cryptocurrencies and Blockchain: Legal Context and Implications for Financial Crime, Money Laundering and Tax Evasion' (2018) European Parliament 15 http://www.europarl.europa.eu/cmsdata/150761/TAX3%20Study%20on%20cryptocurrencies%20and%20blockchain.pdf.

to accelerate the development of their financial infrastructures. Global remittances are a crucial source of funding for emerging economies to assist with weathering harsher economic circumstances.[329] In 2023, the WB reported that global remittances to low- and middle-income jurisdictions reached USD 669 billion.[330] As such, the WB has noted that innovations in cross-border payments are required to reduce operational costs and has identified DLT systems as a potential use case for B2B cross-border payments.[331] Several such solutions have already been piloted, including Visa's B2B Connect[332] and SWIFT's Global Payments Innovation[333] as B2B DLT cross-border payment solutions.

Further, de Filippi has suggested that countries that have unstable currencies, such as Venezuela or Zimbabwe, may make use of Bitcoin to substitute or work alongside their existing payment systems.[334] As such, DLT systems may be used to exchange fiat currencies in a secure and a more rapid manner. For example, in 2018 Ripple piloted xRapid as a cross-border payments solution for use between the US and Mexico.[335] The financial institutions that participated in the pilot reportedly saved between 40% and 70% in foreign exchange costs.[336] xRapid, through Ripple's DTL system, enables the exchange of funds in one bank account from one currency to another with minimal cost in a few seconds.[337] The average payment time recorded was appropriately two minutes, with the majority of the processing time recorded by domestic payment rails, and other intermediary digital asset exchanges. To execute foreign exchange transactions, the Ripple protocol utilises foreign exchange traders participating in the network by creating a succession of transactions between them. The protocol determines the most economical way to proceed with the conversion of funds from one currency to another and then executes and settles the necessary trades using the DLT system.[338]

329. Rodrigo Meija-Ricart, Camillo Tellez & Marco Nicoli, 'Payment Across Borders: Can Distributed Ledgers Bring Us Closer Together?' (*World Bank Blogs*, 26 March 2019), https://blogs.worldbank.org/psd/paying-across-borders-can-distributed-ledgers-bring-us-closer-together.
330. World Bank Press Release, 'Remittance Flows Continue to Grow in 2023 Albeit at Slower Pace' (18 December 2023), https://www.worldbank.org/en/news/press-release/2023/12/18/remittance-flows-grow-2023-slower-pace-migration-development-brief#: ~ :text = In%202023%2C%20remittance%20flows%20to,ability%20to%20send%20money%20home.
331. Rodrigo Meija-Ricart, Camillo Tellez & Marco Nicoli, 'Payment Across Borders: Can Distributed Ledgers Bring Us Closer Together?' (*World Bank Blogs*, 26 March 2019), https://blogs.worldbank.org/psd/paying-across-borders-can-distributed-ledgers-bring-us-closer-together.
332. *See* https://usa.visa.com/partner-with-us/payment-technology/visa-b2b-connect.html.
333. *See* https://www.swift.com/our-solutions/swift-gpi.
334. De Filippi P & Wright A, 'Digital Currencies and Decentralised Payment Platforms' in De Filippi & Wright (eds), *Blockchain and the Law* (Harvard University Press 2018).
335. Rodrigo Meija-Ricart, Camillo Tellez & Marco Nicoli, 'Payment Across Borders: Can Distributed Ledgers bring us Closer Together?' (*World Bank Blogs*, 26 March 2019), https://blogs.worldbank.org/psd/paying-across-borders-can-distributed-ledgers-bring-us-closer-together.
336. Rodrigo Meija-Ricart, Camillo Tellez & Marco Nicoli, 'Payment Across Borders: Can Distributed Ledgers bring us Closer Together?' (*World Bank Blogs*, 26 March 2019), https://blogs.worldbank.org/psd/paying-across-borders-can-distributed-ledgers-bring-us-closer-together.
337. De Filippi P & Wright A, 'Digital Currencies and Decentralised Payment Platforms' in De Filippi & Wright (eds), *Blockchain and the Law* (Harvard University Press 2018).
338. Bryant Gehring, 'How Ripple Works' (*Ripple*, 16 October 2014), https://perma.cc/UM6B-4EPU. *See* Michael T Rosner & Andrew Kang, 'Understanding and Regulating Twenty-First

The broader adoption of DLT through cryptocurrencies as payment rails is however plagued by existing architectural issues, most notably those relating to security, privacy, and scalability.[339] Alternative technologies are also available and being forthwith developed to provide faster and more efficient payments, such as Faster Payment Services. Despite these overarching concerns, DLT through cryptocurrencies remains an alternative payment rail technology which may benefit economies globally.

Century Payment Systems: The Ripple Case Study' (2016) 114(4) Michigan Law Review 649-681 https://doi.org/10.36644/mlr.114.4.understanding.

339. Rodrigo Meija-Ricart, Camillo Tellez & Marco Nicoli, 'Payment Across Borders: Can Distributed Ledgers Bring Us Closer Together?' (World Bank Blogs, 26 March 2019), https://blogs.worldbank.org/psd/paying-across-borders-can-distributed-ledgers-bring-us-closer-together.

CHAPTER 3

Regulatory Competition: A (De)Construction

This chapter provides a theoretical analysis of the theory of regulatory competition. It provides a discussion on the fragmented nature of the attempts to define the theory in the literature. On this basis, it parses apart the essential elements underlining regulatory competition, an endeavour which has not been thoroughly interrogated. In doing so, it conceives a coherent and uniform framework for better understanding regulatory competition. Finally, it provides a discussion of the outcomes of regulatory competition, including the so-called welfare-reducing regulatory races.

3.1 INTRODUCTION

On 23 June 2016, UK citizens were faced with a single question of crucial import, and perhaps largely unknown consequences: 'Should the United Kingdom remain a member of the European Union or leave the European Union?'. Once the historic referendum catapulted the UK further away from its continental European counterparts, financial services and regulation lawyers in London, including myself, experienced a boom in business, given the birth of the commodified 'Brexit Opinion'. As the passporting of regulated financial services from the UK to other EU Member States would not be permitted post-Brexit, financial services firms headquartered in London began their 'forum shopping' of desirable EU Member States. This occurred through weighing up the legal and regulatory advantages and disadvantages present in available EU jurisdictions, with the aim of choosing a sole destination as the seat of their newly incorporated head office.

The result of the UK's decision to leave the EU also contributed to the dawn of a new era in which frameworks globally are fragmented more than ever before. Christine

Lagarde, President of the ECB, noted in 2023 that the world 'is witnessing a fragmentation of the global economy into competing blocs, with each bloc trying to pull as much of the rest of the world closer to its respective strategic interests and shared values'.[340] This global economy fragmentation naturally filters through the decision-making by government authorities responsible for formulating rules which underpin their legal and regulatory systems. Accordingly, the significance and effects of international regulatory competition between sovereign jurisdictions cannot be overstated. To this end, this chapter tackles this familiar trend of fragmentation by providing uniformity to the manner in which the theory of regulatory competition is traditionally understood. This is achieved through deconstructing the essential elements underlining regulatory competition and devising a framework which provides coherence to this area of study.

3.2 DEFINING REGULATORY COMPETITION

Simple, regulatory competition refers to the process through which jurisdictions compete against each other using means targeted to attract identified resources to their jurisdiction, thus directing those same resources away from other competing jurisdictions. While no universally accepted definition of regulatory competition exists, the overwhelming consensus is that the theory is rooted in Charles Tiebout's well-regarded work, 'A Pure Theory of Local Expenditure.' The result of this work was the eponymous Tiebout model, described as the system in which decentralised systems of government, characterised by horizontally arranged jurisdictions competing with one another, lead to efficiency and produce Pareto-optimal outcomes.[341] This model was positioned within the context of the delivery and production of local public goods, such as different tax and benefit structures, used to attract residents.

Since the publication of Tiebout's 1956 paper, the theory of regulatory competition has been widely studied in several academic fields and disciplines primarily to explain the behaviour of governments, private institutions, and consumers. As a result, several approaches to regulatory competition have been developed which have resulted in attempts to define it through both a broad and narrow lens. Expressed in broader terms, regulatory competition has often been defined with reference to normative considerations, in which the nature and objectives of the theory take centre

340. Christina Lagarde, 'Central Banks in a Fragmenting World' (ECB, 17 April 2023), https://www.ecb.europa.eu/press/key/date/2023/html/ecb.sp230417 ~ 9f8d34fbd6.en.html.

341. Charles Tiebout, 'A Pure Theory of Local Expenditures' (1956) 64(5) Journal of Political economy 416. *See also* Richard L Revesz, 'Rehabilitating Interstate Competition: Rethinking the Race-to-the-Bottom Rationale for Federal Environmental Regulation' (1992) 67 New York University Law Review 1210 https://doi.org/10.1086/257839. The Pareto-efficiency or 'optimality principle' denotes a system in which it is impossible to reallocate resources to any one individual or preference criterion without making at least one other individual or preference criterion worse-off (*See* Christopher Phelan & Aldo Rustichini, 'Pareto Efficiency and Identity' (2018) 13 Theoretical Economics 979-1007) https://doi.org/10.3982/te2719.

stage. For example, the theory has been described as encompassing a micro-theory concerned primarily with governmental behaviour.[342] To this end, O'Hara and Ribstein have opined that individual governments are unable to extend their courts' jurisdiction and enforcement powers extra-territorially. As a result, they compete against each other as no individual government can monopolise sovereignty over mobile entities.[343] In alignment with this broad perspective, Morriss has expressed that regulatory competition is 'a feature of our world, and not bug'.[344]

When defined more narrowly, regulatory competition has been explained by focussing on the elements which are required for it to operate. For example, in some instances, emphasis has been placed on the governmental and political systems within which regulatory competition is framed. This is reflected clearly in Tiebout's model in which competition operates intra-nationally between local government units, i.e., municipalities. In other instances, the focus has been on the actors who compete against each other or the parties whose resources form the subject-matter of the competition. For example, Armour has indicated that regulatory competition 'implies that *national legislatures* compete to attract firms to operate subject to their law' (my emphasis added).[345] O'Hara and Ribstein have defined regulatory competition as jurisdictional competition in which 'governing laws can be *chosen by people and firms* rather than mandated by states' (my emphasis added).[346]

There have also been attempts to define regulatory competition with reference to the means used by competing actors to attract identified resources to their respective jurisdictions. For example, Deakin has defined regulatory competition as 'a process whereby legal rules are selected and de-selected through competition between decentralised, rule-making entities'.[347] Emphasis is thus placed on regulatory competition entailing a specific process whereby legal and regulatory rules form the focal point through which competition operates. As such, Deakin seems to suggest that legal rules function not only as a static outcome of governmental processes but are also treated more malleably where adjustment is required as a specific response to competitive pressures. Other means used in the operation of regulatory competition have also been referenced in the attempts to define it. For example, Baldwin and Cave have defined regulatory competition as including not only the competitive use of legal rules but also 'processes, or enforcement regimes in order to secure an advantage'.[348] These

342. Katharina Holzinger & Thomas Sommerer, '"Race to the Bottom" or "Race to Brussels"? Environmental Competition in Europe' (2011) 49(2) Journal of Common Market Studies 322 https://doi.org/10.1111/j.1468-5965.2010.02135.x.
343. Erin A O'Hara & Larry E Ribstein, *The Law Market* (OUP 2009). 66.
344. Andrew P Morris, 'The Role of Offshore Financial Centers in Regulatory Competition' (2008) University of Illinois Law and Economics Research Paper No. LE07-032, 2.
345. John Armour, 'Who Should Make Corporate Law? EC Legislation Versus Regulatory Competition' (June 2005) Law Working Paper No. 54, 8, https://papers.ssrn.com/sol3/papers.cfm?abstract_id = 860444.
346. Erin A O'Hara & Larry E Ribstein, *The Law Market* (OUP 2009) 66.
347. Simon Deakin, 'Legal Diversity and Regulatory Competition' (2006) 12(4) European Law Journal 441.
348. R Baldwin & M Cave, *Understanding Regulation: Theory, Strategy and Practice* (OUP 1999) 180.

approaches to defining regulatory competition are largely viewed through the lens of rules-based competition where the creation of legal rules, hence represented as a product,[349] encompasses but one of several heterogeneous actions taken by governments.[350]

Finally, some definitions prime their focus on the resources which form the subject-matter of the regulatory competition. In the economic literature, this has been expressed as the traditional mobile factors of production: capital, labour, land, and entrepreneurship. More pragmatically, Morriss has referred to this as actors ultimately competing for wealth maximisation through economic activities.[351] In line therewith, O'Hara and Ribstein have described regulatory competition as a process in which 'states compete for *mobile parties and their assets* by attempting to provide the laws that people want' (my emphasis added).[352] While these attempts at defining regulatory competition are helpful and instructive, they have been formulated in a piecemeal fashion, without consideration of the theory through a coherent and consistent understanding. A lack of uniformity in understanding the elements which underline regulatory competition may lead to the overreliance on untested and generalised assumptions, which may impact our ability to understand how actors engaged in regulatory competition compete against each other, and why they do.

To address this gap prevailing in regulatory competition studies, the next section devises a coherent and cohesive framework based on a codification of the essential elements underlining regulatory competition. This framework can be applied to better understand whether regulatory competition operates between competing entities, and if so, on what basis, and to what extent.

3.3 FRAMING REGULATORY COMPETITION

The framework below systematically identifies the essential elements of which regulatory competition is composed. These elements are interrelated and cascade in accordance with the specific context in which regulatory competition is investigated. Overall, the framework intends to provide a cohesive, comprehensive and uniform approach to understanding the nature of regulatory competition, an approach which is lacking in literature in this field.

349. *See*, for example, Roberta Romano, 'Law as a Product: Some Pieces of the Incorporation Puzzle' (1985) 1 Journal of Law, Economics & Organisation 224 https://doi.org/10.1093/oxfordjournals.jleo.a036892 and Horst Eidenmuller, 'The Transnational Law Market, Regulatory Competition, and Transnational Corporations,' (2011) 18(2) Indiana Journal of Global Legal Studies 711 https://doi.org/10.2979/indjglolegstu.18.2.707.
350. *See* Charles Oman, 'Policy Competition for Foreign Direct Investment: A study of Competition Among Governments to Attract FDI' (*OECD*, 2000) 21, https://www.oecd.org/mena/competitiveness//35275189.pdf.
351. Andrew P Morriss, 'The Role of Offshore Financial Centers in Regulatory Competition' (2008) University of Illinois Law and Economics Research Paper No. LE07-032, 3.
352. Erin A O'Hara & Larry E Ribstein, *The Law Market* (OUP 2009).

3.3.1 Environmental Context

Regulatory competition has been studied in several political and social systems. These environments form the contextual spaces which distinguish the different ecosystems in which regulatory competition operates or is intended to operate.[353] They also provide the overarching frame under which key regulatory competition concepts are positioned. In this book, these contexts are referred to as 'Environmental Contexts'. Notably, these Environmental Contexts place restrictions on the actions and behaviour of the actors who directly and indirectly take part in the operation of regulatory competition. These restrictions include, for example, the rules imposed by operating systems of government as well as the cultural systems prevailing in the relevant jurisdictions.[354] Further, every Environmental Context in which regulatory competition operates is limited by the rules imposed by the respective legal system. Finally, at an international level, cooperative measures, including harmonised standards and mutual recognition procedures in federal and quai-federal systems, such as in the US and the EU, place limits on the impact and extent of the operation of regulatory competition.

Overall, the Environmental Context in which regulatory competition operates, and its potential outcomes, are important to understanding how actors compete against each other based on the limits imposed by their respective political and social systems. While regulatory competition has been broadly referenced as operating at a municipal, national, and international level between different governmental and non-government entities, it has not been systematised in the manner explained below. Based on these considerations, the following Environmental Contexts have been identified.

3.3.1.1 Intra-national Regulatory Competition

This type of regulatory competition operates between two or more governmental entities or between two or more governmental entities and NGOs (extra-governmentally) whose actions and behaviours are constrained by their respective legal systems. Here, regulatory competition operates within the confines of a single domestic system in which the entities, or regulatory competition actors compete against each other for the identified resource(s), while adhering to the same legal system in force. Intra-national regulatory competition has been studied predominantly in the context of federal and quasi-federal systems of government.[355] What exactly constitutes 'federalism' is not necessarily clear and has been discussed extensively. However, in 1946 Wheare described their 'federal principle' as encompassing 'the method of dividing powers so that the general and regional governments are each, within a sphere, co-ordinate and independent'.[356]

353. From here on, every reference to 'regulatory competition operates' in a specific environmental context includes a corresponding reference to it being 'intended to operate' or 'perceived to operate' unless specifically indicated otherwise.
354. This book has not been framed using socio-legal considerations and therefore cultural systems fall outside the main scope of this study, but are referred to where appropriate.
355. Daniel C Esty & Damien Geradin, 'Regulatory Co-opetition' in Daniel C Esty & Damien Geradin (eds), *Regulatory Competition and Economic Integration* (OUP 2001) 40.
356. Kenneth Wheare, *Federal Government* (OUP 1946) 11.

Federalism has also been defined with reference to regional and central governments' ability to make final decisions.[357] These broad interpretations are inferred below when references to federalism and quasi-federalism are made in the context of intra-national regulatory competition and 'competitive federalism'.

Intra-national regulatory competition empirical studies have been conducted in several federal jurisdictions including Australia, India and the US, in addition to quasi- or de facto federal jurisdictions such as the UK.[358] Whether the EU project can be classified as operating as a federation remains unclear as scholars have supported this notion,[359] but have also expressed their opposition thereto.[360] In spite of this more granular dissonance, economists and legal scholars alike have treated the EU as a federation for the purpose of their respective regulatory competition empirical studies.[361] With the above in mind, intra-national regulatory competition operates: (i) intra-nationally between governmental entities belonging to the same domestic legal system;[362] and (ii) extra-governmentally between governmental entities and NGOs belonging to the same domestic legal system.[363]

3.3.1.2 International Regulatory Competition

This type of regulatory competition operates between two or more governments or between two or more governments and NGOs (extra-governmentally) whose actions and behaviours are constrained by their respective legal systems. Here, regulatory competition operates within the confines of more than one domestic legal system in which the actors compete against each other for the identified resource(s) while adhering to the same legal system in force.[364] International regulatory competition

357. William Riker, 'Federalism' in Greenstein Fred & Polsby Nelson (eds), *Handbook of Political Science* (Addison-Wesley 1975).
358. John Law, 'How Can We Define Federalism' (2013) 5(3) Perspectives on Federalism 91.
359. *See* Michael Burgess, 'Federalism and European Union: The Building of Europe, 1950-2000' (2000) (Routledge, London); Daniel R Kelemen, 'The Structure and Dynamics of EU Federalism' (2003) 36(1-2) Comparative Political Studies 184, and Stéphanie Chouinard, 'The EU and Federalism' (2014) 24(1) Polities and Policies Compared, Regional and Federal Studies 125-126 https://doi.org/10.1080/13597566.2013.852975.
360. Alan Milward, 'The European Rescue of the Nation-State' (Routledge 1992); Andrew Moravcsik, 'European Federalism: Rhetoric and Reality' in Nicolaidis Kalypso & Howse Robert (eds), *The Federal Vision: Legitimacy and Levels of Governance in the United States and the European Union* (OUP 2001) 161-87 and Philippe Schmitter, 'Some Alternative Futures for the European Polity and Their Implications for European Public Policy' in Yves Mény, Pierre Muller & Jean-Louis Quermonne (eds), *Adjusting to Europe: The Impact of the European Union on National Institutions and Policies* (Routledge 1996) 25-40.
361. *See* William Bratton & Joseph McCahery, 'Fiscal Federalism, Jurisdictional Competition, and Tax Coordination: Translating Theory to Policy in the European Union' in Daniel C Esty & Damien Geradin (eds), *Regulatory Competition and Economic Integration* (OUP 2001) 157.
362. *See* Mark J Roe, 'Delaware's Competition' (2003) 117 Harvard Law Review 591 https://doi.org/10.2307/3651948.
363. Daniel C Esty & Damien Geradin, 'Regulatory Co-opetition' in Daniel C Esty & Damien Geradin (eds), *Regulatory Competition and Economic Integration* (OUP 2001) 44.
364. It should be noted that this does not operate to the exclusion of the use of international law in the operation of RC. However, this description serves primarily to accentuate the operation of

therefore involves sovereign nation-states competing against each other on the global stage for the economic and non-economic activities of parties who may bring about wealth creation. In the economic literature, these activities are referred to as the traditional mobile factors of production, i.e., capital, labour, land and entrepreneurship.[365] In addition to studies measuring regulatory competition empirically between onshore sovereign nation-states, several studies have focussed on whether offshore financial centres (so-called tax havens) compete directly with their onshore equivalents.[366] Studies of this nature have also focussed on measuring competition concerning international securities regulation,[367] labour standards,[368] and environmental[369] regulation and tariff cutting.[370] With the above in mind, international regulatory competition operates: (i) internationally between governmental entities belonging to different domestic legal systems;[371] and (ii) internationally between NGO entities not belonging to any particular domestic or international legal system.

3.3.2 Regulatory Competition Direction

Regulatory competition has also been viewed through the power dynamic relationship which exists between competing actors, based predominantly on the scope of the competences and functions to which they have been assigned. On this basis, the power dynamic relationship is confined to governmental entities, as other competing actors lack the necessary statutory power. On this basis, regulatory competition is classified as operating within a specific dimension which assists with identifying the level and extent of the governmental powers assigned to competing actors. In this book, this power dynamic relationship is referred to as the regulatory competition direction, viewed from both a horizontal and vertical perspective.

RC between *different governmental entities belonging to different sovereign nation-states*, as opposed to governmental entities belonging to the *same sovereign nation-state* (my emphasis).

365. Hans-Werner Sinn, 'The Selection Principle and Market Failure in Systems Competition' (1997) 66 Journal of Public Economics 248 https://doi.org/10.1016/s0047-2727(97)00043-1.
366. *See* Andrew P Morriss, 'The Role of Offshore Financial Centers in Regulatory Competition' (2008) University of Illinois Law and Economics Research Paper No. LE07-032 and Anna M Dionne & Jonathan R Macey, 'Offshore Finance and Onshore Market: Racing to the Bottom or Moving Toward Efficient?' in Andrew P Morriss et al. (eds), *Offshore Financial Centers and Regulatory Competition* (AEI Press 2010).
367. *See* Roberta Romano, 'The Need for Competition in International Securities Regulation' (2001) Faculty Scholarship Series. Paper 1915, http://digitalcommons.law.yale.edu/fss_papers/1915.
368. *See* William Olney, 'A Race to the Bottom? Employment Protection and Foreign Direct Investment' (2013) 91 Journal of International Economics 191 https://doi.org/10.1016/j.jinteco.2013.08.003.
369. *See* Baomin Dong, Jiong Dong & Xin Zhao, 'FDI and Environmental Regulation: Pollution Haven or a Race to the Top?' (2012) 41 Journal of Regulatory Economics 233 https://doi.org/10.1007/s11149-011-9162-3.
370. *See* Pierre-Louis Vezina, 'Race-to-the-Bottom Tariff Cutting' (2014) 22(3) Review of International Economics 444-458 https://doi.org/10.1111/roie.12135.
371. *See* J Samuel Barkin, 'Racing All Over the Place: A Dispersion Model of International Regulatory Competition' (2015) 21(1) European Journal of International Relations 171 https://doi.org/10.1177/1354066114530009.

3.3.2.1 *Horizontal*

The horizontal dimension includes competition between two or more actors operating at the same or similar functional levels of government, and can thus operate between differing states or sovereign-nation states.[372] According to Trachtman, '[i]n horizontal competition, economic institutions at the same horizontal level of social organization compete for economic power and welfare'.[373] Armour has also expressed that the 'horizontal, or domestic, aspect' of regulatory competition concerns selecting the relevant body within a jurisdiction responsible for promulgating rules.[374] The 'exit' of firms from one locale to another to take advantage of the regulatory environment in the former is traditionally a key ingredient for the operation of the horizontal dimension of regulatory competition.[375] Examples of this dimension of regulatory competition include Tiebout's model which focussed on competition operating between different local municipalities.[376] Competition between EU Member States, among US states,[377] and between different sovereign nation-states are also examples of horizontal international regulatory competition.[378]

3.3.2.2 *Vertical*

The vertical dimension includes competition which operates between two or more actors at distinguishing or different levels of government, and can thus operate between local units of government and the national government or between states and the national government[379] The operation of the vertical dimension of regulatory competition is therefore premised on distinguishing levels of power being attributed to different governmental bodies.[380] According to Hornuf, for vertical regulatory competition to operate, the 'supranational legal form', i.e., the European Commission in the EU and the federal government in the US, must promulgate laws and regulations which are exclusive to their domestic counterparts.[381] For example, in the US several

372. *See* Lars Hornuf & Julia Linder, 'End of Regulatory Competition in European Company Law' (2014) Andrássy Working Paper Series No. 33, 12.
373. Joel P Trachtman, 'International Regulatory Competition, Externalization and Jurisdiction' (1993) 34(1) Harvard International Law Journal 51.
374. John Armour, 'Who Should Make Corporate Law? EC Legislation Versus Regulatory Competition' (2005) 58(1) Current Legal Problems 369 https://doi.org/10.1093/clp/58.1.369.
375. *See* Charles Tiebout, 'A Pure Theory of Local Expenditures' (1956) 64(5) Journal of Political economy 416-424.
376. Charles Tiebout, 'A Pure Theory of Local Expenditures' (1956) 64(5) Journal of Political economy 416-424 https://doi.org/10.1086/257839.
377. Lars Hornuf & Julia Linder, 'End of Regulatory Competition in European Company Law' (2014) Andrássy Working Paper Series No. 33 5.
378. Joel P Trachtman, 'International Regulatory Competition, Externalization and Jurisdiction' (1993) 34(1) Harvard International Law Journal 51.
379. *See* Lars Hornuf & Julia Linder, 'End of Regulatory Competition in European Company Law' (2014) Andrássy Working Paper Series No. 33, 12.
380. Joel P Trachtman, 'International Regulatory Competition, Externalization and Jurisdiction' (1993) 34(1) Harvard International Law Journal 53.
381. Lars Hornuf & Julia Linder, 'End of Regulatory Competition in European Company Law' (2014) Andrássy Working Paper Series No. 33 12.

regulatory competition studies have been conducted with reference to competition operating between the federal government and individual states.[382] Competition between the European Commission and individual EU Member States is another example of vertical regulatory competition.[383]

This essential element underlining regulatory competition has not been considered in too much detail. In most instances, it is used as a simple descriptor identifying the different or similar functional units of government considered in the study of regulatory competition. It has also been considered practically as involving the 'selection of the appropriate body' responsible for the formulation of rules.[384] However, this aspect of regulatory competition should also be used to identify the varying degrees of legislative competence and political power of actors engaged in competition. From this perspective, the dimension of regulatory competition is viewed not only as a simple descriptor but also as a marker characterising the power dynamic relationship relevant to the operation of regulatory competition. The power dynamic between competing actors thus provides an interesting perspective on the operation of regulatory competition.

First, this essential element provides an indication of how the respective powers and competences are leveraged as a tool during the operation of regulatory competition. For example, in the vertical dimension actors competing against each other are on an unequal footing as they are vested with distinguished levels of political power and legislative competences, i.e., the federal government as opposed to a state government in the US. These distinguished levels of power and competences provide additional characterisation to the operation of regulatory competition which highlights the relevant power dynamics.

Second, this essential element may be less significant for international regulatory competition where competing actors are positioned in different legal systems, with different legal frameworks and systems of government. However, the overall focus on power dynamics is still relevant for understanding the powers and competences of these competing actors, and how this influences the operation of regulatory competition.

3.3.3 System of Government

The Environmental Contexts in which regulatory competition operates are subject to the limits of the overarching system(s) of government in force. Systems, types, or forms

382. Daniel C Esty, 'Non-governmental Organizations at the World Trade Organisation: Cooperation, Competition, or Exclusion' (1998) 1(1) Journal of International Economic Law 137 https://doi.org/10.1093/jiel/1.1.123.
383. *See* Martina Eckhardt & Wolfgang Kerber, 'Developing Two-tiered Regulatory Competition in EU Corporate Law: Assessing the Impact of the Societas Privata Europaea' (2014) 41(1) Journal of Law and Society 152 https://doi.org/10.1111/j.1467-6478.2014.00660.x and John Armour, 'Who Should Make Corporate Law? EC Legislation Versus Regulatory Competition' (2005) 58(1) Current Legal Problems 369 https://doi.org/10.1093/clp/58.1.369.
384. John Armour, 'Who Should Make Corporate Law? EC Legislation Versus Regulatory Competition' (2005) 58(1) Current Legal Problems 369 https://doi.org/10.1093/clp/58.1.369.

of government refer broadly to the collective of political institutions by which a government is arranged.[385] This governmental collective is ordinarily characterised by the existence of a power source and a power structure.[386] Generally, 'power source' refers to the governmental institutions and individuals exercising authority over a sovereign nation-state and how power is attained, whereas 'power structure' refers to the system by which these players are arranged.[387] Accordingly, the manner in which governments are arranged, and to whom political power is assigned, has a significant impact on how governments behave and how they respond to external forces which affect their designated functions. Democracies,[388] republics, constitutional monarchies, and autocracies, are examples of the most common modern-day systems of government.[389]

The impact of systems of government on regulatory competition has been studied widely. Morriss, for example, has argued that in autocracies the economic freedom brought about by regulatory competition creates alternative centres of power which undermines the control of autocratic governments.[390] Further, in democratic systems of government, regulatory competition can assist with the eradication of regulatory inefficiencies and can act to constrain efforts by governments to redistribute through governmental regulation. A lack of regulatory competition in such systems of government can also lead to increased rent-seeking behaviours by domestic interest groups. As such, regulatory competition has the potential to reduce loss caused by rent-seeking behaviours by minimising barriers which guard off areas of the economy from competition. Also, in jurisdictions where institutions hold a monopoly in certain markets, resulting in the lack of incentive to reduce costs, regulatory competition may act to influence its ability to raise prices directly or indirectly. At the same time, it can spur jurisdictions of this kind to divert resources for product innovation or for offering more efficient services, producing social and welfare gains.[391]

385. Lumen, 'Boundless Political Science: Forms of Government', https://courses.lumenlearning.com/boundless-politicalscience/chapter/forms-of-government/.
386. Lumen, 'Boundless Political Science: Forms of Government', https://courses.lumenlearning.com/boundless-politicalscience/chapter/forms-of-government/.
387. Lumen, 'Boundless Political Science: Forms of Government,' https://courses.lumenlearning.com/boundless-politicalscience/chapter/forms-of-government/.
388. Drew Desilver, 'Despite Global Concerns About Democracy, More Than Half of Countries Are Democratic' (*Pew Research Centre*, 14 May 2019), https://www.pewresearch.org/fact-tank/2019/05/14/more-than-half-of-countries-are-democratic/.
389. *See* Frank E Holman, 'Forms of Government' (1946) 32(4) American Bar Association Journal 190-194.
390. Andrew P Morriss, 'The Role of Offshore Financial Centers in Regulatory Competition' in Andrew P Morriss et al. (eds), *Offshore Financial Centers and Regulatory Competition* (AEI Press 2010).
391. *See* Roberta Romano, 'Law as a Product: Some Pieces of the Incorporation Puzzle' (1985) 1 Journal of Law, Economics & Organisation 224 https://doi.org/10.1093/oxfordjournals.jleo.a036892; Wallace E Oates & Robert M Schwab, 'Economic Competition Among Jurisdictions: Efficiency Enhancing or Distortion Inducing?' (1988) 35 Journal of Public Economics 333 https://doi.org/10.1016/0047-2727(88)90036-9 and Richard L Revesz, 'Rehabilitating Intestate Competition: Rethinking the "Race to the Bottom" Rationale for Federal Environmental Regulation' (1992) 67 New York University Law Review 1210-1254.

The system of government in force therefore impacts how actors, specifically governmental entities, behave in the operation of regulatory competition. In particular, the actions and behaviours of actors would be constrained by the values and principles which underline the system of government in force. For example, democratic governments generally protect rights to private property and free enterprise,[392] whereas autocracies are less committed to enforcing their stated commitments to the rule of law.[393] These differences in the principles and values underlying systems of government, particularly from an economic and legal perspective, have the potential to impact the operation of regulatory competition.

3.3.4 Regulatory Competition Actors

Regulatory competition has been observed and studied primarily through the actions, behaviours and roles of government and non-government entities acting within the perimeter of a particular Environmental Context based on the applicable system(s) of government in form.[394] The government and non-government entities operating in different Environmental Contexts are referred to as regulatory competition Actors. In the literature, these actors are often represented as mere placeholders to contextualise the investigation of the existence of regulatory competition, without placing enough emphasis on the institutional significance of these actors. Accordingly, it is not surprising that more research is required to understand the role of various actors and processes involved in the operation of regulatory competition. Through Tiebout's model, regulatory competition was primarily concerned with the behaviours of 'customers' in a local government setting with emphasis being placed on their decision(s) to relocate to alternative jurisdiction(s) to take advantage of preferred levels of public service goods provision.[395] The conceptualisation of the theory of regulatory competition is rooted in understanding actors other than governments and non-governmental entities.

Only later, and through the prism of competitive federalism, more focus was directed to the actions, behaviours and roles of governments acting within the confines of a particular Environmental Context. However, this dedicated focus on the actions and behaviours of government and sovereign nation-state behaviour has been criticised leading to calls that regulatory competition studies should focus on other competing actors. To this end, the focus of the regulatory competition studies has come full circle. Bearing this in mind, regulatory competition Actors can be divided into the following groups.

392. *See* Karl de Schweinitz Jr, 'Free Enterprise and Democracy' (1953) 20(1) Social Research 55-74.
393. Dan Cao & Roger Lagunoff, 'The Dynamics of Property Rights in Modern Autocracies' (2021) Working Papers Georgetown University, Department of Economics 2, https://drive.google.com/file/d/1VYmFQr6QXt9G_9kQWqp5WMQ-Bl2tM5xT/view.
394. Claudio M Radaelli, 'The Puzzle of Regulatory Competition' (2014) 24 Journal of Public Policy 15 https://doi.org/10.1017/s0143814x04000017.
395. *See* Charles Tiebout, 'A Pure Theory of Local Expenditures' (1956) 64(5) Journal of Political economy 416-424 https://doi.org/10.1086/257839.

3.3.4.1 Primary Actors

Primary Actors in a specific Environmental Context refer to the government entities responsible for the development, execution, and enforcement of promulgated or amended laws, regulations and other regulatory standards and guidelines based on the informed competition policy. Overall, these Actors facilitate the operation of regulatory competition by creating and enforcing the 'means' through which competition takes place. They thus represent the canonical parties between which the regulatory competition operates. The different arms of government as often treated as single units that have formulated a unified approach to regulatory competition. However, it is important to note that several arms of governments partake in decisions which culminate in policy formulation, legislative drafting and enforcement, particularly in democracies. These different arms of government include, in most cases, an executive, a judiciary, and a legislature. To this end, Primary Actors represent government entities as a whole, including those authorised to act on their behalf. This can include, for example, regulatory agencies responsible for regulating key industries and sectors, including regulators who supervise the financial services industry.

The varying governmental arms are also made up of elected politicians motivated, in part, by the decisions of private parties. An increase in the economic activities of these private parties, and the subsequent wealth to citizens, are ordinarily used by politicians when campaigning to secure current or new political appointments.[396] Bearing in mind their functions and competence to make rules, Primary Actors have sometimes been referred to as the 'regulating side' in the literature.[397] In the intra-national regulatory competition, the definitions of the Primary Actors set out below represent the canonical examples of the parties between whom regulation competition operates. These definitions are not an exhaustive list of all the parties involved in regulatory competition. The Primary Actors in the intra-national regulatory competition Environmental Context, include.

3.3.4.1.1 Local Governments[398]

The Oxford Dictionary defines 'local government' to mean the 'administration of a town or other comparatively small district by elected representatives of the people who live there, as distinguished from central government; the governing body responsible

396. Andrew P Morriss, 'The Role of Offshore Financial Centers in Regulatory Competition' in Andrew P Morriss et al. (eds), *Offshore Financial Centers and Regulatory Competition* (AEI Press 2010).
397. Yin Xiao, 'Analysing the Enforcement Dimension of Regulatory Competition: A Cultural Institutionalist Approach' (PhD thesis London School of Economics 2014) 21, http://etheses.lse.ac.uk/1035/1/Xiao_Analysing_the_Enforcement_Dimension_of_Regulatory_Competition.pdf.
398. *See* Joan Costa-Font, Filipe De-Albuquerque & Hristos Doucouliagos, 'Does Inter-Jurisdictional Competition Engender a "Race-to-the-Bottom"? A Meta-Regression Analysis' (2015) 27 Journal of Economics and Politics 490 https://doi.org/10.1111/ecpo.12066.

for this'.[399] This definition is corroborated by Golding's view that local governments are characterised by 'the management of their own affairs by the people of a locality'.[400] Ordinarily, this management often includes the power and authority to govern and implement local government measures, including the autonomy to make policy decisions, subject sometimes to the supervision of the relevant central government.[401] In terms of competences, local governments are responsible for several sectors including education, health and social services, culture and leisure, environment, public safety, housing planning, transportation, and water and waste management.[402] Examples of local governments include boroughs, counties, districts, and municipalities. In the context of the theory of regulatory competition, it is important to point out that local governments are governmental entities in their own right and carry out their functions and competence within the broader political system which includes the overarching central, or national government.

Costa-Font's study found that states engage in expenditure games and strategic expenditure interactions with one another, particularly among municipalities and counties.[403] The principal reason for this is that local governments are usually arranged in decentralised governmental systems where power is dispersed at a national, regional and local level.[404] Local governments, however, also operate in unitary states where the national government is the supreme authority solely empowered to delegate powers and competencies to smaller government units.[405] This distinction is important because it positions local and national governments as separate entities, with varying degrees of legislative competence and political influence, impacting the extent of the operation of regulatory competition. The competences and powers granted to local governments are usually contingent on their constitutional authority, the availability of resources, and the areas of responsibility which require government intervention at a national level.[406]

399. Oxford English Dictionary, 'Local Government', https://www-oed-com.eproxy.lib.hku.hk/view/Entry/109549?redirectedFrom=local+government#eid221893501.
400. Louis Golding, *Local Government* (Leonard Cutts ed., 3rd edn, The English Universities Press Ltd 1964) 19.
401. Louis Golding, *Local Government* (Leonard Cutts ed., 3rd edn, The English Universities Press Ltd 1964) 19 and Britannica, The Editors of Encyclopaedia, 'Local Government' (*Encyclopaedia Britannica*, 8 December 2017), https://www.britannica.com/topic/local-government.
402. *See* Andrew Sancton, 'Canadian Cities in Transition: the Twenty-First Century' in Trudy Bunting & Pierre Filion (eds), *The Municipal Role in the Governance of Canadian Cities* (OUP 2000) 425-442.
403. Joan Costa-Font, Filipe De-Albuquerque & Hristos Doucouliagos, 'Does Inter-jurisdictional Competition Engender a "Race-to-the-Bottom"? a Meta-Regression Analysis' (2015) 27 Journal of Economics and Politics 490.
404. Benjamin Elisha Sawe, 'What is a Unitary State' (*World Atlas*, 1 August 2017), https://www.worldatlas.com/articles/what-is-a-unitary-state.html.
405. Benjamin Elisha Sawe, 'What is a Unitary State' (*World Atlas*, 1 August 2017), https://www.worldatlas.com/articles/what-is-a-unitary-state.html.
406. Patricia A Collins & Michael V Hayes, 'The Role of Urban Municipal Governments in Reducing Health Inequalities: A Meta-Narrative Mapping Analysis' (2010) 9 International Journal of Equity Health 3 https://doi.org/10.1186/1475-9276-9-13.

3.3.4.1.2 *Regional Governments*

The UNESCO's Institute for Statistics describes 'regional governments' as 'the largest geographical area into which the country as a whole may be divided for political or administrative purposes'.[407] To this end, regional governments are ordinarily empowered with the authority to impose and collect taxes within their specific region and to utilise the proceeds thereof in alignment with their specific policies.[408] Examples of regional governments include provinces, states, territories, and regions. In the context of the theory of regulatory competition, the most well-known examples of regional government Actors are states, particularly federated states within a federation. Federated states can be described as partly self-governing polities that have 'joined together for a common purpose'[409] and who are ordinarily empowered with certain levels of constitutionally entrenched autonomous power (i.e., states in Switzerland and the US).

In a similar vein, 'province' can be defined as 'one of the areas that a country or empire is divided into as part of the organization of its government, which often has some control over its own laws'.[410] Of critical importance here, is not the distinctive designation given to the particular regional government, but rather the particular system of government within which it operates, as its powers and competences will be largely dependent on this fact.

Intra-national regulatory competition, particularly the corporate charter competition which took place between US states in the early 1980s until the mid-1990s, is a well-known example of competitive federalism. The study of inter-state competition in the US represents the most comprehensive investigation of regulatory competition and has provided significant insights into the actions and behaviours of regional governments as Primary Actors.

3.3.4.1.3 *Government Departments*

The Collins Dictionary defines government departments, also called 'ministries', to mean the arms, divisions, or sectors of national and state governments responsible for the administration of a particular area of public service provision or governmental function.[411] Government departments are ordinarily led by a senior public official and are provided with the necessary funding, powers and competences to make decisions

407. UNESCO Institute for Statistics Glossary, 'Regional Government' (*UNESCO*, 2021), http://uis.unesco.org/en/glossary-term/regional-government? = undefined&wbdisable = true#: ~ :text = Definition, %2C%20province%2C%20department%20or%20region.
408. UNESCO Institute for Statistics Glossary, 'Regional Government' (*UNESCO*, 2021), http://uis.unesco.org/en/glossary-term/regional-government? = undefined&wbdisable = true#: ~ :text = Definition, %2C%20province%2C%20department%20or%20region.
409. Collins, 'Federated' (*Collins*, 2021), https://www.collinsdictionary.com/dictionary/english/federated.
410. Cambridge Dictionary, 'Province' (*Cambridge Dictionary*, 2021), https://dictionary.cambridge.org/dictionary/english/province.
411. Collins Dictionary, 'Government Department' (*Collins*), https://www.collinsdictionary.com/dictionary/english/government-department.

and execute tasks associated with their particular portfolio of activity.[412] In the context of the theory of regulatory competition, intra-national regulatory competition among governmental departments has not been studied widely, despite research indicating that competition between these Primary Actors is inherent.[413] Breton has indicated that compound governments (such as federations) are made up of autonomous and quasi-autonomous centres of powers (i.e., branches, departments, and ministries) that compete against each other to produce and supply goods and services to citizens.[414]

To support this view, Esty and Geradin have referenced competition operating between the US' Environmental Protection Agency and its Department of Energy based on their differing stances on the design of climate change policies.[415] With the utmost deference to Esty and Geradin, however, the relationship dynamic between these government departments should be classified as 'conflict', rather than competition, as understood in the context of the theory of regulatory competition. Conflict, in which opposing parties express divergent interests concerning the same subject matter, is very different to competition in which opposing parties compete against each other for the same subject matter.[416] As such, diverging policy agendas do not necessarily translate into regulatory competition properly. From this perspective, it is therefore doubtful whether there is much merit to the study of regulatory competition between government departments.

3.3.4.1.4 National Governments

The Oxford Dictionary defines 'national government' as 'a coalition government, especially [sic] one in which party differences are subordinated to the national interest in a time of crisis'.[417] At their base, therefore, national governments are comprised of members affiliated with distinguishing political parties.[418] National governments function primarily as the political authority harnessed with the power to administer the jurisdiction which they control by determining, setting and executing varying agendas. These agendas include those relating to military affairs, domestic and foreign policy, and tax collection. In the context of the theory of regulatory competition, national governments are important Primary Actors as they represent the level of government in which legislative competence and political power are concentrated. Ordinarily, different levels of government within a single system of government have distinguishing

412. Educalingo, 'Ministry (Government Department)' (*Educalingo*), https://educalingo.com/en/dic-en/government-department.
413. *See* Albert Breton, *Competitive Governments: An Economic Theory of Politics and Public Finance* (Cambridge University Press 1996).
414. Albert Breton, *Competitive Governments: An Economic Theory of Politics and Public Finance* (Cambridge University Press 1996) 17.
415. Daniel C Esty & Damien Geradin, 'Regulatory Co-opetition' in Daniel C Esty & Damien Geradin (eds), *Regulatory Competition and Economic Integration* (OUP 2001) 40.
416. Otomar J Bartos & Paul Wehr, *Using Conflict Theory* (Cambridge University Press 2002) 13-14.
417. Oxford English Dictionary, 'National Government', https://www-oed-com.eproxy.lib.hku.hk/view/Entry/125287?redirectedFrom=national+government#eid35384383.
418. Collins Dictionary, 'National Government' (*Collins*), https://www.collinsdictionary.com/dictionary/english/national-government.

levels of competences and powers to set policy and promulgate laws in accordance with their own interests. This political stratification, peculiar to federations and unitary systems of government, impacts the manner in which regulatory competition is directed through the development of policy, laws and regulations.

For example, a local government's competence to legislate over specific areas of the law will determine the extent to which it is able to compete with other Primary Actors, usually including neighbouring local governments, and the national government itself. Similarly, national governments, are usually less concerned with such limited powers as they generally have access to greater funding and superior law-making competences, placing them in a stronger position of power to compete. However, local governments are able to manoeuvre themselves as worthy competitors based on their localised knowledge and expertise.

The Primary Actor in the international regulatory competition Environmental Context, include.

3.3.4.1.5 Sovereign Nation-States

Lexico described 'sovereign state' as a 'state with a defined territory that administers its own government and is not subject to or dependent on another power'.[419] This accords partially with the definition of 'state' under the Montevideo Convention on Rights and Duties of States[420] which classifies the 'state' as a person with a defined territory, a government, a permanent population, and the capability to enter into relations with other states.[421] This definition appears to be purposefully broad, particularly as what 'sovereignty' constitutes precisely remains up for debate. Fowler and Bunck, for example, have expressed that the Montevideo Convention's definition of 'state', while prescriptive, is only a partial indicator of what sovereign states are composed of.[422] In addition to the requirements of the Montevideo Convention, both authors instead argue that sovereignty requires a concerted indication of de facto independence (independence of external authority in foreign matters) or de facto jure independence (state legally separate from other states), coupled most importantly with the determination and approval of the international community at large.[423]

Overall, therefore, what exactly constitutes a 'sovereign state' has still not been settled in the literature, and perhaps for good cause. A strict one size fits all definition would fail to consider geographical and population nuances which fall outside the Montevideo Convention's remit. Further, the bestowment of sovereignty appears to a large extent to involve political processes, the components of which are too bespoke to

419. Lexico, 'Sovereign State', https://www.lexico.com/definition/sovereign_state.
420. Montevideo Convention on Rights and Duties of States adopted by the Seventh International Conference of American States at Montevideo, Uruguay on 26 December 1933.
421. Montevideo Convention on Rights and Duties of States adopted by the Seventh International Conference of American States at Montevideo, Uruguay on 26 December 1933, Art. 1.
422. Michael Ross Fowler & Julie Marie Bunck, 'What Constitutes the Sovereign State?' (1996) 22(4) Review of International Studies 383 https://doi.org/10.1017/s0260210500118637.
423. Michael Ross Fowler & Julie Marie Bunck, 'What Constitutes the Sovereign State?' (1996) 22(4) Review of International Studies 404-405 https://doi.org/10.1017/s0260210500118637.

fit any structured legal definition. In the context of the theory of regulatory competition, sovereign nation-states include both onshore and offshore sovereign states, which have formed the focus of several empirical regulatory competition studies.[424] Empirical studies have also been conducted to measure regulatory competition between different onshore sovereign states at an international level, particularly on the basis of wealth maximisation which may result therefrom.[425] Morriss has stipulated that most politicians, independent of their ideologies and the form of government within which they operate, are directed towards creating wealth within their jurisdictions.[426]

As such, studies at an international level cite regulatory competition between sovereign nation-states competing against each other for economic activity.[427] Regulatory competition at this level appeared to be quite novel based on the origins of measuring intra-national competition at the local, regional and national government within federations and unitary systems of government. These studies were concerned, in particular, with the threat of mobile entities to 'exit' a particular locale, based on the ease with which relocation could be achieved based on geographical considerations. The most likely explanation for the extension of the study of regulatory competition in an international context appears to be the increased globalisation of the world economy in which 'exit' appears to be more threatening based on fewer constraints to the location of economic activity which may now be conducted irrespective of locale based on the proliferation of Internet usage for work and increased digitisation.[428]

3.3.4.2 *Secondary Actors*

Secondary Actors refer broadly to natural and legal persons who are the consumers of the 'means' created and enforced by the Primary Actors in a specific Environmental Context. Primary Actors in their coordinated efforts to compete against each other are therefore centrally concerned with the activity, behaviours, and decisions of Secondary Actors. Overall, Secondary Actors fuel the market for regulatory competition and provide the catalyst for Primary Actors to create the means through which regulatory competition operates. As such, Secondary Actors as often referred to as the 'regulated

424. *See* Andrew P Morriss, 'The Role of Offshore Financial Centers in Regulatory Competition' in Andrew P Morriss et al. (eds), *Offshore Financial Centers and Regulatory Competition* (AEI Press 2010).
425. *See* Anna M Dionne & Jonathan R Macey, 'Offshore Finance and Onshore Market: Racing to the Bottom, or Moving Toward Efficient?' in Andrew P Morris et al. (eds), *Offshore Financial Centers and Regulatory Competition* (AEI Press 2010).
426. Andrew P Morriss, 'The Role of Offshore Financial Centers in Regulatory Competition' in Andrew P Morriss et al. (eds), *Offshore Financial Centers and Regulatory Competition* (AEI Press 2010).
427. Andrew P Morriss, 'The Role of Offshore Financial Centers in Regulatory Competition' in Andrew P Morriss et al. (eds), *Offshore Financial Centers and Regulatory Competition* (AEI Press 2010).
428. *See* J Samuel Barkin, 'Racing All Over the Place: A Dispersion Model of International Regulatory Competition' (2015) 21(1) European Journal of International Relations for a general discussion of the responses to globalisation https://doi.org/10.1177/1354066114530009.

side'[429] or more pragmatically as 'market actors'.[430] This designation, however, is not broad enough to cover the wide spectrum of actors who fall within this category. For example, Secondary Actors do not necessarily have to be *regulated* by any governmental body or authority to qualify as such. The central rationale for this view is that not all Secondary Actors are regulated on the basis of a specific regulatory licence, permit or authorisation which permits them to provide regulated services and products to customers. This may be the case where it is the aim of Primary Actors to attract new Secondary Actors to their market who are authorised in an alternative jurisdiction(s) or who are yet to be authorised. Further, Secondary Actors such as voters do not have to be regulated by any governmental body or authority to display an interest in or have an influence on the way in which Primary Actors create the 'means' through which regulatory competition is enforced and operated. A further distinction can be made between different types of Secondary Actors based on their interests, motivations, and preferences. For example, the interests of firms and voters are broadly distinguishable. On this basis, Secondary Actors in the intra-national regulatory competition include.

3.3.4.2.1 Firms

According to the Oxford Dictionary, 'firm' can be described as 'an association of two or more people for the running of a business. Now more generally: a commercial enterprise, business, or company'.[431] This accords largely with other definitions of 'firm' which place emphasis on the economic purpose of commercial corporations. According to Armour et al., the core characteristics which make-up corporations include centralised management under a board structure, shared ownership by the contributors of capital, legal personality, limited liability, and transferable shares.[432] Other forms of business enterprises that do not possess these core characteristics also exist, such as partnerships and sole proprietorships. In this sense, the concept of 'firm' is an umbrella term, which goes beyond the definition of corporation.

Coarse, in his ground-breaking article 'The Nature of the Firm' directed economists to focus with more precision on the role of the 'firm' in the broader economic system.[433] Coase was of the view that firms exist because they are better-abled than

429. Yin Xiao, 'Analysing the Enforcement Dimension of Regulatory Competition: A Cultural Institutionalist Approach' (PhD thesis London School of Economics 2014) 21, http://etheses.lse.ac.uk/1035/1/Xiao_Analysing_the_Enforcement_Dimension_of_Regulatory_Competition.pdf.
430. *See*, for example, Horst Eidenmuller, 'The Transnational Law Market, Regulatory Competition, and Transnational Corporations,' (2011) 18(2) Indiana Journal of Global Legal Studies 739 https://doi.org/10.2979/indjglolegstu.18.2.707.
431. Oxford English Dictionary, 'Firm', https://www-oed-com.eproxy.lib.hku.hk/view/Entry/70581.
432. John Armour et al., 'What Is Corporate Law?' in Reinier Kraakman et al. (eds), *The Anatomy of Corporate Law: A Comparative and Functional Approach* (OUP 2017).
433. Ronald H Coase, 'The Nature of the Firm' (1937) 16(4) Economica, New Series 386 https://doi.org/10.2307/2626876.

individuals to absorb the transaction costs associated with production and exchange.[434] The impact of Coase's work can be seen through the additional theories which emerged to explain the nature and justification for the existence of the firm. A milestone in this regard is Friedman and Friedman's 'Stakeholder Theory' which justified the firm's existence as being solely for the wealth maximisation of its shareholders.[435] Equally significant, Jensen and Meckling's conception of the firm as a 'nexus of contracts' entered into between a firm's employees, managers, and owners rather than through the wielding of any specific extracontractual authority.[436] In the context of the theory of regulatory competition, firms are the consumers of the 'means' created and enforced by Primary Actors.

The specific legal characterisation given to firms and their particular regulatory designations, regardless of their business form, has an important bearing on the nature and extent of the operation of regulatory competition. In this regard, firms can be distinguished with reference to the following types:

(i) *Incorporated firms* refer to those firms operating within the legal perimeter of a specific sovereign jurisdiction(s) as a whole on the basis of a peremptory certificate of incorporation, enabling such firms to conduct their designated business activity in the relevant sovereign jurisdiction(s).
(ii) *Authorised firms* refer to those firms operating within the legal and regulatory perimeter of a specific sovereign jurisdiction(s) on the basis of a peremptory regulatory licence, permit or authorisation, enabling such firms to provide regulatory products and services to customers in the specific locale(s). In most instances, these firms are also required to be incorporated on the basis of a peremptory certificate of incorporation.
(iii) *Non-incorporated firms* refer to those firms who do not operate within the legal perimeter of a specific sovereign jurisdiction(s) and therefore do not possess the necessary peremptory certificate of incorporation which enables such firms to conduct designated business activity in the relevant sovereign jurisdiction(s).
(iv) *Non-authorised firms* refer to those firms who do not operate within the legal and regulatory perimeter of a specific sovereign jurisdiction(s) and who do not possess a peremptory regulatory licence, permit or authorisation, enabling such firm to provide regulatory products and services to customers in the specific locale(s).

Non-incorporated and non-authorised firms may, however, be contemplating incorporating in an alternative sovereign jurisdiction(s) or submitting an application

434. Ronald H Coase, 'The Nature of the Firm' (1937) 16(4) Economica, New Series 390 https://doi.org/10.2307/2626876.
435. Milton Friedman & Rose D Friedman, *Capitalism and Freedom* (University of Chicago Press 1962).
436. Michael C Jensen & William H Meckling, 'Theory of the Firm: Managerial Behaviour, Agency Costs and Ownership Structure' (1976) 3 Journal of Financial Economics 305 https://doi.org/10.1016/0304-405x(76)90026-x.

for the necessary peremptory regulatory licence, permit or authorisation, to enable such firms to provide regulated products and services to customers in the alternative sovereign jurisdiction(s).

3.3.4.2.2 Voters

According to the Oxford Dictionary 'voter' is simply defined as '[a] person who has the right to vote in an election'.[437] This accords largely with the definition of voter used by the National Institute of Standards and Technology (US Department of Commerce) as encompassing a 'person permitted to cast a ballot'.[438] According to Downs, the two criteria which differentiate types of voters include 'the confidence with which a voter holds his party preference, and the intensity with which he advocates whatever views he has'.[439] Downs further distinguishes different types of voters by placing them within two categories. In the first instance, voters are described with reference to the confidence with which they have decided to vote, including agitators, passives, loyalists, and quasi-informed passives. In the second instance, voters are described with reference to the confidence with which they have decided to abstain from voting, including neutrals, apathetics, quasi-informed neutrals, and the baffled.[440]

In the context of regulatory competition, voters act as Secondary Actors represented ordinarily as eligible voters in the form of individuals or family units who are the consumers of publicly provided goods and services. A clear example of voters as Actors in the regulatory competition context can be viewed through Tiebout's model.[441] In this model, 'consumer-voters' are assumed to be fully mobile and have knowledge of the different expenditure and revenue patterns in several localities.[442] Consumer-voters are therefore seen as facilitating the market for regulatory competition primarily through their relocation decisions based on fiscal policy decisions. The actions and behaviours of voters have also been viewed through the paradigm of their elected representatives and the way they develop and regulate competition policy to retain their power through the electorate.[443]

437. The Oxford Online Dictionary, 'Voter', https://www-oed-com.eproxy.lib.hku.hk/view/Entry/224720?redirectedFrom = voter#eid.
438. National Institute of Standards and Technology (US Department of Commerce), 'Election Terminology Glossary: Draft', https://pages.nist.gov/ElectionGlossary/.
439. Anthony Downs, *An Economic Theory of Democracy* (Harper and Row Publishers, Incorporated 1957) 82.
440. Anthony Downs, *An Economic Theory of Democracy* (Harper and Row Publishers, Incorporated 1957) 85-86.
441. Charles Tiebout, 'A Pure Theory of Local Expenditures' (1956) 64(5) Journal of Political economy 416-424 https://doi.org/10.1086/257839.
442. Henri Tjiong, 'Breaking the Spell of Regulatory Competition: Reframing the Problem of Regulatory Exit' (2002) 66 The Rabel Journal of Comparative and International Private Law 72 (66-96).
443. Bruce G Carruthers & Naomi R Lamoreaux, 'Regulatory Races: The Effects of Jurisdictional Competition' (2016) 54(1) Journal of Economic Literature 63 https://doi.org/10.1257/jel.54.1.52.

3.3.4.3 *Tertiary Actors*

Tertiary Actors refer broadly to non-governmental actors who are neither Primary nor Secondary Actors, but who play an ancillary role in the operation of regulatory competition through their efforts to support a particular agenda, whether representing the interests of the public more broadly or the special interests of a particular group. Tertiary Actors cannot be classified as Primary Actors as they do not possess the necessary legal competence and power to create the means (i.e., legal rules and regulations) through which regulatory competition operates. As representative organisations, however, they can influence the process and outcome of the promulgation and amendment of the means. However, the final arbiter of the means through which regulatory competition operates remains the Primary Actors (governmental institutions).

Tertiary Actors can also not be classified as Secondary Actors as they are not necessarily the consumers of the 'means' created and enforced by the Primary Actors. This is largely because of the purpose for which they are formed and the representative interests which they promote. As a result, Primary Actors in their coordinated efforts to compete against each other, are less concerned with the activity, behaviours, and decisions of Tertiary Actors. Overall, these Actors therefore do not directly fuel the market for regulatory competition and generally do not directly provide the catalyst for Primary Actors to create the 'means' through which regulatory competition operates. However, as indicated above, they can in their representative role influence the way in which the 'means' are promulgated or amended. The Tertiary Actors in both the intra-national and international regulatory competition, include.

3.3.4.3.1 Non-governmental Organisations

The Cambridge Dictionary defines 'non-governmental organisation' to mean 'an organization that tries to achieve social or political aims but is not controlled by a government'.[444] According to the WB, NGOs are 'groups and institutions that are entirely or largely independent of government and characterized primarily by humanitarian or cooperative, rather than commercial, objectives'.[445] Similarly, the UN considers NGOs to be 'any non-profit, voluntary citizens' group which is organised on a local, national or international level'.[446] While there may be no universally accepted definition, the term has been used as an umbrella term to refer to a broad range of organisations with diverse characterisations and mandates.[447] Further, NGOs are

444. Cambridge Dictionary, 'Non-governmental Organisation' (*Cambridge Dictionary*), https://dictionary.cambridge.org/dictionary/english-chinese-traditional/non-governmental-organization.
445. World Bank, 'Operational Directive on NGOs'(No. 14.70, August 1989), https://www.gdrc.org/ngo/wb-ngo-directive.html a.
446. United Nations, 'Civil Society: Who We Are' (2021), https://www.un.org/en/civil-society/page/about-us.
447. Carmen Malena, 'Working with NGOs: A Practical Guide to Operational Collaboration Between the World Bank and Non-governmental Organization' (*World Bank*, March 1995), http://documents1.worldbank.org/curated/en/814581468739240860/pdf/multi-page.pdf.

ordinarily characterised according to three principal factors, being: (i) not-for-profit; (ii) established for humanitarian ends; and (iii) not affiliated or controlled by the government. Other terms used to describe NGOs include stakeholders, civil society organisations, major groups and grassroots organisations.[448] In the context of the theory of regulatory competition, there have been very few studies which focus on the actions and behaviours of NGOs. According to Esty, NGOs can play an important role as 'intellectual competitors' to national governments as they have the necessary analytical tools, spot issues quickly and utilise their resources in response to such issues.[449] Esty cites the efforts of the Environmental Defense Fund in formulating the 'tradable SO2 permit system' which was included in the Clean Air Act 1990[450] as an example of how NGOs can influence policy and law in 'competition' with the prevailing efforts of the government.[451] Esty's argument in this regard is, however, flawed on two accounts.

First, the exact meaning which Esty ascribes to the term NGO is not very clear. However, Esty does reference NGOs in the context of the 'lobbying of a decision-making body' and the concerns that permitting environmental groups to lobby the WTO may lead to disproportionate policy results.[452] Overall, this suggests that Esty has framed NGOs in the prescriptive role of 'interest groups'. This view is supported by a study recently conducted by Schoenefeld which indicated that 'lobby' is one of the focal characteristics associated with interest groups.[453] While Esty's use of NGO in place of 'interest group' may appear to be semantic, the academic literature has drawn a marked distinction between the two terms. Significantly, NGOs are generally formed with a humanitarian and social purpose to defend public interest more broadly, whereas interest groups are helmed by members who lobby governments and their officials on behalf of special interests. There thus appears to be some conflation over exactly whom Esty regards as competing with national governments.

Second, the argument, which was made in section D(a)(iii) in the context of government departments as Primary Actors, can be made here as well. There is a marked conceptual distinction between 'conflict' and 'competition'.[454] Diverging policy agendas between NGOs (and even interest groups) and national governments do

448. Saori Kakihara, 'What is NGO?', Presentation: Young Leaders and International Organisations (27 May 2013), https://slideplayer.com/slide/7040353/.
449. Daniel C Esty, 'Non-governmental Organizations at the World Trade Organisation: Cooperation, Competition, or Exclusion' (1998) 1(1) Journal of International Economic Law 136 https://doi.org/10.1093/jiel/1.1.123. *See also* Daniel C Esty, 'Toward Optimal Environmental Governance' (1999) 6 NYU Law Review 1561.
450. Clean Air Act 1990 (S.1630 101st Congress 1989-1990).
451. Daniel C Esty, 'Toward Optimal Environmental Governance' (1999) 6 NYU Law Review 1561. *See also* Michael H Levin & Barry S Elman, 'The Case for Environmental Incentives' (1990) 7 Environmental Forum 7, 8.
452. Daniel C Esty, 'Non-governmental Organizations at the World Trade Organisation: Cooperation, Competition, or Exclusion' (1998) 1(1) Journal of International Economic Law 138 https://doi.org/10.1093/jiel/1.1.123.
453. Jonas J Schoenefeld, 'Interest Groups, NGOs or Civil Society Organisations? The Framing of Non-State Actors in the EU' (2020) 32(3) International Journal of Voluntary and Nonprofit Organizations 590 https://doi.org/10.1007/s11266-020-00283-w.
454. Otomar J Bartos & Paul Wehr, 'Using Conflict Theory' (Cambridge University Press 2002) 13-14.

not necessarily translate into regulatory competition proper. For example, the exact resources which would be competed for between NGOs and national governments is not clear. Further, there appears to be no opposing and competing 'means' yet in effect at the policy formulation level to spur the operation of regulatory competition. Finally, NGOs have no legally entrenched power and competence to create laws and regulations and only have the ability to influence processes and outcomes. As discussed above, the ultimate arbiter for the creation of the means of regulatory competition is Primary Actors.

3.3.4.3.2 Interest Groups

According to the Oxford Dictionary 'interest group' can be defined as a 'group of individuals possessing a common identifying interest'.[455] This definition is broad in its scope and aligned with Bentley's classic definition of interest group as 'there is no group without its interest. An interest ... is the equivalent of a group ... The group and the interest are not separate'.[456]

According to Britannica, however, interest groups are prescriptive of 'any association of individuals or organizations, usually formally organized, that, on the basis of one or more shared concerns, attempts to influence public policy in its favor ... [t]hey attempt to achieve their goals by lobbying – that is, by attempting to bring pressure to bear on policy makers to gain policy outcomes in their favor'.[457] Interest groups are also sometimes referred to as advocacy groups, special interest groups, and pressure groups. As with any multifaceted technical term, there appears to be no consistent definition of 'interest group'.

In most instances, the term 'interest group' is described with reference to its core characteristics. Baur, for example, is of the view that interest groups are distinguishable from NGOs as they are membership organisations that are conflict-focussed on lobbying for their specific interests.[458] Conversely, NGOs are predominantly non-membership organisations that are consensual-focussed in progressing their ideational and public interests.[459] Yoho provides definition of 'interest group' which considers its nature, why they have been studied in the literature, and their etymological roots. As such, Yoho has indicated 'interest groups are actual organizations, they are private in nature, they attempt to influence public policy, and they are not political parties–i.e., they do not nominate candidates for public office'.[460]

455. Oxford Online Dictionary, 'Interest Group', https://www-oed-com.eproxy.lib.hku.hk/view/Entry/97735?redirectedFrom = interest + group#eid261509.
456. Arthur Fisher Bentley, *The Process of Government* (University of Chicago 1908) 211.
457. Clive S Thomas, 'Interest Group' (*Encyclopedia Britannica*, 9 November 2020), https://www.britannica.com/topic/interest-group.
458. Dorothea Baur, 'Insights from Part IV' (1 January 2012), https://www.researchgate.net/publication/251406954_Insights_from_Part_IV.
459. Dorothea Baur, 'Insights from Part IV' (1 January 2012), https://www.researchgate.net/publication/251406954_Insights_from_Part_IV.
460. James Yoho, 'The Evolution of a Better Definition of the Term "Interest Group" and Its Synonyms' (1998) 35(2) Social Science Journal 231 https://doi.org/10.1016/s0362-3319(98)90042-8.

In the context of the theory of regulatory competition, there have been several studies which focus on the actions and behaviours of interest groups.[461] They have been studied in the context of EU policy formation mechanisms with regard to the instances of asymmetric regulatory standards leading to decision-making deadlock with the European Council.[462] They have also been discussed in the context of the different types of regulatory competition outcomes, specifically regulatory advantage and government responsiveness.[463] In accordance with Tiebout's model, wealth attribution is referenced as being the underlying rationale for government responsiveness to taxpaying parties. This responsiveness is directed at firms and voters. According to Xiao, government responsiveness can also be directed at public interest groups, particularly those interested in the environment, health and safety and labour regulation.[464]

This responsiveness, however, should not be conflated with the way governments treat Secondary Actors, specifically in seeking to create legal and regulatory environments conducive to attracting and retaining the identified resources. For example, government responsiveness associated with interest groups can result in the promulgation and amendment of legal and regulatory rules which ultimately impose higher costs for firms. However, it is important to point out that promulgated and amended laws and regulations would not necessarily be consumed by interest groups in the same sense that they would be by Secondary Actors. As discussed above, Tertiary Actors are characterised largely by their role in representing the interests of others, whether public or private. This representative capacity largely precludes them from operating in environments where legal and regulatory rules would serve them, such as in acting to further regulatory competition.

3.3.5 Regulatory Competition Means

In the operation of regulatory competition, Primary Actors use various means to differentiate themselves from their competitors with the aim to attract (or retain)

461. *See also* William J Carney, 'The Political Economy of Competition for Corporate Charters' (1997) 26(1) Journal of Legal Studies 306 https://doi.org/10.1086/467997; Jonathan Macey, 'Delaware: Home of the World's Most Expensive Raincoat' (2005) 33(4) Hofstra Law Review 1136; Horst Eidenmuller, 'The Transnational Law Market, Regulatory Competition, and Transnational Corporations,' (2011) 18(2) Indiana Journal of Global Legal Studies 732 https://doi.org/10.2979/indjglolegstu.18.2.707 and Bruce G Carruthers & Naomi R Lamoreaux, 'Regulatory Races: The Effects of Jurisdictional Competition' (2016) 54(1) Journal of Economic Literature 55 https://doi.org/10.1257/jel.54.1.52.
462. Alexis Lubow, 'Taming Regulatory Competition: Interest Groups v. Joint-Decision Trap: Four EU Policy Cases on Workers Mobility' (PhD thesis, European University Institute 2017).
463. Yin Xiao, 'Analysing the Enforcement Dimension of Regulatory Competition: A Cultural Institutionalist Approach' (PhD thesis London School of Economics 2014) 28, http://etheses.lse.ac.uk/1035/1/Xiao_Analysing_the_Enforcement_Dimension_of_Regulatory_Competition.pdf.
464. Yin Xiao, 'Analysing the Enforcement Dimension of Regulatory Competition: A Cultural Institutionalist Approach' (PhD thesis London School of Economics 2014) 28, http://etheses.lse.ac.uk/1035/1/Xiao_Analysing_the_Enforcement_Dimension_of_Regulatory_Competition.pdf.

economic activities to their jurisdictions. These means represent the principal mechanisms through which regulatory competition is intended to be facilitated or achieved. Ordinarily, Primary Actors create the means through the designated legal and political processes in force in their respective jurisdictions, such as legislative and policy-making mechanisms and procedures. For the purposes of this book, the primary outputs which result from these processes, and are intended to be used in the operation of regulatory competition, are referred to as the 'Means'. In the literature, regulatory competition Means have been referred to as 'competing measures'.[465] The Means as primary outputs of the actions and behaviours of Primary Actors can be classified largely through the distinction made between: (i) rules-based competition (heterogeneous group of government actions used to attract the traditional factors of production); and (ii) incentives-based competition (fiscal and financial incentives).[466]

Rules-based competition can be understood from a micro and macro perspective. From a micro perspective, Means are presented as primary statutes of law, their accompanying regulations, and regulatory rules. They are informed by government policies and regulatory authority guidelines and approaches. These Means have often been referred to as 'regulatory output' encompassing the laws and decrees adjusted by governments in response to regulatory competition,[467] or created through the drafting of new laws, regulations, and guidelines.[468] They have also been construed as 'instruments of competition' when they are purposefully drafted or amended with the objective of attaining (or retaining) economic and other non-economic activities forming the target of the specific competition policy approach.

Within the context of rules-based competition, regulatory competition Means have also been framed more specifically through the 'law as a product' paradigm, in which legal rules are treated as commodities for which a market exists.[469] According to Eidenmuller, the phenomena of law as a product has arisen broadly across jurisdictions as a result of 'structural changes' to the supply-and-demand of law as a commodity.[470]

465. Yin Xiao, 'Analysing the Enforcement Dimension of Regulatory Competition: A Cultural Institutionalist Approach' (PhD thesis London School of Economics 2014) 25, http://etheses.lse.ac.uk/1035/1/Xiao_Analysing_the_Enforcement_Dimension_of_Regulatory_Competition.pdf.

466. Charles Oman, 'Policy Competition for Foreign Direct Investment: A Study of Competition Among Governments to Attract FDI' (*OECD*, 2000) 21, https://www.oecd.org/mena/competitiveness//35275189.pdf.

467. Katharina Holzinger & Thomas Sommerer, '"Race to the Bottom" or "Race to Brussels"? Environmental Competition in Europe' (2011) 49(2) Journal of Common Market Studies 322 https://doi.org/10.1111/j.1468-5965.2010.02135.x.

468. Katharina Holzinger & Thomas Sommerer, '"Race to the Bottom" or "Race to Brussels"? Environmental Competition in Europe' (2011) 49(2) Journal of Common Market Studies 322 https://doi.org/10.1111/j.1468-5965.2010.02135.x.

469. Horst Eidenmuller, 'The Transnational Law Market, Regulatory Competition, and Transnational Corporations,' (2011) 18(2) Indiana Journal of Global Legal Studies 708 https://doi.org/10.2979/indjglolegstu.18.2.707. *See* Roberta Romano, 'Law as a Product: Some Pieces of the Incorporation Puzzle' (1985) 1(2) Journal of Law, Economics, & Organization 225-283 https://doi.org/10.1093/oxfordjournals.jleo.a036892.

470. Horst Eidenmuller, 'The Transnational Law Market, Regulatory Competition, and Transnational Corporations,' (2011) 18(2) Indiana Journal of Global Legal Studies 709 https://doi.org/10.2979/indjglolegstu.18.2.707.

Through this market activity paradigm, Primary Actors, via their actions and behaviours as governmental entities, represent the 'supplier side' in offering specific Means to Secondary Actors.[471] In supplying or making available the specific Means, Primary Actors compete against each other to attain (or retain) the economic and other non-activities. However, Secondary Actors through their actions and behaviours represent the 'buyer side' in their selection and use of the Means created and offered by Primary Actors.

From a macro-perspective, the specific regulatory output created by Primary Actors represents one component of the overall ecosystem which includes other Means such as educated labour markets, efficient court systems and strengthened rule of law, highly developed infrastructure, and stable legal and political regimes.[472] Primary Actors also create specific microcosmic legal and economic environments as means to compete against other Primary Actors, i.e., special economic zones and export-processing zones to which special laws and regulations apply.[473] Other special legal and political tools, including market deregulation, the liberalisation of investment and trade policies, and the privatisation of state-owned enterprises are also used.[474]

A multitude of studies have been dedicated to considering the mechanisms used by Primary Actors to compete against each other in the context of rules-based competition. For example, in the case of the US corporate charter competition, it has been argued that Delaware 'came up on top' by creating a legal environment, through laws and regulations, which offered more favourable terms to managers leading to shareholder wealth maximisation.[475] This legal environment included, among others, laws and regulations which advance mergers and offer directors surer protection against liability,[476] and a robust and expert judiciary.[477] Further, in the context of labour rights, Primary Actors can create Means by amending the laws regulating the

471. Horst Eidenmuller, 'The Transnational Law Market, Regulatory Competition, and Transnational Corporations,' (2011) 18(2) Indiana Journal of Global Legal Studies 712 https://doi.org/10.2979/indjglolegstu.18.2.707.
472. Andrew P Morriss, 'The Role of Offshore Financial Centers in Regulatory Competition' in Andrew P Morriss et al. (eds), *Offshore Financial Centers and Regulatory Competition* (AEI Press 2010) and Charles Oman, 'Policy Competition for Foreign Direct Investment: A Study of Competition Among Governments to Attract FDI' (*OECD*, 2000) 91, https://www.oecd.org/mena/competitiveness//35275189.pdf.
473. Charles Oman, 'Policy Competition for Foreign Direct Investment: A Study of Competition Among Governments to Attract FDI' (*OECD*, 2000) 21, https://www.oecd.org/mena/competitiveness//35275189.pdf.
474. Charles Oman, 'Policy Competition for Foreign Direct Investment: A Study of Competition Among Governments to Attract FDI' (*OECD*, 2000) 21, https://www.oecd.org/mena/competitiveness//35275189.pdf.
475. Jonathan Macey, 'Delaware: Home of the World's Most Expensive Raincoat' (2005) 33(4) Hofstra Law Review 1132. Easterbrook FH, 'The Race for the Bottom in Corporate Governance' (2009) 95 Virginia Law Review 686.
476. Murali Jagannathan & Adam C Pritchard, 'Do Delaware CEOs Get Fired?' (2017) 74 Journal of Banking and Finance 86 https://doi.org/10.1016/j.jbankfin.2016.10.008.
477. Jonathan Macey, 'Delaware: Home of the World's Most Expensive Raincoat' (2005) 33(4) Hofstra Law Review.

rights of workers, enforcement of existing rules, or sign regional-integrating agreements with neighbouring jurisdictions.[478]

Incentives-based competition has been studied in the context of attracting FDI. For example, a study conducted by Christiansen et al. concluded that incentives are used in Brazil at a regional development level through offering investment incentives in the form of cash grants, loans, start-up assistance, and tax reductions.[479] These incentives were offered as a target policy to attract general or specifically targeted investment projects. Oman et al. has reported that such an approach has proven suitable when used correctly to correct shortcomings present within the particular national system, or where incentive schemes are non-discriminatory. However, using incentives to attract FDI has also proven challenging and risky without the appropriate analytical and regulatory frameworks in place.[480] Other examples of regulatory competition Means within the context of incentives-based competition include reduced capital taxes, subsidies[481] and investment incentives.[482]

3.3.6 Regulatory Competition Drivers

Wealth creation is considered the principal motivator for Primary Actors to compete against each other.[483] To this end, regulatory competition operates so that the actions and behaviours of one Primary Actor are directed towards maximising wealth in their jurisdiction, in response to the actions and behaviours of other Primary Actors.[484] Morriss has indicated that most politicians, independent of ideological stance and form of government, are directed towards creating wealth within their jurisdictions.[485] Further, governments utilise financial resources derived from economic activities to increase the overall well-being of citizens, and in some cases for rent-seeking and

478. Charles Oman, 'Policy Competition for Foreign Direct Investment: A Study of Competition Among Governments to Attract FDI' (*OECD*, 2000) 21, https://www.oecd.org/mena/competitiveness//35275189.pdf.
479. Hans Christiansen, Charles Oman & Andrew Charlton, 'Incentives-based Competition for Foreign Direct Investment: The Case of Brazil' (2003) OECD Working Papers on International Investment 1, https://www.oecd.org/investment/investment-policy/WP-2003_1.pdf.
480. Hans Christiansen, Charles Oman & Andrew Charlton, 'Incentives-based Competition for Foreign Direct Investment: The Case of Brazil' (2003) OECD Working Papers on International Investment 1, https://www.oecd.org/investment/investment-policy/WP-2003_1.pdf.
481. Kim J & Wilson JD, 'Capital Mobility and Environmental Standards: Racing to the Bottom with Multiple Tax Instruments' (1997) 9 Japan and the World Economy 538.
482. Horst Eidenmuller, 'The Transnational Law Market, Regulatory Competition, and Transnational Corporations,' (2011) 18(2) Indiana Journal of Global Legal Studies 712 https://doi.org/10.2979/indjglolegstu.18.2.707.
483. Andrew P Morriss, 'The Role of Offshore Financial Centers in Regulatory Competition' (2008) University of Illinois Law and Economics Research Paper No. LE07-032, 3 and Erin A O'Hara & Larry E Ribstein, *The Law Market* (OUP, 2009) 66.
484. Hans-Werner Sinn, 'The New Systems Competition', Yrjö Jahnsson lectures (Blackwell Publishing Ltd UK 2003).
485. Andrew P Morriss, 'The Role of Offshore Financial Centers in Regulatory Competition' in Andrew P Morriss et al. (eds), *Offshore Financial Centers and Regulatory Competition* (AEI Press 2010).

corruption.[486] In the operation of regulatory competition, wealth creation is achieved through Primary Actors competing and attaining (or retaining) the economic and non-economic activities of Secondary Actors. For the purposes of this study, the benefits, economic or otherwise, intended to be attained (or retained) by Primary Actors through the operation of regulatory competition can referred to as regulatory competition Drivers.

As indicated above, regulatory competition Drivers exist in various forms, represented here in the form of both economic and non-economic activities. As an economic activity, for example, Pavelin and Porter have posited that jurisdictions compete against each other for the 'highly significant economic value' attributed to the activities of multinational corporations resulting from the ease at which they are able to move internationally.[487] This reflects one instance of Primary Actors extracting wealth from Secondary Actors through economic activity. As to non-economic activity, for example, Primary Actors may also compete against each other to attain (or retain) public goods in the form of human capital, such as highly skilled labour.[488]

3.3.6.1 Capital Investment

It is well-documented in the literature that the attainment (or retention) of capital investment serves as the most significant Driver for Primary Actors in their wealth-creation endeavours. Capital investments are significant for jurisdictions as they strengthen domestic financial services industries, and can be key drivers for national economies.[489] For example, Primary Actors may compete with each other to attain (or retain) 'high value-added transactional work creating and managing business entities'.[490] The importance of securing 'high value-added' capital through business, in place of meagre administrative fees, is highlighted by Kamar who has posited that regulatory competition operates 'to attract capital and direct investments in local businesses, rather than incorporations by foreign businesses'.[491] This may be achieved through several economic streams, including portfolio investment, but most notably through FDI. The OECD has defined FDI as a 'category of cross-border investment in which an investor resident in one economy establishes a lasting interest in and a

486. Andrew P Morriss, 'The role of Offshore Financial Centers in Regulatory Competition' in Andrew P Morriss et al. (eds), *Offshore Financial Centers and Regulatory Competition* (AEI Press 2010).
487. Steven Pavelin & Lynda A Porter, 'Race-to-the-Bottom or -Top at Home or Abroad: Health and Safety Standards and the Multinational Firm' (2011) 42(3) The Economic and Social Review 290.
488. Charles Oman, 'Policy Competition for Foreign Direct Investment: A Study of Competition Among Governments to Attract FDI' (*OECD*, 2000) 24, https://www.oecd.org/mena/competitiveness//35275189.pdf.
489. Ehud Kamar, 'Beyond Competition for Incorporations' (2006) Georgetown Law Journal 94(6) 1748 https://doi.org/10.2139/ssrn.720121.
490. Andrew P Morriss, 'The Role of Offshore Financial Centers in Regulatory Competition' in Andrew P Morriss et al. (eds), *Offshore Financial Centers and Regulatory Competition* (AEI Press 2010).
491. Ehud Kamar, 'Beyond Competition for Incorporations' (2006) Georgetown Law Journal 94(6) 1725 https://doi.org/10.2139/ssrn.720121.

significant degree of influence over an enterprise resident in another economy'.[492] Governments rely on these extra-territorial residents and the FDI which they bring for several reasons, but most notably for funding public sector shortfalls and to develop the private sector.[493]

Kerner has posited that governments need to manage their reputations as attractive jurisdictions deserving of investment endowment the more reliant they become on FDI.[494] This is the case, particularly for emerging and developing economies seeking diversified sources of funding.[495] This position, to maintain the 'attractiveness' of one's jurisdiction, finds expression in Albert Hirschman's 'Theory of Institutions'. According to Hirschman, Secondary Actors, i.e., consumers, deal with unattractive institutions, or nation states, through the concepts of 'exit, voice, and loyalty'.[496] Consumers voice their dissatisfaction with governments by threatening to 'exit' through relocation to an alternative jurisdiction should proposed new legal rules be enforced. This mechanism operates so that consumers bait their exit decisions which could result in, among others, capital relocations through the loss of FDI.[497]

The competition for FDI is also made more challenging through the increasingly interconnected and globalised nature of international trade. Oman has posited that the effects of globalisation have served to ease the conducting of international trade and investment, thus significantly increasing competition for FDI.[498] In response to the importance of competing for capital in this context, numerous studies have been conducted to determine the effect, if any, which competing for FDI has on legal rule adjustment. The results of these empirical studies have been varied and divisive, but there is some indication that regulatory competition for FDI has a negative and eroding effect on, for example, employment protection legal rules.[499] However, capital, as a Driver, can take other forms. For example, the attainment (or retention) of franchise

492. Organisation for Economic Co-operation and Development iLibrary, 'Foreign Direct Investment', https://www.oecd-ilibrary.org/finance-and-investment/foreign-direct-investment-fdi/indicator-group/english_9a523b18-en.
493. Andrew Kerner, 'Can Foreign Stock Influence Policymaking' (2015) 48(1) Comparative Political Studies 36 https://doi.org/10.1177/0010414013519411.
494. Andrew Kerner, 'Can Foreign Stock Influence Policymaking' (2015) 48(1) Comparative Political Studies 40 https://doi.org/10.1177/0010414013519411 citing Haggard & Maxfield, 1996; Rodrik, 1989; Wibbels & Arce, 2003.
495. Charles Oman, 'Policy Competition for Foreign Direct Investment: A Study of Competition Among Governments to Attract FDI' (*OECD*, 2000) 7, https://www.oecd.org/mena/competitiveness//35275189.pdf.
496. Albert Hirschman, *Exit, Voice, and Loyalty: Responses to Decline in Firms, Organizations, and States* (Harvard University Press 1970).
497. Katharina Holzinger & Thomas Sommerer, '"Race to the Bottom" or "Race to Brussels"? Environmental Competition in Europe' (2011) 49(2) Journal of Common Market Studies 326 https://doi.org/10.1111/j.1468-5965.2010.02135.x.
498. Charles Oman, 'Policy Competition for Foreign Direct Investment: A Study of Competition Among Governments to Attract FDI' (*OECD*, 2000) 10, https://www.oecd.org/mena/competitiveness//35275189.pdf.
499. *See*, for example, Robert G Blanton & Shannon L Blanton, 'Labour Rights and Foreign Direct Investment: Is There a Race to the Bottom' (2012) 38 International Interactions 267 and William W Olney, 'A Race to the Bottom? Employment Protection and Foreign Direct Investment' (2013) 91 Journal of International Economics 191 https://doi.org/10.1080/03050629.2012.676496.

fees has been cited as spurring the incorporation charter competition which took place between US states throughout the 1980s.[500] In addition, tax revenue as a form of capital, has also been cited as an economic activity over which Primary Actors compete.[501]

3.3.6.2 Human Capital

According to the OECD, 'human capital' can be broadly defined as 'the stock of knowledge, skills and other personal characteristics embodied in the people that helps them to be productive'.[502] Ordinarily, human capital is represented by formal education and work experience. As a regulatory competition Driver, the attainment (or retention) of human capital has been discussed primarily in the context of highly skilled labour. According to Abella, jurisdictions compete for highly skilled labour to achieve various economic goals and to address the needs associated with ageing populations.[503] Jurisdictions that fail to attain (or retain) human capital through highly skilled labour may also risk lagging their competitors in the development of innovative products and services.[504] Global competition for highly skilled labour appears to be particularly relevant for the migration of skilled workers from emerging economies to more advance economies. As such, jurisdictions may compete with one another by easing immigration restrictions usually in force for foreign workers (or exempting them from such restrictions), reducing bureaucratic hindrances for processing visa applications, developing active recruitment programmes, offering equal employment opportunities to spouses of foreign workers, or providing incentives, such as lower incomes taxes.[505]

In the context of the theory of regulatory competition specifically, the literature focusses primarily on how jurisdictions adjust their employment protection rules with the view to attaining (or retaining) highly skilled labour. As such, this focus falls outside the remit of this study which is primarily concerned with financial law and regulation. In addition, the focus on competition for highly skilled labour also falls into the broader field of migration and labour market studies focussing on the monopsony of large firms, rather than regulatory competition. As such, this discussion is not elaborated upon further here.

---

500. Frank Easterbrook, 'The Race for the Bottom in Corporate Governance' (2009) 95 Virginia Law Review 686 and Stephen Bainbridge, 'Does State Corporate Law Race to the Top?' (2003) Journal of Law, Religion, Politics and Culture, https://www.professorbainbridge.com/professorbainbridgecom/2003/09/does-state-corporate-law-really-race-to-the-top.html.
501. Hans-Werner Sinn, 'The Selection Principle and Market Failure in Systems Competition' (1997) 66 Journal of Public Economics 248 https://doi.org/10.1016/s0047-2727(97)00043-1.
502. Organisation for Economic Co-operation and Development, 'Productivity, Human Capital and Educational Policies' https://www.oecd.org/economy/human-capital/.
503. Manolo Abella, 'Global Competition for Skilled Workers' in C Kuptsch & EF Pang (eds) *Competing for Global Talent* (Institute for Labour Studies, International Labour Organisation, Geneva, 2006).
504. Manolo Abella, 'Global Competition for Skilled Workers' in C Kuptsch & EF Pang (eds) Competing for Global Talent (Institute for Labour Studies, ILO, Geneva, 2006).
505. Manolo Abella, 'Global Competition for Skilled Workers' in C Kuptsch & EF Pang (eds) Competing for Global Talent (Institute for Labour Studies, ILO, Geneva, 2006).

3.4 REGULATORY COMPETITION OUTCOMES

The consequences which follow the operation of regulatory competition have been the subject of significant discussion. For the purposes of this book, these consequences are referred to as regulatory competition Outcomes, and are separate to the elements underlining regulatory competition, as set out above. To a large extent, these Outcomes have culminated in the conceptualisation of individual theories which have been used to explain the underlying effects of regulatory competition. As far as possible, the discussion below steers away from considering the normative effects of regulatory competition, including, a general discussion about the 'good' or 'bad' nature of regulatory competition. Instead, the discussion focusses on providing a neutral explanation of the core individual theories which have been developed to explain the potential consequences of regulatory competition, which include: (i) Pareto-efficiency; (ii) Race to the Bottom; and (iii) Race to the Top.

3.4.1 Tiebout Equilibrium

Tiebout's Equilibrium posits that the competitive pressures created by Secondary Actors choosing to relocate to substitute communities would produce efficient outcomes in which governments would be encouraged to set their regulatory products at competitive prices.[506] As such, the threat of 'exit' alone through the mobility of Secondary Actors would act to discipline jurisdictions from passing legal rules which are ineffective or too burdensome, thereby producing an efficient equilibrium.[507] Tiebout's model, however, hinges on two important, if not understated, assumptions. First, the theory assumes that consumer-voters are perfectly mobile and thereby fully capable of relocating to communities whose local governments satisfy their specific preferences. Second, the theory assumes that consumer-voters are harnessed with complete knowledge of the offerings of other communities and thereby order themselves into preferred communities based on the mixed offering of taxes and public services. With these assumptions in mind, it is hypothesised that local governments compete with one another by offering residents mixed offerings as a package of services to attract them.[508]

Competition among local governments in Tiebout's model only finds application if substitute communities are available for consumer-voters to 'exit' to. The threat of exit would act to discipline jurisdictions from passing laws and regulations which are

506. Frank H Easterbrook, 'Antitrust and the Economics of Federalism' (1983) 26 Journal of Law and Economics 29 https://doi.org/10.1086/467024.
507. Robin Hollander & Louise Thornthwaite, 'Competitive Federalism and Workers' Compensation: Do States Race to the Bottom?' (2018) 53(3) Australian Journal of Political Science 338 https://doi.org/10.1080/10361146.2018.1477115.
508. Simon Deakin, 'Legal Diversity and Regulatory Competition' (2006) 12(4) European Law Journal 440, 442 https://doi.org/10.1111/j.1468-0386.2006.00326.x.

ineffective or too burdensome, thereby producing an efficient equilibrium.[509] It is significant to note that the RC literature has highlighted that the threat of firms exiting alone is sufficient to drive policy change, in addition to new entrants to the market choosing to relocate to another jurisdiction.[510] Tiebout's assumption of the mobility of Secondary Actors has been the target of long-standing criticism since the publication of 'A Pure Theory of Local Expenditures'. Deakin, for example, has argued that the conditions for competition in the real world, such as freedom of mobility, are assumed by Tiebout.[511] In Tiebout's defence, reference is made to the fact that consumer-voters are not necessarily perfectly mobile, nor do they have complete knowledge of the offerings of other communities.[512] However, in criticising the lack of interrogation of Tiebout's theoretical assumptions, Deakin has posited that in the 'real' world, three preconditions must exist to make the threat of 'exit' effective, and the intended efficient equilibrium operational.[513] First, the freedom of movement of people and resources must be legally guaranteed. Second, there must be non-discrimination, such as in the form of 'mutual recognition'. Finally, externalities arising as unintended consequences of competition must be accepted.

In a similar vein, Revesz has posited that the assumption of the perfect mobility of individuals and communities is unrealistic when regard is had to the substantial transaction costs involved in moving from one jurisdiction to another.[514] In the present digital age, this criticism has perhaps not aged well. Individuals and businesses are now able to conduct their operations online without any relocation necessary to take advantage of their preferred regulatory environments. Further, Sinn has posited that an efficient equilibrium created through the threat of 'exit' would not necessarily exist if government regulation, in the first instance, is valuable in itself where it assists in overcoming market failure.[515] However, Radaelli has argued that the presence of an efficient equilibrium is only possible in the absence of both political and market

509. Robin Hollander & Louise Thornthwaite, 'Competitive Federalism and Workers' Compensation: Do States Race to the Bottom?' (2018) 53(3) Australian Journal of Political Science 338 https://doi.org/10.1080/10361146.2018.1477115.
510. Bruce G Carruthers & Naomi R Lamoreaux, 'Regulatory Races: The Effects of Jurisdictional Competition' (2016) 54(1) Journal of Economic Literature 53 https://doi.org/10.1257/jel.54.1.52.
511. Richard L Revesz, 'Rehabilitating Interstate Competition: Rethinking the Race-to-the-Bottom Rationale for Federal Environmental Regulation' (1992) 67 New York University Law Review 1236. *See* Steven L Willborn, 'Labor Law and the Race to the Bottom' (2014) 65(2) Mercer Law Review 369-430 https://doi.org/10.2139/ssrn.2339274.
512. Charles Tiebout, 'A Pure Theory of Local Expenditures' (1956) 64 Journal of Political economy 416, 423 https://doi.org/10.1086/257839.
513. Simon Deakin, 'Legal Diversity and Regulatory Competition' (2006) 12(4) European Law Journal 440, 443 https://doi.org/10.1111/j.1468-0386.2006.00326.x.
514. Richard L Revesz, 'Rehabilitating Interstate Competition: Rethinking the Race-to-the-Bottom Rationale for Federal Environmental Regulation' (1992) 67 New York University Law Review 1236. *See* Steven L Willborn, 'Labor Law and the Race to the Bottom' (2014) 65(2) Mercer Law Review 369-430 https://doi.org/10.2139/ssrn.2339274.
515. Hans-Werner Sinn, 'The Selection Principle and Market Failure in Systems Competition' (1997) 66 Journal of Public Economics 247-274 https://doi.org/10.1016/s0047-2727(97)00043-1 and Hans-Werner Sinn, 'The New Systems Competition' Yrjö Jahnsson lectures (Blackwell Publishing Ltd UK 2003).

failures.[516] Barnard has posited that the preconditions for efficient equilibrium are infrequent, even in integrated markets.[517]

Tiebout's contributions have nevertheless been central to the development of the theory of regulatory competition, particularly in the conceptualisation of consumer-voters exiting a particular market to seek opportunities in another. Consequently, it has been central to the development of the field of competitive federalism which has led to a multitude of interdisciplinary studies spanning the fields of economics, public policy, and law.

3.4.2 Race to the Bottom

The Race to the Bottom posits that governments are primarily concerned with increasing economic growth and employment. With this preoccupation in mind, governments react to changes in legal rules in other jurisdictions by weakening their own legal rules.[518] Ordinarily, they do this to attain (and retain) capital and highly skilled labour to the detriment of other jurisdictions.[519] This downward pressure in which different jurisdictions outbid each other through deregulation has also been referred to as the 'Delaware Effect'.[520] The integral components which make up the

516. Claudio M Radaelli, 'The Puzzle of Regulatory Competition' (2014) 24 Journal of Public Policy 2 https://doi.org/10.1017/s0143814x04000017.
517. *See* Catherine Barnard, 'Social Dumping and the Race to the Bottom: Some Lessons for the European Union from Delaware?' (2000) 25 European Law Review 57-78 and Catherine Barnard, 'Regulating Competitive Federalism in the European Union? The Case of EU Social Policy' in Jo Shaw (ed.), *Social Law and Policy in an Evolving European Union* (Hart Publishing 2000) 49-69.
518. Bruce G Carruthers & Naomi R Lamoreaux, 'Regulatory Races: The Effects of Jurisdictional Competition' (2016) 54(1) Journal of Economic Literature 55 https://doi.org/10.1257/jel.54.1.52.
519. Claudio M Radaelli, 'The Puzzle of Regulatory Competition' (2014) 24 Journal of Public Policy 8 https://doi.org/10.1017/s0143814x04000017. Other definitions of 'Race to the Bottom' can be found in Richard L Revesz, 'Rehabilitating Interstate Competition: Rethinking the Race-to-the-Bottom Rationale for Federal Environmental Regulation' (1992) 67 New York University Law Review 1216; Gareth Porter, 'Trade Competition and Pollution Standards: "Race to the Bottom" or "Stuck at the Bottom"?' (1999) 8(2) Journal of Environmental and Development 133 https://doi.org/10.1177/107049659900800203; Jonathan Macey, 'Delaware: Home of the World's Most Expensive Raincoat' (2005) 33(4) Hofstra Law Review 1133-1139; Anna M Dionne & Jonathan R Macey, 'Offshore Finance and Onshore Market: Racing to the Bottom, or Moving Toward Efficient?' in Andrew P Morriss et al. (eds), *Offshore Financial Centers and Regulatory Competition* (AEI Press 2010); Raul Govea et al., 'Emerging Technologies and Ethics: A Race-to-the-Bottom or the Top' (2012) 109 Journal of Business Ethics 553 https://doi.org/10.1007/s10551-012-1430-3; Veerle Heyvaert, 'Regulatory Competition: Accounting for the Transnational Dimension of Environmental Regulation' (2012) 25(1) Journal of Environmental Law 5 https://doi.org/10.1093/jel/eqs019; R Douglas Hecock & Eric M Jepsen, 'Should Countries Engage in a Race to the Bottom? The Effect of Social Spending FDI' (2013) 44 World Development 158; Heather Plumridge Bedi & Louise Tillin, 'Inter-state Competition, Land Conflicts and Resistance in India' (2015) 43(2) Oxford Development Studies 195 https://doi.org/10.1016/j.worlddev.2012.10.016 and Bruce G Carruthers & Naomi R Lamoreaux, 'Regulatory Races: The Effects of Jurisdictional Competition' (2016) 54(1) Journal of Economic Literature 70 https://doi.org/10.1257/jel.54.1.52.
520. Veerle Heyvaert, 'Regulatory Competition: Accounting for the Transnational Dimension of Environmental Regulation' (2012) 25(1) Journal of Environmental Law 7 https://doi.org/10.

Race to the Bottom were developed predominantly through the works of Fischel, Romano and Winter, among others.

The conceptual basis for the Race to the Bottom can be traced back to the US Supreme Court judgment *Louis K Liggett CO v. Lee* in which Justice Louis Brandei opined that 'states where the cost was lowest and the laws least restrictive' resulted in a race 'not of diligence but of laxity'.[521] Since then, the term Race to the Bottom has been used widely, and with particular relevance to the Prisoner's Dilemma game. For example, Revesz has posited that a paradigmatic instance of the Prisoner's Dilemma plays out where two individuals, factually guilty of a felony, are placed into custody separately and are interrogated with the purpose of obtaining confessions. Should neither individual confess, both would be guilty of a misdemeanour and would be given a one-year sentence each. If only one individual confesses, they may be offered a plea bargain that would result in a six-month sentence. The other individual would be found guilty of a felony conviction and be given a ten-year sentence. However, should individuals confess, they would each be convicted of a felony, but would only be given a five-year sentence.[522]

In the regulatory competition context, Primary Actors make 'moves', i.e., relax their laws to outbid each other, which places them in a worse-off position than they would have been had they initially coordinated their respective policies.[523] The worse-off position may result from Primary Actors competing with each other and acting in their own self-interest which leads to collectively irrational and inefficient outcomes,[524] assuming that they are unable to coordinate their responses.[525] In this regard, Carruthers and Lamoreaux have posited that regulatory competition may result in regulatory races

1093/jel/eqs019. *See* Guhan Subramanian, 'The Disappearing Delaware Effect' (2004) 20(1) Journal of Law, Economics, and Organization 32-59 https://doi.org/10.1093/jleo/20.1.32 and Joseph McCahery & Erik Vermeulen, 'Does the European Company Prevent the Delaware Effect' (2005) 11 European Law Journal 785-801 https://doi.org/10.1111/j.1468-0386.2005.00288.x.

521. *Louis K Ligget CO v. Lee* [1933] 288 (US) 517, 557-60.
522. Richard L Revesz, 'Rehabilitating Intestate Competition: Rethinking the "Race to the Bottom" Rationale for Federal Environmental Regulation' (1992) 67 New York University Law Review 1217.
523. *See* Kirsten H Engel, 'State Environmental Standard-Setting: Is there a "Race" and Is It "to the Bottom"?' (1997) 48 Hastings Law Journal 271-398; Simon Deakin, 'Two Types of Regulatory Competition: Competitive Federalism Versus Reflexive Harmonisation. A Law and Economics Perspective on Centros' (1999) 2 Cambridge Yearbook of European Legal Studies 231-260; Daniel A Farber & Philip P Frickey, 'The Jurisprudence of Public Choice' (1987) 65 Texas Law Review 873, 906-907; Peter M Yu, 'To Form a More Perfect Union? Federalism and Informal Interstate Cooperation' (1989) 102 Harvard Law Review 842 https://doi.org/10.5235/152888712802815806 and Richard L Revesz, 'Rehabilitating Intestate Competition: Rethinking the "Race to the Bottom" Rationale for Federal Environmental Regulation' (1992) 67 New York University Law Review 1217. *See* Duncan Snidal, 'Coordination Versus Prisoners' dilemma: Implications for international cooperation and regimes' (1985) 79 American Political Science Review 923-942 https://doi.org/10.2307/1956241.
524. Peter P Swire, 'The Race to Laxity and the Race to Undesirability: Explaining Failures in Competition Among Jurisdictions in Environmental Law' (1996) 14(2) Yale Law and Policy Review 87.
525. Bruce G Carruthers & Naomi R Lamoreaux, 'Regulatory Races: The Effects of Jurisdictional Competition' (2016) 54(1) Journal of Economic Literature 56 https://doi.org/10.1257/jel.54.1.52.

which can be avoided, much in the same manner that coordination among actors in the Prisoner's Dilemma game can avoid negative outcomes.[526] Alternatively, Swire has posited that the traditional remedy for the Prisoner's Dilemma in a Federal System of Government is the enforcement of federal minimum standards.[527]

The Race to the Bottom has been considered both empirically and theoretically. From an empirical perspective, academic scholars and researchers have focussed largely on regulatory competition in the context of finding correlations between the adjustment of legal rules and the tracking of FDI inflows. For example, Olney's study focussed on International Regulatory Competition and the correlation between labour standards and FDI, in the form of business investment.[528] Olney posited that the Race to the Bottom is premised on the following assumptions: (i) multinational corporations choose to locate their investment in jurisdictions with less restrictive legal and regulatory standards; and (ii) jurisdictions compete against each other by undercutting their regulatory standards to attract FDI.[529] Multinational corporations have been the subject of significant focus in the Race to the Bottom regulatory competition literature, particularly because of their international mobile economic power.[530]

However, academic scholars and researchers often reference the corporate charter competition which took place between US states in the 1990s as the canonical example of regulatory competition in the context of the Race to the Bottom. Prior to chartering competition taking off, firms obtained their incorporation charters from the state in which they had originated. At the time firms were not permitted, under state laws, to own securities in other firms and mergers were only permitted if a firm purchased the securities of a firm which had been dissolved for the purpose of a merger.[531] However, this changed when New Jersey formulated a more seamless process for mergers by, for example, facilitating the formation of holding companies permitting one firm to own shares in another. These changes resulted in New Jersey becoming an attractive domicile for mergers and the state was able to substantially

526. Bruce G Carruthers & Naomi R Lamoreaux, 'Regulatory Races: The Effects of Jurisdictional Competition' (2016) 54(1) Journal of Economic Literature 56 https://doi.org/10.1257/jel.54.1.52. *See* Philipp Genschel & Thomas Plumper, 'Regulatory Competition and International Co-operation' (1997) 4(4) Journal of European Public Policy 626-642 and Claudio M Radaelli, 'The Puzzle of Regulatory Competition' (2014) 24 Journal of Public Policy 1-23 https://doi.org/10.1080/135017697344109.

527. Peter P Swire, 'The Race to Laxity and the Race to Undesirability: Explaining Failures in Competition Among Jurisdictions in Environmental Law' (1996) 14:2 Yale Law and Policy Review 87.

528. Robin Hollander & Louise Thornthwaite, 'Competitive federalism and workers' Compensation: Do States Race to the Bottom?' (2018) 53(3) Australian Journal of Political Science 336 https://doi.org/10.1080/10361146.2018.1477115.

529. William Olney, 'A Race to the Bottom? Employment Protection and Foreign Direct Investment' (2013) 91 Journal of International Economics 191 https://doi.org/10.1016/j.jinteco.2013.08.003.

530. Steven Pavelin & Lynda A Porter, 'Race-to-the-bottom or -Top at Home or Abroad: Health and Safety Standards and the Multinational Firm' (2011) 42(3) The Economic and Social Review 290.

531. Bruce G Carruthers & Naomi R Lamoreaux, 'Regulatory Races: The Effects of Jurisdictional Competition' (2016) 54(1) Journal of Economic Literature 70 https://doi.org/10.1257/jel.54.1.52.

increase its revenue from taxes charged to firms based on their authorised capital stock.[532] This move inspired many other states to compete for attracting charters, most notably the state of Delaware.[533] Competition among states ensued not only because it led to increased franchise tax revenues but also because interest groups within states, such as corporate lawyers and corporate managers,[534] benefitted from the increased incorporation activity.[535]

The EU corporate charter competition experience has been somewhat different to that of the US. At a horizontal level, firms have free will to choose the EU Member State in which to incorporate. However, even with the minimisation of trade barriers, subsequent to the creation of the EU, Member States continue to enforce rules upon firms incorporated in neighbouring Member States.[536] In this regard, there have been renewed to harmonise corporate law in the EU, including calls made by powerful interest groups.[537] As early as 1973, Schmitthoff argued that without harmonisation the rules governing shareholder and creditor protection would be eroded, and a Race to the Bottom would ensue in the EU.[538] This rhetoric, together with a number of existing factors, has presented several obstacles to a 'market for incorporations' in the EU. Most significantly, the doctrine of *siège reel*, slightly undercut by the European Court of Justice in 1999,[539] is enforced by most EU Member States. The doctrine provides that firms are required to comply with the incorporation laws of the jurisdiction in which they are headquartered, rather than the jurisdiction in which it is domiciled.[540] In addition, it is still quite challenging for firms to move their registered offices to another

532. *See* Henry N Butler, 'Nineteenth-Century Jurisdictional Competition in the Granting of Corporate Privileges' (1985) 14(1) Journal of Legal Studies 129 https://doi.org/10.1086/467768; Naomi R Lamoreaux, *The Great Merger Movement in American Business 1895-1904* (Cambridge University Press 1985) and Christopher Grandy, 'New Jersey Corporate Chartermongering 1875-1929' (1989) 49(3) Journal of Economic History 677-692 https://doi.org/10.1017/s0022050700008810.
533. *See* Christopher Grandy, 'New Jersey Corporate Chartermongering 1875-1929' (1989) 49(3) Journal of Economic History 677-692 https://doi.org/10.1017/s0022050700008810.
534. William J Carney, 'The Political Economy of Competition for Corporate Charters' (1997) 26(1) Journal of Legal Studies 306 https://doi.org/10.1086/467997.
535. Jonathan R Macey & Geoffrey P Miller, 'Toward and Interest-Group Theory of Delaware Law' (1987) 65 Texas Law Review 469, 502-509.
536. Simon Deakin, 'Regulatory Competition Versus Harmonization in European Company Law' in Daniel C Esty & Damien Geradin (eds), *Regulatory Competition and Economic Integration* (OUP 2001).
537. Bruce G Carruthers & Naomi R Lamoreaux, 'Regulatory Races: The Effects of Jurisdictional Competition' (2016) 54(1) Journal of Economic Literature 76 https://doi.org/10.1257/jel.54.1.52. *See* Alain Viandier, 'Free Movement and Mobility of Companies' (1998) 9 European Business Law Review 301-306 https://doi.org/10.54648/eulr1998037.
538. Clive Schmitthoff, 'The Future of the European Company Law Scene' in Clive Schmitthoff (ed.), *The Harmonization of European Company Law* (UKNCCL 1973) 9.
539. *Centros Ltd v. Erhvervs-og Selskabsstyrelsen* 1999 European Court of Justice (ECJ) 1-1459 and Simon Deakin, 'Regulatory Competition Versus Harmonization in European Company Law' in Daniel C Esty & Damien Geradin (eds), *Regulatory Competition and Economic Integration* (OUP 2001) 203.
540. Helen Xanthaki, 'The Secondary Establishment of Companies Within the EU: Challenge or Missed Opportunity' (1999) 10 European Business Law Review 121 https://doi.org/10.54648/eulr1999014; Simon Deakin, 'Regulatory Competition Versus Harmonization in European Company Law' in Daniel C Esty & Damien Geradin (eds) *Regulatory Competition and Economic Integration* (OUP 2001) 236 and Bruce G Carruthers & Naomi R Lamoreaux, 'Regulatory Races:

EU Member State.[541] However, the Cross-Border Merger Directive,[542] which came into effect in 2005, permits firms to relocate their domiciles by merging with firms in other EU Member States.[543] According to Deakin, a certain degree of harmonisation of the conflict of law rules and practices of EU Member States in relation to incorporation and reincorporation of firms would be required for the US-style competitive federalism to play out in the EU.[544] Carney has argued that the presence of a common market in the US, with the absence of tariffs which provides firms with the option of exiting expensive legal regimes, explains the competitive differences between the US and the EU in competing for corporate charters.[545] Further, the competitive differences may largely be explained by the distinct regulatory competition approaches taken, in the form of competitive federalism and reflexive harmonisation, respectively.[546]

Overall, empirical studies have been unable to provide sufficient evidence to prove the Race to the Bottom hypothesis in which it is assumed that low regulation jurisdictions, regions and states, attract FDI.[547] In the wake of the lack of empirical evidence conclusively pointing to a Race to the Bottom, Carruthers and Lamoreaux have posted that firms instead organise themselves into jurisdictions according to their respective appetites for regulatory oversight, in line with the Tiebout model.[548] The Race to the Bottom has therefore been more useful as a theoretical tool to understand the behaviour of Primary Actors in the operation of regulatory competition. From an

The Effects of Jurisdictional Competition' (2016) 54(1) Journal of Economic Literature 76 https://doi.org/10.1257/jel.54.1.52.

541. Simon Deakin, 'Regulatory Competition Versus Harmonization in European Company Law' in Daniel C Esty & Damien Geradin (eds), *Regulatory Competition and Economic Integration* (OUP 2001).
542. Directive 2005/56/EC of the European Parliament and of the Council of 26 October 2005 on cross-border mergers of limited liability companies.
543. John Armour, 'Who Should Make Corporate Law? EC Legislation Versus Regulatory Competition' (2005) 58(1) Current Legal Problems 369 https://doi.org/10.2139/ssrn.860444 and Simon Deakin, 'Legal Diversity and Regulatory Competition' (2006) 12(4) European Law Journal 450 https://doi.org/10.1111/j.1468-0386.2006.00326.x. *See* Simon Deakin, 'Regulatory Competition Versus Harmonization in European Company Law' in Daniel C Esty & Damien Geradin (eds), *Regulatory Competition and Economic Integration* (OUP 2001); Arianna Ugliano, 'The New Cross-Border Merger Directive: Harmonisation of European Company Law and Free Movement' (2007) 18(3) European Business Law Review 585-617 https://doi.org/10.54648/eulr2007025 and Bruce G Carruthers & Naomi R Lamoreaux, 'Regulatory Races: The Effects of Jurisdictional Competition' (2016) 54(1) Journal of Economic Literature 76 https://doi.org/10.1257/jel.54.1.52.
544. Simon Deakin, 'Regulatory Competition Versus Harmonization in European Company Law' in Daniel C Esty & Damien Geradin (eds), *Regulatory Competition and Economic Integration* (OUP 2001) 216.
545. William J Carney, 'The Political Economy of Competition for Corporate Charters' (1997) 26(1) Journal of Legal Studies 329 https://doi.org/10.1086/467997.
546. *See* Simon Deakin, 'Legal Diversity and Regulatory Competition' (2006) 12(4) European Law Journal 440-454 https://doi.org/10.1111/j.1468-0386.2006.00326.x.
547. Robert JR Elliot & Ying Zhou, 'Environmental Regulation Induced Foreign Direct Investment' (2013) 55 Environmental and Resource Economics 141-158 https://doi.org/10.1007/s10640-012-9620-0.
548. Bruce G Carruthers & Naomi R Lamoreaux, 'Regulatory Races: The Effects of Jurisdictional Competition' (2016) 54(1) Journal of Economic Literature 75 https://doi.org/10.1257/jel.54.1.52. *See* Moshe Cohen, 'Corporate Governance Law: Firm Heterogeneity and the Market for Corporate Domicile' (2012), https://papers.ssrn.com/sol3/papers.cfm?abstract_id=2116536.

empirical perspective, however, the results of regulatory competition studies have been divisive, with little support having been posited in favour thereof.[549]

3.4.3 Race to the Top

The Race to the Top outcome provides that regulatory competition may result from an upward pressure in which stricter legal and regulatory standards in one jurisdiction are passed through, by virtue of economic connectivity, to other jurisdictions.[550] In such a case, governments may feel pressure from, for example, their electorate to emulate the legal and regulatory standards of neighbouring jurisdictions.[551] In the regulatory competition literature, this phenomenon is more widely associated with Vogel's 'California Effect'.[552] The latter term was used in the US when states took the decision to raise their emissions standards, in response to California's own decision to do so.[553] Vogel has stated that the California Effect can be explained by reference to the existence of large and highly regulated markets in the wealthiest jurisdictions in the world.[554] In this regard, the larger the market size of the jurisdiction with stricter legal and regulatory rules relative to that of the jurisdiction with less strict legal and regulatory rules, the more likely the latter is to implement the former's standards.

The Race to the Top therefore operates so that jurisdictions react to a 'first mover' jurisdiction, which raises its legal and regulatory rules, by defensively raising their own legal and regulatory rules to retain market access.[555] On a practical level, larger markets with stricter legal and regulatory rules are free to impose higher costs without being penalised by the market as a result of firms being unable to forego access to them, i.e.,

549. Katharina Holzinger & Thomas Sommerer, '"Race to the Bottom" or "Race to Brussels"? Environmental competition in Europe' (2011) 49(2) Journal of Common Market Studies 316 referring to Suzanne Berger & Ronald Dore, *National Diversity and Global Capitalism* (Ithaca, NY: Cornell University Press 1996) vii https://doi.org/10.1111/j.1468-5965.2010.02135.x; Daniel W Drezner, 'Globalisation and Policy Convergence' (2001) 3 International Studies Review 75; and Thomasa Bernauer & Ladina Caduff, 'In Whose Interest? Pressure Group Politics, Economic Competition and Environmental Regulation' (2004) 24(1) Journal of Public Policy 100 https://doi.org/10.1017/s0143814x04000054.
550. Cristina A Lucier & Brian J Gareau, 'From Waste to Resources: Interrogating "Race to the Bottom" in the Global Environmental Governance of the Hazardous Waste Trade' (2015) 21(2) Journal of World-Systems Research 500 https://doi.org/10.5195/jwsr.2015.11.
551. Robin Hollander & Louise Thornthwaite, 'Competitive Federalism and Workers' Compensation: Do States Race to the Bottom?' (2018) 53(3) Australian Journal of Political Science 339 https://doi.org/10.1080/10361146.2018.1477115.
552. Robin Hollander & Louise Thornthwaite, 'Competitive Federalism and Workers' Compensation: Do States Race to the Bottom?' (2018) 53(3) Australian Journal of Political Science 339. *See* Matthew Potoski, 'Clean Air Federalism: Do States Race to the Bottom?' (2001) 61(3) Public Administration Review 335-343 https://doi.org/10.1111/0033-3352.00034.
553. *See* David Vogel, *Trading Up: Consumer and Environmental Regulation in a Global Economy* (Harvard University Press 1995) and Arthur PJ Mol, 'Ecological Modernization: Industrial Transformations and Environmental Reform' in Michael R Redclift & Graham Woodgate (eds), *The International Handbook of Environmental Sociology* (Elgar Publishing 1997).
554. David Vogel, *Trading Up: Consumer and Environmental Regulation in a Global Economy* (Harvard University Press 1995).
555. Claudio M Radaelli, 'The Puzzle of Regulatory Competition' (2014) 24 Journal of Public Policy 6.

the EU.[556] Firms wishing to export to these larger markets must comply with the relatively stricter legal and regulatory rules. Consequentially, Vogel has posited a condition necessary for the observance of the California Effect is that the costs of changing the legal and regulatory rules, to align them with those of the larger jurisdiction, must be relatively low considering the benefits of market access.[557] This condition finds expression in Princen's study concerning a comparison of the regulations governing genetically modified foods in both the US and Europe.[558] Princen found that the cost of strengthening the US' regulatory rules on the use of the leg-trap ban for trapping wild animals to align it with those enforced in the EU was relatively modest. Contrastingly, the cost of strengthening the US' regulatory rules on the use of the beef hormone ban to align it with those of the EU was substantial. This was similar to the case of the EU's regulations on genetically modified foods. Accordingly, Princen was of the view that the California Effect had occurred in the former case, but not the latter.

As such, the Race to the Top has been the subject of a multitude of both empirical and theoretical regulatory competition studies. Academic scholars and researchers have placed significant focus on studying the effects of regulatory competition in the context of the adjustment of environmental regulation and the Race to the Top. In some instances national, regional, and international competition has led to jurisdictions adopting stricter environmental standards than would have been enforced without the increase of economic interdependency, primarily spurred on by economic openness and capital mobility.[559] A number of jurisdictions have also exhibited behaviour consistent with Vogel's California Effect by moving 'in the direction of political jurisdictions with stricter regulatory standards'.[560] However, this primarily applies to the setting of product standards, which reflects only one component of environmental regulation.[561] Overall, however, the evidence presented by empirical studies on the outcomes of the Race to the Top in which jurisdictions compete against each other in setting environmental regulations is largely inconclusive,[562] with only a handful of case

556. Bruce G Carruthers & Naomi R Lamoreaux, 'Regulatory Races: The Effects of Jurisdictional Competition' (2003) 54(1) Journal of Economic Literature 55 https://doi.org/10.1257/jel.54.1.52.
557. David Vogel & Robert A Kagan, *Dynamics of Regulatory Change: How Globalization Affects National Regulatory Policies* (University of California Press 2002) [9]-[10]. *See* Sebastian Princen, 'A Comparison of the Leghold Trap and the Beef Hormone Issues between the EC and the US and Canada' (1999) Paper read at European Community Studies Association Sixth Biennial International Conference, June 2-5, at Pittsburgh, PA, http://aei.pitt.edu/2367/1/003780.1.pdf.
558. Sebastian Princen, 'A Comparison of the Leghold Trap and the Beef Hormone Issues between the EC and the US and Canada' (1999) Paper read at European Community Studies Association Sixth Biennial International Conference, 2-5 June, at Pittsburgh, PA, http://aei.pitt.edu/2367/1/003780.1.pdf.
559. David Vogel, 'Environmental Regulation and Economic Integration' in Daniel C Esty & Damien Geradin (eds), *Regulatory Competition and Economic Integration* (OUP 2001) 334.
560. David Vogel, 'Environmental Regulation and Economic Integration' in Daniel C Esty & Damien Geradin (eds), *Regulatory Competition and Economic Integration* (OUP 2001) 335.
561. David Vogel, 'Environmental Regulation and Economic Integration' in Daniel C Esty & Damien Geradin (eds), *Regulatory Competition and Economic Integration* (OUP 2001) 338.
562. Bruce G Carruthers & Naomi R Lamoreaux, 'Regulatory Races: The Effects of Jurisdictional Competition' (2016) 54(1) Journal of Economic Literature 64 https://doi.org/10.1257/jel.54.1.52.

study evidence.[563] In addition, despite the natural result of regulatory races leading to regulatory convergence, there still exists considerable variation in environmental regulation and standards.[564] Carruthers and Lamoreaux have also posited that firms are concerned not only with environmental regulation but that other factors such as labour market conditions and geographical location are also important to location decision-making.[565]

The Race to the Top places an overwhelming reliance on the manner and extent to which firms are influenced by costs and expenses in making their decisions to relocate, often ignoring other social and political motivating factors. For example, the cost of relocation may be less of a concern for larger firms who decide to bear the expense of a stricter regulatory regime if it results in smaller firms being put at a competitive disadvantage.[566] Radaelli has however posited that Vogel's California Effect generalises the empirical insights gained from the Race to the Bottom studies in arguing that market integration leads to competition for stricter legal and regulatory rules, thus producing the opposite of a Race to the Bottom.[567] As with the Race to the Bottom, the Race to the Top has therefore been more useful as a theoretical tool to understand the behaviour of Primary Actors in the operation of regulatory competition.

Table 3.1 Summary of the Essential Elements Underlining Regulatory Competition

	RC Essential Element	*Scope*
1.	Environmental Context	Contextual spaces distinguish the different ecosystems in which regulatory competition operates or is intended to operate. They place restrictions on the actions and behaviour of the actors who directly and indirectly take part in the operation of regulatory competition based on the legal system, and cultural and social mores in force.

563. Katharina Holzinger & Thomas Sommerer, '"Race to the Bottom" or "Race to Brussels"? Environmental Competition in Europe' (2011) 49(2) Journal of Common Market Studies citing David Vogel, *Trading Up: Consumer and Environmental Regulation in a Global Economy* (Harvard University Press 1995); Arthur PJ Mol, 'Ecological Modernization: Industrial Transformations and Environmental Reform' in Michale R Redclift & Graham Woodgate (eds), *The International Handbook of Environmental Sociology* (Elgar Publishing 1997); Martin Jänicke, 'Umweltpolitik: global am Ende oder am Ende global? Thesen zu ökologischen Determinanten desWeltmarkts' in Beck Ulrich (ed.), *Perspektiven der Weltgesellschaft* (Frankfurt am Main: Suhrkamp 1998) and Kristine Kern, 'Die Diffusion von Politikinnovationen. Umweltpolitische Innovationen im Mehrebenensystem der USA' (Opladen: Leske & Budrich 2000).
564. Bruce G Carruthers & Naomi R Lamoreaux, 'Regulatory Races: The Effects of Jurisdictional Competition' (2016) 54(1) Journal of Economic Literature 65 https://doi.org/10.1257/jel.54.1.52.
565. Bruce G Carruthers & Naomi R Lamoreaux, 'Regulatory Races: The Effects of Jurisdictional Competition' (2016) 54(1) Journal of Economic Literature 65 https://doi.org/10.1257/jel.54.1.52. *See* Kirsten H Engel, 'State Environmental Standard-Setting: Is There a "Race" and Is It "to the Bottom"?' (1997) 48 Hastings Law Journal 337-347.
566. *See* Dale E Murphy, *The Structure of Regulatory Competition: Corporations and Public Policies in a Global Economy* (OUP 2004).
567. Claudio M Radaelli, 'The Puzzle of Regulatory Competition' (2014) 24 Journal of Public Policy 6 https://doi.org/10.1017/s0143814x04000017.

	RC Essential Element	Scope
2.	Direction	Horizontal or vertical relational dimension of regulatory competition indicating: (i) different or similar functional units of government; and (ii) distinguishing or similar levels of political power and legislative competence among the different actors engaged in regulatory competition.
3.	Systems of Government	Collective of political institutions by which a government is arranged, and which constrains the actions and behaviours of actors taking part in regulatory competition through values and principles which underlie the relevant system of government.
4.	Actors	Government and non-government entities competing against each other and operating in the different Environmental Contexts represented as primary (create and enforce the 'means'), secondary (consumers of the 'means') and tertiary (ancillary role through efforts to support an agenda or cause) RC Actors.
5.	Means	Primary outputs result from the actions and behaviours of Primary Actors through legal and political processes, such as legislative and policy-making mechanisms and procedures intended to be used in the operation of regulatory competition. Examples include rules-based and incentives-based.
6.	Drivers	Benefits, economic or otherwise, intended to be attained (or retained) by Primary Actors through the operation of regulatory competition. Includes wealth creation in the form of economic and non-economic activities such as capital investment and highly skilled labour.

Table 3.2 Summary of the Regulatory Competition Framework Observed in the Literature

Observed RC	*System of Government*	*RC Direction*	*RC Actors*	*RC Means*	*RC Drivers*	*Outcomes*
Tiebout Model	Democracy: Federalism Quasi-federalism	Horizontal	Local Municipality and Local Municipality(ies)	Local public goods, land	Attracting residents to specific locale, tax payments, land use and impact fees, and business revenue	Tiebout Equilibrium, Population size increase
Intra-national – Decentralised governments	Democracy: Federalism Quasi-federalism	Vertical	Local Municipality and State	Reduced labour and operating costs, subsidies, tax breaks, efficient access to transport systems	Attracting business to specific locale, tax payments, business revenue, population	Business operations increase
Competitive Federalism	Democracy: Federalism Quasi-federalism	Horizontal	State and State(s)	Less and more stringent corporate law through adjustment of legal rules, specialised judiciary, and less and more stringent enforcement rules	Incorporate fees, tax payments, and business revue	Regulatory races: To the Bottom and To the Top

Observed RC	*System of Government*	*RC Direction*	*RC Actors*	*RC Means*	*RC Drivers*	*Outcomes*
Competitive Federalism	Democracy Federalism Quasi-federalism	Vertical	State and Federal Government	Less and more stringent incorporation law through adjustment of legal rules, less stringent enforcement rules	Incorporation fees, tax payments, and attracting business	Superior authority in rule setting and amendment
International	Democracy	Horizontal	Sovereign nation-states	Less stringent environmental law through adjustment of legal rules, relaxed domestic anti-trust enforcement, regulatory subsidies	Capital investment (FDI and portfolio) and highly skilled labour	Regulatory races: To the Bottom and To the Top, regulatory coopetition
International	Democracy	Vertical	Sovereign nation-states non-governmental actor(s)	Influence in networking and coordination	International rule setting	Superior authority in rule setting and amendment, Regulatory coopetition

CHAPTER 4

Regulating DLT Financial Products and Services: The SAR of Hong Kong

This chapter provides a narrative analysis of the development of the laws and regulations governing DLT financial products and services in Hong Kong during the key periods of development from 2018-2022. It provides an examination of the actions and behaviours of the HK Government and how competition policy influenced its regulatory approach to DLT Offerings and the formulation of the laws and regulations developed to govern it.

4.1 INTRODUCTION

The SAR of Hong Kong has long been regarded as a top global financial centre. On a geographical basis, it is also considered to be the commercial gateway to Mainland China.[568] As a SAR, HK is governed under the 'one country, two systems' and 'Hong Kong people administering Hong Kong' principles.[569] As an advanced economy, HK has ranked number 4 on the UN's Human Development Index and is regarded as a preeminent Fintech hub globally based on its bustling Fintech ecosystem.[570] This is also buttressed by Mainland China having ranked number 1 in the Global Fintech Ranking 2021.[571] The Basic Law, in effect since 1 July 1997, is the constitutional

568. The Government of the Hong Kong Special Administrative Region (HK Government), 'Hong Kong: China's Global Financial Centre' (2013) 2.
569. HK Government, 'Hong Kong: The Facts', https://www.gov.hk/en/about/abouthk/facts.htm.
570. *See* UNDP, 'Uncertain Times, Unsettled Lives: Shaping our Future in a Transforming World' (8 September 2022) 227, https://hdr.undp.org/content/human-development-report-2021-22#:~:text=DOCUMENT-,Report%20(English),-(5.54%20MB) and The Global Fintech Hub Report, 'The Future of Finance is Emerging: New Hubs, New Landscapes' (2018) 7, 13, https://www.jbs.cam.ac.uk/fileadmin/user_upload/research/centres/alternative-finance/downloads/2018-ccaf-global-fintech-hub-reporteng.pdf.
571. Global Fintech Rankings Report (*Findexable,* 2021) 21, https://findexable.com/wp-content/uploads/2021/06/Global-Fintech-Rankings-2021-v1-23-June-21.pdf.

document for HK setting out the principles by which it is governed.[572] Under the Basic Law, HK is empowered to govern itself with a designated measure of autonomy which includes judicial, executive and legislative independence,[573] composed in the form of an independent judiciary led by a Chief Justice,[574] an executive branch led by the Chief Executive,[575] and a Legislative Council led by a President.[576] Within this system of government, the branches of government empowered to set legal and regulatory rules for the financial services industry, specifically as they apply to DLT Offerings, in addition to formulating competition policy, include the: (i) Legislative Council; (ii) HKMA; and (iii) Securities and Futures Commission.[577] The actions and behaviours of these branches of government form the subject of the regulatory competition analysis in this chapter.

The Legislative Council (LegCo) was established in 1843 under the pre-1997 constitutional framework provided for in the Letters Patent and the Royal Instructions.[578] In 1997, the LegCo Bill was passed to enable the first LegCo of HK to be established. The main function of the LegCo is the amendment, enactment and revocation of HK laws as aligned with the Basic Law and relevant legal procedures.[579] LegCo members are organised into individual standing committees by the House Committee and are responsible for, among other functions, examining new draft laws. The House Committee is also empowered to formulate subcommittees to analyse new draft laws in more detail. Most notably, the House Committee is empowered to designate ad hoc panels tasked primarily with scrutinising the efficacy of government measures and policies.[580] Among these panels, the mandate and scope of work of the Panel on Financial Affairs (LegCo PFA), as determined by its terms of reference, is most relevant for this study. In particular, the LegCo PFA is tasked with monitoring and examining the policies of the HK Government and consider issues relating to financial and finance matters.[581] The LegCo PFA also receives briefings from governmental bodies, including the HKMA, and formulates opinions on significant legislative and financial proposals before those opinions are formally submitted to the LegCo or Finance Committee.[582]

572. *See* https://www.basiclaw.gov.hk/en/basiclaw/facts.html.
573. The Basic Law of the Hong Kong Special Administrative Region of the People's Republic of China (The Basic Law), Art. 2.
574. *See* https://www.hkcfa.hk/en/about/who/judges/chief_justice/index.html.
575. *See* https://www.gov.hk/en/about/govdirectory/govstructure.htm.
576. *See* https://www.legco.gov.hk/en/members/president/roles-of-president.html.
577. There are, however, four principal regulatory authorities are responsible for the supervision of the financial services in Hong Kong SAR, including: the HKMA, the Insurance Authority, the Mandatory Provident Fund System, and the SFC.
578. The National Archives of the UK: Public Record Office C 66/4683.
579. The Basic Law, Art. 73.
580. *See* https://www.legco.gov.hk/en/about-legco/legco-today.html.
581. *See* https://www.legco.gov.hk/en/legco-business/committees/panel.html?financial-affairs&2022#about.
582. *See* https://www.legco.gov.hk/en/legco-business/committees/panel.html?financial-affairs&2022#about.

The HKMA was established in 1993 through the amalgamation of the former offices of the Exchange Fund and the Commissioner of Banking.[583] Under the Exchange Fund Ordinance, the HKMA is empowered to assist the Financial Secretary with the performance of its functions.[584] To this end, the HKMA's mandate comprises four core functions, as set out in an exchange of letters between the HKMA and the Financial Secretary.[585] Among these functions, the HKMA's role in maintaining HK's status quo as an international financial centre is the most relevant for this study. Importantly, this function includes HKMA action and behaviour directed towards formulating competition policy for the financial services industry.[586] On a broader basis, the HKMA derives its competences and powers from several HK legislative ordinances[587] and correspondingly plays a prudential and supervisory role as a financial regulatory authority. As such, the HKMA is responsible for authorising and supervising financial institutions, including banks and other deposit-taking institutions, conducting monetary policy, and managing the Exchange Fund. Finally, the HKMA plays an important collaborative role with the LegCo in promoting accountability and transparency in HK. The HKMA Chief Executive appears before the LegCo PFA on a triannual basis to present the HKMA's ongoing work, and to address questions relating thereto.[588] The HKMA also reports its work to the LegCo PFA through briefing documents.

The SFC was established in May 1989 and was tasked with regulating the futures and securities industry in HK. As an independent statutory body, the SFC operates independently of the HK Government and is funded primarily through fees and transaction levies. The SFC's disciplinary, investigative, and remedial powers and functions are primarily derived from the SFO[589] and other subsidiary legislation.[590] As a financial regulatory authority, the SFC is mandated to perform several functions, including, authorising and supervising intermediaries, such as brokers, investment advisers, and fund managers, and market operators, such as exchanges and alternative trading platforms.[591] The SFC's mandate empowering it to set and enforce market regulation, and investigate breaches and market misconduct, for the financial services industry, is the most relevant function for this study. In performing these functions, the SFC, as a regulatory authority in an international financial centre, is committed to protecting and strengthening the integrity and soundness of HK's futures and securities

583. *See* https://www.hkma.gov.hk/eng/about-us/the-hkma/.
584. Cap 66 Exchange Fund Ordinance, s. 5A and s. 5B.
585. HK Government, 'Functions and Responsibilities in Monetary and Financial Affairs' (25 June 2003), https://www.hkma.gov.hk/media/eng/doc/key-information/press-release/2003/20030627e3a1.pdf.
586. HK Government, 'Functions and Responsibilities in Monetary and Financial Affairs' (25 June 2003), https://www.hkma.gov.hk/media/eng/doc/key-information/press-release/2003/20030627e3a1.pdf. *See also* https://www.hkma.gov.hk/eng/about-us/the-hkma/.
587. This includes, among others, the Banking Ordinance (Cap 155); the Financial Institutions (Resolution) Ordinance (Cap 628); and the Financial Institutions (Resolution) Ordinance (Cap 628).
588. *See* https://www.hkma.gov.hk/eng/data-publications-and-research/legislative-council-issues/.
589. Cap 571 Securities and Futures Ordinance (SFO).
590. *See* https://www.sfc.hk/en/About-the-SFC/Our-role.
591. *See* https://www.sfc.hk/en/About-the-SFC/Our-role.

markets to benefit investors and the industry. Finally, the SFC has described its approach to regulation as 'innovative' through its facilitation of innovation where it is beneficial for investors and market efficiency.[592] Taking this into consideration, the SFC ensures that its regulations are effective against new technologies, and the potential risks which they may bear.

4.1.1 Input: 2008-2017

The analysis below sets out the actions and behaviours of the HK Government in directing the advancement of competition policy within the context of the emergence of Fintech, and its position of importance on legal and policy agendas.

4.1.1.1 Competition Policy and the Role of Fintech

HK's competitiveness, both regionally and internationally, forms an integral HK Government policy objective, directed largely through its financial services industry, marked as one of HK's four traditional pillar industries.[593] In levying this policy agenda, the HK Government's role has been stated as formulating policies favourable to market competition for the purposes of standing out against competitive forces.[594] For example, in its 2008-09 Policy Address, the HK Government referred to the increased regional competition in the securities market. In response, the HK Government directed that it would develop HK's securities market by, among others, enhancing the efficiency of listings and attracting new and large firms from Eastern Europe and Russia to list in HK.[595] Overall, however, the actions and behaviours of the HK Government in directing its competition policy are underscored primarily by its overarching policy objective to strengthen and maintain HK's status quo as an international financial centre for, among others, financial services.[596] In this regard, the HK Government has initiated several policy responses aimed at attracting international capital, financial products, financial institutions and highly skilled labour.[597] Notably, these responses include the promulgation of legal and regulatory rules aimed at strengthening the regulatory regime for financial institutions.[598] The HK Government's response to competitive pressures is therefore well-documented as an integral policy objective required to strengthen HK's reputation as a leading financial centre.[599]

592. *See* https://www.sfc.hk/en/About-the-SFC/Our-role/How-we-function/Regulatory-approach.
593. HK Government, 'The 2010-11 Policy Address: Sharing Prosperity for a Caring Society' (2010) 29.
594. HK Government, 'The 2008-2009 Policy Address: Embracing New Challenges' (2008) 3.
595. HK Government, 'The 2008-2009 Policy Address: Embracing New Challenges' (2008) 7.
596. HK Government, 'The 2008-2009 Policy Address: Embracing New Challenges' (2008) 5 and HK Government, 'The 2009-10 Policy Address: Breaking New Ground Together' (2009) 19.
597. HK Government, 'The 2009-10 Policy Address: Breaking New Ground Together' (2009) 6.
598. HK Government, 'The 2008-2009 Policy Address: Policy Agenda' (2008) 9 and HK Government, 'The 2010-11 Policy Address: Policy Agenda' (2010) 26.
599. HK Government, 'The 2008-2009 Policy Address: Policy Agenda' (2008) 3, 5.

During the time period 2008-2010, the HK Government was concerned primarily with promoting HK as a regional hub, and as such directed action to support initiatives including financing cooperative projects and participating in crisis management in the Asia-Pacific region. This objective formed a regular feature on the HK Government's policy agenda, as reflected in the HKMA's tri-annual briefings to the LegCo PFA. This regional focus also extended to the concern that the increased focus on the development of Shanghai as a financial centre posed a competitive threat.[600] During the same time period, one of the key strategies adopted by the HK Government to challenge competitive pressure was to adopt closer economic ties with Mainland China.[601]

In collaboration with Mainland China, the HK Government developed the bond market in the Asia-Pacific region to highlight HK's position as a preeminent international financial centre.[602] For example, through the Institutional Bond Issuances Programme, HK banks operating in Mainland China were permitted to issue renminbi bonds in HK to expand the renminbi as a funding source.[603] Action was also taken to develop HK as a regional payment services hub, including facilitating renminbi use outside of Mainland China via transactions between HK and Mainland Chinese businesses.[604] Overall, the HK Government noted the 'need to innovate and enhance [our] competitiveness in response to competition from other cities in the region',[605] and the challenges posed by global competitive pressures.[606]

During the time period 2011-2014, the HK Government directed action to promote the competitiveness of its asset management industry aimed to emphasise HK's reputation as a leading asset management hub. In this regard, the HK Government initiated promotion campaigns targeting asset and fund managers in Canada, Europe, the Middle East, Southeast Asia, the US, and Mainland China.[607] Most notably, and highlighting HK's competitive edge, the HKMA convinced the board of directors of a sizeable North American pension fund to establish itself in HK.[608] The HK Government has referenced the rule of law, freedom of information, and its ties to the international community, as HK's competitive edge,[609] representative of the Means through which it chooses to participate in regulatory competition.

600. HK Government, 'The 2009-10 Policy Address: Breaking New Ground Together' (2009) 3.
601. HK Government, 'The 2008-09 Policy Address: Policy Agenda' (2008) 3.
602. HKMA, 'Briefing to the Legislative Council Panel on Financial Affairs' (29 January 2008) 37; HKMA, 'Briefing to the Legislative Council Panel on Financial Affairs' (28 April 2008) 10 and HKMA, 'Briefing to the Legislative Council Panel on Financial Affairs' (21 November 2008) 54.
603. HKMA, 'Briefing to the Legislative Council Panel on Financial Affairs' (21 May 2009) 52 and HKMA, 'Briefing to the Legislative Council Panel on Financial Affairs' (19 November 2009) 60 and HKMA, 'Briefing to the Legislative Council Panel on Financial Affairs' (1 February 2010) 50.
604. HKMA, 'Briefing to the Legislative Council Panel on Financial Affairs' (2 February 2009) 55.
605. HK Government, 'The 2009-10 Policy Address: Policy Agenda' (2009) 3.
606. HK Government, 'The 2010-11 Policy Address: Policy Agenda' (2010) 6.
607. HKMA, 'Briefing to the Legislative Council Panel on Financial Affairs' (1 March 2011) 63; HKMA, 'Briefing to the Legislative Council Panel on Financial Affairs' (23 May 2011) 62; HKMA, 'Briefing to the Legislative Council Panel on Financial Affairs' (19 November 2012) 60 and HKMA, 'Briefing to the Legislative Council Panel on Financial Affairs' (5 May 2014) 64.
608. HKMA, 'Briefing to the Legislative Council Panel on Financial Affairs' (19 November 2012) 60 and HKMA, 'Briefing to the Legislative Council Panel on Financial Affairs' (5 May 2014) 64.
609. HK Government, 'The 2009-10 Policy Address: Breaking New Ground Together' (2009) 49.

In 2012, the London-HK RMB Forum was established to facilitate the internationalisation of the renminbi (RMB),[610] through the efforts of banks in both cities encouraging corporations to make use thereof. This initiative led to an overall increase in the number of renminbi corporate accounts and foreign exchange transactions. Increasing HK's presence regionally and internationally through cooperation on financial initiatives, also formed an important tenet of the HK Government's policy agenda.[611] Further, in 2013, the HK Government established the FSDC mandated to foster the progression of the financial services industry in HK and to formulate a roadmap for its future strategic development.[612]

From an international perspective, the HK Government directed its policy agenda to attract firms from Europe, the US and other emerging economies (i.e., Secondary Actors) to list in HK by amending the existing regulatory regime by requiring, for example, listed firms to disclose price sensitive information (i.e., the Means).[613] Correspondingly, in June 2014 the HKMA implemented its ECF for private wealth management (later extended to banks) to enhance risk management proficiencies through voluntary professional competence, compliance and ethical standards.[614] The HKMA remarked that the ECF is 'conducive to maintaining the competitiveness of Hong Kong as an international financial centre'.[615]

During the time period 2015-2017, the HK Government expressed concern regarding competitive pressures arising from other jurisdictions, and the need to 'develop a high value-added and diversified economy'.[616] As such, it was indicated that measures were required to progress the creative, innovation, and technology sectors in HK. Accordingly, the HK Government pledged to fund an HKD 2 billion Innovation and Technology Venture Fund to encourage investment in innovation and technology start-ups in HK.[617] At the same time, the HKMA directed action towards further developing the financial services industry, as one of its 'most internationally competitive pillar industries',[618] including establishing a cross-sector resolution regime for HK financial institutions, aligned with FSB standards.[619]

610. HKMA, 'First Meeting of Hong Kong: London Forum to Promote Cooperation on Development of International RMB Business' (22 May 2012), https://www.hkma.gov.hk/eng/news-and-media/press-releases/2012/05/20120522-4/.
611. HKMA, 'Briefing to the Legislative Council Panel on Financial Affairs' (6 May 2013) 68.
612. *See* Financial Services Development Council (FSDC), 'Vision & Mission' (2021), https://www.fsdc.org.hk/en/about-us/vision-mission/.
613. HK Government, 'The 2011-12 Policy Address: From Strength to Strength' (2011) 49.
614. HKMA, 'Briefing to the Legislative Council Panel on Financial Affairs' (3 November 2014) 58 and HKMA, 'Briefing to the Legislative Council Panel on Financial Affairs' (6 February 2017) 64.
615. HKMA, 'Enhanced Competency Framework' (16 December 2021), https://www.hkma.gov.hk/eng/key-functions/international-financial-centre/soft-infrastructure/enhanced-competency-framework/.
616. HK Government, 'The Chief Executives 2017 Policy Address: We Connect for Hope and Happiness' (2017) 19.
617. HK Government, 'The 2016 Policy Address: Innovate for the Economy, Improve Livelihood, Foster Harmony, Share Prosperity' (2016) 24.
618. HK Government, 'The 2016 Policy Address: Innovate for the Economy, Improve Livelihood, Foster Harmony, Share Prosperity' (2016) 3 and 12.
619. HKMA, 'Briefing to the Legislative Council Panel on Financial Affairs' (4 May 2015) 59.

In early 2015, the HK Government directed its policy agenda to develop HK into a Fintech hub, based on its overarching policy objective to maintain HK as an international financial centre.[620] For this specific purpose, the HK Government established the Steering Group on Financial Technologies (Fintech SG) in April 2015. The Fintech SG delivered its foundational report on 26 February 2016 (Fintech SG Report), in which it recommended five key areas 'for nurturing a conducive ecology for Fintech development' in HK based on its analysis of the experiences of Mainland China and overseas jurisdictions.[621] Notably, one key area was expressed as 'promotion', defined as 'how a strong and consistent promotional message may be formulated to appeal to talents, startups, funding and financial institutions'.[622]

In this regard, the Fintech SG Report recommended that the HK Government, in line with Fintech Hubs elsewhere, develop a clear Fintech strategy to help industry actors better understand HK's Fintech environment. It was further recommended that the HK Government establish an annual Fintech event to highlight HK's Fintech environment with the aim of attracting local and overseas talent to HK. This recommendation culminated in the establishment of the annual HK Fintech Week, with its inaugural event being hosted by the HKMA in October 2017. At this inaugural event, the HKMA published its second whitepaper on DLT was published, and hosted technical workshops on, among others, payments and DLT.[623] At the heart of the strategy encapsulated in the Fintech SG report was developing HK's competitiveness as a leading financial centre. In particular, the press release to the Fintech SG Report highlighted that HK's Fintech sector should be developed to ensure that its financial services industry 'can stay ahead of the competition'.[624] Most significantly, the Fintech SG Report noted that competition 'to attract Fintech activities is keen among advanced economies, and the conduciveness of the local Fintech ecology could determine the outcome of this race for talents, enterprises, funding and, ultimately, innovations'.[625] To this end, the Fintech SG Report highlighted the Fintech development strategies, policy approaches and promotion initiatives undertaken in Mainland China, Singapore and the UK.[626]

The nature of HK's competitiveness as a Fintech Hub was also addressed in the LegCo's FinTech Working Group's (LegCo FinTech WG) response to the Fintech SG Report.[627] In particular, the LegCo FinTech WG Response specified that HK's Fintech

620. Financial Secretary, 'The 2015-16 Budget' (25 February 2015) 14, https://www.budget.gov.hk/2015/eng/pdf/e_budgetspeech2015-16.pdf.
621. HK Government, 'Report of the Steering Group on Financial Technologies' (26 February 2016), 5-6.
622. HK Government, 'Report of the Steering Group on Financial Technologies' (26 February 2016) 6.
623. HKMA, 'Briefing to the Legislative Council Panel on Financial Affairs' (6 November 2017) 65.
624. HK Government, 'Steering Group on Fintech Releases Report' (26 February 2016), https://www.info.gov.hk/gia/general/201602/26/P201602260497.htm.
625. HK Government, 'Report of the Steering Group on Financial Technologies' (26 February 2016) 37.
626. HK Government, 'Report of the Steering Group on Financial Technologies' (26 February 2016) 39 and 63.
627. Legislative Council (Information Technology), 'Response to the Report of the Steering Group on Financial Technologies' (April 2016).

sector had overall received inadequate investment, when compared to other leading international financial centres, such as London and NY.[628] To counter this lack of financial capital in the HK Fintech sector, the LegCo's Fintech Working Group suggested that tax incentives could possibly be deployed to attract Fintech sector investment. This regulatory competition Means was deployed similarly by the UK Government in July 2015 when it announced that interest earnings on P2P would be tax-free.[629]

In accordance with the HK Government's policy approach, the HKMA announced in 2016 that developing Fintech in HK was one of its key drivers.[630] In accordance therewith, the HKMA launched its Fintech Facilitation Office tasked with developing the Fintech sector in HK by, for example, facilitating the exchange of new Fintech developments.[631] In tandem with these efforts, on 1 March 2016, the SFC launched its Fintech Contact Point to be used as a platform to connect itself with Fintech businesses. The SFC also launched its Fintech Advisory Group tasked with, among others, keeping abreast of Fintech trends and assessing the benefits and risks of Fintech, including relevant regulatory perimeter repercussions.[632]

Fintech sector development was furthered through the launches of the HKMA's Fintech Supervisory Sandbox in September 2016 and the SFC's and Insurance Authority's Supervisory Sandbox in September 2017, enabling an experimental pilot project environment in HK.[633] In 2017, the London-HK Financial Services Forum, previously called the London-HK RMB Forum, expanded its scope to include cooperation concerning Fintech matters.[634] In the same year, the HKMA announced its Smart Banking Initiative, which included the Faster Payment System aimed to enhance payments and settlements on a real-time basis in HK.[635] The HKMA also reported that several banks in HK were developing trade finance platforms using DLT to automate trade finance mechanisms.[636]

The HK Government's wide-ranging policy initiative to develop HK into a Fintech hub was directed in alignment with its overarching policy objective of maintaining and strengthening HK as an international financial centre. To this end, in developing a

628. Legislative Council (Information Technology), 'Response to the Report of the Steering Group on Financial Technologies' (April 2016), paras 4 and 11.
629. Legislative Council (Information Technology), 'Response to the Report of the Steering Group on Financial Technologies' (April 2016), para. 11.
630. HKMA, 'Diversified Fintech' (11 November 2016).
631. HKMA, 'How the HKMA Sees FinTech: "Risk-based, Tech-neutral"' (21 March 2016). *See* https://www.hkma.gov.hk/eng/key-functions/international-financial-centre/fintech/.
632. SFC, 'SFC Establishes the FinTech Contact Point' (1 March 2016). *See* https://www.sfc.hk/en/Welcome-to-the-Fintech-Contact-Point/Fintech-Advisory-Group.
633. HKMA, 'Circular on Fintech Supervisory Sandbox' (6 September 2016), https://www.hkma.gov.hk/media/eng/doc/key-information/guidelines-and-circular/2016/20160906e1.pdf and HK Government, 'The Chief Executives 2017 Policy Address: We Connect for Hope and Happiness' (2017) 33.
634. HKMA, 'Briefing to the Legislative Council Panel on Financial Affairs' (6 February 2017) 74.
635. HKMA, 'Briefing to the Legislative Council Panel on Financial Affairs' (6 November 2018) 67.
636. HKMA, 'Briefing to the Legislative Council Panel on Financial Affairs' (6 November 2017) 66. eTradeConnect was established launched on 27 September 2018. *See* HKMA, 'Briefing to the Legislative Council Panel on Financial Affairs' (5 November 2018) 68.

'headquarters economy' in HK,[637] the government stressed that HK's competitiveness in international markets should be maintained and that steps should be taken to deter acts which harm the business and investment environment in HK.[638] In assessing its own competitive prowess, the HK Government expressed that HK is an 'ideal place for the development of financial technologies' bearing in mind its advanced information and communication technology sector.[639]

4.1.1.2 Discussion

These actions and behaviours considered above are examined below by identifying the significant themes which delineate the HK Government's approach to competition policy for the financial services industry, and the extent of its 'competitive appetite' in relation thereto.

4.1.1.2.1 Competition Policy

The actions and behaviours directed by the HK Government during the time period 2008-2017 evidenced a clear and distinct policy agenda aimed at positioning the HK Government as a Primary Actor, both internationally and regionally, in the Environmental Context of international regulatory competition. The analysis evidenced that, in considering this competitive landscape, the HK Government was cognisant of both: (i) its position relative to other competing Primary Actors; and (ii) the position of competing Primary Actors relative to others. The HK Government deployed several branches of government to direct its competition policy objectives, using several regulatory competition Means to attract (and retain) the regulatory competition Drivers directed to Secondary Actors.

The HK Government's awareness of its own competitiveness is reflected primarily through its competition policy goal of strengthening and maintaining HK's status as an international financial centre. This is buttressed by the government's consideration of the competitive pressures presented by competing Primary Actors, and how the HK Government responds thereto. The competitiveness of these Primary Actors has also been considered by the HK Government in advancing competition policy, as reflected by an inclination to benchmark the policy directives of competing jurisdictions. This is illustrated by the Fintech SG Report's review of the approaches taken by several governments to develop their Fintech industries, noting in particular the UK.

In marketing HK's competitiveness, the HK Government has described its role as a promoter in its 'Government-to-Government' interchanges. Accordingly, the actions

637. HKMA, 'Briefing to the Legislative Council Panel on Financial Affairs' (5 February 2017) 75.
638. HK Government, 'The 2015 Policy Address: Uphold the Rule of Law, Seize the Opportunities, Make the Right Choices, Pursue Democracy, Boost the Economy, Improve People's Livelihoods' (2015) 5.
639. HK Government, 'The Chief Executives 2017 Policy Address: We Connect for Hope and Happiness' (2017) 33 and HK Government, 'The Hong Kong Special Administrative Region of the People's Republic of China: The Chief Executive's 2017 Policy Address – Policy Agenda' (2017) 9.

and behaviours directing competition policy objectives are executed by several branches of government responsible for promoting and developing HK's competitiveness as an international financial centre. These include, most notably, the LegCo, FSDC and the HKMA. For example, the LegCo's Fintech WG was particularly influential in spearheading additional investment into HK's Fintech sector, comparing it as inadequate to the investment levels of London and NY. The HKMA's Market Outreach Division was specifically mandated to target and engage investors to attract both international and Mainland Chinese capital investment.

The HK Government executed its competition policy through heterogeneous actions and behaviours, most notably the introduction of legal and regulatory rules and voluntary standards aimed at enhancing the institutional frameworks for the financial services industry. These regulatory competition Means have been described by the HK Government as offering measures which 'strive for excellence through unceasing efforts to enhance [our] competitiveness and improve the business environment'.[640] The Means were targeted at international and regional Secondary Actors, including firms in North America, Europe and Mainland China, to attract and retain regulatory competition Drivers, primarily in the form of capital investment and highly skilled labour.[641]

4.1.1.2.2 Significant Policy Themes

An analysis of the actions and behaviours directed by the HK Government during the time period 2008-2017 highlighted several significant themes, including an identification of a broad set of factors influencing the development of the Fintech industry in HK, and the advancement of competition policy. These significant themes are important as they highlight the HK Government's: (i) level of awareness of competition pressures from other Primary Actors; and (ii) the extent to which they were concerned about these competitive pressures. The level of concern regarding the competitive pressures is primarily represented by the actions which the HK Government directed in response thereto. These significant themes include the following:

> *International financial centre*. The HK Government's overarching policy objective was strengthening and maintaining HK's reputation as an international financial centre for financial services. Accordingly, the actions and behaviours directed by the relevant branches of the HK Government were executed in accordance with this strategic basis. In particular, the government viewed its role as staving off the threat of competition from international and regional Primary Actors, primarily through formulating favourable legal and regulatory rules and policies to withstand such competitive forces.[642] The HK

640. HK Government, 'The 2016 Policy Address: Innovate for the Economy, Improve Livelihood, Foster Harmony, Share Prosperity' (2016) 3.
641. HK Government, 'The Hong Kong Special Administrative Region of the People's Republic of China: The Chief Executive's 2017 Policy Address – Policy Agenda' (2017) 3 and 18.
642. HK Government, 'The 2008-2009 Policy Address: Embracing New Challenges' (2008) 3.

Government has referenced the rule of law, freedom of information, and its ties to the international community, as HK's 'competitive edge'.[643]

Strengthening economic ties with Mainland China. A key strategy implemented by the HK Government to counter competitive pressures experienced with respect to international and regional Primary Actors was to adopt closer economic ties with Mainland China. This strategy took the form of several economic cooperation initiatives aimed at facilitating HK's overarching policy objective and strengthening its position as a regional hub. These initiatives included the Institutional Bond Issuances Programme and development of HK into a regional payment hub, aimed to facilitate increased use of the renminbi outside Mainland China. Further, the London-HK RMB Forum was formed to facilitate the internationalisation of the RMB.

International Fintech Hub. The HK Government directed its policy agenda to develop HK into a Fintech hub, in advancement of its overarching policy objective. The Fintech SG spearheaded this policy objective with its report setting out the development strategies, policy approaches and promotion initiatives taken by Primary Actors, such as the UK. The HKMA and the SFC also played an important role in driving Fintech development through various initiatives, including the establishment of its Fintech Facilitation Office and Fintech Contact Point, and its respective regulatory sandboxes. With this in mind, the Fintech SG Report provided the blueprint for HK to develop its own approach to Fintech, in part based on Fintech initiatives applied in competing jurisdictions.

4.1.2 Process: 2015-2018

The analysis below sets out the actions and behaviours of the HK Government directed towards formulating a regulatory approach to the governance of Fintech and DLT Offerings in its jurisdiction.

4.1.2.1 Developing a Regulatory Approach to DLT

The HK Government's initial regulatory response to virtual currencies erred on the side of caution as illustrated by its conservative stance. The HKMA issued a consumer warning characterising Bitcoin as a 'virtual commodity' which could not be accepted as legal tender. The HKMA reminded consumers of the risks associated with Bitcoin trading, and directed, most notably, that it does not regulate virtual currencies, including Bitcoin.[644] To this end, the HKMA expressed that its regulatory approach to the burgeoning Fintech sector was based on its 'risk-based and technology-neutral'

643. HK Government, 'The 2009-10 Policy Address: Breaking New Ground Together' (2009) 49.
644. HKMA, 'The HKMA Reminds the Public to Be Aware of the Risks Associated with Bitcoin' (11 February 2015), https://www.hkma.gov.hk/eng/news-and-media/press-releases/2015/02/20150211-3/.

principle.[645] This principle entailed the implementation of regulatory frameworks based on the specific risks derived from conducting financial activities, in place of imposing exemptions or strict requirements. The HKMA acknowledged concerns that HK's approach to Fintech was 'backward' and highlighted that its challenge was to balance the development of Fintech by providing enough flexibility, with the needs of consumers to be protected from the risks presented by new financial products and services.[646] To this end, the HKMA used DLT as an example, expressing the need to scrutinise its potential risks and benefits once it has been deployed more widely on a retail and institutional basis. Overall, the HKMA noted that its responsibility was to consider new developments by first considering their possible disadvantages. Taken together, these considerations reflected an overall cautious approach to the development of the Fintech sector in HK.

In February 2016, the Fintech SG published its report providing the basis for the HK Government's regulatory approach to Fintech. In particular, it was noted that regulation was necessary to develop HK as a Fintech hub by understanding 'how the regulatory framework can better keep up with the fast-evolving technological environment'.[647] Further, the report recommended that the HK Government and financial regulatory authorities adopt a flexible approach in its consideration of whether existing legislation should be amended, or whether new legislation should be promulgated to govern Fintech Offerings in HK.[648] In considering this approach, the report indicated that consumer protection should be of primary importance.[649] The Fintech SG Report also recommended that financial regulatory authorities in HK should assist the Fintech sector to better understand the existing regulatory environment.[650] This led to the establishment of the HKMA's Fintech Facilitation Office and the SFC's Fintech Contact Point and its Fintech Advisory Group, to connect these financial regulatory authorities with the stakeholders in the Fintech sector. With respect to DLT specifically, the report noted that Blockchain Technology could be utilised as an underlying technology to benefit 'a low-cost and transparent transaction infrastructure'.[651] Further, it highlighted HK's potential to become a 'Blockchain hub' based on its pre-existing financial services and technology industries.[652]

In April 2016, the LegCo's Fintech Working Group provided its response to the HK Fintech Steering Group Report and endorsed the majority of the recommendations

645. HKMA, 'How the HKMA Sees FinTech: "Risk-based, Tech-neutral"' (21 March 2016).
646. *See* HK Government, 'Report of the Steering Group on Financial Technologies' (26 February 2016) 7.
647. HK Government, 'Report of the Steering Group on Financial Technologies' (26 February 2016) 38.
648. HK Government, 'Report of the Steering Group on Financial Technologies' (26 February 2016) 8.
649. HK Government, 'Report of the Steering Group on Financial Technologies' (26 February 2016) 20.
650. HK Government, 'Report of the Steering Group on Financial Technologies' (26 February 2016) 10.
651. HK Government, 'Report of the Steering Group on Financial Technologies' (26 February 2016) 26.
652. HK Government, 'Report of the Steering Group on Financial Technologies' (26 February 2016) 26.

made. However, the LegCo's Fintech Working Group expressed the view that 'more substantive measures should be included to update the regulations for Fintech innovations'.[653] To this end, the Fintech Working Group indicated that it conducted a survey on the current state of Fintech in HK in which its regulatory environment was indicated as one of three major obstacles to HK's Fintech competitiveness.[654] In particular, it recommended that existing regulations should be reviewed and updated urgently to serve Fintech Offerings in HK.[655]

At this initial stage, regulatory initiatives undertaken by financial regulatory authorities in HK focussed on educating the Fintech industry and consumers about the potential uses to which DLT could be put. The HKMA led these regulatory initiatives, with its President highlighting DLT's possible use cases in financial services and cementing the HKMA's 'risk-based, technology-neutral' approach.[656] In particular, the HKMA President noted that DLT would have to be assessed to gather an understanding of its potential use before a formal regulatory response could be provided. To this end, on 11 November 2016, the HKMA, in collaboration with the ASTRI, published its first Whitepaper on DLT (HKMA Whitepaper) as the first step in the larger DLT research project to educate the Fintech industry.[657] The HKMA Whitepaper set out an explanation of DLT's key features, its potential benefits and risks, and identified its use cases for the financial services industry. Further, it identified important legal questions to be considered when considering the manner in which DLT Offerings should be regulated in HK. Save for this specific consideration, the HKMA Whitepaper did not make any recommendations regarding the specific manner in which DLT Offerings should be regulated in HK, or which regulatory approach to DLT should be adopted. This position, however, was consistent with the HK Government's approach, as indicated by the Chief Executive that 'the HKMA needs to have a better understanding of these issues before DLT can be adopted for wide application in the banking sector'.[658]

In April 2016, the LegCo PFA published a discussion paper setting out the government's approach to fostering the development of Fintech more pointedly, establishing a four-pronged approach to developing Fintech in HK, none of which included creating a new and bespoke legal and regulatory framework for Fintech Offerings.[659] The LegCo PFA, however, indicated its resolve to continue its engagement with the Fintech industry, and to monitor its dynamic developments.[660] Accordingly,

653. Legislative Council (Information Technology), 'Response to the Report of the Steering Group on Financial Technologies' (April 2016).
654. Legislative Council (Information Technology), 'Response to the Report of the Steering Group on Financial Technologies' (April 2016), paras 3 and 12.
655. Legislative Council (Information Technology), 'Response to the Report of the Steering Group on Financial Technologies' (April 2016) 4, para. 12.
656. HKMA, 'Diversified FinTech' (11 November 2016), https://www.hkma.gov.hk/chi/news-and-media/insight/2016/11/20161111.
657. HKMA and Applied Sciences and Technology Research Institute, 'Whitepaper on Distributed Ledger Technologies' (11 November 2016) 3.
658. HKMA, 'HKMA Fintech Day' (11 November 2016), https://www.hkma.gov.hk/eng/news-and-media/speeches/2016/11/20161111-1.
659. Legislative Council Panel on Financial Affairs (LegCo PFA), 'Strategies and Measures to Develop Financial Technologies' (11 April 2016) 3.
660. LegCo PFA, 'Strategies and Measures to Develop Financial Technologies' (11 April 2016) 5.

the policy approach to developing Fintech in HK veered away from promulgating a new and bespoke legal and regulatory framework for Fintech Offerings towards developing the industry by nurturing new talent and encouraging financial institutions to innovate new Fintech Offerings.[661]

This non-legislative approach was evidenced through the actions and behaviours of several HK Government branches responsible for fostering economic development in HK. For example, the HK Government advised the FSDC to appoint a dedicated senior officer to lead the FSDC Secretariat's objectives bearing in mind, among others, dynamic changes in the Fintech industry.[662] To this end, the FSDC's 2017 mandate included exploring initiatives that maintain HK's competitiveness, including the development of Fintech. This mandate did not, however, support any directives to develop a legal and regulatory framework for DLT Offerings in HK. The FSDC's view on the position of Fintech in HK aligned with the HKMA, in that Fintech development must be balanced with consumer protection.[663]

In 2017, the HK Government accelerated its efforts to develop a regulatory approach to DLT Offerings.[664] In May 2017, the FSDC published two reports aiming to support the development of the Fintech sector in HK.[665] The FSDC's first report focussed on how HK's Fintech sector should be developed and provided an overview of such development in other jurisdictions. Again, it was expressed that financial regulation in HK presents an obstacle to the development of the Fintech sector, for which reform was required. It was emphasised that financial regulation in HK centres on traditional business models and was less suitable for the Fintech sector. Further, the non-standardised approach to regulating financial institutions through institution-specific regulation presented obstacles.[666]

The FSDC's second report focussed specifically on the DLT development in HK. Most notably, this report recommended that the HK Government and the financial services industry should, among others, embrace virtual currency development in HK.[667] In embracing DLT, the HK Government would provide support to the financial

661. LegCo PFA, 'Report of the Panel on Financial Affairs for Submission to the Legislative Council' (29 June 2016) 8-9.
662. LegCo PFA, 'Updated Background Brief on Financial Services Development Council' (3 January 2017) 6.
663. LegCo PFA, 'Updated Background Brief on Financial Services Development Council' (3 January 2017) 8.
664. HKMA, 'Blockchain and Majong' (31 March 2017), https://www.hkma.gov.hk/chi/news-and-media/r-and-m-column/2017/03/column-20170331/.
665. Financial Services Development Council (FSDC), 'FSDC Releases Reports to Promote Further Development of Financial Technology in Hong Kong' (9 May 2017), https://www.fsdc.org.hk/en/media/fsdc-releases-reports-to-promote-further-development-of-financial-technology-in-hong-kong.
666. FSDC, 'The Future of FinTech in Hong Kong' (9 May 2017) 21, https://www.fsdc.org.hk/media/auznib1l/fsdc-paper_fintech_e.pdf.
667. FSDC, 'FSDC Releases Reports to Promote Further Development of Financial Technology in Hong Kong' (9 May 2017) 2, https://www.fsdc.org.hk/en/media/fsdc-releases-reports-to-promote-further-development-of-financial-technology-in-hong-kong.

services industry, and promote HK's openness to harnessing DLT in business. However, the report noted that the financial services industry would play a crucial role in taking the initiative to make use of DLT.[668] Most notably, the report set out a four-pronged approach to develop DLT in HK, which included the recommendation that the HK Government adapt existing legislative and regulatory frameworks to bring virtual currencies within their remit.[669]

In October 2017, the HKMA, in collaboration with the ASTRI, published its second Whitepaper on DLT, providing a pragmatic perspective on the development of DLT in HK (HKMA Whitepaper 2.0).[670] The whitepaper set out several core principles which could be applied to DLT control measures, governance, and security management. Further, it provided a discussion on the common compliance and legal obstacles associated with DLT and stipulated a set of recommendations which could potentially overcome those obstacles.[671] In alignment with its conservative approach, the HKMA Whitepaper 2.0 indicated that no specific regulatory regime for DLT had been developed in HK because of its ever-evolving nature, and the lack of a complete comprehension of its associated risks.[672] Nevertheless, the HKMA Whitepaper 2.0 specified that DLT Offerings could potentially trigger the application of existing legal and regulatory requirements based on its compliance risks and governance controls.[673] To this end, the HKMA Whitepaper 2.0 foreshadowed the potential regulatory regime for DLT Offerings in HK. However, the whitepaper focussed largely on providing a regulatory response to DLT use through developmental initiatives such as proof-of-concept projects in HK and exploring the use of DLT for CBDCs. However, at the HKMA's inaugural Fintech Day, it was noted that the HKMA would collaborate with the Fintech sector to formulate practical guidelines based on the HKMA Whitepaper 2.0's recommendations.[674]

The LegCo PFA was largely responsible for directing the HK Government's Fintech policy initiatives, predominantly in the form of reports setting out measures and strategies to develop Fintech and its annual policy addresses. This policy approach was informing of the work undertaken by financial regulatory authorities in HK in developing their regulatory responses to virtual currencies in HK. In particular, the HK Government's enthusiasm to promulgate new and bespoke laws and regulations for Fintech Offerings was largely inhibited by its view that the existing regulatory framework in HK could be applied to Fintech firms. The HK Government also

668. FSDC, 'Hong Kong: Building Trust using Distributed Ledger Technologies' (9 May 2017) 2.
669. FSDC, 'Hong Kong: Building Trust using Distributed Ledger Technologies' (9 May 2017) 6.
670. HKMA and Applied Sciences and Technology Research Institute, 'Whitepaper 2.0 on Distributed Ledger Technology' (25 October 2017) 6.
671. HKMA and Applied Sciences and Technology Research Institute, 'Whitepaper 2.0 on Distributed Ledger Technology' (25 October 2017) 26 and 42.
672. HKMA and Applied Sciences and Technology Research Institute, 'Whitepaper 2.0 on Distributed Ledger Technology' (25 October 2017) 26.
673. HKMA and Applied Sciences and Technology Research Institute, 'Whitepaper 2.0 on Distributed Ledger Technology' (25 October 2017) 26 and 30.
674. HKMA, 'A New Era of Smart Banking: Step Forward' (25 October 2017), https://www.hkma.gov.hk/chi/news-and-media/insight/2017/10/20171025#.

impressed that the existing regulatory framework was sufficient to protect consumers and firms where they formed the targets of Fintech Offerings.[675] The non-legislative approach proposed by the HK Government to the regulation of DLT Offerings did not go without opposition. Some members of the LegCo PFA expressed that the HK Government should implement a bespoke regulatory framework and should abstain from applying its 'technology neutral' principle nor over-regulate.[676] Further, it was argued that HK had fallen behind in its development of Fintech in comparison to other jurisdictions, whether as a result of the inadequacy of the existing regulatory regime, or the inability of financial regulatory authorities to cope with Fintech sector development in HK.[677] It was also suggested that a working group be established to regularly review and harmonise legal and regulatory rules governing Fintech Offerings in HK, including guidelines issued by financial regulatory authorities.[678]

During 2018, additional policy initiatives aimed to grow the Fintech sector were undertaken by the HKMA, in particular the further development of its Fintech Supervisory Sandbox and Chatroom, and the introduction of virtual banking through the Guideline on Authorisation of Virtual Banks.[679] A Fintech Career Accelerator Scheme 2.0 was also launched to grow the Fintech talent network in HK[680] Additional work was carried out on the Banking Made Easy Task Force to identify and simplify legal and regulatory rules which may act as an obstacle to technological progress. The HKMA also entered into a Fintech cooperation agreement with the Monetary Authority of Singapore to develop a DLT interface to act as a connector for the domestic trade finance platforms of the two cities.[681]

In November 2018, the SFC set out a conceptual framework for the possible regulation of virtual asset trading platforms principally through the application of regulatory rules comparable to those which apply to licensed automated trading services.[682] This potential regulation was spurred on by international developments, in addition to concerns regarding investor protection represented through the use of such platforms. The SFC indicated that virtual asset trading platforms eager to comply with high levels of standards and practices would set them apart from their peers operating outside the SFC's regulatory perimeter. Accordingly, a study of a possible conceptual framework was undertaken with those virtual asset trading platforms through the SFC's regulatory sandbox.

675. LegCo PFA, 'Report of the Panel on Financial Affairs for Submission to the Legislative Council' (29 June 2016) 8.
676. LegCo PFA, 'Report of the Panel on Financial Affairs for Submission to the Legislative Council' (29 June 2016) 3.
677. LegCo PFA, 'Report of the Panel on Financial Affairs for Submission to the Legislative Council' (29 June 2016) 3-4.
678. LegCo PFA, 'Report of the Panel on Financial Affairs for Submission to the Legislative Council' (29 June 2016) 4.
679. HKMA, 'Briefing to the Legislative Council Panel on Financial Affairs' (5 February 2018) 58.
680. HKMA, 'Briefing to the Legislative Council Panel on Financial Affairs' (15 May 2018) 69.
681. HKMA, 'Briefing to the Legislative Council Panel on Financial Affairs' (5 February 2018) 67.
682. SFC, 'Statement on the Regulatory Framework for Virtual Asset Portfolio Managers, Fund Distributors, and Trading Platform Operators' (1 November 2018) 4.

4.1.2.2 *Discussion*

The actions and behaviours considered above are examined below through an identification of the regulatory approach adopted by the HK Government, together with the competition policy considerations which formed part of the approach adopted.

4.1.2.2.1 Regulatory Approach

The actions and behaviours directed by the HK Government during the time period 2015-2018 evidenced a cautious regulatory response to the governance of Fintech and DLT Offerings in HK. In particular, the HK Government instituted a fact-finding enquiry to better appraise itself, and the Fintech industry, of the uses to which DLT could be put, together with its risks and benefits. The HK Government also indicated that existing regulatory frameworks could be appropriately applied to Fintech firms and were sufficient to protect consumers, in line with its 'risk-based and technology-neutral' principle. The government also indicated that HK could be developed into a 'Blockchain hub' but indicated that its regulatory environment could impede its Fintech sector's competitiveness.

4.1.2.2.2 Underlying Principles

Several key factors influenced the government's cautious regulatory response to the governance of Fintech and DLT Offerings. These key themes are important as they highlight the HK Government's: (i) actions and behaviours in the form of regulatory and policy initiatives which drove the development of Fintech in HK; (ii) underlying rationale for adopting a cautious approach to formulating a regulatory response to the governance of Fintech and DLT Offerings in HK; and (iii) consideration of competition policy in formulating its regulatory response. The key factors underlining this regulatory approach include:

> *Fact-finding enquiry.* The HK Government approached the development of Fintech through the guise of a fact-finding enquiry, directed primarily through a two-prong approach. First, through regulatory and policy initiatives, the HK Government directed to educate the Fintech sector of DLT's principal features and uses. This is reflected clearly through the work of the HKMA, including its public addresses and published whitepapers. Second, through its own investigation, the HK Government educated itself on DLT 'basics', including its risks, benefits and use cases for the financial services industry. From a policy perspective, the government also investigated the approaches to Fintech and DLT adopted by competing jurisdictions.
>
> *Risk-based and technology-neutral.* The HKMA indicated that it adopted a 'risk-based and technology-neutral' approach to new products and services created using emerging technologies. This approach was described as implementing regulatory frameworks based on the specific risks presented by

undertaking financial services, in place of enforcing exemptions or strict requirements to allow new technologies to be used in providing those financial services. This approach is reflected largely by the HKMA's mandate to protect customers and is represented by its warning to customers regarding Bitcoin trading, as opposed to banning such trading altogether. To this end, the HKMA indicated it would always first consider the disadvantages of new products and services.

Balancing consumer protection and Fintech development. The HK Government highlighted the challenging task of having to balance the development of Fintech by providing enough flexibility, with the needs of consumers to be protected from the risks presented by new financial products and services. This balancing exercise formed the hallmark feature of the government's regulatory approach to the governance of Fintech and DLT Offerings, underscored wholly by its 'risk-based and technology-neutral' principle. As such, DLT was represented as a case study illustrating the government's approach in carefully scrutinising the advantages and risks of the DLT Offerings once employed in the retail and institutional finance sectors.

Regulatory and policy initiatives. The HK Government deployed several regulatory and policy initiatives to develop the Fintech sector. In particular, the HKMA and LegCo PFA continued their engagement with the Fintech industry, in addition to implementing initiatives aimed at fostering new talent and encouraging financial institutions to innovate new Fintech Offerings. Further, the HKMA developed its Fintech Supervisory Sandbox and Chatroom and introduced virtual banking through the Guideline on Authorisation of Virtual Banks.[683] A Fintech Career Accelerator Scheme 2.0 was also launched to grow the Fintech talent network in HK, in addition to working on the Banking Made Easy Task Force.

Competition policy. The HK Government considered competition policy concerns in the formulation of its regulatory approach to Fintech, and specifically to DLT. It was noted that HK had the potential to develop into a 'Blockchain hub' based on its existing financial services and technology industries. It was also noted that by embracing the use of DLT, the government would provide the necessary support to the financial services industry, which would in turn promote HK's openness to harness the use of DLT in business. Most significantly, it was indicated that HK's regulatory environment significantly impeded the competitiveness of HK's Fintech sector and that existing regulations needed to be reviewed and updated, to provide regulatory certainty.

Non-legislative intervention. The HK Government, in place of formulating a bespoke regulatory regime to govern DLT Offerings, indicated that existing regulatory frameworks could be applied to Fintech firms, and were sufficient to protect consumers where they formed the targets of Fintech Offerings. This non-legislative approach was undertaken despite opposition thereto in the

683. HKMA, 'Briefing to the Legislative Council Panel on Financial Affairs' (5 February 2018) 53.

government and the Fintech industry. Several governmental bodies either recommended that the government adapt existing legislative and regulatory frameworks to bring virtual currencies within its remit or develop a bespoke regulatory regime for Fintech Offerings, including virtual currencies.

4.1.3 Output: 2017-2019

The analysis below sets out the actions and behaviours of the HK Government directed to issuing regulatory rules and guidance which had the effect of formalising the regulations governing DLT Offerings.

4.1.3.1 Regulatory Rules

4.1.3.1.1 Initial Coin and STOs

On 5 September 2017, the SFC issued its Statement on ICOs which was catalysed by the increased use in HK and elsewhere of ICOs as an alternative funding mechanism.[684] The statement indicated that ICOs, subject to the circumstances of each case, may fall within the regulatory perimeter of the SFC and thus be subject to the securities laws of HK should digital tokens be offered or sold as 'securities', as defined in the SFO. Ordinarily, ICOs encompass digital tokens described as 'virtual commodities', which are not in themselves a 'security'. However, the SFC indicated that at the time ICOs incorporated digital tokens which have terms and features which may characterise them as securities, debentures, or interests in CIS. 'Securities' are defined broadly by the SFO to include shares, debentures, and interests in CIS.[685] According to the SFC, digital tokens in an ICO which exemplify equity or ownership interests in a firm may be characterised as 'shares'. For example, digital tokens conferring token holders with shareholders' rights, including the right to receive dividends. Digital tokens used to create or acknowledge a debt or liability owed by the issuer may be characterised as a 'debenture'.[686] For example, digital tokens conferring token holders repayment of the principal investment on a fixed date or upon redemption, including interest. Token proceeds invested and managed collectively by an ICO operator enabling token holders to participate in a share of returns may be characterised as a CIS.[687]

Accordingly, dealing in or advising on digital tokens, as part of an ICO, which fall into the SFO's definition of securities, or managing or marketing a fund investing in those digital tokens, may constitute a regulated activity as per Part 1 of Schedule 5 of the SFO. Parties engaged in these regulated activities must be licensed by or registered with the SFC if the relevant business activities are directed to targeting the HK public,

684. SFC, 'Statement on Initial Coin Offerings' (5 September 2017), https://www.sfc.hk/en/News-and-announcements/Policy-statements-and-announcements/Statement-on-initial-coin-offerings.
685. Cap 571 Securities and Futures Ordinance, s. 1, pt I, Sch. 1.
686. Cap 571 Securities and Futures Ordinance, s. 1, pt I, Sch. 1.
687. Cap 571 Securities and Futures Ordinance, s. 1, pt I, Sch. 1.

and they would be required to comply with the necessary SFC licensing and conduct regulatory rules. The SFC's regulatory framework may also apply to cryptocurrency exchanges; parties selling and purchasing digital tokens on cryptocurrency exchanges; and ICOs encompassing offers to the HK public to acquire securities or to participate in a CIS.[688]

On 28 March 2019, the SFC issued a statement clarifying its position on STOs.[689] These offerings are ordinarily structured with features similar to traditional security offerings, and encompass security tokens, offered to professional investors only, as digital representations of asset ownership or economic rights, using DLT. According to the SFC, security tokens are likely to qualify as securities, as defined in the SFO, which fall within the SFC's regulatory perimeter, and which are subject to the security laws of HK. Distributing and marketing STOs involving security tokens characterised as securities may constitute a regulated activity as per Part 1 of Schedule 5 of the SFO for which a licence is required, or registration for a Type 1 regulated activity (dealing in securities). The SFC indicated that intermediaries engaged in distributing, and marketing security tokens must comply with all necessary SFC licensing and conduct regulatory rules. This includes, in particular, the Code of Conduct for Persons Licensed by or Registered with the SFC COC suitability (reasonable advice) requirement,[690] supplemented by the suitability frequently asked questions.[691] Additional investor protection measures would also apply based on security tokens qualifying as 'complex products' under the Guidelines on Online Distribution and Advisory Platforms and the SFC COC.[692] Intermediaries must also comply with the Circular to Intermediaries on the Distribution of Virtual Asset Funds relating to: (i) selling restrictions; (ii) due diligence; and (iii) information for clients.

4.1.3.1.2 Fund Distribution

On 1 November 2018, the SFC published a circular reminding intermediaries of the legal and regulatory rules applicable to the distribution of virtual asset funds under their management and the practices and standards expected by the SFC relating thereto.[693] This was primarily directed at intermediaries licensed or registered for Type 1 regulated activity (dealing in securities) and Type 9 regulated activity (asset management) and engaged in the distribution of virtual assets funds under their

688. Cap 571 Securities and Futures Ordinance, pt IV.
689. SFC, 'Statement on Security Token Offerings' (28 March 2019), https://www.sfc.hk/en/News-and-announcements/Policy-statements-and-announcements/Statement-on-Security-Token-Offerings.
690. SFC, 'Code of Conduct for Persons Licensed by or Registered with the Securities and Futures Commission' (September 2020) 11, para. 5.2.
691. SFC, 'Frequently Asked Questions on Triggering of Suitability Obligations', https://www.sfc.hk/en/faqs/intermediaries/supervision/Triggering-of-Suitability-Obligations/Triggering-of-Suitability-Obligations.
692. SFC, 'Code of Conduct for Persons Licensed by or Registered with the Securities and Futures Commission' (September 2020) 12, para. 5.5; and SFC, 'Guidelines on Online Distribution and Advisory Platforms' (July 2019).
693. SFC, 'Circular to Intermediaries: Distribution of Virtual Asset Funds' (1 November 2018).

management, including carrying on a business in the distribution of interests in a CIS. The SFC highlighted that these licensing or registration requirements would apply whether or not the underlying virtual assets constitute securities or futures contracts under the SFO. Accordingly, intermediaries who distribute virtual asset funds, whether authorised by the SFC or not, must comply with the suitability (reasonable advice) requirement,[694] supplemented by the suitability frequently asked questions.[695] They must also comply with the complex product requirements under the Guidelines on Online Distribution and Advisory Platforms and paragraph 5.5 of the SFC COC.[696] A set of additional requirements apply to intermediaries engaged in the distribution of virtual asset funds not authorised by the SFC, but who have: (i) an indicated investment aim to invest in virtual assets (or intend to invest); or (ii) have invested more than 10% of their GAV in virtual assets directly, or indirectly. Some of the key features of these additional requirements relate to selling restrictions and concentration assessments, due diligence on virtual asset funds not authorised by the SFC, and providing specific information to clients.

4.1.3.1.3 Futures Contracts and Investment Products

On 11 December 2017, the SFC issued a circular reminding intermediaries of the legal and regulatory rules applicable to providing financial services relating to Bitcoin futures contracts and cryptocurrency-related investment products.[697] This circular was issued by the SFC in its consideration of the introduction of the first Bitcoin Futures by regulated US futures and commodities exchanges in December 2017. This refers, in particular, to the launch of the Bitcoin exchange-trade fund BITO, the first to be approved by the SEC, traded on Chicago Mercantile Exchange.[698] Once launched, the SFC noted that investors in HK would be able to trade in Bitcoin Futures through intermediaries holding membership with these exchanges. Futures contracts are defined by the SFO as including 'a contract or an option on a contract made under the rules or conventions of a futures market'.[699] According to the SFC, Bitcoin Futures have features characteristic of conventional futures contracts. As such, Bitcoin Futures traded subject to the rules of and trading on regulated exchanges are regarded as futures contracts within the remit of the SFO. This position applies despite the assets

694. SFC, 'Code of Conduct for Persons Licensed by or Registered with the Securities and Futures Commission' (September 2020) 11, para. 5.2.
695. SFC, 'Frequently Asked Questions on Triggering of Suitability Obligations', https://www.sfc.hk/en/faqs/intermediaries/supervision/Triggering-of-Suitability-Obligations/Triggering-of-Suitability-Obligations.
696. SFC, 'Code of Conduct for Persons Licensed by or Registered with the Securities and Futures Commission' (September 2020) 12, para. 5.5; and SFC, 'Guidelines on Online Distribution and Advisory Platforms' (July 2019).
697. SFC, 'Circular to Licensed Corporations and Registered Institutions on Bitcoin Futures Contracts and Cryptocurrency-Related Investment Products' (11 December 2017).
698. Karamfil Todorov, 'Launch of the First US Bitcoin ETF: Mechanics, Impact and Risks' (*Bank for International Settlements*, 6 December 2017), https://www.bis.org/publ/qtrpdf/r_qt2112t.htm.
699. Cap 571 Securities and Futures Ordinance, s. 1, pt I, Sch. 1.

underlying Bitcoin Future falling outside the SFC's regulatory remit. Accordingly, dealing in Bitcoin Futures as a business activity, including relaying or routing Bitcoin Futures orders, may constitute a regulated activity as per Part 1 of Schedule 5 of the SFO for which a licence for Type 2 (dealing in futures) regulated activity is required.

The SFC also indicated that marketing a fund investing in Bitcoin Futures may constitute a regulated activity as per Part 1 of Schedule 5 of the SFO for which a licence for Type 1 regulated activity (dealing in securities) is required. In addition, managing a fund investing in or providing advisory services relating to Bitcoin Futures may also comprise a regulated activity for which a licence for Type 9 regulated activity (asset management) or Type 5 regulated activity (advising on futures contracts) respectively, is required. Finally, parties advising on, dealing in, or managing cryptocurrency-related investment products must comply with all necessary SFC licensing and conduct regulatory rules should these products qualify as securities within the remit of the SFO, including CFDs,[700] options and swaps. In particular, intermediaries and parties providing regulated financial services in relation to cryptocurrency-related investment products must comply with SFC COC KYC requirements governing investor characterisation;[701] suitability (reasonable advice);[702] and derivatives products.[703] Further, cryptocurrency exchanges offering such products must comply with specific requirements related to automated trading services and to recognised exchange companies set out in Part III of the SFO. Finally, the SFC's licensing or registration requirements may apply where parties provide financial services in relation to cryptocurrency-related products which constitute an invitation to the HK public to purchase securities or structured products or to participate in a CIS as per the SFO.

Despite its specific intention to *remind* parties of the legal and regulatory rules applicable to providing financial services relating to Bitcoin Futures Contracts and cryptocurrency-related investment products, the circular instead set outs out the SFC's view on the application of its existing regulatory framework to these products, with scant reference to the rules applicable to such parties. Its primary concern, however, is represented in the form of warning the public of the inherent risks in investing in such products. Bearing this in mind, on 6 November 2019, the SFC issued an additional warning to investors concerning the risks inherent in purchasing virtual asset (e.g., Bitcoin) futures contracts, with the exception of those traded on US exchanges regulated by the Commodity Futures Trading Commission and authorised by the SFC.[704] These risks, associated with virtual assets futures contracts, relate primarily to their highly leveraged nature and the volatile nature of the virtual asset prices underlying these future contracts. Further, the SFC stated that these complex products

700. Authorised under Cap 148 Gambling Ordinance.
701. SFC, 'Code of Conduct for Persons Licensed by or Registered with the Securities and Futures Commission' (September 2020) 10, para. 5.1A.
702. SFC, 'Code of Conduct for Persons Licensed by or Registered with the Securities and Futures Commission' (September 2020) 11, para. 5.2.
703. SFC, 'Code of Conduct for Persons Licensed by or Registered with the Securities and Futures Commission' (September 2020) 11, para. 5.3.
704. SFC, 'SFC Issues Warning on Virtual Asset Futures Contracts' (6 November 2019).

and their inherent risks may even be challenging for the average investor to comprehend. As such, reference is made to other jurisdictions contemplating a ban on the sale of virtual assets futures contracts to retail investors. Despite no such ban being in place in HK or being contemplated, the SFC indicated that it is unlikely to license or authorise any parties to conduct such business in HK bearing in mind their risk nature, and to protect the public therefrom.[705]

4.1.3.1.4 Portfolio Management

On 1 November 2018, the SFC issued a statement providing guidance on the application of the existing regulatory framework to virtual asset portfolio managers,[706] fund distributors, and trading platform operators.[707] This guidance was prompted by increased investor interest in virtual assets and unlicensed trading platforms operating in HK. The SFC noted that while virtual assets do not currently represent a significant threat to financial stability, there appears to be consensus among financial regulatory authorities that they do represent significant threats to investor protection. This is represented predominantly through increased investment in virtual asset portfolios managed by unregulated portfolio managers or via unregulated trading platforms to which the protections proffered by the SFO do not apply. Bearing in mind this state of affairs, the SFO formulated an approach to incorporate unregulated virtual asset portfolio management activities into its regulatory perimeter. The statement therefore pronounces that firms who distribute a fund under its management which invests solely in virtual assets not encompassing securities or futures contracts, require a licence for Type 1 regulated activity (dealing in securities). Further, firms who manage a fund of funds, irrespective of whether each fund invests solely or partially in virtual assets not encompassing securities or futures contracts, require a licence for Type 9 regulated activity (asset management). As such, these firms will be subject to the SFC's supervisory oversight and licensing conditions.

All licensed portfolio managers who intend to invest in virtual assets must therefore comply with the same set of regulatory rules. This includes portfolio managers managing portfolios which invest solely or partially in virtual assets which constitute securities or futures contracts. The rationale for this approach is based on the SFC's view that 'virtual assets, as an asset class, have similar features and risk characteristics, whether or not they amount to "securities" or "futures contracts"'.[708] To this end, the SFO developed a set of principles-based terms and conditions encompassing the essential regulatory rules to be adhered to by virtual asset portfolio managers, imposed by way of licensing conditions, subject to amendments and

705. SFC, 'SFC Issues Warning on Virtual Asset Futures Contracts' (6 November 2019).
706. This includes portfolio managers who manage CIS per SFC, 'Regulatory Standards for Licenced Corporations Managing Virtual Asset Portfolio' (1 November 2018) 1.
707. SFC, 'Statement on the Regulatory Framework for Virtual Asset Portfolio Managers, Fund Distributors, and Trading Platform Operators' (1 November 2018).
708. SFC, 'Regulatory Standards for Licenced Corporations Managing Virtual Asset Portfolio' (1 November 2018).

elaborations based on the relevant business model.[709] As such, on 1 November 2018, the SFC published its Regulatory Standards for Licensed Corporations Managing Virtual Asset Portfolio. These standards, reflected as licensing conditions, apply to licensed firms who manage (or plan to manage) portfolios with: (i) an indicated investment aim to invest in virtual assets; and (ii) an intention to invest 10% or more of the portfolio's GAV in virtual assets (together the '*de minimis* threshold'). Overall, these standards primarily concern licensed firms': (i) management of portfolios (or portions thereof) investing in virtual assets (subject to de minimis threshold); and (ii) financial resources should they plan to hold virtual assets not encompassing securities or futures contracts on behalf of portfolios which they manage.[710]

The SFC provided its remarks on the licensing process, including a requirement imposed on licensed applicants and licensed firms to notify the SFC if they presently manage or plan to manage portfolios investing in virtual assets.[711] Once notified, the SFC will discuss the firm's proposed or present business activities, and will thereafter issue a set of bespoke terms and conditions reasonable and appropriate for the firm's business model. Once a firm has agreed to these bespoke terms and conditions, they will be imposed as licensing conditions. A firm's non-agreement with the proposed terms and conditions will result in the SFC rejecting its licence application. Further, a licensed firm's non-agreement with the proposed terms and conditions will be required to unwind its existing virtual asset portfolio. The SFC provided a high-level summary of these standard terms and conditions in its document published on 1 November 2018[712] including those relating to liquid capital;[713] portfolio evaluation;[714] risk management;[715] and the safeguarding of assets.[716] However, in October 2019, the SFC published a complete set of proforma terms and conditions (Proforma T&Cs) fleshing out its previously provided high-level summary thereof.[717] In particular, the Proforma T&Cs defined 'virtual assets' quite broadly to include digital embodiments of value represented as digital tokens, other crypto-assets, virtual commodities or other assets

709. SFC, 'Regulatory Standards for Licenced Corporations Managing Virtual Asset Portfolio' (1 November 2018).
710. SFC, 'Regulatory Standards for Licenced Corporations Managing Virtual Asset Portfolio' (1 November 2018) 2.
711. SFC, 'Statement on the Regulatory Framework for Virtual Asset Portfolio Managers, Fund Distributors, and Trading Platform Operators' (1 November 2018) 3. Also *see* SFC, 'Circular to Intermediaries on Compliance with Notification Requirements' (1 June 2018).
712. SFC, 'Regulatory Standards for Licenced Corporations Managing Virtual Asset Portfolio' (1 November 2018).
713. SFC, 'Regulatory Standards for Licenced Corporations Managing Virtual Asset Portfolio' (1 November 2018) 6.
714. SFC, 'Regulatory Standards for Licenced Corporations Managing Virtual Asset Portfolio' (1 November 2018) 4.
715. SFC, 'Regulatory Standards for Licenced Corporations Managing Virtual Asset Portfolio' (1 November 2018) 5.
716. Securities and Futures Commission, 'Regulatory Standards for Licenced Corporations Managing Virtual Asset Portfolio' (1 November 2018) 3.
717. SFC, 'Proforma Terms and Conditions for Licensed Corporations Which Manage Portfolios Which Invest in Virtual Assets' (October 2019) 3.

similarly natured, irrespective of whether they fall within the definition of securities or futures contracts per the SFO.[718]

At the outset, the Proforma T&Cs set out eight General Principles which virtual asset fund managers are required to comply with in their management of a virtual asset fund. These principles include acting honestly and fairly, and in the best interests of their clients; acting with due care and diligence; avoiding conflicts of interests; properly accounting for and safeguarding fund assets; and providing clear and timely disclosures to investors. Overall, these general principles reflect generally well-established conduct requirements expected of firms in the financial services industry.[719] The most impactful features of the Proforma T&Cs include standards relating to: (i) organisation and management; (ii) virtual asset fund management; (iii) custody; (iv) operations; (v) dealing with funds and fund investors; and (vi) fees and expenses.

4.1.3.1.5 Trading Platforms

On 6 November 2019, the SFC published its position paper introducing a new opt-in regulatory framework for virtual asset trading platforms consisting of comprehensive regulatory standards comparable to those applicable to licensed automated trading services and securities brokers.[720] The SFC clarified that the trading of non-security virtual assets falls outside its regulatory perimeter, and accordingly the regulatory standards only apply to firms operating platforms enabling clients to trade security virtual assets. Virtual asset trading platforms may therefore choose to remain unregulated by operating platforms trading non-security virtual assets only. Therefore, clients should be able to easily draw a distinction between regulated and unregulated virtual asset trading platforms. Accordingly, a centralised online trading platform offering at least one security token on its platform will require a licence for Type 1 regulated activity (dealing in securities) or Type 7 regulated activity (providing automated trading services).[721] The SFC indicated that it would only consider licence applications from centralised online trading platforms providing virtual asset trading, clearing and settlement services, and who keep control of their investors' assets.[722] As such, it would not accept licence applications from trading platforms: (i) offering a direct P2P marketplace for executing transactions by investors who keep control of their assets; and (ii) trading virtual assets for clients, but who do not provide any automated trading services.[723]

718. SFC, 'Proforma Terms and Conditions for Licensed Corporations Which Manage Portfolios Which Invest in Virtual Assets' (October 2019) 4.
719. SFC, 'Proforma Terms and Conditions for Licensed Corporations Which Manage Portfolios Which Invest in Virtual Assets' (October 2019) 6.
720. SFC, 'Position Paper: Regulation of Virtual Asset Trading Platforms' (6 November 2019).
721. SFC, 'Position Paper: Regulation of Virtual Asset Trading Platforms' (6 November 2019), para. 32.
722. SFC, 'Position Paper: Regulation of Virtual Asset Trading Platforms' (6 November 2019), para. 33.
723. SFC, 'Position Paper: Regulation of Virtual Asset Trading Platforms' (6 November 2019), para. 33.

Under the SFC's supervision, a licensed trading platform's conduct of virtual asset trading activities, core fitness and properness,[724] and its infrastructure will be considered in its entirety. The SFO is empowered to consider the 'state of affairs' of any other business of a licensed firm[725] and to inspect any documents concerning transactions affecting a licensed firm's business.[726] Its supervisory remit will cover both security and non-security virtual asset trading, as they are likely to be interconnected, and 'form part and parcel of an integrated business'.[727] As such, a licensed trading platform's non-security virtual asset trading activities, even where they constitute an insignificant part of the business, will be considered by the SFC as part of its initial and ongoing fitness and properness assessments. Licensed trading platforms are required to structure all virtual asset trading activities undertaken by its group of companies conducted in or marketed to investors in HK under a single corporate entity licensed by the SFC.[728] This includes both on and off-platform activities, and any activities ancillary to trading services provided, but excludes the distribution of virtual asset funds, management of virtual asset portfolios, and all activities unrelated to virtual asset trading. The overall purpose of this arrangement should ensure that the SFC is able to exercise robust supervisory oversight of the licensed trading platform's virtual asset business activities, acting to reduce ambiguity regarding which parts of the trading platform's business fall within the SFC's licensing and supervisory remit.

Upon granting a licence, the SFC will impose licensing conditions relevant to the specific risks associated with a trading platform's business, including: (i) only engage professional investors; (ii) compliance with the Terms and Conditions for Virtual Asset Trading Platform Operators (Virtual Asset Trading Platform T&Cs); (iii) SFC's prior written approval for any material changes to services or activities, and new or incidental services offered; (iv) SFC's prior written approval for products added to a trading platform; (v) monthly reports to the SFC covering business activities; and (vi) annual report by an independent professional firm confirming all licensing conditions and applicable legal and regulatory requirements are satisfied.[729] The most impactful features of the Virtual Asset Trading Platform T&Cs include requirements relating to: (i) safe custody of assets; (ii) KYC and AML/CTF; (iii) prevention of market manipulative and abusive activities; (iv) virtual assets for trading; and (v) risk management.

4.1.3.2 Discussion

The actions and behaviours considered above are examined below through the guise of the salient regulatory features instituted by the HK Government.

724. Cap 571 Securities and Futures Ordinance, s. 116.
725. Cap 571 Securities and Futures Ordinance, s. 129.
726. Cap 571 Securities and Futures Ordinance, s. 180.
727. SFC, 'Position Paper: Regulation of Virtual Asset Trading Platforms' (6 November 2019), para. 34.
728. SFC, 'Position Paper: Regulation of Virtual Asset Trading Platforms' (6 November 2019), para. 39.
729. Cap 571 Securities and Futures Ordinance, s. 116(6).

4.1.3.2.1 *Regulatory Framework*

An analysis of the actions and behaviours directed by the HK Government during the time period 2017-2019 evidenced the development of a regulatory framework for DLT Offerings, specifically for virtual assets, as underlined by the provisions of the SFO and the AML Ordinance (Cap 615) through the supervision of the SFC and the HKMA.[730] The HK Government adopted the specific term 'virtual assets', which has been defined broadly under the provisions of the SFO. Accordingly, HK has adopted a non-legislative approach, opting to apply its existing regulatory framework to virtual asset activities. A firm undertaking activities related to virtual assets which fall within the definition of securities under the SFO may require a licence to conduct those activities.

4.1.3.2.2 *Central Components*

Several factors influenced the development of the regulatory framework governing DLT Offerings. These central components are crucial as they highlight: (i) the severity or laxity of the regulatory rules and guidance introduced by the HK Government; and (ii) whether the actions and behaviours directed towards developing a regulatory framework for DLT Offerings were consistent with the regulatory approach established in the Process analysis, which included competition policy considerations. The central components underlining the development of the regulatory framework governing DLT Offerings include:

> *Regulatory remit*. The regulatory framework developed for the governance of DLT Offerings, specifically virtual assets, included a number of regulatory activities, for which a licence is required. These regulated activities include dealing in securities, advising on securities, dealing in futures, advising on futures, asset management, and providing automated trading services. Accordingly, the regulatory framework includes within its remit a broad range of virtual asset activities relating to ICOs, STOs, fund distribution of virtual funds, futures contracts and investment products, virtual asset portfolio management and virtual asset trading platforms. The SFC's regulatory remit is quite broad but limited to regulated activities involving virtual assets which constitute 'securities' under the SFO.
>
> *Regulatory rules*. The regulatory framework developed for the governance of DLT Offerings, specifically virtual assets, is underlined by a risk-based approach and an extension of regulatory protections to consumers, on the basis of the SFC's principle of 'same business, same risks, same rules'. According to this principle, the same regulatory standards which apply to brokers and other automated trading services, apply to virtual currency activities, ensuring a level playing field for all operations. The regulatory rules impose sweeping provisions to the business of firms undertaking virtual asset activities including requirements relating to organisation and management,

730. Cap 615 Anti-Money Laundering and Counter Terrorist Finance Ordinance.

safe custody of assets, operations marketing activities, KYC, risk management and conflicts of interests.

AML rules. The regulatory framework developed for the governance of DLT Offerings, specifically virtual assets, includes AML rules to be adhered to by firms undertaking virtual currency activities. In particular, the AML requirements applicable to licensed firms, such as the Guideline on AML and Counter-Financing of Terrorism, were extended to virtual asset portfolio managers and trading platforms. Notably, virtual asset fund managers must comply with the specified AML requirements, even if the funds they manage do not constitute securities or futures contracts per the SFO. The HK Government indicated that it was one of the first international financial centres to comprehensively regulate virtual asset trading platforms to address AML and consumer protection concerns.

Flexibility. The regulatory framework developed for the governance of DLT Offerings, specifically virtual assets, is characterised by a measure of flexibility regarding the application of the SFC's regulatory rules. This is evidenced by the SFC's voluntary opt-in regime for virtual asset trading platforms trading at least one virtual asset constituting a security under the SFO. This opt-in regime did not apply to virtual asset trading platforms trading non-security virtual assets. In addition, the terms and conditions developed by the SFC for firms undertaking virtual asset activities were flexible and bespoke, based on the requirements of the specific firm. Overall, this flexibility is illustrative of the HK Government's cautious regulatory approach to its governance of DLT Offerings.

4.1.3.2.3 Regulatory Approach

The analysis of actions and behaviours directed by the HK Government during the time period 2017-2019 evidenced a cautious approach to the regulation of DLT Offerings, specifically virtual assets, consistent with the regulatory approach established in the Process analysis. In particular, the HK Government's cautious regulatory approach, underlined by its non-legislative approach, was reflected by the application of its 'same business, same risks, same rules' evidenced by the extension of its existing regulatory framework to firms conducting virtual asset activities. Further, its staged regulatory approach was highlighted through its establishment of regulatory initiatives underscored by a measure of flexibility, such as the opt-in regime for virtual asset trading platforms.

Applying the cautious regulatory approach to the regulatory framework developed for DLT Offerings, also furthered the HK Government's fact-finding enquiry, allowing the government to provide the necessary regulatory protections for consumers in real time. It also permitted the HK Government to observe the ongoing regulatory environment for virtual asset activities and to gain the necessary supervisory experience to assist it with developing a future strategy to regulate virtual asset activities. Further, the regulatory framework developed considered competition policy concerns, with the SFC indicating that HK was one of the first jurisdictions to implement a comprehensive regulatory framework for virtual asset trading platforms.

4.1.4 Feedback 2019-2022

The analysis below sets out the actions and behaviours of the HK Government directed at modifying the initial regulatory response governing DLT Offerings.

4.1.4.1 Trading Platforms

In November 2020, the SFC announced the HK Government's proposed licensing regime under the AML Ordinance for virtual asset trading platforms trading any type of cryptoasset, including those not constituting securities under the SFO.[731] The SFC indicated that the 'opt-in' regime, formulated by the regulatory framework established for virtual asset trading platforms in November 2019, represented a significant limitation.[732] Under this approach, trading platforms were able to operate outside the SFC's regulatory perimeter simply by trading cryptoassets not constituting securities as defined by the SFO. With the new licensing regime, however, trading platforms trading any type of cryptoasset operating in HK, or targeting HK investors, would need to be licensed by the SFC.[733] The proposed licensing regime will trigger the SFC's regulatory functions through its assessment of licence applications, ensuring compliance with relevant regulatory rules and their enforcement, supervising firms' day-to-day operations, and investigating irregularities.[734] Once in force, virtual asset trading in HK will be regulated under two licensing regimes: (i) opt-in regulatory framework; and (ii) proposed licensing regime under the AML Ordinance, under the principle 'same business, same risks, same rules'.[735] The SFC indicated that this new regime would enable it to provide adequate protection to investors through mitigating risks posed to them, while simultaneously complying with its international commitments involving AML/CFT.[736] In December 2020, the SFC announced that it had granted its first licence to a virtual asset trading platform allowing it to provide services to professional investors only and being subject to bespoke regulatory requirements akin to those

731. HK Government, 'Government Launches Consultation on Legislative Proposals to Enhance Anti-money Laundering and Counter-Terrorist Financing Regulation' (3 November 2020) and SFC, 'Fintech: The Regulatory Response to Evolving Challenges. Keynote Address at Hong Kong FinTech Week' (3 November 2020).
732. SFC, 'Fintech: The Regulatory Response to Evolving Challenges. Keynote Address at Hong Kong FinTech Week' (3 November 2020) 2.
733. SFC, 'Fintech: The Regulatory Response to Evolving Challenges. Keynote Address at Hong Kong FinTech Week' (3 November 2020) 2.
734. SFC, 'Fintech: The Regulatory Response to Evolving Challenges. Keynote Address at Hong Kong FinTech Week' (3 November 2020) 2.
735. SFC, 'Fintech: The Regulatory Response to Evolving Challenges. Keynote Address at Hong Kong FinTech Week' (3 November 2020) 2.
736. SFC, 'Fintech: The Regulatory Response to Evolving Challenges. Keynote Address at Hong Kong FinTech Week' (3 November 2020) 2.

applicable to automated trading venues and securities brokers.[737] The SFC highlighted that it was one of the first major jurisdictions to issue a comprehensive regulatory framework for virtual asset trading platforms in line with the recommendations of international standard-setting organisations, such as IOSCO. It also noted plans by other major jurisdictions to regulate virtual asset trading platforms directed to alleviate concerns associated with AML and consumer protection.[738]

4.1.4.2 Virtual Asset Service Providers

On 21 May 2021, the FSTB published its consultation conclusions on legislative proposals to enhance AML/CTF in HK.[739] The consultation period commenced on 3 November 2020 and concluded on 31 January 2021 considering, among others, a licensing regime for virtual asset service providers. The FSTB noted that there was extensive support for the HK Government to bolster HK's AML/CTF regime in line with global standards, thereby maintaining HK's reputation as an international financial centre.[740] Accordingly, a licensing regime under the AML Ordinance, in compliance with FATF standards, would 'harness opportunities presented by financial innovation while ensuring the healthy and orderly development of the market'.[741] Under the new virtual asset service provider regime, the business of operating a virtual asset exchange would constitute a regulated virtual activity under the AML Ordinance, for which a licence would be required from the SFC to conduct such business.[742] The proposed regime would only apply to exchanges dealing in virtual assets, and not to other types of virtual asset service providers such as wallet providers and custodians.[743] Under the proposed licensing conditions, only locally incorporated firms with a permanent place of business in HK will be eligible for a virtual asset service provider licence, in addition to passing a fit and proper test.[744] Virtual asset service providers must comply with the AML/CTF requirements set out in Schedule 2 of the AML Ordinance (notably customer due diligence and record-keeping requirements).[745]

Virtual asset providers must only offer their services to professional investors, in addition to enforcing strict criteria permitting virtual assets to be included on their platforms. In addition, they must comply with prescribed regulatory requirements

737. SFC, 'SFC Licenses First Virtual Asset Trading Platform' (16 December 2020).
738. SFC, 'SFC Licenses First Virtual Asset Trading Platform' (16 December 2020) 1.
739. Financial Services and Trade Bureau (FSTB), 'Public Consultation on Legislative Proposals to Enhance AML and CFT in Hong Kong' (21 May 2021).
740. FSTB, 'Public Consultation on Legislative Proposals to Enhance AML and CFT in Hong Kong' (May 2021), para. 1.3.
741. FSTB, 'Public Consultation on Legislative Proposals to Enhance AML and CFT in Hong Kong' (May 2021), para. 2.3.
742. FSTB, 'Public Consultation on Legislative Proposals to Enhance AML and CFT in Hong Kong' (May 2021), para. 2.5.
743. HKMA, 'Discussion Paper on Cryptoassets and Stablecoins' (January 2022), para. 4.1.
744. FSTB, 'Public Consultation on Legislative Proposals to Enhance AML and CFT in Hong Kong' (May 2021), para. 2.10 and para. 2.12.
745. FSTB, 'Public Consultation on Legislative Proposals to Enhance AML and CFT in Hong Kong' (May 2021), para. 2.10 and para. 2.14.

relating to financial resources, financial reporting and disclosure, knowledge and experience, prevention of conflicts of interests, market manipulative and abusive activities, risk management, segregation and management of client assets and soundness of the business.[746] It is also proposed that virtual asset providers be granted an 'open-ended' licence, continuing as valid until revoked by the SFC.[747] As such, the SFC will be empowered as the supervisory authority of licensed virtual asset service providers, ensuring their compliance with their AML Ordinance.[748] The FSTB presented its legislative proposals to the LegCo PFA on 7 February 2022,[749] directing to submit an amendment bill to the LegCo in the second quarter of 2022.[750] The proposed virtual asset service providers regime aims to bring virtual asset exchanges within the SFC's regulatory perimeter, however, will fail to capture stablecoins within its remit. This includes the primary functions present in an ordinary stablecoin arrangement including: (i) issuance and redemption of tokens; (ii) effecting of transactions; (iii) token custody and operation; (iv) value stabilisation and reserve management; (v) transaction validation; and (vi) fund transmission.[751]

4.1.4.3 Stablecoins

In January 2022, the HKMA commenced its consultation exercise inviting views from the financial services industry and the public on the manner in which payment-related stablecoins should be regulated in HK.[752] In its Discussion Paper, the HKMA set out the risks unique to stablecoins[753] and indicated that appropriate regulation should be introduced to govern such tokens.[754] In this regard, it proposed that regulation should be introduced to ensure financial and monetary stability, user protection, and the reduction of regulatory arbitrage.[755] To this end, an 'agile' regulatory approach, together with a risk-based and proportionate regulation should be used as guiding principles in establishing a regulatory regime for stablecoins in HK.[756]

746. FSTB, 'Public Consultation on Legislative Proposals to Enhance AML and CFT in Hong Kong' (May 2021), para. 2.10 and para. 2.14.
747. FSTB, 'Public Consultation on Legislative Proposals to Enhance AML and CFT in Hong Kong' (May 2021), para. 2.10 and para. 2.18.
748. FSTB, 'Public Consultation on Legislative Proposals to Enhance AML and CFT in Hong Kong' (May 2021), para. 2.23.
749. LegCo PFA, 'Anti-Money Laundering and Counter-Terrorist Financing (Amendment) Bill 2022' (7 February 2022).
750. HKMA, 'Discussion Paper on Cryptoassets and Stablecoins' (January 2022), para. 4.1 and Financial Services and Treasury Board, 'Letter to Forerunners of the Virtual Asset Industry: Embracing Regulation, Development, Tradition and Innovation' (17 March 2022) and LegCo PFA, 'Anti-Money Laundering and Counter-Terrorist Financing (Amendment) Bill 2022' (7 February 2022), para. 24.
751. HKMA, 'Discussion Paper on Cryptoassets and Stablecoins' (January 2022), para. 4.1.
752. HKMA, 'Discussion Paper on Cryptoassets and Stablecoins' (January 2022).
753. HKMA, 'Discussion Paper on Cryptoassets and Stablecoins' (January 2022), para. 5.1.
754. HKMA, 'Discussion Paper on Cryptoassets and Stablecoins' (January 2022), para. 5.2.
755. HKMA, 'Discussion Paper on Cryptoassets and Stablecoins' (January 2022), para. 5.2(i).
756. HKMA, 'Discussion Paper on Cryptoassets and Stablecoins' (January 2022), para. 5.2(ii).

4.1.4.4 *Fund Distribution*

In November 2021, the SFC mapped out some of the aspects of its future approach to regulating DLT Offerings noting that it would continue approaching regulation from a practical perspective to provide a 'well-defined regulatory environment' which encourages innovation, investor protection, and market expansion.[757] In particular, it indicated that it was in the process of reviewing the regulatory regime for virtual assets which it introduced in 2018 to assess whether it was still 'fit for purpose, and whether any modifications are required'.[758] This process would be executed in collaboration with the HKMA, in alignment with the adoption 'same business, same risks and rules' principle.[759] This collaboration culminated in the publication of the SFC and HKMA joint circular in January 2022. The joint circular was published by the SFC and the HKMA subsequent to its review of the existing regulatory framework and consideration of queries from the industry and market developments.[760] This culminated in updated guidance to intermediaries engaged in the distribution of virtual assets and virtual asset-related products. The joint circular defines virtual assets according to the definition set out in the SFC's Proforma T&Cs, excluding central bank digital currencies.[761] Virtual asset-related products are defined as investment products: (i) having a principal investment strategy to invest in virtual assets; (ii) deriving their value primarily from the value and features of virtual assets; or (iii) tracking or replicating investment returns closely corresponding to virtual assets.[762] This joint circular, which supersedes the SFC's circular addressed to intermediaries distributing virtual assets issued on 1 November 2018, contains several impactful features setting out requirements related to: (i) complex products; (ii) additional investor protection obligations; (iii) suitability obligations; (iv) dealing services; (v) advisory services.

4.1.4.5 *Discussion*

The actions and behaviours considered above are examined below through the adaptations and/or amendments effected to the regulatory approaches and regulatory frameworks, respectively, established by the HK Government to govern DLT Offerings.

757. SFC, 'Fintech: Metamorphosis of the Financial Industry Keynote Address at Hong Kong FinTech Week 2021' (3 November 2021) 5.
758. SFC, 'Fintech: Metamorphosis of the Financial Industry Keynote Address at Hong Kong FinTech Week 2021' (3 November 2021) 5.
759. SFC, 'Fintech: Metamorphosis of the Financial Industry Keynote Address at Hong Kong FinTech Week 2021' (3 November 2021) 5.
760. SFC and HKMA, 'Joint Circular on Intermediaries' Virtual Asset-Related Activities' (28 January 2022) 1, note 1.
761. SFC and HKMA, 'Joint Circular on Intermediaries' Virtual Asset-Related Activities' (28 January 2022) 1, note 1.
762. SFC and HKMA, 'Joint Circular on Intermediaries' Virtual Asset-Related Activities' (28 January 2022) 1, note 2.

4.1.4.5.1 Updated Regulatory Response

Several changes were effected to the regulatory framework developed to govern DLT Offerings, while the regulatory approach established remained largely unchanged. Most significantly, the SFC expanded the virtual asset trading platform regime to include the trading of any type of virtual asset, including those not constituting securities for the purposes of the SFO, through the AML Ordinance. The SFC indicated that this expansion would aid it in providing adequate protection for investors, in addition to fulfilling its international AML and CTF commitments. The 'opt-in' regime created for virtual asset trading would, however, be retained. The FSTB also proposed a new regulatory regime for firms operating a virtual asset exchange, which would constitute a regulated activity under the auspices of the AML Ordinance. Under this proposal, only locally incorporated firms with a permanent place of business in HK would be eligible to apply for a virtual asset service provider 'open-ended' licence. These service providers would only be permitted to offer their services to professional investors. This proposed new regulatory regime, however, would not be applicable to stablecoins. Accordingly, the SFC proposed a regulatory regime for stablecoins with the purpose of ensuring financial and monetary stability, user protection, and reducing regulatory arbitrage.

The initial regulatory approach established for the governance of DLT Offerings in HK remained unchanged. In particular, the SFC indicated that it would embark on a review of the regulatory regime for virtual assets introduced in 2018 with the aim of considering whether it was still 'fit for purpose, and whether any modifications are required'. This approach was consistent with the fact-finding enquiry approach undertaken by the HK Government in monitoring market developments and providing an appropriate regulatory response thereto when needed. The SFC and HKMA also applied the 'same business, same risks, same rules' principle in adapting the initial regulatory framework governing DLT Offerings, in alignment with its non-legislative approach. Overall, the actions and behaviours of the HK Government directed to amending the initial response to the regulatory framework governing DLT Offerings were effected to extend the SFC regulatory perimeter to specific virtual asset business which previously fell outside its remit, therefore filling the existing regulatory gaps. To this end, the rationale underlying the amendment of the initial response to the regulatory framework developed was to provide enhanced regulatory protections for investors and to apply international standards for AML/CTF. In effecting these amendments to the regulatory framework, the HK Government applied largely the same regulatory approach, however, it undertook to consult more with the financial services industry in proposing legislative and regulatory amendments.

4.1.4.5.2 Competition Policy Influence

Competition policy considerations influenced the amendments effected to regulatory framework developed for governing DLT Offerings. In particular, the SFC noted that its continuous approach to regulating virtual assets in HK was viewed from a practical perspective to provide a 'well-defined regulatory environment' which encourages innovation, investor protection, and market expansion.[763] The SFC highlighted that HK was one of the first major jurisdictions to develop a comprehensive regulatory framework for virtual asset trading platforms in line with internationally recommended standard-setting organisations, such as IOSCO. The FSTB also highlighted that there was wide-ranging support for the HK Government to reinforce HK's AML/CTF rules in alignment with international standards, thereby maintaining and strengthening HK's reputation as an international financial centre.[764] In particular, the FSTB noted that the regulatory regimes introduced by the AML Ordinance would provide a solid legislative framework for the regulation of virtual assets in HK, which would assist with developing and expanding the virtual asset industry through harnessing, among others, HK's advantages as an international financial centre.[765] The solid legislative framework would thus act to bolster market confidence and would provide a map forward for the virtual asset sector's sustainable development.

763. SFC, 'Fintech: Metamorphosis of the Financial Industry Keynote Address at Hong Kong FinTech Week 2021' (3 November 2021) 5.
764. FSTB, 'Public Consultation on Legislative Proposals to Enhance AML and CFT in Hong Kong' (May 2021), para. 1.3.
765. FSTB, 'Public Consultation on Legislative Proposals to Enhance AML and CFT in Hong Kong' (May 2021), para. 1.3.

CHAPTER 5

Regulating DLT Financial Products and Services: The City of London, United Kingdom

This chapter provides a narrative analysis of the development of the laws and regulations governing DLT financial products and services in London during the key periods of development from 2018-2022. It provides an examination of the actions and behaviours of the UK Government and how competition policy influenced its regulatory approach to DLT Offerings and the formulation of the laws and regulations developed to govern it.

5.1 INTRODUCTION

London has been recognised as a leading global and regional financial centre since the nineteenth century.[766] The UK's convenient time zone and location have been touted as geographical advantages critical to elevating London into a top financial hub. As an advanced economy, the UK has ranked 13th on the UN's Human Development Index[767] and is recognised for its robust legal and institutional frameworks, having ranked 13th on the World Justice Project's 2020 Rule of Law Index.[768] Globally, the UK ranks high in terms of competitiveness, having placed 18th on the IMD World Competitiveness

766. *See* Simon Mollan & Ranald Michie, 'The City of London as an International Commercial and Financial Center since 1900' (2012) 13(3) Enterprise & Society 538-587 https://doi.org/10.1093/es/khr072.
767. Global Human Development Indicators, *United Nations Development Programme* (December 2020), https://hdr.undp.org/en/countries.
768. World Justice Project, 'World Justice Project Rule of Law Index: 2020 Insights' 6, https://worldjusticeproject.org/sites/default/files/documents/WJP%20Insights%202020%20-%20Online%20.pdf.

Ranking.[769] Notably, it also ranked 2nd on the 2021 Global Fintech Rankings and is widely recognised for its Fintech development efforts.[770] The UK adopts a democratic system of government as a parliamentary democracy and a constitutional monarchy, without a written constitutional instrument.[771] Instead, constitutional competence and power are derived from the common law and legislation.[772] The UK state is divided into three separate branches including: (i) the Executive, comprised of the Crown and Her Majesty's Government;[773] (ii) parliament; and (iii) the judiciary.[774] Within this system of government, the branches of government empowered to set legal and regulatory rules for the financial services industry, specifically as they apply to DLT Offerings, in addition to formulating competition policy, include: (i) Her Majesty's Treasury; (ii) Parliament; (iii) the BoE; and (iv) the FCA.

Her Majesty's Treasury (HM Treasury), also referred to as the Exchequer, is the economic and finance ministry responsible for developing and implementing the UK Government's economic and public finance policy.[775] HM Treasury's responsibilities most relevant for this study include setting financial services policy (i.e., banking and financial services regulation), ensuring financial stability, and promoting London's competitiveness. To this end, it is responsible for economic growth, fostering financial inclusion, and improving financial services regulation to protect consumers. The HM Treasury's objectives include ensuring the stability of the UK's macro-economic growth, and competitiveness across the UK.[776]

The DIT was established in 2016 as the ministerial department responsible for securing the UK's and global prosperity through promoting and financing international trade and investment, in the championship of free trade.[777] The DIT replaced key functions in the UK Government including the Defence Security Organisation, the GREAT Campaign, and UK Export Finance.[778] Most notably, the DIT absorbed the functions of UKTI, including its responsibility to promote UK outward and inward investment, for the purpose of fostering economic growth.[779] The DIT was therefore

769. World Competitiveness Ranking 2021, https://www.imd.org/centers/world-competitiveness-center/rankings/world-competitiveness/.
770. Global Fintech Rankings Report (*Findexable*, 2021) 21, https://findexable.com/wp-content/uploads/2021/06/Global-Fintech-Rankings-2021-v1-23-June-21.pdf.
771. *See* https://www.commonwealthofnations.org/sectors-united_kingdom/government/.
772. UK Courts and Tribunals Judiciary, 'The Justice System and the Constitution', https://www.judiciary.uk/about-the-judiciary/the-judiciary-the-government-and-the-constitution/jud-acc-ind/justice-sys-and-constitution/.
773. *See* United Kingdom Government (UK Government), 'How Government Works', https://www.gov.uk/government/how-government-works.
774. UK Courts and Tribunals Judiciary, 'The Justice System and the Constitution', https://www.judiciary.uk/about-the-judiciary/the-judiciary-the-government-and-the-constitution/jud-acc-ind/justice-sys-and-constitution/.
775. *See* https://www.gov.uk/government/organisations/hm-treasury/about.
776. *See* https://www.gov.uk/government/organisations/hm-treasury/about.
777. *See* https://www.gov.uk/government/organisations/department-for-international-trade/about.
778. *Sir* Martin Donnelly, 'Establishing the Department for International Trade: Balancing the Urgent and the Important' (1 November 2016), https://quarterly.blog.gov.uk/2016/11/01/establishing-the-department-for-international-trade-balancing-the-urgent-and-the-important/.
779. Theresa May, 'Machinery of Government Changes' (18 July 2016), https://questions-statements.parliament.uk/written-statements/detail/2016-07-18/HCWS94.

largely responsible for directing the UK's competition, trade and investment policy, and London's role therein.[780]

The UK Parliament was established in the fourteenth century and comprises two houses, namely the HOC and the HOL. It functions primarily to promulgate laws and fulfils the 'checks and balances' role for the Executive.[781] The HOC comprises 650 democratically elected members of parliament responsible for debating draft legislation and relevant political issues, predominantly through bespoke committees.[782] The HOL is the second chamber of the UK Parliament and comprises approximately 800 members appointed by the Queen/King, as advised by the Prime Minister, and is tasked with complementing the work of the HOC.[783] The HOL operates independently of the HOC and is also responsible for examining and challenging public policy through Select Committees.[784]

The BoE was established in 1694 as the private bank of the UK State.[785] At present it functions as the UK's central bank by 'promoting the good of the people of the United Kingdom by maintaining monetary and financial stability'.[786] The BoE's constitution is set out in several legislative acts, including the Bank of England Act 1694, the Bank of England Act 1998, and the Financial Services Act 2012.[787] The BoE is mandated to: (i) issue banknotes in England and Wales; and (ii) set interest rates to account for inflation through monetary policy.[788] It is also responsible for maintaining the UK's financial system's stability, principally through its FPC which identifies, monitors and implements initiatives to eliminate systemic risks.[789]

The PRA was established in 2013 as a subsidiary of the BoE[790] and is primarily responsible for authorising and regulating all large banks, building societies, credit unions, insurers and investment firms in the UK.[791] In the aftermath of the 2008 GFC, the PRA was tasked with setting the prudential policies for regulated firms, in addition

---

780. In February 2023, the DIT merged with the Department for Business, Energy and Industrial Strategy to form the Department for Business and Trade. However, this is not material to this book whose subject-matter is framed within the period 2008-2022.
781. *See* https://www.parliament.uk/.
782. UK Parliament, 'The Work of the House of Commons', https://www.parliament.uk/business/commons/what-the-commons-does/.
783. UK Parliament, 'Members and their Roles', https://www.parliament.uk/business/lords/whos-in-the-house-of-lords/members-and-their-roles/.
784. UK Parliament, 'What the Lords Does', https://www.parliament.uk/business/lords/work-of-the-house-of-lords/what-the-lords-does/.
785. Bank of England (BoE), 'Our History', https://www.bankofengland.co.uk/about/history.
786. BoE, 'Our Code: Our Commitment to How We Work' (September 2017) 1, https://service.betterregulation.com/sites/default/files/upload/2018-08/ourcode.pdf.
787. BoE, 'The Bank of England Act 1998, the Charters of the Bank and Related Documents' (June 2018) 3, https://www.bankofengland.co.uk/-/media/boe/files/about/legislation/boe-charter.pdf.
788. BoE, 'About Us' (17 March 2022), https://www.bankofengland.co.uk/about.
789. BoE, 'Financial Policy Committee', https://www.bankofengland.co.uk/about/people/financial-policy-committee. As of 1 March 2017, the BoE and Financial Services Act established the PRA as a Committee in the BoE, and thus removed its status as a subsidiary.
790. Financial Services and Markets Act 2000 (FSMA), pt 1A.
791. BoE, 'About Us' (17 March 2022), https://www.bankofengland.co.uk/about.

to supervising their business activities.[792] The PRA's rules for firms which it supervises are set out in its Rulebook.[793] Through its micro-prudential regulation, the PRA works in tandem with the FPC, tasked with facilitating macro-prudential regulation.[794] The PRA executes its mandate through bespoke supervision, adopting a forward-looking approach, and seeing the bigger picture.[795]

The FCA was established in 2013 as an independent statutory body which replaced the former Financial Services Authority.[796] The FSMA sets out the FCA's strategic objectives as including ensuring that markets, including markets for regulated financial services, function well.[797] To this end, the FCA is specifically mandated to protect consumers and financial markets, in addition to promoting competition in accordance with the interests of consumers.[798] For example, the FCA issues warnings to the public regarding firms carrying on activities without being authorised to do so.[799] Resultantly, the FCA is responsible for authorising firms who wish to carry on specific activities, together with supervising the conduct of these authorised firms.[800] The FCA is also responsible for prudentially supervising firms not regulated by the PRA.[801] To this end, the FCA and the PRA work collaboratively to regulate and supervise financial institutions and other firms in the UK. Among its competencies and powers, the FCA's mandate to make rules, prepare and issue codes, and provide general guidance under the FSMA, is the most relevant for this study.[802] This rule-making competence is represented most significantly by the FCA Handbook, which contains a complete record of the rules which FCA authorised and non-authorised financial services firms are required to adhere to.[803] Finally, under FSMA the FCA is empowered with wide-ranging enforcement capabilities, including issuing fines and withdrawing authorisations.[804]

5.1.1 Input

The analysis below sets out the actions and behaviours of the UK Government directed to formulating and implementing competition policy within the context of the emergence of Fintech, and its position of importance on legal and policy agendas.

792. BoE, 'What is the Prudential Regulation Authority (PRA)?', https://www.bankofengland.co.uk/knowledgebank/what-is-the-prudential-regulation-authority-pra.
793. *See* https://www.prarulebook.co.uk/.
794. BoE, 'What is the Prudential Regulation Authority (PRA)?', https://www.bankofengland.co.uk/knowledgebank/what-is-the-prudential-regulation-authority-pra.
795. BoE, 'What is the Prudential Regulation Authority (PRA)?', https://www.bankofengland.co.uk/knowledgebank/what-is-the-prudential-regulation-authority-pra.
796. FSMA, pt 1A.
797. FSMA, pt 1B(2).
798. FSMA, pt 1B(3).
799. Financial Conduct Authority (FCA), 'Protecting Customers' (19 April 2016), https://www.fca.org.uk/about/protecting-consumers.
800. FCA, 'About the FCA' (20 April 2016), https://www.fca.org.uk/about/the-fca.
801. FCA, 'About the FCA' (20 April 2016), https://www.fca.org.uk/about/the-fca.
802. FSMA, pt 1B(9).
803. *See* https://www.handbook.fca.org.uk/.
804. FSMA, pt 1(L).

5.1.1.1 *Competition Policy and the Role of Fintech*

London has long been regarded as the centre of the UK's financial services industry. Its competitiveness with former European finance centres, particularly Amsterdam and Paris, is well-documented historically,[805] hallmarking London's endurance as a global finance hub. Internationally, the UK's competitiveness is reflected primarily through its ability to maintain London as an international financial centre, offering a business environment which is 'the best place to do business'.[806] As such, the UK Government has marketed its business environment, innovation, and international connections as key drivers.[807] Its success in advancing this policy objective is evidenced by having been recognised as a top exporter of financial services globally.[808] The actions and behaviours of the UK Government in directing competition policy are underscored primarily by its policy aim to strengthen the UK's financial services industry through promoting the UK's interests globally.[809] This forms a key hallmark of the UK's economy and is central to the UK Government's foreign and economic policy.[810] The UK's ability to attract foreign investment has also been highlighted as an important feature of its capability to produce successful firms.[811] To this end, the UK Government has focussed its competition policy on attracting 'high value foreign direct investment to the UK' through various means.[812] Accordingly, the UK Government uses considerable resources to attract inward investment and to enhance UK firms' competitiveness via overseas investment and trade channels.[813]

During the time period 2008-2010, the UK Government, as with other affected countries, grappled with the aftermath of the 2008 GFC. As such, the UK Government's policy agenda focussed on economic recovery through growth and reducing economic deficit.[814] Its approach to international competition was also viewed through this lens, particularly in light of attracting foreign investment, a cornerstone of the UKTI's

805. *See* Simon Mollan & Ranald Michie, 'The City of London as an International Commercial and Financial Center since 1900' (2012) 13(3) Enterprise & Society 538-587 and BoE, 'London as an International Financial Centre' (November 1989), https://www.bankofengland.co.uk/-/media/boe/files/quarterly-bulletin/1989/london-as-an-international-financial-centre.pdf.
806. United Kingdom Trade and Investment (UKTI), 'Departmental Report and Resource Accounts 2008-09' (20 July 2009) 12.
807. UKTI, 'Departmental Report and Resource Accounts 2008-09' (20 July 2009) 12.
808. *See* The City UK, 'Key Facts about the UK as an International Financial Centre 2019' (December 2019) 3, https://www.thecityuk.com/media/wympuijs/key-facts-about-the-uk-as-an-international-financial-centre-2022.pdf.
809. UK Government, 'The Queen's Speech to Both Houses of Parliament' (3 December 2008) 3 and UKTI, 'Britain Open for Business: Growth Through International Trade and Investment' 63, https://assets.publishing.service.gov.uk/government/uploads/system/uploads/attachment_data/file/294090/Britain_open_for_business_-_UKTI_s_five_year_strategy_1_.pdf.
810. UK Government, 'The Queen's Speech to Both Houses of Parliament' (3 December 2008) 3 and UKTI, 'Britain Open for Business: Growth Through International Trade and Investment' 63, https://assets.publishing.service.gov.uk/government/uploads/system/uploads/attachment_data/file/294090/Britain_open_for_business_-_UKTI_s_five_year_strategy_1_.pdf.
811. UKTI, 'Departmental Report and Resource Accounts 2008-09' (20 July 2009) 12.
812. UKTI, 'Departmental Report and Resource Accounts 2008-09' (20 July 2009) 19.
813. UKTI, 'Departmental Report and Resource Accounts 2008-09' (20 July 2009) 74.
814. UK Government, 'The Queen's Speech to Both Houses of Parliament' (25 May 2010) https://www.gov.uk/government/speeches/queens-speech-2010.

strategy. For example, the UKTI reported that London's position as the 'top global financial centre' was fraught with increased competition from alternative financial centres motivated to attract foreign investment.[815] The UKTI, together with the Financial Services Strategy Advisory Board, developed specific marketing targeted at, among others, Mainland China and NY.[816]

The success of London's financial services industry, and its competitive edge against other international financial centres, has been noted for its legal and regulatory environments, and its ease of access for foreign investors.[817] In formulating its competition policy, London illustrated its awareness of the effects of globalisation on the competitiveness of its financial centre and hence its need to market itself effectively.[818] In particular, it noted the rise of cities into 'world cities', which focus on developing expertise in a wide variety of services, including NY, Tokyo and Paris.[819] NY is highlighted as London's main rival, particularly in respect of the international nature of the equities listed on the London Stock Exchange.[820]

Overall, this period saw the UK Government focus on strengthening the economy by restructuring the financial sector, through employment programmes and by fostering responsible investment.[821] The UK Government proposed, in particular, the legislative reform of the financial sector to strengthen governance and to place restrictions on its reward systems.[822] Further, in 2010 the UKTI announced its five-year strategy 'Britain Open for Business' to refocus its efforts on growing, among others, the UK's ability to attract foreign investment by targeting high-quality FDI and institutional investors, such as overseas sovereign wealth and pension funds.[823] In the same year, the UK Government announced plans to promulgate legislation to reform financial regulation in accordance with the lessons learned from the 2008 GFC.[824]

During the time period 2011-2014, the UKTI focussed on several initiatives to bolster the UK's reputation domestically and internationally, including developing innovation.[825] This approach retained the UKTI's messaging that the UK is a 'springboard

815. UKTI, 'Departmental Report and Resource Accounts 2008-09' (20 July 2009) 30.
816. UKTI, 'Departmental Report and Resource Accounts 2008-09' (20 July 2009) 30.
817. Greater London Authority (GLA) Economics, 'London's Central Business District: Its Global Importance' (2008) 5 and 46, https://www.london.gov.uk/sites/default/files/gla_migrate_files_destination/londons-cbd-jan08.pdf.
818. GLA, 'The Major's Economic Development Strategy for London' (May 2010) 18 and 28, https://www.london.gov.uk/sites/default/files/gla_migrate_files_destination/Economic-Development-Strategy.pdf.
819. GLA Economics, 'London's Central Business District: Its Global Importance' (2008) 46, https://www.london.gov.uk/sites/default/files/gla_migrate_files_destination/londons-cbd-jan08.pdf.
820. GLA, 'The Major's Economic Development Strategy for London' (May 2010) 19.
821. UK Government, 'The Queen's Speech to Both Houses of Parliament' (18 November 2009) 1.
822. UK Government, 'The Queen's Speech to Both Houses of Parliament' (18 November 2009) 2.
823. UK Trade and Investment, 'Departmental Report and Resource Accounts 2010-11' (14 July 2011) 15.
824. UK Government, 'The Queen's Speech to Both Houses of Parliament' (25 May 2010), https://www.gov.uk/government/speeches/queens-speech-2010.
825. UKTI, 'Britain Open for Business: Growth Through International Trade and Investment' 63, https://assets.publishing.service.gov.uk/government/uploads/system/uploads/attachment_data/file/294090/Britain_open_for_business_-_UKTI_s_five_year_strategy_1_.pdf.

for growth' based on its business-friendly environment and global reach.[826] At the same time, the UK Government indicated that work needed to be done to counterbalance the UK's reputation as being less developed in the technology and innovation sectors.[827] The UKTI also acknowledged that competition for inward investment was becoming increasingly challenging.[828] As such, its strategy to continue the UK's growth was to secure high-quality foreign investment from mostly advanced economies, with a particular focus on the US.[829]

In 2012, the LEP, a non-incorporated mayoral appointed body, published a report concerning the protection and promotion of London's competitiveness. Once again, it was noted that London was facing increased competition from other international financial centres, including HK and NY.[830] To maintain London's competitiveness, it was recommended that developments were required, among others, to progress innovation.[831] To this end, during the time period 2012-2014, the UKTI's strategy evolved to include targeting the development of innovation, culminating in the launch of Science and Innovation in November 2012, Innovate UK in March 2013, and the Innovation Hub at the end of 2013.[832] The strengthening of the UK's international competitiveness formed a key feature of the UK Government's approach to developing its economy, particularly through the prism of developing innovation and technology. This policy aim was reflected in the UK Government's 2013 Industrial Strategy which mapped out 'Eight Great Technologies' to be used in the long-term growth of the economy.[833] The UKTI included this Industrial Strategy in the next phase of its 'Britain Open for Business' strategic objective.[834] The importance of the UK's competitiveness was also highlighted in the Queen's 2014 speech which reported that legislative measures would be taken to ensure that the UK is 'the most attractive place to start, finance and grow a business'.[835]

826. UKTI, 'Britain Open for Business: Growth Through International Trade and Investment' 63, https://assets.publishing.service.gov.uk/government/uploads/system/uploads/attachment_data/file/294090/Britain_open_for_business_-_UKTI_s_five_year_strategy_1_.pdf.
827. UKTI, 'Britain Open for Business: Growth Through International Trade and Investment' 63, https://assets.publishing.service.gov.uk/government/uploads/system/uploads/attachment_data/file/294090/Britain_open_for_business_-_UKTI_s_five_year_strategy_1_.pdf.
828. UKTI, 'Britain Open for Business: Growth Through International Trade and Investment' 25, https://assets.publishing.service.gov.uk/government/uploads/system/uploads/attachment_data/file/294090/Britain_open_for_business_-_UKTI_s_five_year_strategy_1_.pdf.
829. UKTI, 'Britain Open for Business: Growth Through International Trade and Investment' 25, https://assets.publishing.service.gov.uk/government/uploads/system/uploads/attachment_data/file/294090/Britain_open_for_business_-_UKTI_s_five_year_strategy_1_.pdf.
830. London Enterprise Panel, 'LEP Priorities: Competitiveness Options Appraisal' (29 May 2012) 5, https://www.london.gov.uk/moderngovmb/documents/s10056/Competitiveness%20paper.rtf?CT=2.
831. London Enterprise Panel, 'LEP Priorities: Competitiveness Options Appraisal' (29 May 2012) 2, https://www.london.gov.uk/moderngovmb/documents/s10056/Competitiveness%20paper.rtf?CT=2.
832. UKTI, 'Departmental Report and Resource Accounts 2012-13' (27 June 2013) 10 and UKTI, 'Departmental Report and Resource Accounts 2012-13' (26 June 2014) 18.
833. UK Government, 'Industrial Strategy: Government and Industry in Partnership Progress Report' (April 2014) 38.
834. UK Government, 'Britain Open for Business: The Next Phase' (24 January 2014) 25.
835. UK Government, 'The Queen's Speech to Both Houses of Parliament' (4 June 2014).

The significance of the development of innovation and technology for the long-term growth of the UK economy during the time period 2011-2014, coincided with a pointed interest in developing Fintech in the UK's financial services industry. For example, in July 2014 the FCA published a 'Call for Input' on its proposed initiative, Project Innovate.[836] This project would operate to assist firms with bringing innovative ideas to the financial services industry through an incubator and an innovation hub. In proposing to launch Project Innovate, the FCA was motivated in part by the 'application of digital technology and the corresponding growth of the fintech sector' and the role of innovation in fostering efficient competition.[837]

In August 2014, former Chancellor George Osborne announced the launch of the UK Government's new trade body for Fintech 'Innovate Finance'. Notably, the Chancellor highlighted the policy objective to 'make London the Fintech capital of the world'.[838] To ensure the UK's competitiveness, the UKTI was tasked with promoting the UK as the 'destination of choice for setting up a FinTech company' and with encouraging firms globally to move to the UK 'as the springboard for internationalising their FinTech business'.[839] It was also recognised that international competition for Fintech was fiercely competitive, and that, among others, legal and regulatory rules which were 'pro-innovation' were required for developing the Fintech sector in the UK. The FCA published its 'Call for Input' Feedback Statement in October 2014. This statement highlighted that legal uncertainty regarding the applicability of the FCA's regulatory regime to Fintech firms acted to reduce the degree of enthusiasm to experiment with innovative products and services.[840] Further, the lack of certainty as to whether the UK Government would regulate digital currencies deterred businesses from testing related technologies.[841] In response, the FCA stated that it would provide appropriate guidance and clarification to Fintech firms as needed.[842] It noted it would continue to work in collaboration with the UK Government in deciding the appropriate form of regulation which would act to foster digital currency innovation.[843]

During the time period 2015-2017, the UK Government continued to promote the development of the Fintech sector in the UK and its competitiveness. In March 2015, the UK Government's Chief Scientific Adviser published a report on the future of Fintech in the UK providing a strategic plan for the development of the sector up until 2025 (Fintech Future Report).[844] Most notably, the report highlights the UK Government's policy aim of becoming one of the world's hubs for innovation in finance.[845] The report stated that

836. Financial Conduct Authority (FCA), 'Project Innovate: Call for Input Feedback Statement' (October 2014).
837. FCA, 'Project Innovate: Call for Input Feedback Statement' (October 2014) 5.
838. UK Government, 'Chancellor on Developing FinTech' (6 August 2014).
839. UK Government, 'Chancellor on Developing FinTech' (6 August 2014).
840. FCA, 'Project Innovate: Call for Input Feedback Statement' (October 2014) 14.
841. FCA, 'Project Innovate: Call for Input Feedback Statement' (October 2014) 15.
842. FCA, 'Project Innovate: Call for Input Feedback Statement' (October 2014) 6 and 7.
843. FCA, 'Project Innovate: Call for Input Feedback Statement' (October 2014) 7 and 32.
844. UK Government Chief Scientific Adviser, 'FinTech Futures: The UK as a World Leader in Financial Technologies' (March 2015).
845. UK Government Chief Scientific Adviser, 'FinTech Futures: The UK as a World Leader in Financial Technologies' (March 2015) 5.

this policy aim would be achieved using the UK's competitive edge based on its position as a leading international financial centre, its regulatory framework's promotion of innovation, and its scientific research abilities.[846] On a practical basis, the Fintech Future Report noted that the 'best investment environment, the right tax system, the appropriate regulatory framework and the best infrastructure' would be required for Fintech firms to succeed in the UK.[847] Notably, it was indicated that a supportive regulatory environment based on principles-based regulation, which considers consumer interests, could provide increased economic growth through the generation of tax revenues.[848] The report recommended that the UKTI continue promoting the UK's competitiveness by developing it as a global Fintech Hub and attracting innovators to the UK.[849] Finally, the report highlighted Blockchain and digital currencies as a key technology grouping that would foster development in the UK Fintech sector.[850]

In May 2016, the FCA announced the opening of its Regulatory Sandbox, as a part of the Project Innovate initiative.[851] The Regulatory Sandbox, dubbed as the first of its kind, was described as a 'safe space' for firms to test innovative business models, products, and services, and to deliver those measures with the ensured protection of consumers. The establishment of the Regulatory Sandbox was meant to facilitate the fostering of innovation with consumer interests in mind, while at the same time promoting competition through the use of disruptive technology. Successful firms participating in the Regulatory Sandbox would be provided with a host of tools including a bespoke authorisation process for new firms in the testing phase, and regulatory guidance for ideas falling outside the existing regulatory regime. In the same year, the Queen's Speech highlighted the UK Government's policy aims to develop its Fintech sector, noting that '[l]egislation will be introduced to improve Britain's competitiveness and make the United Kingdom a world leader in the digital economy'.[852] To this end, in February 2016, the UK Government published its 'UK FinTech On the Cutting Edge: An Evaluation of the International FinTech Sector' report (UK Fintech Report) comparing the UK's Fintech ecosystem with those existing around the world, with the purpose of drawing lessons therefrom.[853] The report thus benchmarked seven Fintech ecosystems, including HK and NY, using the benchmarking factors: talent, capital, policy and demand.

The UK Fintech Report defined policy as 'government policy across regulation, tax and sector growth initiatives', including a regulatory regime providing support to

846. UK Government Chief Scientific Adviser, 'FinTech Futures: The UK as a World Leader in Financial Technologies' (March 2015) 11.
847. UK Government Chief Scientific Adviser, 'FinTech Futures: The UK as a World Leader in Financial Technologies' (March 2015) 55.
848. UK Government Chief Scientific Adviser, 'FinTech Futures: The UK as a World Leader in Financial Technologies' (March 2015) 16.
849. UK Government Chief Scientific Adviser, 'FinTech Futures: The UK as a World Leader in Financial Technologies' (March 2015) 11.
850. UK Government Chief Scientific Adviser, 'FinTech Futures: The UK as a World Leader in Financial Technologies' (March 2015) 20.
851. FCA, 'Financial Conduct Authority's Regulatory Sandbox Opens to Applications' (9 May 2016).
852. UK Government, 'Queen's Speech 2016' (18 May 2016).
853. UK Government, 'UK FinTech on the Cutting Edge: An Evaluation of the International FinTech Sector' (26 February 2016) 3.

new market entrants and innovative business models.[854] To this end, the report highlights that the UK's Fintech policy environment is conducive to supporting Fintech development through the role of the FCA, tax incentives, and government programmes.[855] In contrast, however, the report indicated that the policy environments in both HK and the US were intricate, cautious, and in some instances obscure.[856] In particular, it noted that HK's Fintech ecosystem was nascent and emerging, with a predominant focus on capital markets. The US Government was characterised for their traditional approach, and for providing limited industry support.[857]

Overall, the UK Fintech Report concluded that policy initiatives were central to supporting Fintech sector growth and served as a primary differentiator between the benchmarked Fintech ecosystems and the UK.[858] To this end, increased policy initiatives and financial centre specialisations were highlighted as posing challenges to the UK's leading Fintech policy initiative position.[859] Resultantly, the report proposed seven recommendations, including maintaining the FCA's position in developing the Fintech sector and widening tax incentives to promote the growth of investment.[860] This report and its recommendations were built into the UK's Digital Strategy 2017, while it grappled with its decision to leave the EU. The UK's Digital Strategy 2017 sets out seven objectives for the development of the UK's digital economy.[861] Overall, Fintech is highlighted as a key component to developing the UK's digital economy. For example, Fintech's position is made central through the objective of ensuring that the UK is the prime location for start-ups and growth for digital businesses. To this end, the strategy highlights several initiatives executed by the UK Government and the BoE to support the development of the UK Fintech sector. The specific efforts of the UK Government in the development of the UK Fintech sector align with its approach to maintain London as a competitive international financial centre, through its recognition as an international Fintech Hub.

5.1.1.2 Discussion

The actions and behaviours considered above are examined below through an identification of the significant themes delineating the UK Government's approach to

854. UK Government, 'UK FinTech on the Cutting Edge: An Evaluation of the International FinTech Sector' (26 February 2016) 8 and 9.
855. UK Government, 'UK FinTech on the Cutting Edge: An Evaluation of the International FinTech Sector' (26 February 2016) 8 and 11.
856. UK Government, 'UK FinTech on the Cutting Edge: An Evaluation of the International FinTech Sector' (26 February 2016) 11.
857. UK Government, 'UK FinTech on the Cutting Edge: An Evaluation of the International FinTech Sector' (26 February 2016) 11.
858. UK Government, 'UK FinTech on the Cutting Edge: An Evaluation of the International FinTech Sector' (26 February 2016) 16.
859. UK Government, 'UK FinTech on the Cutting Edge: An Evaluation of the International FinTech Sector' (26 February 2016) 16.
860. UK Government, 'UK FinTech on the Cutting Edge: An Evaluation of the International FinTech Sector' (26 February 2016) 74 and 79.
861. UK Government, 'UK Digital Strategy 2017' (1 March 2017).

competition policy for the financial services industry, and its 'competitive appetite' in relation thereto.

5.1.1.2.1 Competition Policy

The actions and behaviours directed by the UK Government during the time period 2008-2017 are illustrative of a focussed competition policy approach placing the UK Government as a Primary Actor internationally, in the Environmental Context of international regulatory competition. The analysis evidenced that, in considering this competitive landscape, the UK Government is cognisant of both: (i) its position relative to competing Primary Actors (the UK's own competitiveness); and (ii) the position of competing Primary Actors relative to others (other Primary Actors competitiveness). The UK Government deploys several branches of government to direct its competition policy objectives, using several regulatory competition Means to attract (and retain) the Drivers through Secondary Actors.

The UK Government's awareness of its own competitiveness is reflected primarily through its competition policy aim of strengthening the UK's economy, and London's position as a leading international financial, through the development of its Fintech sector. This is supported by the UK Government's consideration of competitive forces, particularly in the form of increased competition from alternative financial centres, such as HK and NY. The competitiveness of these Primary Actors has also been considered by the UK Government in progressing competition, as reflected by the UK Fintech Report's benchmarking, undertaken to review the Fintech development strategies adopted by other jurisdictions.

In promoting the UK's competitiveness, the UK Government undertakes the role of the promoter of the UK economy. Further, the FCA serves as the primary contact point for the Fintech sector. Accordingly, the actions and behaviours directing competition policy were executed by several branches of the UK Government responsible for promoting and developing London's competitiveness as an international financial centre, most notably, the UKTI, DIT and the FCA. For example, the UKTI and the DIT's main function was to spearhead various marketing initiatives aimed at attracting foreign inward investment. The FCA established Project Innovate, tasked with fostering innovation in the financial services industry, as a source of London's competitiveness.

The UK Government executed its competition policy through several heterogeneous actions and behaviours, most notably establishing several policy initiatives to support the development of innovation and technology in the UK. In developing the Fintech sector, the UK Government also placed a premium on developing 'pro-innovation' legal and regulatory rules. Overall, the UK Government markets the role of the FCA, tax incentives, and government programmes,[862] via overseas investment and

862. UK Government, 'UK FinTech on the Cutting Edge: An Evaluation of the International FinTech Sector' (26 February 2016) 8 and 11.

trade channels,[863] as the regulatory competition Means. These Means are targeted at foreign and institutional investors, including overseas sovereign wealth and pension funds, to attract and retain RC Drivers, primarily in the form of high-quality foreign inward investment.

5.1.1.2.2 Significant Policy Themes

An analysis of the actions and behaviours directed by the UK Government during the time period 2008-2017 highlighted several significant themes, including an identification of a broad set of factors influencing the development of the Fintech industry in the UK, and the advancement of competition policy. These significant themes are important as they highlight the UK Government's: (i) level of awareness of competitive pressures from other Primary Actors; and (ii) the extent to which they were concerned about these competitive pressures. The level of concern regarding the competitive pressures is primarily represented by the actions which the UK Government levied in response thereto. These significant themes include the following:

> *Promotion of the UK's interests abroad.* The UK Government's central policy aim was strengthening the UK's financial services industry by promoting its economic interests globally. This policy aim represents one of the cornerstones of the UK's economy and is integral to the UK Government's foreign and economic policy. It is executed using, among others, marketing strategies through overseas and investment trade channels targeted primarily at advanced economies. To this end, the UK Government consistently makes use of the messaging that the UK is a 'springboard for growth' and the 'best place to do business', as part of its promotion activities. The UK's ability to attract foreign investment has been highlighted as an important feature of its capability to produce successful firms.[864]
>
> *Fostering innovation in the UK.* The UK Government directed to strengthen the UK's international competitiveness, and thereby its economy, through the prism of developing innovation and technology. This policy aim culminated in directing policy initiatives towards growing the UK's Fintech sector, in particular, to develop London into the 'FinTech capital of the world'.[865] These policy initiatives resulted in the establishment of several governmental bodies and initiatives aimed to support the development of the Fintech sector, including Science and Innovation, Innovate UK, Project Innovate, Innovation Hub, and the FCA's Regulatory Sandbox. Further, the UK Government expended resources and research efforts on developing a clear and distinct Fintech strategy for the UK.
>
> *The role of regulation.* The UK Government indicated that the development of applicable legislation and regulation was one of the principal factors which

863. UKTI, 'Departmental Report and Resource Accounts 2008-09' (20 July 2009) 74.
864. UKTI, 'Departmental Report and Resource Accounts 2008-09' (20 July 2009) 12.
865. UK Government, 'Chancellor on Developing FinTech' (6 August 2014).

ensured the resilience of the UK's economy.[866] The UK's competitiveness was also viewed through the prism of legislative and regulatory measures meant to foster an attractive environment to start, finance and grow a business.[867] The success of the financial services industry in London, and its competitive edge against other international financial centres, was also noted for its legal and regulatory environment. Overall, it was highlighted that a supportive regulatory environment premised on principles-based regulation characterised as 'pro-innovation', would act to strengthen the UK's economy.

5.1.2 Process: 2014-2017

The analysis below sets out the actions and behaviours of the UK Government directed towards formulating a regulatory approach to the governance of Fintech and DLT Offerings in its jurisdiction.

5.1.2.1 Developing a Regulatory Approach to DLT

The UK Government directed its regulatory and policy initiatives towards DLT Offerings by adopting a cautious approach. This was reflected by the UK Government's 'Call for Information', in which the benefits and risks of digital currencies were surveyed, its use as a payment rail, in addition to uncovering the underlying rationale for the increased ownership and use of Bitcoins in the UK.[868] Most notably, the 'Call for Information' was focussed on gathering the views of the financial services industry and consumers as to whether digital currencies should be regulated in the UK, and if so, what kind of regulation was required. The 'Call for Information' received 120 submissions from a variety of stakeholders including academic researchers, banks, consultancies, and financial firms.[869]

Several stakeholders expressed that one of the key barriers to the development of the digital currency sector in the UK was a lack of an appropriate regulatory framework.[870] In response, the UK Government sought to clarify how pre-existing legal and regulatory rules could be applied to digital currency firms and users.[871] To this end, the UK Government proposed to apply AML regulation to digital currency exchanges in the UK with the aim of fostering appropriate innovation and also preventing the criminal use of digital currencies.[872] Notably, the UK Government indicated that, because digital currency use was not widespread in the UK, proportionate regulation presented a suitable solution for the absence of a regulatory framework for digital currencies in the

866. UK Government, 'The Queen's Speech to Both Houses of Parliament' (3 December 2008) 3.
867. UK Government, 'The Queen's Speech to Both Houses of Parliament' (4 June 2014).
868. UK Government, 'Digital Currencies: 5 Reasons We're Calling for Information' (3 November 2014), https://www.gov.uk/government/news/digital-currencies-5-reasons-were-calling-for-information.
869. UK Government, 'Digital Currencies: Response to the Call for Information' (March 2015).
870. UK Government, 'Digital Currencies: Response to the Call for Information' (March 2015) 8.
871. UK Government, 'Digital Currencies: Response to the Call for Information' (March 2015) 3.
872. UK Government, 'Digital Currencies: Response to the Call for Information' (March 2015) 4.

UK.[873] The UK Government also indicated that a framework setting out best practice standards for consumer protection could address the risks associated with digital currencies, without imposing burdensome regulation on the digital currency sector.[874] Further, the UK Government noted that it would collaborate with the BSI to develop voluntary standards for digital currency firms for consumer protection.[875] To this end, the BSI commissioned a report to assist it in developing a DLT/Blockchain standards strategy, in light of the needs of the stakeholders in the UK.[876] In furtherance of the UK Government's fact-finding process, the report also set out an overview of the DLT landscape, with a focus on its developmental issues.[877]

In April 2017, the FCA published a Discussion Paper on DLT considering its view on DLT through a 'technology neutral' approach to regulating financial services in the UK.[878] According to the FCA, this approach entailed regulating the *activities* which technology enables, and not the *technology* itself, in order to foster innovation, and to avert regulatory arbitrage (my emphasis).[879] To this end, the FCA highlighted its role in regulating competition for the benefit of consumers, while supporting the development of innovation. In particular, it was noted that DLT's potential to spur competition should be balanced with the FCA's mandate to protect consumers and uphold market integrity.[880] In conducting this balancing exercise, a consideration of how DLT applies to regulated financial products and services was therefore required. The FCA indicated that this balancing exercise could be facilitated by Project Innovate, encompassing a regulatory offering providing support and advice, a regulatory sandbox and the use of regulatory technology (RegTech). Overall, the FCA stated that its 'technology neutral' approach may need to be adapted where its regulatory requirements were not an appropriate fit for DLT Offerings, thereby not impeding DLT Offering development for the benefit of customers.[881] However, at that stage, the FCA expressed the view that it did not see the need to amend its regulatory framework to enable it to apply to DLT Offerings specifically.[882] Instead, the FCA indicated that it would continue gathering information on DLT models, their potential benefits and risks, and how they operate within the existing regulatory framework.

In December 2017, the FCA published its Feedback Statement on its DLT Discussion Paper noting in particular that its regulatory framework did not require adaptation as it was accommodating enough to apply to DLT Offerings provided by regulated firms.[883] In particular, the feedback it received highlighted that no specific

873. UK Government, 'Digital Currencies: Response to the Call for Information' (March 2015) 9.
874. UK Government, 'Digital Currencies: Response to the Call for Information' (March 2015) 19.
875. UK Government, 'Digital Currencies: Response to the Call for Information' (March 2015) 19.
876. Rand Europe, 'Understanding the Landscape of Distributed Ledger Technologies/Blockchain' (2017) i and ix, https://www.rand.org/pubs/research_reports/RR2223.html.
877. Rand Europe, 'Understanding the Landscape of Distributed Ledger Technologies/Blockchain' (2017), https://www.rand.org/pubs/research_reports/RR2223.html.
878. FCA, 'Discussion Paper on Distributed Ledger Technology' (April 2017) 5.
879. FCA, 'Discussion Paper on Distributed Ledger Technology' (April 2017) 7.
880. FCA, 'Discussion Paper on Distributed Ledger Technology' (April 2017) 7.
881. FCA, 'Discussion Paper on Distributed Ledger Technology' (April 2017) 7.
882. FCA, 'Discussion Paper on Distributed Ledger Technology' (April 2017) 8.
883. FCA, 'Distributed Ledger Technology: Feedback Statement on Discussion Paper 17/03' (December 2017) 4.

regulatory rules needed to be altered, and that the current regulatory regime did not pose any barriers to the provision of DLT Offerings. In regard to ICOs, the feedback was consistent with the FCA's view that ICOs needed to be considered on a case-by-case basis.[884] As to the next steps, the FCA indicated that it would not propose any changes to its rules to accommodate DLT Offerings but would keep its eye on market developments.[885] In alignment with the FCA, the PRA also adopted a 'technology neutral' approach towards technology that is targeted to a specific outcome. According to the BoE, this approach entailed focussing on 'whether the operational processes and governance of any use of technology adequately mitigates any risks that may arise'.[886] In applying this approach to DLT, the PRA considered both the benefits and risks of the technology, specifically in the context of the financial and monetary stability of the UK. The PRA also considered how DLT could potentially impact firms which it regulates, and how it could potentially use DLT to fulfil its mandate. To this end, the BoE developed a number of Proof-of-Concepts using DLT, including a renewed RTGS service capable of supporting systems built on DLT.[887]

During the time period 2018-2019, the UK Government directed its actions and behaviours towards developing a firm regulatory response to the increased interest in the use and adoption of digital currencies in the financial services industry. To this end, in February 2018, the House of Commons Treasury Committee (Treasury Committee) launched an enquiry into cryptoassets. The underlying objective of this enquiry was to assess: (i) the function of digital currencies in the UK; (ii) the effect of DLT on financial infrastructure and institutions; and (iii) how the UK Government, the FCA, the BoE have responded to digital currencies, particularly bearing in mind the need to balance the promotion of innovation, with consumer protection.[888] In September 2018, the Treasury Committee published its final report having conducted its enquiry primarily through hearing oral evidence on, among others, the regulation of cryptoassets, and through receiving written submissions (Final Report).[889] As a basis, the Final Report provided an overview of the cryptoasset ecosystem, in addition to outlining the use cases and applications of DLT, particularly in financial services. The Final Report also highlighted the UK's regulatory response to the development of the cryptoassets industry, including the risks presented by its broader use and adoption, such as its high price volatility, cyber security risks, accessibility and use of exchanges and digital wallets, and the likelihood of price coordination manipulation. The Final Report specified further that the continued development of the cryptoasset industry could

884. FCA, 'Distributed Ledger Technology: Feedback Statement on Discussion Paper 17/03' (December 2017) 5.
885. FCA, 'Distributed Ledger Technology: Feedback Statement on Discussion Paper 17/03' (December 2017) 5.
886. BoE, 'Financial Policy Committee Statement from Its Meeting: 12 March 2018' (16 March 2018), https://www.bankofengland.co.uk/statement/fpc/2018/financial-policy-committee-statement-march-2018.
887. BoE, 'RTGS Renewal Proof of Concept: Supporting DLT Settlement Models' (2018), https://www.bankofengland.co.uk/-/media/boe/files/payments/rtgs-renewal-proof-of-concept.pdf.
888. House of Commons Treasury Committee (Treasury Committee), 'Crypto-assets' (19 September 2018) 3.
889. Treasury Committee, 'Crypto-assets' (19 September 2018).

affect financial stability. Notably, it stated that cryptoassets could be regulated in the UK either through the existing regulatory framework or through a new tailored regulatory framework separate from the existing regime.[890] In particular, for the existing regulatory framework to apply, cryptoasset activities would need to be specified as a regulated activity in the FSMA RAO. Such a step would not be novel and has been undertaken by the FCA in the past in respect of other Fintech Offerings. For example, as of April 2014, P2P lending (i.e., crowdfunding) became a regulated activity under the auspices of Article 36H of the RAO.

The Treasury Committee indicated that amending the RAO to include cryptoassets as a regulated activity could be the correct approach to regulating the industry,[891] and would also be the most time-efficient method for including cryptoassets within the FCA's regulatory perimeter. The second option to regulate cryptoassets through the adoption of a new tailored regulatory framework, could be tailored based on industry requirements, but would be time-consuming based on the amendments that would be required to be made to existing legislation.[892] Accordingly, the Treasury Committee recommended that the UK Government consider the nature of the cryptoasset-regulated activities to be specified in the RAO, which should include at a minimum, provisions relating to ICOs and cryptoasset exchange services.[893] To this end, the Treasury Committee recommended that regulation should be introduced as a matter of urgency, particularly considering the growing risks associated with cryptoassets, and the need to protect consumers.[894] Accordingly, the Final Report noted that once the RAO has been amended to include cryptoassets as a specified investment, the FCA would consult on its approach to regulating this new activity, culminating in new rules and regulations.[895] It also expressed the view that developing a new tailored regulatory framework for cryptoassets would require more time but could be modelled on the regime imposed for P2P lending, which includes minimum prudential requirements for firms, conduct of business rules, and rules which regulate how disputes are resolved.[896] A number of stakeholders and governmental bodies provided written submissions to the HM Treasury on the development of the cryptoasset industry in the UK. These submissions were particularly informative for the Treasury Committee and provided a sound basis for its recommendations on the manner in which the cryptoasset industry could be regulated in the UK in the future. A number of important written submissions were made including by the CLC, BSI, the BoE, and the FCA. These written submissions focussed on a central question: whether the UK Government was correctly balancing the regulation of cryptoassets with its mandate to protect consumers without impeding the promotion of innovation.

In April 2018, the FCA provided its written submission to the Treasury Committee setting out its view on the role of digital assets in the UK, highlighting in particular the

890. Treasury Committee, 'Crypto-assets' (19 September 2018) 35.
891. Treasury Committee, 'Crypto-assets' (19 September 2018) 36.
892. Treasury Committee, 'Crypto-assets' (19 September 2018) 36.
893. Treasury Committee, 'Crypto-assets' (19 September 2018) 36.
894. Treasury Committee, 'Crypto-assets' (19 September 2018) 36.
895. Treasury Committee, 'Crypto-assets' (19 September 2018) 36.
896. Treasury Committee, 'Crypto-assets' (19 September 2018) 35.

benefits and risks presented through broader cryptoasset use and adoption.[897] Notably, the FCA provided its preliminary view of the application of its regulatory perimeter to cryptoasset activities in the UK. First, it noted that the application of its regulatory perimeter was dependent upon the specific cryptoasset under consideration, and thus that determinations would be made on a case-by-case basis. This approach was consistent with the FCA's actions and behaviours directed at the regulation of ICOs and CFDs. For example, in September 2017, the FCA published a consumer warning alerting potential investors of the risks of purchasing digital tokens as part of an ICO.[898] The consumer warning specified that ICOs were largely outside the purview of the FCA's regulatory perimeter unless they were structured to include regulated investments, such as transferable securities. However, the FCA did exhibit a more defined stance regarding specific classes of cryptoasset activity use. For example, in November 2017 the FCA published a consumer warning alerting potential investors of the high risk and speculative nature of CFDs with cryptocurrencies forming the underlying financial instrument.[899] Unlike its stance on ICOs, the FCA indicated specifically that its regulatory perimeter applied to traded cryptoasset CFDs. Second, the FCA indicated that its position on cryptoasset activities would be evaluated on an ongoing basis, having regard to the 'complex and evolving' nature of the application of the FCA's regulatory perimeter to cryptoasset activities. Accordingly, the FCA indicated that it would work with other regulatory bodies and take necessary action where consumer interests need protection. This would include collaboration with European and other supranational regulatory bodies, and global standard-setting bodies to an international response to cryptoasset activities. In addition, it indicated that it would continue working with stakeholders and innovative firms in assessing the appropriateness of the application of the existing regulatory framework to cryptoassets and DLT.

In the same month, the CLC provided its written submission to the Treasury Committee focussing primarily on the role of cryptoassets in the development of the financial services industry in London.[900] First, the CLC highlighted London's position as a leading international financial centre and its objective to attract investment and new business. In seeking to maintain this position, the CLC highlighted that London should be positioned as the leader of technology-driven financial and professional products and services. The CLC also indicated that it was concerned with the nature and extent of the proposed regulation of cryptoasset activities, cautioning against adopting a 'heavy-handed' approach which would act to counter innovation and competition in the UK.

897. FCA, 'Financial Conduct Authority's Written Submission on Digital Currencies' (April 2018), data.parliament.uk/WrittenEvidence/CommitteeEvidence.svc/EvidenceDocument/Treasury/Digital currencies/written/81677.html.
898. FCA, 'Initial Coin Offerings' (12 September 2017), https://www.fca.org.uk/news/statements/initial-coin-offerings.
899. FCA, 'Consumer Warning about the Risks of Investing in Cryptocurrency CFDS' (14 November 2017), https://Www.Fca.Org.Uk/News/News-Stories/Consumer-Warning-About-Risks-Investing-Cryptocurrency-Cfds.
900. City of London Corporation, 'Memorandum from the City of London Corporation' (April 2018), data.parliament.uk/WrittenEvidence/CommitteeEvidence.svc/EvidenceDocument/Treasury/Digital currencies/written/82205.html.

In May 2018, the BoE provided its written submission focussing on the potential impact of cryptoassets on financial and monetary stability in the UK. In particular, it noted that extensive use of cryptoassets in the UK was unlikely to impact its influence on setting monetary policy as cryptoassets fail to meet the three functional requirements to be classified as money. The BoE also noted that cryptoassets did not represent a substantial threat to financial stability in the UK. This position had been reached by the FPC in March 2018 on the basis that cryptoassets' use for payments was minimal, cryptoasset stock was relatively small, and systemically important UK financial institutions had negligible exposures to cryptoassets.[901] From a policy perspective, the BoE noted ongoing initiatives at both a domestic and international level. At a domestic level, the BoE highlighted its role, alongside the FCA, in the UK Government's Cryptoasset Taskforce to assess the benefits and risks of the broader use of DLT in financial services. At a global level, the BoE highlighted its engagement with the G20 and the FSB, and the continued efforts to monitor cryptoassets and their related risks. From a rulemaking perspective, the BoE's written submission indicated that the PRA was considering how existing prudential regulation could potentially apply to cryptoassets held by banks and financial institutions. In addition, the PRA was considering whether additional rules would be required to counter risks associated with cryptoasset activities.

The Cryptoassets Taskforce was launched in March 2018 by the HM Treasury Chancellor in collaboration with the FCA and the BoE. This work culminated in the publication of a final report in October 2018 setting out the manner in which cryptoassets could potentially be regulated in the UK going forward (CATF Report).[902] The report reiterated the strategy for the UK to become the world's most innovative economy, as set out in the 2017 Digital Strategy Plan. The CAFT also highlighted the UK Government's competition policy goal to maintain its position as a leading international financial centre through, among others, its robust regulatory frameworks and the fostering of innovation in the financial services industry. The CATF Report provided an outline for the development and implementation of the UK's proposed policy and regulatory approach to cryptoasset activities. This approach included actions to be taken by the BoE and FCA to provide greater clarity concerning the application of its existing regulatory perimeter. These actions included FCA-led consultations on: (i) the proposed ban on the sale of derivatives referencing specific types of cryptoassets; and (ii) regulatory guidance on the application of the existing regulatory perimeter to cryptoassets activities.[903] In addition, it was stated that the HM Treasury would consult on possible extensions of the existing regulatory perimeter to cryptoassets which have features similar to specified investments, but which do not fall within the perimeter. The CATF Report concluded that the development of DLT for use in the financial services industry was still at a nascent stage. It did, however, emphasise the potential

901. BoE, 'Financial Policy Committee Statement from Its Meeting: 12 March 2018' (16 March 2018), https://www.bankofengland.co.uk/statement/fpc/2018/financial-policy-committee-statement-march-2018.
902. HM Treasury, BoE, and the FCA, 'Crypto-asset Taskforce: Final Report' (October 2018).
903. HM Treasury, BoE, and the FCA, 'Crypto-asset Taskforce: Final Report' (October 2018) 40.

benefits which could be realised through DLT's broader adoption and use in the financial services industry. As such, it highlighted the HM Treasury, the BoE and the FCA's ongoing role in supporting DLT's development.[904] At the same time, the report highlighted the immediate concern for authorities to mitigate the risks posed by cryptoasset activity to consumers and market integrity, in addition to averting its use for illicit purposes.[905] In this regard, it indicated that a robust regulatory response was required to manage cryptoasset-related risks which fall within existing regulatory frameworks.[906]

In January 2019, the FCA published its Guidance on Cryptoassets Consultation Paper (Proposed Guidance) in fulfilment of its first commitment set out in the CATF Report.[907] The primary purpose of the consultation was to provide clarity to market participants on how the FCA's existing regulatory perimeter applies to cryptoasset activities, and as such whether performing those activities required authorisation.[908] The consultation was relevant for a host of market participants, including firms creating, issuing, and marketing cryptoasset products and services.[909] Overall, the Proposed Guidance provided an unbinding, but persuasive view on whether cryptoasset tokens, as categorised in the CATF Report as either exchange, security, or utility tokens, fell within the FCA's regulatory perimeter.[910]

The consultation period closed on 5 April 2019, after which the FCA received 92 responses from, among others, large banks, Fintech firms, token issuers, and cryptocurrency exchanges.[911] The FCA reported that the majority of the respondents supported the proposals set out in the Proposed Guidance, and as such the Final Guidance on Cryptoassets published in July 2019, did not differ significantly.[912] Certain adjustments were, however, made with the purpose of providing further clarity, and to ensure that proposed policy objectives were achieved. This included a reframing of the cryptoasset taxonomy to take into consideration observations from the market; additional clarity provided on stablecoins; and additional guidance on when tokens may be considered e-money.[913] The FCA's feedback to the respondents focussed on regulated and unregulated tokens and market observations. In particular, the FCA noted that respondents' views calling for a new regime for exchange tokens fell outside the scope of the Proposed Guidance, but that these views would inform the HM Treasury's work on unregulated cryptoassets.[914] Some respondents also indicated that the distinction between exchange and utility tokens was not clear, and therefore requested further

904. HM Treasury, BoE, and the FCA, 'Crypto-asset Taskforce: final report' (October 2018) 2.
905. HM Treasury, BoE, and the FCA, 'Crypto-asset Taskforce: Final Report' (October 2018) 3.
906. HM Treasury, BoE, and the FCA, 'Crypto-asset Taskforce: Final Report' (October 2018) 3.
907. FCA, 'Guidance on Cryptoassets: Consultation Paper CP19/3' (January 2019).
908. FCA, 'Guidance on Cryptoassets: Consultation Paper CP19/3' (January 2019) 4-5.
909. FCA, 'Guidance on Cryptoassets: Consultation Paper CP19/3' (January 2019) 5.
910. HM Treasury, BoE, and FCA, 'Crypto-asset Taskforce: Final Report' (October 2018) 11 and FCA, 'Guidance on Cryptoassets: Consultation Paper CP19/3' (January 2019) 16.
911. FCA, 'Guidance on Crypto-assets Feedback and Final Guidance to CP 19/3' (July 2019).
912. FCA, 'Guidance on Crypto-assets Feedback and Final Guidance to PS 19/22' (July 2019) 7.
913. FCA, 'Guidance on Crypto-assets Feedback and Final Guidance to PS 19/22' (July 2019) 7.
914. FCA, 'Guidance on Crypto-assets Feedback and Final Guidance to PS 19/22' (July 2019) 10.

guidance. To this end, the FCA agreed to make changes which would clearly distinguish the categories of regulated and unregulated cryptoassets. For example, e-money tokens would be separated from utility and security tokens and would be accorded its own regulated e-money token category.[915]

In July 2019, the FCA published its Consultation Paper proposing a ban on the retail sale of derivatives and exchange-trade notes that reference specific types of unregulated, transferable cryptoassets in fulfilment of its second commitment (Proposed Rules).[916] The primary purpose of the consultation was to propose rules prohibiting the distribution, marketing, and sale to retail clients of derivatives and exchange-trade notes that reference specific types of unregulated, transferable cryptoassets.[917] The proposed ban was based on the FCA's consideration that retail consumers are not able to reliably assess the risks associated with those products. Without this reliable knowledge, retail consumers could potentially suffer harm from unexpected losses resulting from purchasing these products.[918] The Proposed Rules indicated that the consultation was relevant for a host of market participants, including firms creating, issuing, and marketing cryptoasset products and services.[919] Overall, the Proposed Rules therefore sought to minimise harm to retail consumers suffered as a consequence of the sale of derivatives and ETNs referencing specific types of unregulated, transferable cryptoassets, in line with its FSMA operational objective to protect consumers. The proposed ban would only apply in respect of retail customers and would not apply to professional or eligible counterparty clients; derivatives or exchange-trade notes referencing other tokens; and collective investment undertakings.[920]

The consultation period closed on 3 October 2019, after which the FCA received 527 responses from, among others, exchanges offering crypto-derivatives and unregulated cryptoassets, firms that issue and sell cryptoassets, and retail consumers.[921] The FCA reported that the majority of the respondents opposed the proposed ban on the basis, among others, that: (i) cryptoassets do have intrinsic value; (ii) retail consumers have the capability to value cryptoassets; and (iii) a ban would be disproportionate with other measures able to achieve the same objectives. The FCA, however, indicated that having taken into consideration the necessary feedback, the rules as consulted would be confirmed, subject to minor technical adjustments, culminating in the

915. FCA, 'Guidance on Crypto-assets Feedback and Final Guidance to PS 19/22' (July 2019) 13.
916. FCA, 'Prohibiting the Sale to Retail Clients of Investment Products that Reference Cryptoassets: Consultation Paper CP19/22' (July 2019).
917. FCA, 'Prohibiting the Sale to Retail Clients of Investment Products that Reference Cryptoassets: Consultation Paper CP19/22' (July 2019) 4.
918. FCA, 'Prohibiting the Sale to Retail Clients of Investment Products that Reference Cryptoassets: Consultation Paper CP19/22' (July 2019) 3.
919. FCA, 'Prohibiting the Sale to Retail Clients of Investment Products that Reference Cryptoassets: Consultation Paper CP19/22' (July 2019) 4.
920. FCA, 'Prohibiting the Sale to Retail Clients of Investment Products that Reference Cryptoassets: Consultation Paper CP19/22' (July 2019) 5.
921. FCA, 'Prohibiting the Sale to Retail Clients of Investment Products that Reference Cryptoassets: Consultation Paper CP19/22' (July 2019) 3.

publication of its Policy Statement in October 2020.[922] The FCA's feedback to the respondents centred on the perceived value of cryptoassets. The FCA reiterated the view that cryptoasset prices are determined through speculative behaviour and sentiment.[923] In particular, it opposed the respondents' view that cryptoassets exchanged for fiat currency endows it with intrinsic value as the underlying medium of exchange remains the relevant fiat currency.[924] The respondents submitted alternative valuation models to support the argument that retail consumers are able to reliably value cryptoassets. On a review of these models, the FCA concluded that the variety of factors and techniques used to value cryptoassets, which included subjective inputs, in fact, supported its view that cryptoassets cannot be reliably valued.[925]

5.1.2.2 Discussion

The actions and behaviours considered above are examined below through an identification of the regulatory approach adopted by the UK Government, together with the competition policy considerations which formed part of the approach adopted.

5.1.2.2.1 Regulatory Approach

The actions and behaviours directed by the UK Government to develop a regulatory approach for the governance of Fintech and DLT Offerings were underlined primarily by its policy aim of making the UK the global centre for financial innovation. To this end, the UK Government adhered to a 'watch and learn' approach to the burgeoning area of cryptoassets.[926] This approach was undertaken primarily through the guise of two strategic objectives, which included: (i) a fact-finding process levied to fully understand DLT as an emerging type of Fintech, particularly the risks it posed, and use cases for the financial services industry; and (ii) continuous engagement with consumers and the financial services industry.

5.1.2.2.2 Underlying Principles

Several key factors influenced the government's adoption of a staged and proportionate regulatory response to the governance of Fintech and DLT Offerings in the UK. These key themes are important as they highlight the UK Government's: (i) actions and

922. FCA, 'Prohibiting the Sale to Retail Clients of Investment Products that Reference Cryptoassets: Policy Statement PS20/10' (October 2020).
923. FCA, 'Prohibiting the Sale to Retail Clients of Investment Products that Reference Cryptoassets: Policy Statement PS20/10' (October 2020) 8.
924. FCA, 'Prohibiting the Sale to Retail Clients of Investment Products that Reference Cryptoassets: Policy Statement PS20/10' (October 2020) 8.
925. FCA, 'Prohibiting the Sale to Retail Clients of Investment Products that Reference Cryptoassets: Policy Statement PS20/10' (October 2020) 10.
926. House of Commons Library, 'Cryptocurrencies: Bitcoin and Other Exchange Tokens' Briefing Paper No. 8780 (19 February 2020) 19.

behaviours in the form of regulatory and policy initiatives which drove the development of Fintech in the UK; (ii) underlying rationale for adopting a 'watch and learn' approach to formulating a regulatory response to the governance of Fintech and DLT Offerings in the UK; and (iii) a consideration of competition policy in formulating its regulatory response. The key factors underlining this regulatory approach include:

> *Fact-finding enquiry*. The UK Government approached the development of Fintech and DLT in the UK, specifically London, through policy and regulatory initiatives geared to gathering information on DLT's benefits, risks, business models and uses cases for the financial services industry. This investigation took the form of the publication of government reports and discussion papers, through the UK Government's 'Call for Information', the FCA's discussion papers, the Treasury Committee's enquiry on cryptoassets, and the Cryptoasset Taskforce. It also included continuous monitoring of market developments based on the complex and evolving nature of the cryptoasset industry to allow financial regulatory authorities to observe how cryptoasset activities could fall within its existing regulatory frameworks.
>
> *Technology-neutral approach*. The FCA and the PRA adopted a 'technology-neutral' approach to responding to financial services and products underlined by the emerging technology. In particular, this approach comprised the regulation of the financial services activities conducted by firms through the use of the emerging technology, and not the regulation of the technology itself. The underlying purpose of this approach is to facilitate the development of innovation, but at the same time is applied to prevent regulatory arbitrage in relation thereto through possible regulatory gaps. To this end, the 'technology-neutral' approach is applied with flexibility and may be adapted where necessary, such as when its application would act to stifle the development of innovation.
>
> *Balancing consumer protection and fostering innovation*. The UK Government's regulatory approach to Fintech and DLT is underlined predominantly by the need to balance the protection of consumer interests with the fostering of innovation for the benefit of consumers. The FCA's mandate includes promoting competition through DLT's potential balanced with its duty to protect consumers and uphold market integrity. Practically, the actions and behaviours of the FCA advanced both interests through its consumer warnings on ICOs and CFDs, and through encouraging innovation and considering all ancillary risks through its Project Innovate. This balancing exercise also formed the focal point of consideration in the Treasury Committee's enquiry on cryptoassets.
>
> *Industry and stakeholder engagement*. The UK Government's regulatory approach was developed through its continuous engagement with the financial services industry, consumers and other relevant stakeholders. This engagement formed an integral component of the UK Government's fact-finding enquiry, most notably represented by the written submissions forming part of the 'Call for Information', the Treasury Committee's enquiry into

cryptoassets, and the FCA's consultation processes conducted for its Proposed Guidance and Proposed Rules. Industry and stakeholder engagement played a particularly pivotal role in directing whether cryptoassets should be regulated in the UK, and what form that regulation should take once it is implemented.

Competition policy. The UK Government considered competition policy concerns in developing a regulatory approach to the governance of DLT Offerings, specifically cryptoassets. This consideration was directed in the context of the UK Government's overall policy aim of strengthening and maintaining London as a leading international financial centre and as a leader of technology-driven financial and professional services. This approach was consistent with the UK Government's strategic objective to make the UK the world's most innovative economy. Notably, the Cryptoassets Taskforce highlighted that the overall policy aim could be achieved through, among others, its robust regulatory frameworks and fostering innovation in the financial services industry.

Non-legislative intervention. The UK Government's initial response to the governance of DLT Offerings was to apply light touch regulation, such as its proposal to apply AML regulation to cryptoasset exchanges. The application of proportionate regulation was based on the limited use of cryptoassets in the UK and to prevent burdening the industry with too many regulatory requirements. This initial view extended to applying the existing regulatory framework to cryptoassets through proposed regulatory guidance, as opposed to developing a new tailored regulatory framework which would be time-consuming. The UK Government indicated that the existing regulatory framework could be appropriately applied to cryptoassets and could provide sufficient protection to consumers.

5.1.3 Output: 2019-2020

The analysis below sets out the actions and behaviours of the UK Government directed to issuing regulatory rules and guidance which had the effect of formalising the regulations governing DLT Offerings.

5.1.3.1 Regulatory Rules

5.1.3.1.1 Perimeter Regulatory Guidance on Cryptoassets

In July 2019, the FCA published its final guidance clarifying the application of its existing regulatory perimeter to different types of cryptoassets; the corresponding obligations for firms; and the regulatory protections to which consumers are entitled (Final Guidance).[927] Overarchingly, the Final Guidance provides market participants

927. FCA, 'Guidance on Cryptoassets: Feedback and Final Guidance to CP 19/3' (July 2019) para. 1.2.

with clarity on whether different types of cryptoasset tokens fall within the FCA's regulatory perimeter by virtue of its qualification as: (i) a 'specified investment' under the RAO; (ii) a 'financial instrument' under MiFID II; and (iii) 'electronic money' under the EMRs. The guidance also sets out the FCA's view on the application of the PSRs to cryptoasset activities. Accordingly, the Final Guidance clarifies the FCA's expectations for firms conducting cryptoasset activities, and for which authorisation or registration is required.[928] The guidance is thus relevant to, among others, firms creating, holding, issuing, and marketing cryptoasset products and services, such as custodian wallet providers, exchanges and trading platforms.[929] The guidance is not legally binding on UK courts but instead represents the persuasive views of the FCA.[930] Even so, firms acting in accordance with the Final Guidance would be treated as 'having complied with the relevant rule or requirement' by the FCA.[931] Notably, the FCA has expressed that the guidance would progress cryptoasset market activity, and boost competition in favour of consumers.[932]

The FCA's regulatory perimeter comprises the financial services activities which require FCA authorisation (or registration) before firms may carry on such activities 'by way of business' in the UK. Ostensibly, therefore, the perimeter draws the boundary between activities which are regulated by the FCA, and those which are not. The FCA derives its regulatory perimeter powers on the basis of the general prohibition set out in section 19 of the FSMA which states that no person is permitted to carry on a regulated activity unless they are an authorised or an exempt person. As such, firms carrying on regulated activities, or claiming to do so, involving cryptoassets by way of business in the UK, must ensure they have the correct FCA permissions before conducting those activities.[933]

The FCA's regulatory perimeter is delineated primarily by the specified activities and investments set out in the FSMA and the RAO. The Markets in Financial Instruments Directive (MiFID II) also specifies a range of financial instruments which constitute different categories of investments to which MiFID II applies. These financial instruments fall within the FCA's regulatory perimeter by virtue of their transposition into UK law under the RAO. The FCA's regulatory perimeter is also, however, informed by reference to ancillary legislation, most notably, the issuing of e-money under the auspices of the EMRs,[934] and the provision of payment services within the remit of the PMRs.[935] Firms carrying on regulated activities, or claiming to do so, involving

928. FCA, 'Guidance on Cryptoassets: Feedback and Final Guidance to CP 19/3' (July 2019) para. 1.4 and para. 1.20.
929. FCA, 'Guidance on Cryptoassets: Feedback and Final Guidance to CP 19/3' (July 2019) para. 1.4 and para. 1.14.
930. FCA, 'Guidance on Cryptoassets: Feedback and Final Guidance to CP 19/3' (July 2019) para. 1.4 and para. 1.21.
931. FCA, 'Guidance on Cryptoassets: Feedback and Final Guidance to CP 19/3' (July 2019) para. 1.4 and para. 1.21.
932. FCA, 'Guidance on Cryptoassets: Feedback and Final Guidance to CP 19/3' (July 2019) para. 1.4 and para. 1.18.
933. FCA, 'Guidance on Cryptoassets: Feedback and Final Guidance to CP 19/3' (July 2019) para. 26.
934. Electronic Money Regulations 2011.
935. Payment Services Regulations 2017 (PSRs).

cryptoassets, must ensure they have the correct FCA permissions before conducting those activities only if those activities are conducted by way of business in the UK. The FCA's Perimeter Guidance Manual (PERG) provides guidance on the meaning of 'by way of business', but indicative factors include whether a person receives compensation (monetary or non-monetary) and whether the activity is carried on regularly and with a commercial objective.[936] The decentralised nature of cryptoassets and inherent cross-border elements may provide challenges to this geographically-based requirement. However, a regulatory activity may still be regarded as being conducted in the UK even if a part of the activity is conducted outside UK borders.[937] The most significant features of the FCA's Final Guidance include explanations related to: (i) specified investments; (ii) financial promotions; (iii) unregulated tokens; (iv) stablecoins; (v) regulated payment services; and (vi) regulated tokens.

5.1.3.1.2 *Prohibiting the Sale to Retail Clients of Investment Products That Reference Cryptoassets*

In October 2020, the FCA published its policy statement setting out its final position and the applicable Handbook Rules banning the distribution, marketing and sale in or from the UK of derivatives and ETNs referencing specific kinds of unregulated, transferable cryptoassets to retail clients.[938] The ban served to minimise harm to retail clients' experiences with purchasing these investment products on the basis that retail clients are unable to reliably assess the benefits and risks thereof.[939] The proposed ban is relevant to, among others, firms creating, distributing, issuing, and marketing cryptoasset products and services, such as custodian wallet providers, exchanges and trading platforms. The FCA's rules on this ban came into force on 6 January 2021 upon which firms were required to cease related activities.[940]

The FCA's ban was effected legislatively by amendments to its COBS through the Conduct of Business (Cryptoasset Products) (Amendment) and Associated Exiting the European Union Amendments Instrument 2020.[941] The ban applies specifically to: (i) MiFID investment firms, save for collective portfolio management investment firms; (ii) branches of third country investment firms; (iii) MiFID optional exemption firms; and (iv) temporary permission firms who are EEA MiFID Investment firms, save for collective portfolio management investment firms.[942] COBS 22.6 notes that 'marketing'

936. *See* FCA PERG 2.3.
937. FCA PERG 2.4.
938. FCA, 'Prohibiting the Sale to Retail Clients of Investment Products that Reference Cryptoassets' (October 2020) PS20/10.
939. FCA, 'Prohibiting the Sale to Retail Clients of Investment Products that Reference Cryptoassets' (October 2020) PS20/10, para. 1.11.
940. FCA, 'Prohibiting the Sale to Retail Clients of Investment Products that Reference Cryptoassets' (October 2020) PS20/10, para. 1.5 and para. 1.8.
941. Conduct of Business (Cryptoasset Products) Instrument 2020 (FCA 2020/34), annex B.
942. FCA, COBS 22.6.1 (1)-(4).

includes communicating and approving financial promotions,[943] and 'distribution or sale' includes any dealing of cryptoassets derivatives and ENTs.[944]

5.1.3.2 Discussion

The actions and behaviours considered above are examined below through the guise of the salient regulatory features instituted by the UK Government.

5.1.3.2.1 Regulatory Framework

An analysis of the actions and behaviours directed by the UK Government during the time period 2019-2020 evidenced the development of a regulatory framework for DLT Offerings, specifically for cryptoassets, as underlined by the provisions of the FSMA, RAO, EMRs and the PSRs, through the supervision of the FCA and the PRA. The UK Government adopted the specific term 'cryptoasset', categorised into three cryptoasset token types: exchange, security, and utility tokens.[945] Accordingly, the UK has adopted a non-legislative approach, opting to apply its existing regulatory framework to cryptoasset activities. Generally, a firm undertaking activities related to cryptoassets which constitute a 'specified investment' under the RAO, may require a licence to conduct those activities.

5.1.3.2.2 Central Components

Several factors influenced the development of the regulatory framework governing DLT Offerings. These central components are crucial as they highlight: (i) the severity or laxity of the regulatory rules and guidance introduced by the UK Government; and (ii) whether the actions and behaviours directed towards developing a regulatory framework for DLT Offerings were consistent with the regulatory approach established in the Process analysis, which included competition policy considerations. The central components underlining the development of the regulatory framework governing DLT Offerings include:

> *Regulatory remit*. The regulatory framework developed for the governance of DLT Offerings, specifically cryptoassets, was clarified predominantly through the FCA's Final Guidance. To this end, firms who undertake activities involving cryptoasset tokens may require a licence by virtue of those activities being qualified as: (i) a 'specified investment' under the RAO; (ii) a 'financial instrument' under MiFID II; (iii) 'electronic money' under the EMRs; (iv) or application of the PSRs. Accordingly, the regulatory framework includes within its remit a broad range of cryptoassets relating to firms creating,

943. FSMA, s. 21(13) and Financial Services and Markets Act 2000 (Financial Promotion) Order 2005 (SI 2005/1529) (FPO), Art. 6(d).
944. RAO, para. 2, Sch. 2.
945. HM Treasury, BoE, and FCA, 'Crypto-asset Taskforce: Final Report' (October 2018) 11.

holding, issuing, and marketing crypto-asset products and services, such as custodian wallet providers, exchanges and trading platforms.

Regulatory rules. The regulatory framework developed for the governance of DLT Offerings, specifically cryptoassets, is provided predominantly in the form of regulatory guidance which clarifies the FCA's expectations for firms conducting cryptoasset activities, and for which authorisation is required. In delineating the remit of the FCA's regulatory perimeter, the Final Guidance distinguishes between regulated and unregulated tokens. Accordingly, firms who act in accordance with the Final Guidance are treated as 'having complied with the relevant rule or requirement' by the FCA. The FCA's regulatory rules include the ban on the sale to retail clients of investment products that reference cryptoassets, underlined by the policy aim of minimising harm which may be caused to these clients.

AML. The regulatory framework developed for the governance of DLT Offerings, specifically cryptoassets, included proposed plans by the UK Government to transpose the 5AMLD into UK law.[946] The UK Government indicated that its transposition would go beyond the scope of the 5AMLD to include activities relating to, among others, exchange services between one cryptoasset and another, cryptoasset automated teller machines, and the issuance of new cryptoassets, such as through ICOs. The AML regime under the transposed 5AMLD will apply to activities, irrespective of their status as falling within the FCA's regulatory perimeter. To this end, businesses related to unregulated tokens, such as exchange tokens, would be included in the AML regime.

Supervisory objectives. The regulatory framework developed for the governance of DLT Offerings, specifically cryptoassets, is underlined by the FCA's supervisory objectives, among others, consumer protection and competition harms. The Final Guidance should enable consumers to identify whether a cryptoasset falls within the FCA's regulatory perimeter and is thus subject to applicable regulatory rules, and regulatory protections. To this end, consumers are permitted to use the FCA Register to determine whether firms have the necessary permissions for the regulated activities which they are conducting. Notably, the Final Guidance is underlined by the policy aim of reducing legal uncertainty, which may foster cryptoasset market development and enhance competition for the benefit of consumers.

5.1.3.2.3 Regulatory Approach

The analysis of actions and behaviours directed by the UK Government during the time period 2019-2020 evidenced a light touch approach to the regulation of DLT Offerings, specifically cryptoassets, consistent mostly with the regulatory approach established in the Process analysis. In particular, the 'watch and learn' regulatory approach was

946. Directive (EU) 2018/843 on the prevention of the use of the financial system for the purposes of money laundering or terrorist financing.

evidenced through the UK Government's fact-finding enquiry illustrated through its ongoing work to establish a regulatory framework for cryptoassets in the UK, including the HM Treasury's consultation on whether additional regulation would be required for the cryptoasset market, in particular unregulated cryptoassets, and the transposition and extension of the 5AMLD into UK law.

The FCA's Final Guidance was consistent with the UK Government's non-legislative approach to developing a regulatory framework for the governance of DLT Offerings. However, the HM Treasury's consultations may alter this approach through new legislation regulating unregulated cryptoasset tokens. The Final Guidance was also consistent with the FCA's aim to protect consumers, such as the application of its financial promotion rules. Competition policy concerns were also highlighted, with the FCA noting that its Final Guidance would progress the cryptoasset market activity, and boost competition in favour of consumers.[947] The application of the FCA's technology-neutral approach, however, was less evident, as also illustrated by the ban on the sale of derivatives referencing cryptoassets.

5.1.4 Feedback

The analysis below sets out the actions and behaviours of the UK Government directed to modifying the initial regulatory response governing DLT Offerings.

5.1.4.1 Regulatory Rules

5.1.4.1.1 Money Laundering and Regulatory Arbitrage

The broader use and adoption of cryptoassets in the UK, and internationally, spurred on concerns regarding the potential for regulatory arbitrage, and associated money laundering activities. In particular, the FCA highlighted that the global nature of permissionless DLT systems, unencumbered by geographical limitations, may easily exploit the gaps existing in the regulatory framework for cryptoassets worldwide.[948] For example, several leading cryptoasset exchanges have relocated across jurisdictions, while others have no permanent address, maintaining their service offerings to their customers through their use of cloud server storage.[949] To this end, the FCA indicated that it was working in collaboration with the FATF to address issues of this nature. The FCA indicated that it expects cryptoasset exchanges to comply with the same AML obligations applicable to firms in traditional markets.[950] This would include the performance of KYC checks for onboarding clients, using transaction monitoring

947. FCA, 'Guidance on Cryptoassets: Feedback and Final Guidance to CP 19/3' (July 2019) para. 1.4 and para. 1.18.
948. FCA, 'Unstable Coins: Cryptoassets, Financial Regulation and Preventing Financial Crime in the Emerging Market for Digital Assets' (6 March 2020).
949. FCA, 'Unstable Coins: Cryptoassets, Financial Regulation and Preventing Financial Crime in the Emerging Market for Digital Assets' (6 March 2020) 4.
950. FCA, 'Unstable Coins: Cryptoassets, Financial Regulation and Preventing Financial Crime in the Emerging Market for Digital Assets' (6 March 2020) 5.

tools to ensure that funds held do not constitute the proceeds of crime, and actively examining users for any suspicious activity.[951] According to the FCA, tackling illicit use cases of cryptoassets is beneficial for financial innovation, as opposed to comprising a 'zero sum game'.[952] Accordingly, the HM Treasury incorporated the 5AMLD domestically through the amendment of the Money Laundering Regulations[953] designating the FCA as the supervisor for specified cryptoasset business activities, including ICOs.[954]

Accordingly, firms engaged in one of the specified cryptoasset business activities, must comply with several AML obligations including: (i) conducting a comprehensive risk assessment identifying the money laundering risks in their business, and establishing policies and procedures tackling these risks;[955] (ii) conducting customer due diligence for all transactions;[956] (iii) monitoring transactions executed on behalf of clients to identify potential suspicious or unusual transactions indicating money laundering risks;[957] (iv) retaining records for a period of at least 5 years subsequent to the termination of business relationships, but no longer than 10 years;[958] and (v) transmitting suspicious activity reports to the UK National Crime Agency. The FCA's cryptoasset AML regime came into effect on 10 January 2020.

5.1.4.1.2 *Cryptoasset Promotions*

In July 2020, the HM Treasury published its consultation document on the UK Government's proposal to include the promotion of specified kinds of cryptoassets within the scope of the FCA's financial promotion regime.[959] According to the HM Treasury, such an approach would benefit consumer protection, while simultaneously 'promoting responsible innovation'.[960] To this end, the HM Treasury referenced the Cryptoasset Taskforce's conclusion that a lack of appropriate information and misleading advertising, particularly for retail customers, were material threats to consumer protection.[961] The FCA's consumer research confirmed this position, noting in particular that consumers less knowledgeable of cryptoassets, were more likely to be predisposed to advertisements.[962] The HM Treasury proposed to bring unregulated cryptoassets into the remit of the FCA's financial promotion regime by including them in the list of controlled investments and amending the number of controlled activities,

951. FCA, 'Unstable Coins: Cryptoassets, Financial Regulation and Preventing Financial Crime in the Emerging Market for Digital Assets' (6 March 2020) 5.
952. FCA, 'Unstable Coins: Cryptoassets, Financial Regulation and Preventing Financial Crime in the Emerging Market for Digital Assets' (6 March 2020) 5.
953. Money Laundering, Terrorist Financing and Transfer of Funds (Information on the Payer) Regulations 2017 (ML Regulations).
954. FCA, 'Unstable Coins: Cryptoassets, Financial Regulation and Preventing Financial Crime in the Emerging Market for Digital Assets' (6 March 2020) 6.
955. ML Regulations, reg 18.
956. ML Regulations, reg 27.
957. ML Regulations, reg 33.
958. ML Regulations, reg 40(3)-(4).
959. HM Treasury, 'Cryptoasset Promotions Consultation' (July 2020).
960. HM Treasury, 'Cryptoasset Promotions Consultation' (July 2020), para. 1.1.
961. HM Treasury, 'Cryptoasset Promotions Consultation' (July 2020), para. 3.7 and para. 3.8.
962. FCA, 'Research Note: Crypto Consumer Research 2020' (30 June 2020).

to which the FPO[963] currently applies.[964] Schedule 1 of the FPO specifies the list of controlled investments, such as futures, options and government and public securities, and controlled activities, such as dealing in securities, arranging deals in investments and managing investments. Security tokens falling within the RAO's regulatory perimeter are also subject to the remit of FPO as 'controlled investments', as are e-money tokens regulated under the EMRs.[965] The addition of unregulated cryptoassets to the list of controlled investments specified in Part 2 of Schedule 1 of the FPO, would extend the financial promotion prohibition to inducements or invitations to exercise any rights bestowed by unregulated cryptoassets to obtain, dispose of, underwrite or convert the same.[966] The proposed definition of 'unregulated cryptoasset' ('qualifying cryptoasset') includes only those which are fungible and transferable as material features which raise the possibility of customer protection issues,[967] thereby excluding digital collectibles, and customer loyalty points as tokens on a DLT system.[968] In addition, the HM Treasury proposed to extend the list of controlled activities to include buying, selling, subscribing for or underwriting of qualifying cryptoassets.[969]

In April 2021, the FCA published its Discussion Paper on financial promotions for high-risk investments.[970] While the Discussion Paper largely relates to high-risk investments currently falling within its remit of the FPO, the FCA did indicate that as new high-risk investments emerge or are brought within the regulatory perimeter of the financial promotion regime, it has to consider how to label them for the purpose of its financial promotion rules. Bearing this in mind, the FCA indicated that the issues covered in the Discussion Paper may bear relevance to the HM Treasury's proposal to bring cryptoassets into the remit of the financial promotion regime. As part of this proposal, the FCA would need to categorise cryptoassets within the scope of its financial promotion rules.[971]

In January 2022, the FCA published its Consultation Paper on financial promotion rules for high-risk investments, including cryptoassets.[972] High-risk investments are those subject to the marketing restrictions under the FCA's rules including, NRRS and PTPA.[973] Cryptoassets will be categorised as such once brought within the remit of the financial promotion regime.[974] The FCA indicated that it intends to apply the

963. Financial Services and Markets Act 2000 (Financial Promotion) Order 2005.
964. HM Treasury, 'Cryptoasset Promotions Consultation' (July 2020), para. 4.14.
965. HM Treasury, 'Cryptoasset Promotions Consultation' (July 2020), para. 4.10.
966. HM Treasury, 'Cryptoasset Promotions Consultation' (July 2020), para. 4.16.
967. HM Treasury, 'Cryptoasset Promotions Consultation' (July 2020), para. 4.22 and para. 4.24.
968. HM Treasury, 'Cryptoasset Promotions Consultation' (July 2020), paras 4.26-7.
969. HM Treasury, 'Cryptoasset Promotions Consultation' (July 2020), para. 4.30.
970. FCA, 'Strengthening Our Financial Promotion Rules for High-Risk Investments and Firms Approving Financial Promotions' (April 2021).
971. FCA, 'Strengthening Our Financial Promotion Rules for High-Risk Investments and Firms Approving Financial Promotions' (April 2021), para. 3.10.
972. FCA, 'Strengthening Our Financial Promotion Rules for High-Risk Investments, Including Cryptoassets' (January 2022).
973. FCA, 'Strengthening Our Financial Promotion Rules for High-Risk Investments, Including Cryptoassets' (January 2022), para. 1.7.
974. FCA, 'Strengthening Our Financial Promotion Rules for High-Risk Investments, Including Cryptoassets' (January 2022), para. 1.7.

existing rules applicable to NRRS and PTPA to cryptoassets as well, to be referred to together as 'restricted mass market investments'.[975] As such, cryptoasset financial promotions will need to adhere to the existing rules in COBS 4, in addition to the requirements for promotions to be clear, fair and not misleading.[976] Further, in January 2022, the HM Treasury published its consultation response to its proposal to bring unregulated cryptoassets within the remit of the FPO, with a majority of the 25 respondents indicating their support for the UK Government's proposed approach.[977] While some respondents indicated their approval of the government's 'risk-based, incremental approach' to the regulation of cryptoassets in the UK, others opined that this approach would best be served alongside a comprehensive tailored cryptoasset regulatory regime.[978] The HM Treasury indicated that since the publication of its consultation document, consumers have been faced with increased cryptoasset risks, particularly bearing in mind the increased ownership thereof, providing a case for governmental intervention.[979]

As security tokens and e-money tokens already fall within the remit of the FCA's financial promotion regime, extending this regime to qualifying cryptoassets would close the current gap resulting in unregulated cryptoassets, such as utility and exchange tokens, having to comply with these rules. The primary concern relating to these high-risk investments is the potential harm which they may cause to consumers. At the same time, regulation should not operate to restrict consumers unnecessarily in making their investment decisions. As such, in directing its Consumer Investment Strategy,[980] the FCA aims to provide regulation which enables consumers to access and identify investments suited to their context and risk attitude.[981]

5.1.4.1.3 Stablecoins

In January 2021, the HM Treasury published its consultation document requesting views on the UK's regulatory approach to cryptoassets, and to challenges presented by stablecoins.[982] On a broader basis, the UK Government proposed that cryptoasset regulation would be designed and implemented by regulators using their 'agile powers' to issue rules and codes of practice.[983] The HM Treasury would not seek to detail cryptoasset requirements through legislative proposals but instead, with the UK

975. FCA, 'Strengthening Our Financial Promotion Rules for High-Risk Investments, Including Cryptoassets' (January 2022), para. 1.12.
976. FCA, 'Strengthening Our Financial Promotion Rules for High-Risk Investments, Including Cryptoassets' (January 2022), para. 1.12.
977. HM Treasury, 'Cryptoasset Promotions: Consultation Response' (January 2022), para. 3.10.
978. HM Treasury, 'Cryptoasset Promotions: Consultation Response' (January 2022), para. 3.11.
979. HM Treasury, 'Cryptoasset Promotions: Consultation Response' (January 2022), para. 3.14 and para. 3.16.
980. FCA, 'Consumer Investments: Strategy and Feedback Statement' (14 September 2021).
981. FCA, 'Strengthening Our Financial Promotion Rules for High-Risk Investments, Including Cryptoassets' (January 2022), para. 1.3.
982. HM Treasury, 'UK Regulatory Approach to Cryptoassets and Stablecoins. Consultation and Calls for Evidence' (January 2021).
983. HM Treasury, 'UK Regulatory Approach to Cryptoassets and Stablecoins. Consultation and Calls for Evidence' (January 2021), para. 2.3.

Government, would delineate the extent of the regulatory perimeter, and the objectives and principles underlying it.[984] This approach would allow regulators to respond better to market developments and would provide flexibility to update the regime to incorporate work being carried out on an international basis.[985] The HM Treasury indicated that without appropriate regulation and oversight, stablecoins could pose a series of risks, including financial and market stability, and consumer and competition risks.[986] Accordingly, the HM Treasury proposed the establishment of a regulatory regime for stablecoins as a means of payment, covering the issuing of stablecoins, and the provision of services ancillary thereto.[987] This regime would cover cryptoasset tokens 'which could be reliably used for retail or wholesale transactions', and would exclude algorithmic stablecoins akin to unbacked exchange tokens (i.e., Bitcoin), security tokens and e-money tokens.[988] The proposed high-level requirements which would apply include authorisation, prudential, maintenance and management of reserves requirements.[989]

In April 2022, the HM Treasury published its response to its consultation document confirming the UK Government's legislative proposals to extend the regulatory perimeter to include activities relating to issuing or facilitating the use of stablecoins as a means of payment.[990] Such an extension would be in line with the UK Government's 'same risk, same regulatory outcome' approach.[991] The proposal would entail amending the EMRs and the PSRs (to include stablecoin issuance and provision of wallets and custody services); Part 5 of the Banking Act 2009 (to include stablecoin activities where risks may be classed as systemic); and the Financial Services (Banking Reform) Act 2013 (to subject stablecoin-based payments systems to competition regulation by the Payment Systems Regulator).[992]

Some respondents conveyed concerns regarding the UK's competitiveness based on the proposed approach to be adopted in regulating cryptoasset activities in the UK. In particular, it was highlighted that innovation and competition should be prioritised

---

984. HM Treasury, 'UK Regulatory Approach to Cryptoassets and Stablecoins. Consultation and Calls for Evidence' (January 2021), para. 2.5.
985. HM Treasury, 'UK Regulatory Approach to Cryptoassets and Stablecoins. Consultation and Calls for Evidence' (January 2021), para. 2.4.
986. HM Treasury, 'UK Regulatory Approach to Cryptoassets and Stablecoins. Consultation and Calls for Evidence' (January 2021), para. 3.7.
987. HM Treasury, 'UK Regulatory Approach to Cryptoassets and Stablecoins. Consultation and Calls for Evidence' (January 2021), para. 3.9.
988. HM Treasury, 'UK Regulatory Approach to Cryptoassets and Stablecoins. Consultation and Calls for Evidence' (January 2021), paras 3.16-18.
989. HM Treasury, 'UK Regulatory Approach to Cryptoassets and Stablecoins. Consultation and Calls for Evidence' (January 2021), para. 3.23.
990. HM Treasury, 'UK Regulatory Approach to Cryptoassets, Stablecoins, and Distributed Ledger Technology in Financial Markets. Response to the Consultation and Call for Evidence' (April 2022) 2.
991. HM Treasury, 'UK Regulatory Approach to Cryptoassets, Stablecoins, and Distributed Ledger Technology in Financial Markets. Response to the Consultation and Call for Evidence' (April 2022), para. 2.42.
992. HM Treasury, 'UK Regulatory Approach to Cryptoassets, Stablecoins, and Distributed Ledger Technology in Financial Markets. Response to the Consultation and Call for Evidence' (April 2022) 2-3.

by the UK Government with the purpose of attracting innovative firms to the UK, particularly bearing in mind the UK's exit from the EU.[993] In addition, it was stated that the UK Government should ensure that its regulation of cryptoasset activities is 'not more onerous than that' of the regulation in other jurisdictions.[994] As such, it was argued that the approach adopted should place the UK in a strong competitive position directed to attracting investment and new business.[995] In response, the HM Treasury stated that the proposed 'agile approach' would enable the UK to exploit the 'freedoms gained by the EU', allowing regulators to adjust to market developments, based on rules appropriate for consumers and market actors.[996] The HM Treasury stated that the proposed approach would foster conditions necessary for stablecoin industry growth, in alignment with the UK Government's policy objective of placing the UK financial services industry 'at the forefront of cryptoasset technology and innovation'.[997] Once the proposed legislative changes have been made, the UK Government would 'deliver a world-leading' stablecoin regulatory regime,[998] which would promote competition and innovation in a rapidly evolving sector through clear and proportionate regulation.[999]

5.1.4.2 *Discussion*

The actions and behaviours considered above are examined below through the adaptations and/or amendments effected to the regulatory approaches and regulatory frameworks, respectively, established by the UK Government to govern DLT Offerings.

5.1.4.2.1 Updated Regulatory Response

Several changes were effected to the regulatory framework developed to govern DLT Offerings, while the regulatory approach established remained largely unchanged.

993. HM Treasury, 'UK Regulatory Approach to Cryptoassets, Stablecoins, and Distributed Ledger Technology in Financial Markets. Response to the Consultation and Call for Evidence' (April 2022), para. 2.17.
994. HM Treasury, 'UK Regulatory Approach to Cryptoassets, Stablecoins, and Distributed Ledger Technology in Financial Markets. Response to the Consultation and Call for Evidence' (April 2022), para. 2.22.
995. HM Treasury, 'UK Regulatory Approach to Cryptoassets, Stablecoins, and Distributed Ledger Technology in Financial Markets. Response to the Consultation and Call for Evidence' (April 2022), para. 2.22.
996. HM Treasury, 'UK Regulatory Approach to Cryptoassets, Stablecoins, and Distributed Ledger Technology in Financial Markets. Response to the Consultation and Call for Evidence' (April 2022), para. 2.25.
997. HM Treasury, 'UK Regulatory Approach to Cryptoassets, Stablecoins, and Distributed Ledger Technology in Financial Markets. Response to the Consultation and Call for Evidence' (April 2022) 3.
998. HM Treasury, 'UK Regulatory Approach to Cryptoassets, Stablecoins, and Distributed Ledger Technology in Financial Markets. Response to the Consultation and Call for Evidence' (April 2022) 3.
999. HM Treasury, 'UK Regulatory Approach to Cryptoassets, Stablecoins, and Distributed Ledger Technology in Financial Markets. Response to the Consultation and Call for Evidence' (April 2022), para. 1.14.

Most significantly, the HM Treasury incorporated the 5AMLD domestically through the amendment of the Money Laundering Regulations, with the FCA's cryptoasset AML regime coming into effect on 10 January 2020. The underlying purpose for the domestic transposition of the 5AMLD was to tackle illicit use cases of cryptoassets, which the HM Treasury noted was beneficial for financial innovation. As such, firms engaged in one of the specified cryptoasset business activities would have to comply with the AML Regulations. Further, the HM Treasury announced its proposal to include the promotion of unregulated cryptoassets within the scope of the FCA's financial promotion regime, on the basis that it would provide greater consumer protection and promote responsible innovation. To this end, the FCA initiated its consultation process on the financial promotion rules applicable to high-risk investments, which would include cryptoassets once categorised as such. The rules applicable to NRRS and PTPA would apply to cryptoassets and would together be referred to as 'restricted mass market investments'. Once in effect, cryptoasset financial promotions must comply with the existing rules specified in COBS 4, in addition to the requirements for promotions to be clear, fair, and not misleading.

Finally, the HK Treasury entered into a consultation process requesting views on the UK's regulatory approach to cryptoassets, specifically the challenge presented by stablecoins. The HM Treasury thus proposed to create a regulatory regime for stablecoins as a means of payment. To this end, it was indicated that the legislative proposals for the new stablecoin regulatory regime would include extending the regulatory perimeter to include issuing or facilitating stablecoin use as a means of payment. The extension of the perimeter in this regard would accord with the UK Government's 'same risk, same regulatory outcome' approach. Specific legislative amendments would thus be effected to the EMRs, the PSRs, Part 5 of the Banking Act 2009, and the Financial Services (Banking Reform) Act 2013.

The initial regulatory approach established for the governance of DLT Offerings in the UK remained largely unchanged. In particular, the UK Government indicated that the proposed cryptoasset regulation would be designed and implemented by regulators using their 'agile powers' to issue rules and codes of practice. This view accorded with the UK Government's fact-finding enquiry through which the cryptoasset market was continuously monitored, allowing financial regulatory authorities to be agile in responding to regulatory issues as they unfold. The purpose of this approach was thus to allow financial regulatory authorities to respond better to market developments and be provided with the flexibility to update the regulatory approach to incorporate work being carried out on an international basis, where relevant. To this end, the UK Government continued to undertake its non-legislative approach in which in place of seeking to detail cryptoasset requirements through legislative proposals, the UK Government delineated the application of the existing regulatory perimeter to the particular cryptoasset business activity. This approach was evidenced by the HM Treasury's proposal to establish a regulatory regime for stablecoins. At the same time, however, the UK Government departed from its non-legislative approach through legislative measures and proposals thereof. This approach was evidenced by the domestic transposition of the 5AMLD and the proposed extension of the financial promotions regime to unregulated cryptoassets. Overall, the actions and behaviours of the HK Government directed to amending the initial response to the regulatory framework governing DLT Offerings were effected to regulate cryptoasset business activity which previously fell outside its remit, therefore filling the existing regulatory gaps. In effecting these amendments to the regulatory framework, the UK Government applied largely the same staged and proportionate regulatory response, by considering where risks and opportunities are most urgent or acute. Further, this approach ensured that the regulatory response is agile, enabling financial regulatory authorities to consider the international developments, in plotting its future strategy for financial services and payments regulation.

5.1.4.2.2 Competition Policy Influence

Competition policy considerations influenced the amendments effected to the regulatory framework developed for governing DLT Offerings. In particular, the FCA expressed its concern regarding the global nature of permissionless DLT systems, ripe for potential regulatory arbitrage, spurring its collaboration with the FATF to address this issue. On a similar basis, the HM Treasury expressed its concern over the unregulated nature of stablecoins which could pose, among others, competition risks, leading to its proposals to establish a new regulatory regime by extending the existing regulatory perimeter. The financial services industry expressed the view that innovation and competition should be prioritised by the UK Government with the purpose of attracting innovative firms to the UK, particularly bearing in mind the UK's exit from the EU.[1000] In response, the HM Treasury indicated that the UK Government's 'agile approach' would allow the UK to exploit the 'freedoms gained by the EU', and permit regulators to respond to market developments, based on rules appropriate for consumers and market actors.[1001] In particular, it noted that the UK Government's approach would support the conditions required for stablecoin industry growth, in line with the UK Government's policy objective of placing the UK financial services industry 'at the forefront of cryptoasset technology and innovation'.[1002]

1000. HM Treasury, 'UK Regulatory Approach to Cryptoassets, Stablecoins, and Distributed Ledger Technology in Financial Markets. Response to the Consultation and Call for Evidence' (April 2022), para. 2.17.
1001. HM Treasury, 'UK Regulatory Approach to Cryptoassets, Stablecoins, and Distributed Ledger Technology in Financial Markets. Response to the Consultation and Call for Evidence' (April 2022), para. 2.25.
1002. HM Treasury, 'UK Regulatory Approach to Cryptoassets, Stablecoins, and Distributed Ledger Technology in Financial Markets. Response to the Consultation and Call for Evidence' (April 2022) 3.

CHAPTER 6

Regulating DLT Financial Products and Services: The State of New York, United States

This chapter provides a narrative analysis of the development of the laws and regulations governing DLT financial products and services in New York during the key periods of development from 2018-2022. It provides an examination of the actions and behaviours of the New York State Government and how competition policy influenced its regulatory approach to DLT Offerings and the formulation of the laws and regulations developed to govern it.

6.1 INTRODUCTION

NY is traditionally regarded as the centre of American finance, and a leading financial centre often paralleled with London, its enduring competitor. Its reputation as the financial powerhouse of the US developed principally through the growth of its commercial and trading markets.[1003] Its subsequent reputation as a leading financial centre has been attributed to a multitude of factors, including its dominance as an international trade finance hub, characterised by the presence of specialists in foreign financial institutions.[1004] The formalisation of the NY Stock and Exchange Board, later

1003. Adam Church, 'The Rise-and-Fall of Leading International Financial Centers: Factors and Applications' (2018) 7(2) Michigan Business and Entrepreneurial Law Review 299 https://doi.org/10.36639/mbelr.7.2.rise.

1004. Adam Church, 'The Rise-and-Fall of Leading International Financial Centers: Factors and Applications' (2018) 7(2) Michigan Business and Entrepreneurial Law Review 300 https://doi.org/10.36639/mbelr.7.2.rise. *See* generally Charles P Kindleberger, *The Formation of Financial Centers: A Study in Comparative Economic History* (Princeton Studies in International Finance No. 36, Princeton University Press 1974).

the NY Stock Exchange, in 1817 also acted to cement NY's status as an influential global financial hub. Its reputation is further bolstered by being a state within the US' federal system of government. The US has ranked high at number 17 on the UN's Human Development Index.[1005] Further, the US scored high on global competitiveness having ranked number 10 on the IMD World Competitiveness Ranking.[1006] Most notably, the US is well-known for its entrepreneurial and start-up culture, having ranked number 1 on the 2021 Global Fintech Ranking.[1007] It is also regarded as having a robust legal and institutional regime, having ranked number 21 on the World Justice Project's 2020 Rule of Law Index.[1008] NY has its own constitution, which is subject to the Constitution of the US, ratified in June 1788. The US adopts a democratic system of government in the form of a representative democracy and a republic, underlined by a common law legal system.[1009] It is divided into three separate branches (at both a state and federal level) of government including the: (i) Executive branch, headed by a governor in each state, and the president at a federal level; (ii) Legislative branch made of up a bicameral parliament (with the exception of Nebraska); and (iii) Judicial branch led by the Supreme Court.[1010] Within this state system of government, the branch of government empowered to set legal and regulatory rules for the financial services industry, specifically as they apply to DLT Offerings, in addition to formulating competition policy, include the: (i) NY State Legislature; and (ii) NY State Department of Financial Services.[1011]

The NY State Legislature was established in the 1770s and comprises two houses, namely the State Senate and the State Assembly, under the auspices of NY's Constitution.[1012] It functions primarily to propose draft laws in the form of bills, subject to the limits set by the Constitution of the US and specific federal statutes and treaties. The State Senate comprises a varying number of members as authorised by NY's Constitution, whereas the State Assembly comprises 150 members, elected from the NY state districts for a two-year term. Bills may be introduced by either house but must be passed in the same form by both houses before it is presented to the Governor for their assent. The Legislature also performs a check function in respect of the Governor, acting in their executive authority.

The NYDFS was established in October 2011, upon the dissolution of the NYBD and the NY State Insurance Department, and is empowered to exercise the powers and

1005. Global Human Development Indicators, *United Nations Development Programme* (December 2020), https://hdr.undp.org/en/countries.
1006. World Competitiveness Ranking 2021, https://www.imd.org/centers/world-competitiveness-center/rankings/world-competitiveness/.
1007. Global Fintech Rankings Report (*Findexable*, 2021) 21, https://findexable.com/wp-content/uploads/2021/06/Global-Fintech-Rankings-2021-v1-23-June-21.pdf.
1008. World Justice Project Rule of Law Index: 2020 Insights (2020) 6, https://worldjusticeproject.org/sites/default/files/documents/WJP%20Insights%202020%20-%20Online%20.pdf.
1009. *See* https://worldpopulationreview.com/country-rankings/democracy-countries.
1010. *See* https://www.whitehouse.gov/about-the-white-house/our-government/state-local-government/.
1011. At the federal level this notably includes the: (i) US Congress; (ii) Securities and Exchange Commission; and (iii) Commodity Futures Trading.
1012. *See* https://www.nysenate.gov/branches-government-new-york-state.

perform the functions of both former departments.[1013] The NYDFS was created under the auspices of the Financial Services Law,[1014] to 'modernize regulation by allowing the agency to oversee a broader array of financial products and services, rather than the previous system of limiting regulation to services provided by only certain types of institution'.[1015] To this end, the NYDFS is the licensing, regulatory and supervisory financial regulator for, among others, banks, insurance companies, and other financial institutions in NY.[1016]

The Financial Services Law provides the NYDFS with broad powers to take any action which, among others, fosters the growth of NY's financial services industry, encourages economic development in NY through regulation and supervision, and protects consumers.[1017] Among these functions, the NYDFS' competence in creating regulatory rules is the most relevant for this study. The Financial Services Law also empowers the NYDFS with broad powers to investigate financial crimes. The NYDFS Superintendent is empowered to investigate activities in violation of the Financial Services Law when it has 'a *reasonable suspicion* that a person or entity has engaged, or is engaging, in fraud or misconduct with respect to the banking law, the insurance law' or other relevant laws.[1018]

6.1.1 Input: 2008-2013

The analysis below sets out the actions and behaviours of the NY Government in directing the advancement of competition policy within the context of the emergence of Fintech, and its position of importance on legal and policy agendas.

6.1.1.1 Competition Policy and the Role of Fintech

NY is well regarded as one of the top international financial centres, and the financial hub of the US. Its development into a leading international financial centre and its 'competitive spirit' has been researched extensively.[1019] In the mid-1780s its pre-eminence as America's financial hub was however forestalled by Philadelphia's first-mover advantage in establishing the US' first federally chartered bank, and its oldest stock exchange.[1020] However, NY made use of its geographical location as a port city, and the formalisation of its Stock and Exchange Board to overtake Philadelphia to become the US' hub of financial activities. It continues to leverage its position as a

1013. *See* https://www.dfs.ny.gov/About_Us.
1014. NY Laws FIS Financial Services Law §2812 (1 February 2011) (Financial Services Law).
1015. *See* http://www.dfs.ny.gov/about/history.html.
1016. *See* https://www.dfs.ny.gov/who_we_supervise.
1017. Financial Services Law, Art. 2, §201.
1018. Financial Services Law, Art. 4.
1019. *See* generally Charles P Kindleberger, *The Formation of Financial Centers: A Study in Comparative Economic History* (Princeton Studies in International Finance No. 36, Princeton University Press 1974).
1020. *See* Historical Society of Pennsylvania. 'Philadelphia Stock Exchange Papers' (2006), https://hsp.org/sites/default/files/legacy_files/migrated/findingaid3070phlx.pdf.

leading international financial centre through competition policy and related initiatives.

Overall, however, the actions and behaviours of the NY Government in directing its competition policy are underscored primarily through highlighting that NY is crucially important for leading financial services on a global scale for the generation of significant economic activity for its jurisdiction, and the US overall.[1021] To this end, competition from several Primary Actors has highlighted the competitive pressures challenging NY's position as a leading international financial centre.[1022] The NY Government, and its regulators, are therefore cognisant of competition from other Primary Actors. In response, the NY Government has initiated several policy and regulatory initiatives, with the aim of maintaining NY's position as a leading financial centre. Such policy and regulatory initiatives include, for example, the NYESD, established in 1995 subsequent to the consolidation of the NY Department of Economic Development, and the NY State Urban Development Corporation.[1023] The NYESD operates primarily to promote the economic growth of NY, to support business investment, and to create jobs.[1024] The NYESD aims to support the retention and development of existing and new businesses, and to foster the development of an 'innovation-based economy'. While the efforts of the NYESD promote the growth of NY's economy by providing a competitive landscape, its mandate is not directly focussed on fostering financial services industry growth.

In 2007, the Major of NY and the US Senate commissioned McKinsey & Company to survey the competitiveness of the US' financial services industry, with a particular emphasis on NY.[1025] McKinsey's resulting report set out recommendations in the form of actions required to strengthen and maintain NY's leadership role in international financial services.[1026] In particular, it highlighted London's increased competitiveness as a Primary Actor over NY, specifying that working and living conditions were more competitive in London.[1027] Further, competition from European and Asian markets were highlighted as possibly undermining NY's pre-eminent position in international financial services.[1028]

During the time period 2008-2010, the NY Government grappled with the 2008 GFC and its related consequences. Accordingly, the focus during this time period was largely on financial regulatory reform legislation, with NY having promulgated specific legislation to protect homeowners from the fallout of the mortgage crisis.[1029] In addition, the NYBD stepped up its efforts to oversee the mortgage industry. Despite this focus on the aftermath of the 2008 GFC, NY governmental policy continued to be

1021. McKinsey and Company, 'Sustaining New York's and the US's Global Financial Services and Leadership' (2007) Report commissioned by Major Michael R Bloomberg and Charles E Schumer (McKinsey Report) 9.
1022. McKinsey Report, 9-11.
1023. *See* https://esd.ny.gov/about-us.
1024. *See* https://esd.ny.gov/about-us.
1025. McKinsey Report.
1026. McKinsey Report, 18.
1027. McKinsey Report, 14.
1028. McKinsey Report, 9-11.
1029. New York State Banking Department (NYSBD), '2009 Annual Report' (15 September 2010) 3.

geared towards strengthening and maintaining NY's position as 'a center for the financial industry' and ensuring that financial regulatory authorities remain at the forefront of financial services regulation.[1030] Accordingly, during this time period the NYBD, and the US federal government more broadly, focussed their efforts primarily on domestic initiatives aimed to facilitate economic recovery from the 2008 GFC through maintaining the stability of the economy, protecting consumers, preventing unnecessary foreclosures, and expanding banking products.[1031] These initiatives resulted in the promulgation of the Dodd-Frank Wall Street and Consumer Act in July 2010, representing the most significant financial regulatory reform legislation during this time period.[1032] Further, the NYBD continued to maintain contact with the supervisory authorities of the 136 foreign bank branches incorporated in NY, as a key component of its regulatory strategy.

During the time period 2011-2014, the policy focus shifted to rebuilding the financial services industry in NY through job creation, improved protection for consumers, and increased regulatory oversight of financial products and services falling into regulatory gaps.[1033] This renewed focussed resulted in the establishment of the NYDFS in October 2011, tasked to facilitate the policy objective of maintaining NY's status as the 'world financial capital by modernizing the regulation of financial services'.[1034] To achieve these goals, the NYDFS was divided into five divisions including, most notably, the Markets Division, responsible for monitoring developments in the financial services industry, to enable to NYDFS to respond appropriately to rapidly evolving financial products and services.[1035] During 2011, the NYDFS executed several initiatives to protect consumers, including mortgage servicing reform, reducing costs of court delays in respect of mortgage foreclosure proceedings, and launching an investigation into force-place insurance investigation.[1036] The NYDFS also increased efforts to promote the NY state bank charter, in favour of the US federal bank charter. In particular, it was highlighted that NY regulatory authorities were more flexible and knowledgeable of the specific home markets of banks.[1037] NYDFS noted that NY continues to be an attractive prospect for foreign banks, having been approached by banks in India, Mainland China, Europe and South America to open an agency, branch or representative office in NY, despite global economic distress.[1038]

During 2012, the NYDFS continued to perform its role by protecting consumers and promoting the progression of fair and sound financial services.[1039] In particular, the NYDFS took steps to promote smart, strong and targeted regulation including

1030. NYSBD, '2008 Annual Report' (15 September 2009) 3.
1031. NYSBD, '2010 Annual Report' (15 September 2011) 3.
1032. NYSBD, '2010 Annual Report' (15 September 2011) 3.
1033. New York State Financial Services Department (NYDFS), 'First Annual Report of the Superintendent to the Governor and Legislature' (15 May 2012) 3.
1034. NYDFS, 'First Annual Report of the Superintendent to the Governor and Legislature' (15 May 2012) 4.
1035. NYDFS, '2011 Annual Report' (15 May 2012) 5.
1036. NYDFS, '2011 Annual Report' (15 May 2012) 6-7.
1037. NYDFS, '2011 Annual Report' (15 May 2012) 13.
1038. NYDFS, '2011 Annual Report' (15 May 2012) 22.
1039. NYDFS, '2012 Annual Report' (13 June 2013).

investigating Standard Chartered Bank for money-laundering violations resulting in the laundering of hundreds of billions of dollars for Iran and safeguarding the fairness of capital requirements for community and regional banks.[1040] The NYDFS indicated that NY's foreign and wholesale banking industry continued to grow having been approached by banks from Asia, Europe and South America to open an agency, branch or representative office in NY. The NYDFS also continued its work to promote the NY state bank charter.[1041]

During 2013, the NYDFS increased its efforts to encourage the growth of the financial services industry in NY by promoting its state bank charter, resulting in three banks converting their federal bank charters to NY state bank charters.[1042] The NYDFS also recognised the significance of community and regional banks for the financial services industry in NY, culminating in the publication of its Community Banking Report in February 2013. Most notably, the NYDFS launched a department-wide initiative with the goal of improving cyber security in the financial services industry.[1043] To this end, the NYDFS engaged with a wide range of financial services firms to understand the cyber security challenges and threats affecting the industry.

6.1.1.2 Discussion

The actions and behaviours considered above are examined below through an identification of the significant themes delineating the NY Government's approach to competition policy for the financial services industry, and its 'competitive appetite' in relation thereto.

6.1.1.2.1 Competition Policy

The actions and behaviours directed by the NY Government during the time period 2008-2017 are illustrative of a tempered approach to competition policy positioning the NY Government as a Primary Actor internationally, in the Environmental Context of International regulatory competition. The analysis evidenced that, in considering this competitive landscape, the NY Government is cognisant of both: (i) its position relative to competing Primary Actors (NY's own competitiveness); and (ii) the position of competing Primary Actors relative to others (other Primary Actors competitiveness). The NY Government deployed the NYDFS primarily to direct its competition policy objectives for the financial services industry, using available regulatory competition Means to attract (and retain) Drivers through Secondary Actors.

The NY Government's awareness of its own competitiveness is reflected primarily through its policy objective of strengthening and maintaining NY's leadership role in international finance. This is supported by the NY Government's awareness of competitive forces, particularly in the form of increased competition from other

1040. NYDFS, '2012 Annual Report' (13 June 2013) 2.
1041. NYDFS, '2012 Annual Report' (13 June 2013) 3.
1042. NYDFS, '2013 Annual Report' (15 June 2014) 2.
1043. NYDFS, '2013 Annual Report' (15 June 2014) 3.

international financial centres, particularly London. While the NY Government appears to be cognisant of competitive pressures, its policy initiatives were driven more inwardly focussing on economic growth through job creation, consumer protection and increasing regulatory oversight of financial products and services falling outside the remit of the regulatory framework.

The NY Government executed its competition policy objective of maintaining NY as a leading financial centre through several heterogeneous actions and behaviours, focussing on implementing policy and regulatory initiatives supporting the growth of NY's economy. In particular, the NYDFS focussed on growing NY's banking sector through the promotion of its state bank charter and meeting with foreign banks to establish an agency, branch or representative office in NY, as the regulatory competition Means. These Means were targeted at banks with a federal charter and overseas foreign banks, to attract and retain Drivers, primarily in the form of chartering and other business and licensing fees, and taxes.

6.1.1.2.2 Significant Policy Themes

An analysis of the actions and behaviours directed by the NY Government during the time period 2008-2013 highlighted several significant themes, including an identification of a broad set of factors influencing the development of the financial services industry in NY, and the advancement of competition policy. These significant themes are important as they highlight the NY Government's: (i) level of awareness of competitive pressures from other Primary Actors; and (ii) the extent to which they were concerned about these competitive pressures. The level of concern regarding the competitive pressures is primarily represented by the actions which the NY Government levied in response thereto. These significant themes include the following:

> *Recovering from the 2008 GFC.* The NY Government directed its policy and regulatory initiatives to support NY's economic recovery and growth following the 2008 GFC. The initiatives were aimed at maintaining the stability of the economy, protecting consumers, preventing unnecessary foreclosures, and expanding banking products. This included legislative measures, such as the promulgation of financial regulatory reform legislation to protect homeowners from the fallout of the mortgage crisis, and the Dodd-Frank Wall Street and Consumer Act in July 2010. The NYBD also stepped up its efforts to oversee the mortgage industry and continued its engagement with the supervisory authorities of the 136 foreign bank branches incorporated in NY.
>
> *World financial capital.* The NY Government's primary policy objective was strengthening and maintaining NY's leadership role in international financial services. This policy objective was directed by the NY Government through several policy and regulatory initiatives, underlined by the NYDFS' role in promoting the growth of the financial services industry in NY. The NYDFS focussed its efforts inwardly to create jobs and increase the protection of consumers and expended much of its efforts developing and maintaining its banking sector. Further, the NYDFS focussed its efforts on improving cyber

security through the launch of a department-wide initiative. Among others, the NYDFS engaged a variety of financial services firms to understand the cyber security challenges and threats affecting the financial services industry. *First-mover advantage.* In promoting NY's competitiveness, the NYDFS played the primary role of implementing policy and regulatory initiatives to maintain NY's reputation as a leading international financial centre. In accordance with this policy objective, the NYDFS directed to increase its regulatory oversight to include virtual currency activity falling outside its regulatory remit. To this end, the actions and behaviours of the NYDFS accorded with its mandate to modernise the regulation of finance in NY. From this perspective, the NYDFS played an important role in progressing regulatory initiatives for emerging Fintech Offerings and was one of the first financial regulatory authorities in the world to do so. Other than spearheading the regulation of virtual currencies, the NYDFS did not direct any distinct competition policy agenda.

6.1.2 Process: 2013-2014

The analysis below sets out the actions and behaviours of the NY Government directed towards formulating a regulatory approach to the governance of Fintech and DLT Offerings in its jurisdiction.

6.1.2.1 Developing a Regulatory Approach to DLT

During the time period 2013-2014, the new regulatory focus on virtual currencies was precipitated through the growing recognition of the use of virtual currencies for illicit purposes. The online marketplace 'Silk Road', used for the sale of illegal drugs through the use of Bitcoin, the fallout from the Mt. Gox Bitcoin exchange theft, and a Ponzi scheme involving Bitcoin, are noteworthy events which spurred on discussions surrounding virtual currency use in the mid-2010s. In August 2013, the Senate Committee on Homeland Security and Governmental Affairs (Senate Committee) sent a letter to the Department of Homeland Security, among others, requesting it to disclose its policies on virtual currencies, in response to the increased illicit use of Bitcoin, and increased investor interest. The Senate Committee also requested information on how those policies had been developed, how agencies were coordinating with each other, and their proposed plans for virtual currency regulation.[1044] These letters were issued subsequent to two months of interviews conducted by the Senate Committee with academic scholars, government officials, and stakeholders in the financial services and technology industries.[1045] The Senate Committee's approach highlighted its concern

1044. *See* letter from Senate Committee on Homeland Security and Governmental Affairs addressed to Secretary of Homeland Security (12 August 2013), https://www.hsgac.senate.gov/imo/media/doc/Virtual%20Currency%20Letter%20REDACTED.pdf.
1045. Zachary Warmbrodt, 'Congress Starts Looking into Bitcoin' (*Politico*, 13 August 2013), https://www.politico.com/story/2013/08/congress-starts-looking-into-bitcoin-095464.

about the risks posed by emerging technologies which in its view should be managed expeditiously. Adopting a proactive approach to regulating virtual currencies would enable its benefits and efficiencies to be captured, in place of imposing stricter regulatory rules at a later stage which may diminish those benefits.[1046]

On 12 August 2013, the NYDFS launched a fact-finding enquiry into virtual currencies to consider whether regulation, on top of existing money transmission regulations, was required.[1047] The NYDFS indicated that it recognised virtual currencies' potential to build innovative platforms and improve the efficiency of the financial system, but indicated that this needed to be balanced against the risks which virtual currencies present. In August 2013, the NYDFS issued subpoenas to 20 virtual currency industry stakeholders to gather information on the manner in which they operate, and the customer protection safeguards which they have in place. Further, in November 2013 the NYDFS announced its intention to hold public hearings and to introduce a regulatory framework through a 'BitLicense'.[1048] In November 2013, the NYDFS issued its 'Notice of Intent to Hold Hearings on Virtual Currencies' (Notice of Intent). The Notice of Intent indicated that the issuing of a BitLicense would be considered, in addition to related AML and consumer protection requirements for licensed entities.[1049] The NYDFS highlighted that its enquiry was directed particularly at the 'cloak of anonymity' which virtual currencies provided to support criminal activity, including drug smuggling and money laundering.[1050] In alignment with these efforts, the Senate Committee marked its formal enquiry into virtual currencies which culminated in the congressional hearing 'Beyond Silk Road: Potential Risks, Threats, and Promises of Virtual Currencies' held on 18 November 2013.[1051]

The Senate Committee's congressional hearing was explorative in nature and focussed primarily on the potential benefits and risks of virtual currencies for the US Government, and broader society.[1052] Overall, the witness testimony of a number of government officials, including the director of the Financial Crimes Enforcement Network (FinCEN), provided the Senate Committee with foundational information regarding the use of virtual currencies, including how it operates practically, its related risks and threats, and the potential value which it may create for society.[1053] The

1046. Zachary Warmbrodt, 'Congress Starts Looking into Bitcoin' (*Politico*, 13 August 2013), https://www.politico.com/story/2013/08/congress-starts-looking-into-bitcoin-095464.
1047. NYDFS, '2013 Annual Report' (15 June 2014) 9.
1048. NYDFS, '2013 Annual Report' (15 June 2014) 9.
1049. NYDFS, 'Notice of Intent to Hold Hearing on Virtual Currencies' (14 November 2013).
1050. Daniel Cawrey, 'New York State Is Considering Issuing "BitLicenses" to Bitcoin Businesses' (*Coindesk*, 15 November 2013), https://www.coindesk.com/markets/2013/11/14/new-york-state-is-considering-issuing-bitlicenses-to-bitcoin-businesses/.
1051. Committee on Homeland Security and Governmental Affairs United States Senate, 'Beyond Silk Road: Potential Risks, Threats, and Promises of Virtual Currencies' (18 November 2013), https://www.govinfo.gov/content/pkg/CHRG-113shrg86636/pdf/CHRG-113shrg86636.pdf.
1052. Committee on Homeland Security and Governmental Affairs United States Senate, 'Key Senate Committee Holds First Congressional Hearing on Virtual Currencies' (18 November 2013), https://www.hsgac.senate.gov/media/majority-media/key-senate-committee-holds-first-congressional-hearing-on-virtual-currencies.
1053. Committee on Homeland Security and Governmental Affairs United States Senate, 'Key Senate Committee Holds First Congressional Hearing on Virtual Currencies' (18 November 2013) 44,

FinCEN had been particularly proactive in its regulatory response to the emergence of DLT and virtual currencies, having provided regulatory guidelines for virtual currencies as early as March 2013.[1054] The proactive approach adopted by the FinCEN is mirrored by the regulatory approach undertaken by the NYDFS in its response to the emergence of DLT and virtual currencies. In January 2014, the NYDFS held its public virtual currency regulation hearings. Benjamin Lawsky, Superintendent of the NYDFS at the time, stipulated that the purpose of the hearings was to provide a bird's eye view of the virtual currency business, including a consideration of its benefits and risks.[1055] The two-day hearing session consisted of five panels including academic scholars, cryptocurrency investors, and law enforcement.[1056] The panel discussions focussed on the virtual currency environment, including deliberations on appropriate definitions, cryptocurrency use for illicit purposes, and the potential for innovation.[1057]

The central question posed at the hearings was whether existing financial regulation should be extended to virtual currencies firms, or whether a bespoke regulatory regime should be created.[1058] The investors' panel led by, among others, the Winklevoss twins, advocated that regulation would spur the growth of the virtual currency industry, but cautioned that a new regulatory regime was not needed. They also asserted that the recent prosecutions associated with the illicit use of virtual currencies indicated that current law enforcement techniques were effective in rooting out criminal virtual currency use.[1059] Both the NY District Attorney and the South District of NY Deputy US Attorney disagreed stating that illicit use posed challenges falling outside the contemplation of existing frameworks. At the conclusion of the public hearings, the NYDFS directed that it would most likely create a bespoke regulatory regime, BitLicense, considering the need to promote innovation and prevent the criminal use of virtual currencies. On 11 February 2014, the NYDFS provided additional details of its proposed regulation of the virtual currency business at a cryptocurrency conference in Washington D.C.[1060] They stressed that the existing money transmitter regulations were not wholly appropriate for virtual currency

https://www.hsgac.senate.gov/media/majority-media/key-senate-committee-holds-first-congressional-hearing-on-virtual-currencies.

1054. Financial Crimes Enforcement Network (FinCEN), 'Application of FinCEN's Regulations to Persons Administering, Exchanging, or Using Virtual Currencies' (18 March 2013).

1055. Benjamin Lawsky, 'Cryptocurrencies: State of Play' (February 2014), https://www.youtube.com/watch?v=zhIZd9b2-Qs&ab_channel=NewAmerica.

1056. NYDFS, 'Virtual Currency Business', https://www.dfs.ny.gov/virtual_currency_businesses#bitlicense-faqs.

1057. Keith Miller & Dax Hansen, 'New York DFS Virtual Currency Hearings Point to New "BitLicense" Law' (*Perkins Coie*, 14 February 2014), https://www.virtualcurrencyreport.com/2014/02/new-york-dfs-virtual-currency-hearings-point-to-new-bitlicense-law/.

1058. Keith Miller & Dax Hansen, 'New York DFS Virtual Currency Hearings Point to New "BitLicense" Law' (*Perkins Coie*, 14 February 2014), https://www.virtualcurrencyreport.com/2014/02/new-york-dfs-virtual-currency-hearings-point-to-new-bitlicense-law/.

1059. Keith Miller & Dax Hansen, 'New York DFS Virtual Currency Hearings Point to New "BitLicense" Law' (*Perkins Coie*, 14 February 2014), https://www.virtualcurrencyreport.com/2014/02/new-york-dfs-virtual-currency-hearings-point-to-new-bitlicense-law/.

1060. Keith Miller & Dax Hansen, 'New York DFS Virtual Currency Hearings Point to New "BitLicense" Law' (*Perkins Coie*, 14 February 2014), https://www.virtualcurrencyreport.com/2014/02/new-york-dfs-virtual-currency-hearings-point-to-new-bitlicense-law/.

business, but that components of these regulations and existing banking regulation could be used to establish a bespoke BitLicense regulatory regime. This regime would include, among others, capital requirements and consumer disclosures to be complied with by virtual currency firms.

On 13 February 2014, Lawsky addressed the current 'State of Play' of virtual currency business in NY at a press conference.[1061] In particular, they addressed the question of why, in the absence of a robust federal and international response to their use in financial services, the NYDFS concerned itself with how virtual currency business should be regulated. Acknowledging that the use of virtual currencies did not pose any systemic risks, Lawsky highlighted its emergence clearly reflected the necessity for innovation in the financial regulatory and technological ecosystems. To this end, it was highlighted that the NYDFS strives to be a 'modern innovative financial regulator' different from other regulators, leading the way forward in effectively regulating virtual currencies.[1062] On 11 March 2014, the NYDFS issued a Public Order pronouncing its intention to consider applications and formal proposals for the establishment of regulated virtual currency exchanges conducting their business in NY.[1063] The NYDFS described the issuance of this Public Order as 'the next phase' of its public enquiry into establishing 'appropriate regulatory guardrails' for virtual currency firms.[1064] Further, the press release announcing the Public Order stipulated that approved applicants would be required to comply with the proposed bespoke BitLicense regulatory framework, to be issued by the NYDFS in the second quarter of 2014.[1065] It was also indicated that the NYDFS would, in the near future, consider applications and proposals from virtual currency firms conducting business other than exchanges. The NYDFS reiterated that its primary goal in developing a bespoke BitLicense regulatory framework was to balance the need to provide appropriate regulatory protections for consumers while ensuring simultaneously that innovation is not stifled. To this end, Lawsky opined that virtual currencies were 'unlikely to disappear entirely', and that 'turning a blind eye and failing to put in place guardrails or virtual currency firms while consumers use that product' is not a justifiable regulatory approach for financial regulatory authorities.[1066] As such, the underlying rationale for establishing a bespoke BitLicense regulatory framework would be to have strong oversight of virtual currency firms which would include 'robust standards for consumer protection, cyber security, and AML compliance'.[1067]

1061. Benjamin Lawsky, 'Cryptocurrencies: State of Play' (February 2014), https://www.youtube.com/watch?v=zhIZd9b2-Qs&ab_channel=NewAmerica.
1062. Benjamin Lawsky, 'Cryptocurrencies: State of Play' (February 2014), https://www.youtube.com/watch?v=zhIZd9b2-Qs&ab_channel=NewAmerica.
1063. Order Pursuant to New York Banking Law§§2-B, 24, 32, 102-A, and 4001-B and Financial Services Law§§301(C) and 302(A) (11 March 2014).
1064. NYDFS, 'NYDFS Issues Public Order on Virtual Currency Exchanges' (11 March 2014), https://www.dfs.ny.gov/reports_and_publications/press_releases/pr1403111.
1065. NYDFS, 'NYDFS Issues Public Order on Virtual Currency Exchanges' (11 March 2014), https://www.dfs.ny.gov/reports_and_publications/press_releases/pr1403111.
1066. NYDFS, 'NYDFS Issues Public Order on Virtual Currency Exchanges' (11 March 2014), https://www.dfs.ny.gov/reports_and_publications/press_releases/pr1403111.
1067. NYDFS, 'NYDFS Issues Public Order on Virtual Currency Exchanges' (11 March 2014), https://www.dfs.ny.gov/reports_and_publications/press_releases/pr1403111.

The NYDFS' virtual currency enquiry, which spanned over an eleven-month period, culminated in the publication of a draft regulatory framework on 17 July 2014 establishing a BitLicense governing virtual currency business activity in NY.[1068] This proposal was both a 'first-in-the-nation' regulatory framework for virtual currencies,[1069] in addition to being the first formal financial services regulatory regime for virtual currencies worldwide.[1070] This move by the NYDFS has been described as 'the leading government voice on a technology that has befuddled regulators and terrified law enforcement personnel'.[1071] The proposed BitLicense regulatory rules were published in the July 2014 edition of the NY State Register, which also initiated a 45-day inspection period for public comment.[1072] The proposed BitLicense regulatory rules specified that such a licence would be required by firms engaging in virtual currency business activity in NY, which includes the sale and purchase of virtual currencies as a customer business; receiving or transmitting virtual currency on behalf of customers; and securing, storing or maintaining custody or control of virtual currency on behalf of customers. On a practical basis, this would include virtual currency exchanges, digital wallet service providers, and merchant services providers within the remit of NYDFS' regulatory perimeter. However, merchants and consumers who use virtual currency to purchase or sell goods or services would be excluded from the remit of the proposed BitLicense regulatory framework.

The BitLicense regulatory framework obliged virtual currency firms to comply with a host of regulatory requirements, including those related to business continuity and capital requirements; consumer protection (disclosures and policies); and cyber security tailored specifically for virtual currency firms.[1073] Most significantly, regulated virtual currency firms would be required to comply with AML requirements relating to the collection and maintenance of transaction information, including the names and addresses of all parties to a transaction, and transaction descriptions and monetary value. This proposed requirement challenged the inherent anonymous and decentralised character of Bitcoin and the intent with which it was originally created. On 21 August 2014, the NYDFS doubled the 45-day inspection period for public comment, extending the deadline to 21 October 2014 after having received nearly 4,000 letters

1068. NYDFS, 'NYDFS Releases Proposed BitLicense Regulatory Framework for Virtual Currency Firms', (17 July 2014) https://www.dfs.ny.gov/reports_and_publications/press_releases/pr 1407171.
1069. NYDFS, '2014 Annual Report' (4 May 2015) 6.
1070. NYDFS, 'NYDFS Releases Proposed BitLicense Regulatory Framework for Virtual Currency Firms' (17 July 2014), https://www.dfs.ny.gov/reports_and_publications/press_releases/pr 1407171.
1071. Michael Bobelian, 'New York's Financial Regular, Benjamin Lawsky, Maintains Lead on Bitcoin Regulation' (*Forbes*, 24 June 2014), https://www.forbes.com/sites/michaelbobelian/2014/07/25/new-yorks-financial-regulator-benjamin-lawsky-maintains-lead-on-bitcoin-regulation/?sh=4fe6c7157e2e.
1072. New York State Register, 'Rule Making Activities' (23 July 2014) 14, https://dos.ny.gov/july-23-2014-rule-making-activities.
1073. NYDFS, 'NYDFS Releases Proposed BitLicense Regulatory Framework for Virtual Currency Firms' (17 July 2014), https://www.dfs.ny.gov/reports_and_publications/press_releases/pr 1407171.

from the virtual currency industry.[1074] On 18 December 2014, the NYDFS published its remarks on the revised BitLicense regulatory framework.[1075] Lawsky noted that the draft BitLicense regulatory framework would be updated to provide virtual currency start-ups with more flexibility, based on public concern regarding the effect of compliance costs. The NYDFS indicated that the draft BitLicense regulatory framework would also be updated to provide for a two-year transitional BitLicense tailored for start-ups and small businesses unable to comply with all the requirements for a BitLicense.[1076]

The NYDFS indicated that the two-year transitional BitLicense would provide 'start-ups an on-ramp as they build up their operations'.[1077] To encourage angel investment in virtual currencies, the draft BitLicense regulatory framework would also be updated to permit licensees to apply to the NYDFS to determine that certain parties should not be considered 'control parties' when they are not involved in the day-to-day operations of a firm, or its major management decisions. Such a determination would prevent the triggering of a host of regulatory requirements applicable to 'control parties'.[1078] Significantly, licensees would also no longer be required to acquire the addresses and transaction data of parties to a transaction, as this requirement was deemed to be 'not workable' in the context of virtual currencies.[1079] The NYDFS also indicated that the draft BitLicense regulatory framework would be updated to clearly demarcate the categories of firms and persons to whom it does not apply. For example, software developers who create and provide digital wallets; virtual currency miners; and individual holders of virtual currency would not need to be authorised by the NYDFS under the BitLicense regulatory framework. Merchants who accept virtual currencies as a medium of payment for goods and services, and their customers, as their sole virtual currency activity, would also not be required to obtain a BitLicense. Finally, customer loyalty programmes, gift cards, and rewards which are denominated in fiat currency would fall outside the remit of the BitLicense regulatory framework.[1080]

On 4 February 2015, the NYDFS published the revised version of the draft BitLicense regulatory framework with the inclusion of some of the considerations expressed by the virtual currency industry during the inspection period. In the same year, NYDFS Superintendent Lawsky, speaking at the BIT Emerging Payments Forum

1074. Davis Polk, 'New York's Final "BitLicense Rule": Overview and Changes from July 2014 Proposal' (5 June 2015) 2.
1075. NYDFS, 'Superintendent Lawsky's Remarks on Revised BitLicense Framework for Virtual Currency Regulation and Trends in Payments Technology' (18 December 2014).
1076. NYDFS, 'Superintendent Lawsky's Remarks on Revised BitLicense Framework for Virtual Currency Regulation and Trends in Payments Technology' (18 December 2014) and Davis Polk, 'New York's Final "BitLicense Rule": Overview and Changes from July 2014 Proposal' (5 June 2015) 4.
1077. NYDFS, 'Superintendent Lawsky's Remarks on Revised BitLicense Framework for Virtual Currency Regulation and Trends in Payments Technology' (18 December 2014).
1078. NYDFS, 'Superintendent Lawsky's Remarks on Revised Bitlicense Framework for Virtual Currency Regulation and Trends in Payments Technology' (18 December 2014).
1079. NYDFS, 'Superintendent Lawsky's Remarks on Revised BitLicense Framework for Virtual Currency Regulation and Trends in Payments Technology' (18 December 2014).
1080. NYDFS, 'Superintendent Lawsky's Remarks on Revised BitLicense Framework for Virtual Currency Regulation and Trends in Payments Technology' (18 December 2014).

in Washington D.C., noted that drafting regulation should be approached on a creative basis, by avoiding the conventional approach to placing emerging technologies into 'existing regulatory boxes'.[1081] To this end, Lawsky stated that financial regulatory authorities should avoid calls to simply ban or dismiss emerging technologies which they are not familiar with, but should instead conduct investigations into these innovations as they develop.[1082]

6.1.2.2 Discussion

The actions and behaviours considered above are examined below through an identification of the regulatory approach adopted by the NY Government, together with the competition policy considerations which formed part of the approach adopted.

6.1.2.2.1 Regulatory Approach

The actions and behaviours directed by the NY Government to develop a regulatory approach for the governance of Fintech and DLT Offerings were underlined by a pre-emptive response by proposing to establish a comprehensive regulatory framework for virtual currencies. To this end, the NY Government adhered to a 'proactive' approach to the burgeoning area of virtual currencies. This approach was undertaken primarily through the guise of specified strategic objectives, which included: (i) engagement with the financial services industry in formulating a regulatory response; (ii) establishing regulatory rules to act as guardrails to prevent the illicit use of virtual currencies; protecting consumers; and (iii) encouraging the growth of the virtual currency industry in NY.

6.1.2.2.2 Underlying Principles

Several key factors influenced the NY Government's adoption of a proactive regulatory response to the governance of Fintech and DLT Offerings in NY. These key themes are important as they highlight the NY Government's: (i) actions and behaviours in the form of regulatory and policy initiatives which drove the development of Fintech in NY; (ii) underlying rationale for adopting a 'proactive' approach to formulating a regulatory response to the governance of Fintech and DLT Offerings in NY; and (iii) a consideration of competition policy in formulating its regulatory response. The key factors underlying this regulatory approach include:

> *Fact-finding enquiry.* The NY Government, primarily through the NYDFS, approached the development of DLT, specifically virtual currencies in NY, through accelerated policy and regulatory initiatives geared to considering

1081. NYDFS, 'NYDFS Announces Final BitLicense Framework for Regulating Digital Firms' (3 June 2015).
1082. NYDFS, 'NYDFS Announces Final BitLicense Framework for Regulating Digital Firms' (3 June 2015).

whether regulation, on top of existing money transmission regulations, was required to regulate virtual currency firms and their business activities. The NYDFS also aimed to gather information on the manner in which virtual currency firms operate, and the customer protection safeguards in place. The NYDFS was concerned, in particular, with the use of virtual currencies for illicit purposes, but also with its potential to spur innovation. The NYDFS undertook its fact-finding enquiry through several initiatives including issuing subpoenas requesting information from various stakeholders on current approaches and responses to DLT Offering uses and holding public hearings.
Industry engagement. The NY Government, primarily through the NYDFS, engaged with the financial services industry as an integral component of its fact-finding enquiry. This industry engagement was clearly expressed through several policy and regulatory initiatives, most notably its issuance of subpoenas and public hearings and feedback received on the initial draft and revised versions of the BitLicense regulatory framework. The NYDFS' response to its engagement with the industry was represented through a measured approach. In particular, it noted the industry's view that regulation was not necessary for virtual currency business activities but nevertheless developed such regulation. In spite thereof, the NYDFS incorporated several industry concerns into the later iterations of its BitLicense regulations.
Balancing illicit virtual currency use with promoting innovation. The NY Government's regulatory approach to virtual currency was largely informed by the increased publicity received regarding its illicit use, in particular, the online marketplace 'Silk Road', the fallout from the Mt. Gox Bitcoin exchange theft, and the Senate Committee's increased interest therein. Accordingly, in creating its BitLicense regulatory framework, the NYDFS considered the need to root out criminal use of virtual currencies while simultaneously developing regulation which does not stifle innovation. The need to root out criminal use of virtual currencies was underlined in particular by the NYDFS' regulatory mandate to protect consumers.
Competition policy. The NY Government's regulatory approach was marked by an accelerated timetable for the adoption of virtual currency regulation. This proactive approach resulted in a first-mover advantage characterised by the BitLicense regulatory framework constituting the first formal financial services regulatory regime for virtual currencies worldwide. The first-mover advantage was underlined by the policy aim that regulation would spur the growth of the virtual currency industry through regulatory certainty created by the introduction of the BitLicense. Despite a lack of an international response to the use of virtual currencies in financial services, the NYDFS indicated that it aimed to be a 'modern innovative financial regulator' distinguished from others and leading the way forward in effectively regulating virtual currencies.
Legislative intervention. The NY Government, principally the NYDFS, proposed to establish a new and bespoke regulatory framework for virtual currency firms, resulting in the proposal of the BitLicense. This proposed new

regulatory framework aimed to provide appropriate guardrails for virtual currency firms underlined by the existing money transmission and banking regulatory rules. The guardrails would provide strong oversight of virtual currency firms, including strong standards for consumer protection, cyber security and AML compliance. The proposal of a new and bespoke regulatory framework accorded with NYDFS' mandate to modernise regulation and close regulatory gaps, as inspired by the events which transpired from the 2008 GFC.

6.1.3 Output: 2014-2015

The analysis below sets out the actions and behaviours of the NY Government directed to issuing regulatory rules and guidance which had the effect of formalising the regulations governing DLT Offerings.

6.1.3.1 BitLicense Regulatory Framework

On 3 June 2015, the NYDFS published the third and final BitLicense regulatory framework (BitLicense Regulations), described as 'the first comprehensive framework for regulating digital currency firms', setting out bespoke regulatory rules relating to AML, consumer protection, and cyber security for virtual currency firms.[1083] In particular, the BitLicense Regulations requires the licensing of, and compliance with minimum standards of conduct by, any person engaged in a virtual currency business activity involving NY, or a NY resident.[1084] Financial intermediaries conducting virtual currency business activities are thus captured by the regulation, but software developers and virtual currency miners, to the extent that they do not engage in such activities, fall outside its remit.[1085] Accordingly, the most significant features of the BitLicense Regulations include provisions related to: (i) definition of virtual currency; (ii) licensing application; (iii) capital requirements; (iv) custody and protection of customer assets; (v) material changes to business; (vi) change of control, mergers and acquisitions; (vii) books and record; (viii) examinations; (ix) AML programme; (x) cyber security programme; (xi) business continuity and disaster discovery; (xii) advertising and marketing; and (xiii) consumer protection.

6.1.3.2 Discussion

The actions and behaviours considered above are examined below through the guise of the salient regulatory features instituted by the NY Government.

1083. Official Compilation of Codes, Rules and Regulations of the State of New York, Title 23, Financial Services, Ch. I, Regulations of the Superintendent of Financial Services, Part 200 Virtual Currencies (23 CRR-NY).
1084. 23 CRR-NY, s. 200.(3)(a) read with s. 200.(2)(q).
1085. 23 CRR-NY, s. 200.(2)(q).

6.1.3.2.1 Regulatory Framework

An analysis of the actions and behaviours directed by the NY Government during the time period 2014-2015 evidenced the development of a regulatory framework for DLT Offerings, specifically for cryptoassets, as underlined by the provisions of the BitLicense Regulations, through the supervision of the NYDFS. The NY Government adopted the specific term 'virtual currency', defined broadly under the auspices of the BitLicense Regulations. Accordingly, the NY Government has adopted a legislative approach, opting to create a new and bespoke regulatory framework for virtual currency business activity. Generally, a firm undertaking virtual currency business activity as defined under the BitLicense Regulations, may require a licence to conduct those activities.

6.1.3.2.2 Central Components

Several factors influenced the development of the regulatory framework governing DLT Offerings. These central components are crucial as they highlight: (i) the severity or laxity of the regulatory rules and guidance introduced by the NY Government; and (ii) whether the actions and behaviours directed towards developing a regulatory framework for DLT Offerings were consistent with the regulatory approach established in the Process analysis, which included competition policy considerations. The central components underlining the development of the regulatory framework governing DLT Offerings include:

> *Regulatory remit*. The regulatory framework developed for the governance of DLT Offerings, specifically virtual currency, was created through a bespoke regulatory regime in the form of the BitLicense Regulations. To this end, firms who undertake virtual currency business activities involving NY, or a NY resident require a licence. The BitLicense Regulations thus apply to financial intermediaries undertaking virtual currency business activity but exclude software developers and virtual currency miners from its application. Accordingly, the regulatory framework includes within its remit a broad range of virtual currency business activity, including those related to, among others, receiving or transmitting virtual currency; and storing and holding custody or control of virtual currency for others.
>
> *Regulatory rules*. The regulatory framework developed for the governance of DLT Offerings, specifically virtual currency, is provided through a new and bespoke regulatory regime in the form of the BitLicense Regulations. This regulatory framework was developed from existing money transmitter and banking regulations, adapted to apply to virtual currency businesses, out of the internet age. In particular, the BitLicense Regulations set out the licensing requirements and minimum standards of conduct to be complied with by any person engaging in virtual currency business activities in NY or to a NY resident. These standards of conduct include requirements relating to capital,

custody and protection of customer assets, material changes to business, books and records, advertising and marketing.

AML and consumer protection. The regulatory framework developed for the governance of DLT Offerings, specifically virtual currency, includes specific provisions which underlie the purpose for which it was created. In particular, firms conducting virtual currency business activities are required to establish an AML programme based on an initial risk assessment considering all compliance, financial, legal and reputational risks related to its activities the parties whom it engages with, and its geographic location. As to consumer protection, all licensees are required to make clear disclosures in writing to their customers, relating to the licensees' activities, products and services, and to virtual currencies generally, among others.

Competition policy. The regulatory framework developed for the governance of DLT Offerings, specifically virtual currency, constituted the first formal regulatory framework for virtual currencies in the world. The establishment of the BitLicense Regulations represented a 'first mover' advantage, during a time period absent any response to the regulation of DLT Offerings internationally or from the US federal government. The draft BitLicense Regulations were also amended to consider the impact of the regulatory framework on start-ups and small businesses. In particular, it was amended to make provision for a two-year conditional BitLicense, as a competitive feature, permitting start-ups and small businesses unable to fully comply with all of the provisions of the BitLicense Regulations to operate under a conditional licence.

6.1.3.2.3 Regulatory Approach

The analysis of actions and behaviours directed by the NY Government during the time period 2014-2015 evidenced a proactive approach to the regulation of DLT Offerings, specifically virtual currency, consistent with the regulatory approach established in the Process analysis. In particular, the proactive approach was evidenced through the NY Government's accelerated timeline for the promulgation of regulatory rules, with the NYDFS having initiated its fact-finding enquiry in August 2013, and the BitLicense Regulations being published in June 2015. The establishment of a new and bespoke regulatory framework governing virtual currency business activity is also representative of the NYDFS' legislative approach.

The specific provisions of the BitLicense Regulations were framed in alignment with the NY Government's approach to balance the prevention of illicit virtual currency use with promoting innovation. This is reflected through the BitLicense Regulations imposing AML obligations on firms conducting virtual currency business activities, in addition to the two-year conditional BitLicense geared at start-ups and small businesses. The issuing of the BitLicense Regulations also represents a first-mover advantage for the NY Government, providing regulatory certainty for the virtual currency industry, which could potentially spur innovation, and economic development in NY.

The BitLicense Regulations were also reflective of the NYDFS' aim to be a 'modern innovative financial regulator' distinguished from other regulators.

6.1.4 Feedback

The analysis below sets out the actions and behaviours of the UK Government directed to modifying the initial regulatory response governing DLT Offerings.

6.1.4.1 Market Manipulation and Fraud

On 7 February 2018, the NYDFS issued guidance on the prevention of market manipulation and other wrongful activity (the Guidance) applicable to all virtual currency firms licensed under 23 NYCRR Part 200 or chartered as limited purpose trust companies under the NY Banking Law (together 'VC Firms').[1086] In particular, the Guidance was directed to remind VC Firms of their obligations to establish processes to detect, prevent and respond to fraud, attempted fraud and similar wrongdoing. Further, VC Firms were reminded to be particularly vigilant of market manipulation bearing in mind the significant risks which virtual currency poses to consumers and to the safety and soundness of financial services institutions. All VC Firms must establish effective processes to detect, prevent and respond to fraud, attempted fraud and similar wrongdoing based on an evaluation of the specific risks faced by it. These effective processes must be constituted in a written policy which addresses, among others, the allocation of responsibility for monitoring risks and the establishment of procedures and controls protecting against identified risks. VC Firms must also ensure that fraud, market manipulation and other wrongdoing, whether actual or suspected, is investigated effectively. In addition, VC Firms must report details of any wrongdoing to the NYDFS immediately upon discovery and update the NYDFS on an ongoing basis of any significant developments related to the original report.

6.1.4.2 New Virtual Currency Listing Regime

On 11 December 2019, the NYDFS announced its proposal to establish a regulatory regime for new coin listings executed by VC Firms with the aim of facilitating the periodical offer and use of new coins to their existing products.[1087] This proposal marked the NYDFS' first step in its review of the BitLicense virtual currency regime in consideration of market developments over the four-year period since the regime's inception in 2015. The policy objective underlying the proposed new listing regime was stated as ensuring that NY, as the centre of both consumer protection and innovation, adapts to the rapid pace of development of its dynamic financial services industry, and

1086. NYDFS, 'Guidance on the Prevention of market Manipulation and Other Wrongful Activity' (7 February 2018).
1087. NYDFS, 'Financial Services Superintendent Linda A. Lacewell Announces New Proposed Regime for Listing of Virtual Currencies' (11 December 2019).

speedily delivers services to the market. The NYDFS proposed two new options for coin listings and as such requested feedback from the public. First, coins which the NYDFS has approved for permitted use would be listed on its website. VC Firms would thus be permitted to list such coins with the requisite notice given to the NYDFS. Second, the NYDFS would provide a proposed model framework for the formation of company coin-listing policies. VC Firms would be required to formulate a bespoke model framework having regard to their risk profile and business activities and submit a coin-listing policy to the NYDFS for its approval. Once the NYDFS has granted its approval, firms may self-certify listings of new coins subject to its coin-listing policy and with prior written notice to the NYDFS.

A VC Firm's proposed coin-listing policy must be comprised of robust mechanisms which address procedures entailing the approval and review of virtual currency concerned with its virtual currency business activities.[1088] At a minimum, the proposed coin-listing policy must comprise provisions which relate to governance, risk, and monitoring. In particular, it was proposed that a VC Firm's board of directors would have to approve its coin-listing policy, review and executive decisions relating to each new coin listing, avoid conflicts of interests, and keep minutes of board meetings. In addition, it was proposed that risk assessments should be conducted and documented for each coin-listing to ensure it is free of any conflicts of interests. On 24 June 2020, the NYDFS published its revised proposed guidelines following a consideration of the feedback received from the public during the consultation period, which broadly reflected support for the new proposed regulatory regime.[1089] Accordingly, the NYDFS revised its guidelines resulting in the creation of two separate frameworks for VC Firms to adopt or list new coins. Such an approach would improve the efficiency and speed of the processes used by VC Firms in adopting or listing new coins. It would also enable the objective of developing innovation based on safety and soundness considerations, and consumer protection. These two frameworks comprise the following impactful features:

> *Coin-listing policy general framework*. Policies must be formulated to permit the approval of a coin by a VC Firm only if it is determined that its use or adoption would be subject to safety and soundness considerations and the standards set out in 23 NYCRR Part 200. Accordingly, VC Firms are not permitted to self-certify any coin intended to assist with the concealment of their customer's or counterparty's identity. VC Firms must ensure that appropriate governance arrangements are in place, including the annual review of their coin-listing policy. They must also conduct a robust risk assessment to ensure that the coin is used subject to the standards set out in 23 NYCRR Part 200, in addition to conducting ongoing monitoring of the uses to which the coin is put.[1090]

1088. NYDFS, 'Proposed Guidance Regarding Adoption or Listing of Virtual Currencies' (11 December 2019).
1089. NYDFS, 'Guidance Regarding Adoption or Listing of Virtual Currencies' (24 June 2020).
1090. NYDFS, 'Guidance Regarding Adoption or Listing of Virtual Currencies' (24 June 2020) 2-3.

Greenlisting coins general framework. The NYDFS will keep a record of all approved coins, and their specific uses, whether approved by the NYDFS or through the self-certification process by VC Firms. Coins which have received approval for specific uses by three unrelated and different VC Firms (Greenlist Threshold) will be added to the Greenlist for the specified use by the NYDFS. There will also be a six-month Greenlist waiting period from the date of the NYDFS' announcement until other VC Firms who have not previously received approval can use the coin. As with the coin-listing policy framework, VC Firms are required to monitor the use of any coins (on the Greenlist) ensuring that its ongoing use remains prudent.[1091]

6.1.4.3 Conditional BitLicense

In June 2020, the NYDFS announced a set of virtual currency initiatives in alignment with its review of the BitLicense regulatory framework culminating in its engagement with the industry and other experts to facilitate the ease with which VC Firms operate in NY.[1092] According to Superintendent Lacewell, these initiatives were targeted at fostering innovation, advancing NY's economy, and facilitating NY in continuing 'to blaze a trail in the virtual currency marketplace'.[1093] One such initiative is the memorandum of understanding entered into between the NYDFS and the SUNY indicating the intent to establish a SUNY-related virtual currency programme directed to assist emerging virtual currency entities from local communities. The NYDFS announced that virtual currency entities participating in the SUNY programme would operate through a proposed conditional licensing framework. This regime would allow persons to apply for a conditional licence to conduct virtual currency business activity where they are collaborating with an existing NYDFS-authorised firm. The existing NYDFS authorised firm would supply the conditional licensee with operational, staff and other relevant support until such time as the conditional licensee is able to acquire a complete NYDFS BitLicense or a limited purpose trust charter of its own accord. Overall, the proposed conditional licence regime aligns with the NYDFS' purpose to encourage financial institutions to operate, remain and expand in NY.[1094] The NYDFS indicated that the proposed conditional licence framework could be used by new entrants such as start-ups, growth-stage companies, existing NY firms currently not engaged in any virtual currency business activity, and incumbent virtual currency firms operating outside of NY.[1095] The NYDFS Superintendent is empowered with the authority to suspend or revoke a conditional licence granted, and may also levy reasonable conditions which 'may be subject to heightened review, whether in regard

1091. NYDFS, 'Guidance Regarding Adoption or Listing of Virtual Currencies' (24 June 2020) 3-4.
1092. NYDFS, 'Superintendent Lacewell Launches Series of Virtual Currencies Initiatives' (24 June 2020).
1093. NYDFS, 'Superintendent Lacewell Launches Series of Virtual Currencies Initiatives' (24 June 2020).
1094. Financial Services Law §102(a).
1095. NYDFS, 'Request for Comments on a Proposed Framework for a Conditional BitLicense' (24 June 2020).

to the scope and frequency of examination of otherwise'.[1096] Conditional licensee applicants are required to notify the NYDFS of its intention to collaborate with an authorised VC Firm and to provide a draft version of their service level agreement.

6.1.4.4 BitLicense Application Procedures

In June 2020, the NYDFS announced new practices for its review of BitLicense applications, to counter concerns expressed by the industry relating to the duration of and the transparency exhibited during the BitLicense application review process.[1097] The NYDFS indicated that these concerns were borne primarily from submissions of incomplete BitLicense applications, often experienced through the omission of necessary documents and information. To this end, the NYDFS introduced two new practices aiming to support efficiency and transparency during its application review process. Ordinarily, BitLicense applications are submitted through the Nationwide Multistate Licensing System and Registry which provides a checklist of requirements, application process steps, and a description of the documents required.

First, the NYDFS announced that it would only review applications substantively ready as characterised by its inclusion of all necessary checklist documents and the application being adequate on its face through its detail and organisation. Applications not complying with this requirement, would be deemed unready for substantive review and would only be considered once missing documents and information have been provided. Applications may also be deemed unready for substantive review if, at a later stage, it is discovered that required documents are missing, or significant issues materialise which would mark an in-depth application review as inappropriate. The NYDFS expressed the view that this practice would expedite its application review process and would make efficient use of NYDFS resources.

Second, the NYDFS announced that it would inform applicants of any deficiencies in their submitted applications once the substantive review process has commenced. This would be conveyed through deficiency letters (most likely emails) which would indicate the return date by which an applicant would be required to respond to the NYDFS. The NYDFS is permitted, without any further notice, to deny an application if all deficiencies have not been fully addressed at the end of the indicated response period for the third deficiency letter requesting them to be addressed. This practice would allow the NYDFS to use its resources more effectively and would benefit applicants attentively progressing their applications under substantive review.

6.1.4.5 Stablecoin Guidance

On 8 June 2022, the NYDFS published its guidance to VC Firms issuing US dollar-backed stablecoins under its supervision setting out the baseline requirements to be

1096. 23 NYCRR 200.4(c).
1097. NYDFS, 'Notice of Virtual Currency Business Activity License Application Procedures' (24 June 2020).

complied with in doing so.[1098] The NYDFS indicated that it has levied controls, requirements and standards on stablecoins issued by authorised entities since 2018, particularly when it approved the first issuance of stablecoins by Gemini Trust Company LLC and Paxos Trust Company LLC.[1099] The guidance aims to assist authorised entities currently issuing stablecoins, or who may be interested in doing so, to better under the general requirements which they are required to comply with. It should be noted that the guidance is only applicable to stablecoins backed by US dollars issued under NYDFS supervision. The most impactful features of the guidance includes:

> *Backing and redeemability.* Stablecoins must be fully backed by a reserve of assets. The market value of the reserve must be equal to at least the nominal value of the remaining stablecoin units at the end of each business day. Issuers of stablecoins (Issuer) must establish and maintain clear redemption policies which have been approved by the NYDFS in writing. The redemption policy must specify that lawful holders of stablecoins are entitled to redeem stablecoin units from the Issuer at par in a timely fashion. The policy must also clearly define the terms 'redemption' and 'timely' or expressly adopt the default definition of these terms as provided by the NYDFS. In exception cases, the NYDFS may require a redemption of stablecoins which it considers as not qualifying as timely.
>
> *Reserve.* Issuers are required to segregate the reserve assets from the issuing entity's proprietary assets. The reserve must be held in custody with: (i) a US state or federally chartered depository institution, with deposits insured by the Federal Deposit Insurance Corporation; and/or (ii) asset custodians with the prior written approval of the NYDFS. At all times, the reserve assets must be held by the aforementioned custodians for the benefit of the holders of the stablecoin units. The reserve must only include US treasury bills; reverse repurchase agreements; government money-market funds; and US state or federally charted deposit institution deposit accounts; subject to additional requirements being met. Finally, issuers must manage the reserve's liquidity risk in line with the redemption requirements.
>
> *Attestation.* At least once per month, the reserve must undergo an examination of management's assertions by an independent, US-licensed and CPA through the application of the attestation standards of the American Institute of Certified Public Accounts. The CPA must be appointed with the prior written approval of the NYDFS. The management's assertions to be included in the attestation include, among others, the end-of-day market value of the reserve and outstanding stablecoin units. The attestation should also include management's assertions applicable to the effectiveness of internal controls,

1098. NYDFS, 'Guidance on the Issuance of US Dollar-Back Stablecoins' (8 June 2022).
1099. NYDFS, 'DFS Continues to Foster Responsible Growth in New York's Fintech Industry with New Virtual Currency Product Approvals' (10 September 2018).

structure, and procedures relating to the previously mentioned management's assertions. The reports of the CPA should be made public by the Issuer.

6.1.4.6 *Discussion*

The actions and behaviours considered above are examined below through the adaptations and/or amendments effected to the regulatory approaches and regulatory frameworks, respectively, established by the NY Government to govern DLT Offerings.

6.1.4.6.1 Updated Regulatory Response

Several changes were effected to the regulatory framework developed to govern DLT Offerings, while the initial regulatory approach established remained largely unchanged. Most significantly, the NYDFS announced its review of the BitLicense Framework which it introduced in 2015, resulting in several policy and regulatory initiatives in accordance therewith. The underlying purpose of the review was stated as ensuring that NY, as the centre of both consumer protection and innovation, adapts to the rapid pace of development of its dynamic financial services industry, and speedily delivers services to the market. In accordance with this review, the NYDFS established a new coin listing regime culminating in the creation of two separate frameworks for VC Firms to adopt or list new coins, through a coin-listing policy or a greenlisting coin general framework. The NYDFS indicated that the purpose of this new coin listing regime was to improve the efficiency and speed of the processes used by VC Firms in adopting or listing new coins. Further, the new coin listing regime would enable the objective of developing innovation based on safety and soundness considerations, and consumer protection. The NYDFS also implemented two new practices aiming to support efficiency and transparency during its BitLicense application review process. A new conditional licensing framework allowing persons to apply for a conditional licence to conduct virtual currency business activity in collaboration with an existing NYDFS-authorised firm was also proposed. The NYDFS indicated that this new conditional licence could be used by new entrants, such as start-ups, growth-stage companies, existing NY firms currently not engaged in any virtual currency business activity, and incumbent virtual currency firms operating outside of NY. Further, the NYDFS published its guidance to virtual currency firms issuing US dollar-backed stablecoins which set out the general requirements which they are required to comply with in order to undertake such virtual currency business activity. Finally, the NYDFS issued guidance on the prevention of market manipulation and other wrongful activity acting as a reminder to virtual currency firms of their obligations to establish processes to detect, prevent and respond to fraud, attempted fraud and similar wrongdoing. In particular, these firms were reminded to be watchful of market manipulation considering the significant risks it poses to consumers and to the safety and soundness of financial services institutions. To this end, the NYDFS highlighted that virtual currency firms are required to create and implement a written policy setting out effective processes to detect, prevent and respond to fraud, attempted fraud and similar wrongdoing based on an evaluation of the specific risks faced by it.

The initial regulatory approach established for the governance of DLT Offerings in NY remained largely unchanged. In particular, the review of the BitLicense Framework accorded with the NY Government's continuous fact-finding enquiry through accelerated policy and regulatory initiatives considering market developments. The NYDFS, in particular, focussed on how processes could be made more efficient, such as to facilitate BitLicense applications and the adoption or listing of new coins. Further, the NY Government implemented initiatives to reinforce its position on preventing the use of virtual currency for illicit purposes, such as the NYDFS' reminder to VC Firms to be vigilant of market manipulation and to establish processes to detect, prevent and respond to fraud. Overall, the actions and behaviours of the NY Government directed to amending the initial response to the regulatory framework governing DLT Offerings were effected primarily to update the NYDFS' BitLicense Framework to take into account market developments and feedback since its introduction in 2015. Further, the amendments were effected to reinforce the NYDFS' mandate to provide the necessary guardrails, through regulation, to prevent the illicit use of virtual currency, while balancing the promotion of innovation in the virtual currency industry, such as through the introduction of the new conditional licence. In effecting the amendments to the regulatory framework, the NY Government largely applied its proactive approach to the regulation of DLT Offerings.

6.1.4.6.2 Competition Policy Influence

Competition policy considerations influenced the amendments effected to the regulatory framework developed for governing DLT Offerings. In particular, the NYDFS indicated that the policy objective underlying its review of the BitLicense Framework was to ensure that NY, as the centre of both consumer protection and innovation, adapts to the rapid pace of development of its dynamic financial services industry, and speedily delivers services to the market. This underlying policy objective accords squarely with the NYDFS' regulatory approach, in which it proactively responds to market developments through appropriate regulation. In particular, the NYDFS noted that its review of the BitLicense Framework, conducted partly through its engagement with the financial services industry and other stakeholders, also aimed to facilitate the ease with which virtual currency firms operate in NY. To this end, NYDFS' Superintendent Lacewell stated that its policy and regulatory initiatives undertaken during the review were targeted at fostering innovation, advancing NY's economy, and facilitating NY in continuing 'to blaze a trail in the virtual currency marketplace'.[1100] In particular, the NYDFS indicated that its new conditional licence regime accords with its purpose to encourage financial institutions to operate, remain and expand in NY.

1100. NYDFS, 'Superintendent Lacewell Launches Series of Virtual Currencies Initiatives' (24 June 2020).

CHAPTER 7

The Dog That Never Barks: Regulatory Competition Between International Financial Centres

This chapter provides a view on whether HK, London, and NY were engaged in regulatory competition with one another concerning their regulation of financial products and services underlined by DLT during the period 2008-2022. This view is set out through the formulation of three overarching themes which examine the extent of any regulation competition between the aforementioned jurisdictions. Finally, this chapter sets out the lessons distilled from the impact which regulatory competition may have on the development of regulation governing financial products and services underlined by burgeoning technologies.

7.1 INTRODUCTION

This chapter is concerned primarily with answering the question: to what extent were HK, London, and NY engaged in regulatory competition with one another through their regulation of financial products and services underlined by DLT during the period 2008-2022? This question is answered through the prism of the four institutional lenses, including: (i) Input; (ii) Process; (iii) Feedback; and (iv) Output. Collectively, these institutional lenses provide the frame within which the actions and behaviours of the concerned jurisdictions are examined to measure the influence of competition policy on their regulation of DLT Offerings. To this end, a visual representation of the key actions and behaviours of the authorities in the concerned jurisdictions are tabulated for each institutional lens. These key actions and behaviours are plotted in tables to reflect key data sources which have been reviewed and examined as part of the discussions set out in previous chapters. In particular, they act to illustrate the absence or emergence of any specific patterns, such as the concentration of any activity, or the lack thereof, and any overlapping actions and behaviours. The result is an identification of two specific patterns, including patterns of convergence and divergence.

First, these patterns are primarily concerned with whether the jurisdictions purposefully amended or developed their legislative and regulatory frameworks governing DLT Offerings in response to the influence of regulatory competition, or the threat thereof. The patterns of convergence were reviewed in two forms, either as: (i) a downward convergence, in the form of the implementation of reduced regulatory standards; or (ii) an upward convergence, in the form of the implementation of stricter regulatory standards. Further, the patterns of divergence were reviewed through the jurisdictions adopting specific legislative, regulatory, and policy initiatives intended to distinguish themselves from other Primary Actors in their governance of DLT Offerings.

Second, and more broadly, the patterns were secondarily concerned with the actions and behaviours of the jurisdictions relating to the manner in which they developed their competition policy and regulatory responses to the governance of DLT Offerings in their respective jurisdictions, in response to the influence of regulatory competition, or the threat thereof. First, patterns of convergence were reviewed in the form of the adoption of similar competition policy and regulatory approaches to the governance of DLT Offerings, and the underlying bases thereof. Second, patterns of divergence were reviewed in the form of the adoption of distinguishing competition policy and regulatory approaches to the governance of DLT Offerings, and the underlying bases thereof.

This analysis is examined to identify any underlying thematic observations evidencing the extent to which the concerned leading international financial centres were engaged in regulatory competition with one another. In conclusion, this chapter sets out the lessons distilled from the analysis of the potential impact of regulatory competition on the development of rules for financial products and services underlined by novel technologies.

7.1.1 Input

As previously indicated, the Input analysis entailed an evaluation of the governmental actions and behaviours of the concerned jurisdictions directed to formulating and implementing competition policy within the context of the emergence of Fintech and its position of importance on legal and policy agendas during the time period 2008-2017. This section examines those actions and behaviours with the aim of identifying any patterns of convergence and divergence which support the existence of any regulatory competition between the concerned jurisdictions in their regulation of DLT Offerings. To this end, Figure 7.1 provides a visual aid through data points which represent the key governmental actions and behaviours which have been reviewed in the analysis set out in previous chapters. External factors which may have influenced the concerned jurisdiction's approach to Fintech, to the exclusion of competition policy concerns, are also discussed but have not been tabulated in Figure 7.1 below.

Figure 7.1 Input Analyses of Governmental Actions and Behaviours for the Time Period 2008-2017

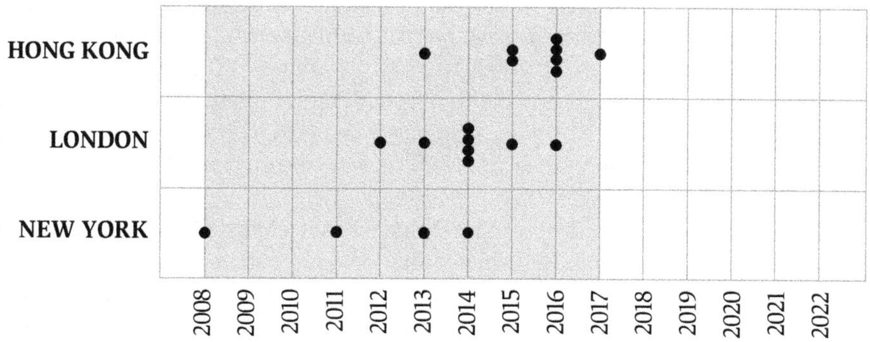

7.1.1.1 Converging Patterns

First, the analysis evidenced that competition policy was a significant driver in maintaining and developing the financial services industries of the concerned jurisdictions. Notably, the analysis evidenced that the jurisdictions were cognisant of their position relative to other competing Primary Actors. This was illustrated principally through the policy objective of maintaining the position of the concerned jurisdictions as leading global financial centres. Correspondingly, the financial regulatory authorities in each of the jurisdictions played an integral role in implementing policy and regulatory initiatives which advanced this underlying policy objective. In HK, this policy objective was framed as maintaining and strengthening the city's status as a leading centre for financial services, both regionally and internationally. To achieve this policy objective, the LegCo, FSDC and the HKMA implemented several policy and regulatory initiatives. In the UK, this policy objective was set as strengthening the UK's economy, with emphasis being placed on London's position as a leading international financial centre. The UKTI and the DIT served as the primary branches of the UK Government responsible for spearheading various marketing initiatives aimed at attracting foreign inward investment. In NY, this policy objective was framed as maintaining the city as the world's financial capital. The NYDFS played a significant role in promoting the competitiveness of NY's financial services industry, particularly through its modernisation of financial regulation.

The degree of significance of competition policy as a driver for the development of the financial services industries was different among the concerned jurisdictions. This was illustrated through: (i) the level of awareness of other Primary Actors' competitiveness; and (ii) the corresponding potential threat of competition from those actors. Greater emphasis was placed on the aforementioned factors where competition policy was considered significant for the development of the relevant financial services industry. This was most evident in the case of HK, where the competitiveness of other Primary Actors was considered by the HK Government in their advancement of competition policy, reflected primarily by a propensity to benchmark the policy directives of competing jurisdictions. In the case of London, the UK Government considered competitive forces, particularly those presented in the form of increased competition from other leading financial centres, including both HK and NY. These external competitive forces were measured through benchmarking initiatives, particularly those to review the Fintech development strategies adopted by other Primary Actors. The NY Government also exhibited an awareness of potential competitive forces in the form of increased competition from other international financial centres, most significantly London. However, its policy initiatives overall, were focussed less on maintaining NY as the world's financial capital, directed instead to progressing inwardly directed economic growth.

Second, the analysis evidenced that the emergence of Fintech played a significant role in the formulation and implementation of competition policy. Notably, the analyses evidenced that several policy and regulatory initiatives were formulated and implemented in response to the emergence of Fintech. In the case of HK and London, these initiatives were underlined by the policy objective of developing the cities into global Fintech and innovation hubs. In HK, this policy objective was framed as developing HK into a Fintech hub, underlined by its goal of maintaining and strengthening HK's reputation as a leading international financial centre. In the case of London, this policy objective was framed as developing the UK's Fintech sector, particularly to develop London into the 'FinTech capital of the world', thereby advancing the UK's international competitiveness. In the case of both HK and London, these actions and behaviours directed at formulating and implementing competition policy within the context of the emergence of Fintech appeared to illustrate a converging pattern of 'step-wise' or parallel movement. This is evidenced through the policy and regulatory initiatives implemented, as illustrated in Figure 7.1 above. To this end, analogous governmental actions and behaviours were evidenced in both HK and the UK establishing Fintech strategies in February and March 2013, respectively, and regulatory sandboxes in September and May 2016, respectively.

7.1.1.2 Diverging Patterns

In promoting NY's competitiveness, the NYDFS played the primary role of implementing policy and regulatory initiatives to maintain NY's reputation as a leading international financial centre. However, the advancement of this policy objective was directed principally towards regulatory initiatives, rather than implementing policy to grow NY's Fintech industry, as was the case with both HK and NY. For example, the NYDFS directed to increase its regulatory oversight to include virtual currency activity falling outside its regulatory remit, in accordance with its mandate to modernise the regulation of finance services. To this end, the NYDFS advanced a 'first mover advantage' approach to progressing regulatory initiatives for emerging Fintech Offerings, and one of the first financial regulatory authorities in the world to do so. This focus on the importance of regulation, rather than on policy, was also evidenced by the behaviours of the UK Government, albeit on a superficial level, based on the absence of any concrete regulatory proposals put forth by the government. It was, however, indicated that the development of applicable legislation and regulation was one of the principal factors which ensured the resilience of the UK's economy,[1101] fostering an attractive environment to start, finance and grow a business. In particular, London's financial services industry and its competitive edge against other international financial centres was noted for its legal and regulatory environment. However, the Input analysis evidenced no governmental actions and behaviours, or proposals, to direct competition policy to the emergence of Fintech on the basis of any specific legislative and regulatory measures.

7.1.1.3 External Factors

The NY Government's lack of focus on developing the Fintech industry in NY may potentially be explained by the NYDFS' principal aim of stimulating economic recovery as a result of the 2008 GFC. During the time period 2008-2014, the NYDFS focussed on implementing policy and regulatory initiatives which furthered the growth of its banking industry, such as its state bank charter and the establishment of new foreign banks in NY. It was also tasked with modernising NY financial services regulation and closing legal and regulatory lacunae, such as those which may have caused the 2008 GFC. To this end, aside from furthering the policy objective of maintaining NY as the world financial capital, the NYDFS' proactive regulatory stance could be explained by its mandate to close regulatory gaps within its framework, rather than responding exclusively to the competitive pressures presented by both HK and London.

The HK Government's policy objective of maintaining and strengthening HK's reputation as an international financial centre was also influenced by its goal to strengthen economic ties with Mainland China. To this end, a central strategy implemented by the HK Government to counter competitive pressures experienced by international and regional Primary Actors was to adopt closer economic ties with the Mainland. This resulted in the implementation of several economic cooperation initiatives aimed at facilitating HK's overarching policy objective and strengthening its position as a regional hub. As a result, the actions and behaviours of the HK Government directed to formulate and implement competition policy should be reflective of this additional policy dimension.

7.1.2 Process

As previously indicated, the Process analysis entailed an evaluation of the governmental actions and behaviours of the concerned jurisdictions directed towards formulating and implementing a regulatory approach to the governance of DLT Offerings for their respective jurisdictions during the time period 2013-2020. This section examines those actions and behaviours with the aim of identifying any patterns of convergence and

1101. UK Government, 'The Queen's Speech to Both Houses of Parliament' (3 December 2008) 3, https://assets.publishing.service.gov.uk/government/uploads/system/uploads/attachment_data/file/243346/9780101563123.pdf.

divergence which support the existence of any regulatory competition between the concerned jurisdictions through their regulation of DLT Offerings. To this end, Figure 7.2 provides a visual aid with the data points representing the key governmental actions and behaviours represented which have been reviewed in the regulatory competition analysis set out in Chapters 4, 5, and 6.

Figure 7.2 Process Analyses of Governmental Actions and Behaviours for the Time Period 2013-2020

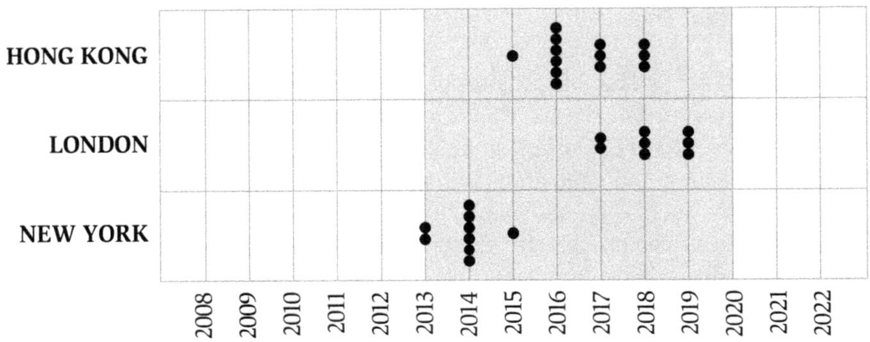

7.1.2.1 Converging Patterns

First, the Process analysis of the actions and behaviours directed by the Concerned Jurisdictions during the time period 2013-2020 evidenced that a fact-finding enquiry was conducted by the governments regarding DLT's use in the financial services industry prior to establishing an appropriate regulatory response. Notably, the analysis evidenced that the governments in the concerned jurisdictions implemented policy and regulatory initiatives marked to comprehend DLT's basics, its risks and benefits, and use cases for the financial services industry. The policy and regulatory initiatives were implemented through distinguishing actions and behaviours. In HK, the HKMA sought to educate the Fintech sector of DLT's underlying features and uses first, followed by its own DLT investigations. In the case of London, the UK Government undertook an information-gathering exercise on DLTs benefits, risks, business models and uses cases for the financial services industry, principally through the Treasury Committee and the Cryptoasset Taskforce. In NY, the fact-finding enquiry was directed through accelerated policy and regulatory initiatives geared to considering whether regulation, on top of existing money transmission regulations, was required to govern virtual currency firms. The NYDFS undertook its fact-finding enquiry through several initiatives including issuing subpoenas and holding public hearings. In the case of HK and the UK, the governments' fact-finding enquiries were marked by continuous monitoring of the respective Fintech markets, accounting for their dynamic and rapid development.

Second, the analysis evidenced that the financial regulatory authorities engaged with their respective financial services industries in developing their regulatory approaches to Fintech and DLT Offerings. In particular, the UK Government engaged continuously with the financial services industry, consumers and other relevant stakeholders, represented primarily in the form of written submissions and feedback provided to consultation processes. In NY, the NYDFS engaged with the financial services industry through several policy and regulatory initiatives, most notably through the issuance of subpoenas, public hearings and feedback received on the draft and revised versions of the BitLicense regulations. Third, the analysis evidenced that the financial regulatory authorities mostly adopted a technology-neutral approach to their regulation of financial services products underlined by emerging technologies. Notably, the HKMA adopted a 'risk-based and technology-neutral' approach in which regulatory frameworks were implemented based on specific risks posed by undertaking financial services, in place of posing bans or strict requirements to use the technology. In the UK, the FCA and the PRA also adopted this approach comprising the regulation of the financial services activities conducted by firms through the use of the emerging technology, and not the regulation of the technology itself.

Fourth, the analysis evidenced that the financial regulatory authorities aimed to balance their mandate to protect consumers with the policy goal of promoting innovation. In HK, the HK Government sought to balance the development of Fintech with the needs of consumers to be protected from the risks presented by new financial products and services. In the case of London, this balancing exercise was performed by the FCA through its mandate to protect consumer interests with the goal of fostering innovation for their benefit. In NY, the NYDFS performed a similar balancing exercise but focussed on developing regulations which did not stifle innovation, while preventing the illicit use of virtual currency. Finally, the analysis evidenced that competition policy was considered in the formulation of their regulatory approaches to Fintech and DLT Offerings. The HK Government expressed HK's potential to be developed into a 'Blockchain hub', promoting HK's openness to harnessing DLT in the financial services industry. In the case of London, the UK Government directed to maintain London as a leading international financial centre, and as a leader of technology-driven financial and professional services. Finally, the NYDFS marketed itself as a 'modern innovative financial regulator' distinguished from other financial regulatory authorities and leading the way forward in regulating virtual currencies.

7.1.2.2 Diverging Patterns

While the governmental actions and behaviours directed by the concerned jurisdictions in formulating a regulatory response to governing Fintech and DLT Offerings resulted in converging patterns, the regulatory responses themselves varied among the cities. This diverging pattern was marked primarily by the proposal to either regulate DLT Offerings through existing regulatory frameworks or through a newly created and bespoke regulatory regime. To this end, the NYDFS adopted a 'proactive' regulatory response culminating in the proposal of a new and bespoke regulatory framework for virtual currency business activity in NY. Adopting this approach was novel at the time when virtual currencies posed no discernible risk to financial and monetary stability, on a domestic and international basis. In the interests of not stifling innovation, the NYDFS indicated that the BitLicense regulations provided the necessary guardrails, however referenced its purpose as providing the NYDFS with strong oversight of virtual currency firms. As mentioned previously, the formulation of a new and bespoke regulatory framework accorded with NYDFS' mandate to modernise financial regulation, and to close regulatory gaps, most likely inspired by the 2008 GFC fallout and calls for more robust regulation and oversight of the financial services industry. On the other end of the spectrum, the UK Government adopted a 'watch and learn' approach representing a light-touch perspective to the governance of DLT Offerings through the proposed application of the existing regulatory framework. To this end, the UK Government proposed that the FCA's existing regulatory framework could be appropriately applied to cryptoassets and could provide sufficient protection to consumers. Further, the UK Government continued to monitor the cryptoasset market, and did not rule out possible legislative measures, should it become necessary. The 'cautious' regulatory approach adopted by the HK Government represented a middle ground between that applied by the UK and NY Governments. In particular, as with the UK, the HK Government proposed that the existing regulatory framework could be applied to Fintech firms and was sufficient to protect consumers where they formed the targets of Fintech Offerings but proposed to provide more robust regulatory guidance.

The regulatory responses formulated by the HK and UK Governments were premised on the view that cryptoassets did not pose a systemic risk as the markets in both jurisdictions were too small, obviating the need for a comprehensive legislative response. The NYDFS came to a similar view but nevertheless proposed to formulate a new and bespoke regulatory regime for virtual currency. This accentuated the NYDFS' 'proactive' approach, and its 'first mover advantage' among the leading international financial centres. The approaches of the HK and NY Governments are clearly distinguished by Figure 7.2 illustrating that in 2015 when the revised BitLicense regulations were issued, the HKMA issued a consumer warning apprising the public of the risks associated with Bitcoin. Finally, while the HK Government engaged with the industry and stakeholders in formulating its regulatory approach to governing DLT Offerings in its jurisdiction, it focussed primarily on the actions and behaviours of the branches of government through the policy and regulatory initiatives directed by them. As such, the analysis illustrated less engagement with the industry than directed by the HK Government, when compared to London and NY. Further, while the financial regulatory authorities in HK and the UK prominently stated their technology-neutral approach, the NYDFS was less direct about endorsing this approach. Former Superintendent Lawsky has, however, in the past indicated that financial regulation should be neutral, but that technology-specific regulations were sometimes warranted, where reasonable and appropriately tailored.[1102]

1102. Benjamin Lawsky, 'Regulating Digital Currency: BitLicense and the Internet of Value' (14 October 2014) Speech: Cardoza Law School, https://yu.hosted.panopto.com/Panopto/Pages/Embed.aspx?id=01b5be00-c8df-4688-a1dc-5302b6ca3c7e.

7.1.3 Output

As previously indicated, the Output analysis entailed an evaluation of the governmental actions and behaviours of the concerned jurisdictions directed to promulgating legal and regulatory rules, or to the issuance of regulatory guidance based on the pre-existing regulatory framework, which had the effect of formalising the rules governing DLT Offerings during the time period 2014-2020. This section examines those actions and behaviours with the aim of identifying any patterns of convergence and divergence which support the existence of any regulatory competition between the concerned jurisdictions through their regulation of DLT Offerings. To this end, Figure 7.3 provides a visual aid with the data points representing the key governmental actions and behaviours represented which have been reviewed in the regulatory competition analysis set out in Chapters 4, 5, and 6.

Figure 7.3 Output Analyses of Governmental Actions and Behaviours for the Time Period 2014-2020

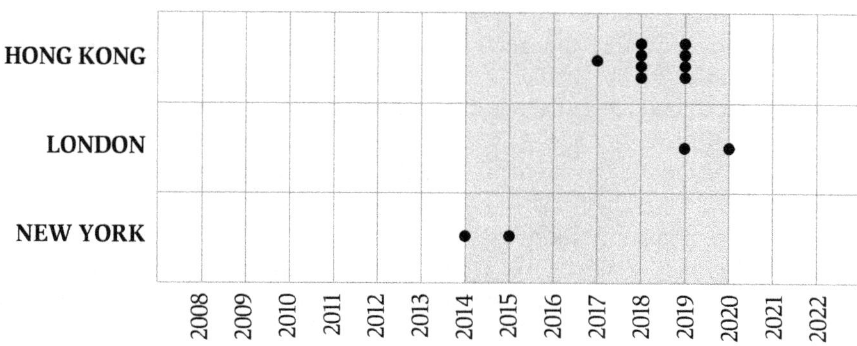

7.1.3.1 Converging Patterns

First, the Output analysis of the actions and behaviours directed by the concerned jurisdictions evidenced that the legal and regulatory rules promulgated, or regulatory guidance issued, had the effect of delineating the regulatory frameworks for DLT Offerings. Notably, the analysis evidenced that the concerned jurisdictions set out regulatory frameworks which detailed the regulatory activities involving DLT Offerings, which required a licence, and those unregulated activities for which a licence was not required. In HK, the regulatory remit evidenced was quite broad including the regulated activities of dealing in securities, advising on securities, dealing in futures, advising on futures, asset management, and providing automated trading services. At the same time, the application of the regulatory perimeter in HK was limited to regulated activities involving virtual assets constituting 'securities' under the SFO. In the case of London, it was evidenced that the regulatory remit included a wide range of regulated activities involving creating, holding, issuing, and marketing crypto-asset products and services. However, the regulatory perimeter was limited to activities involving cryptoasset tokens qualified as: (i) a 'specified investment' under the RAO; (ii) a 'financial instrument' under MiFID II; (iii) 'electronic money' under the EMRs; or (iv) application of the PSRs. In NY, it was evidenced that the regulatory remit included a broad range of virtual currency business activity, including those related to, among others, receiving or transmitting virtual currency.

Second, the analysis evidenced regulatory frameworks which focussed on imposing AML regulatory requirements on firms providing DLT Offerings. In HK, licensed firms undertaking virtual currency activities were required to comply with AML requirements, including those set out in the Guideline on AML and Counter-Financing of Terrorism. In the case of London, the UK Government proposed to transpose the 5AMLD into domestic law, in addition to going beyond its provisions by imposing AML requirements to all cryptoasset activities, whether regulated or not. In NY, virtual currency firms are required to establish an AML programme based on an initial risk assessment conducted. Third, the analysis evidenced regulatory frameworks which provided protection to consumers by protecting them against the risks posed by DLT Offerings. In the UK, the FCA's supervisory objectives include consumer protection and competition harms. To this end, the FCA's Final Guidance was formulated to assist consumers in identifying whether a cryptoasset falls within the FCA's regulatory perimeter and is thus subject to applicable regulatory rules, and regulatory protections. In the case of NY, the BitLicense Regulations contain several provisions providing regulatory protections for consumers, including the right to receive a host of disclosures from virtual currency firms.

Finally, the regulatory frameworks developed by the HK and NY Governments included a measure of flexibility, which could be characterised as 'competitive advantages'. In HK, this was representative of the application of the SFC's regulatory rules, illustrated largely by the SFC's opt-in regime for virtual asset trading platforms trading at least one virtual asset constituting a 'security' under the SFO. Further, the terms and conditions developed by the SFC for firms undertaking virtual asset activities were flexible and bespoke, based on firm requirements. This measure of flexibility accorded with the NYDFS' conditional BitLicense which permitted start-ups and small businesses unable to fully comply with all of the provisions of the BitLicense Regulations to operate under a conditional licence.

7.1.3.2 Diverging Patterns

While the governmental actions and behaviours directed by the Concerned Jurisdictions in formulating a regulatory framework to governing Fintech and DLT Offerings resulted in converging patterns, the mode of delivery of the regulatory rules underlining those regulatory frameworks varied among the concerned jurisdictions. This diverging pattern was marked primarily by the application of the non-legislative and legislative approaches adopted by the concerned jurisdictions. To this end, the NYDFS promulgated a new and bespoke regulatory regime in the form of the BitLicense

Regulations, based on the money transmission and banking regulations but adapted for virtual currency business. The regulatory rules set out applicable licensing requirements and minimum standards of conduct.

In the case of London, the regulatory framework developed for the governance of cryptoassets was provided in the form of regulatory guidance which clarified the FCA's expectations for firms conducting cryptoasset activities, and for which authorisation is required. As such, the FCA's conduct of business rules, as set out in its Handbook, would apply to firms carrying on cryptoasset activities by way of business in the UK. The regulatory framework formulated for virtual assets in HK was underlined by a risk-based approach and an extension of regulatory protections to consumers, on the basis of the SFC's principle 'same business, same risks, same rules'. The regulatory rules informing this framework impose sweeping provisions on licensed firms undertaking virtual asset activities in HK.

Figure 7.3 illustrates additional diverging patterns regarding the regulatory frameworks developed for governing DLT Offerings. In particular, the NYDFS' finalised its regulatory framework in 2015, without any further amendments thereto, in contrast to the actions and behaviours directed by the HK and UK Governments in their continuous market monitoring, evidencing their cautious and proportionate regulatory approaches. Further, the regulatory frameworks developed by HK and UK Governments can be contrasted based on the sheer quantity of regulatory documents issued. HK financial regulatory authorities issued several circulars and statements reinforcing its regulatory position, whereas the UK Government adopted a minimalist approach, consistent with its light-touch regulatory response.

7.1.4 Feedback

As previously indicated, the Feedback analysis entailed an evaluation of the governmental actions and behaviours of the concerned jurisdictions directed to modifying the initial regulatory response to governing DLT Offerings during the time period 2018-2022. This section examines those actions and behaviours with the aim of identifying any patterns of convergence and divergence which support the existence of any regulatory competition between the concerned jurisdictions through their regulation of DLT Offerings. To this end, Figure 7.4 provides a visual aid with the data points representing the key governmental actions and behaviours represented which have been reviewed in the regulatory competition analysis set out in Chapters 4, 5, and 6.

Figure 7.4 Feedback Analyses of Governmental Actions and Behaviours for the Time Period 2014-2022

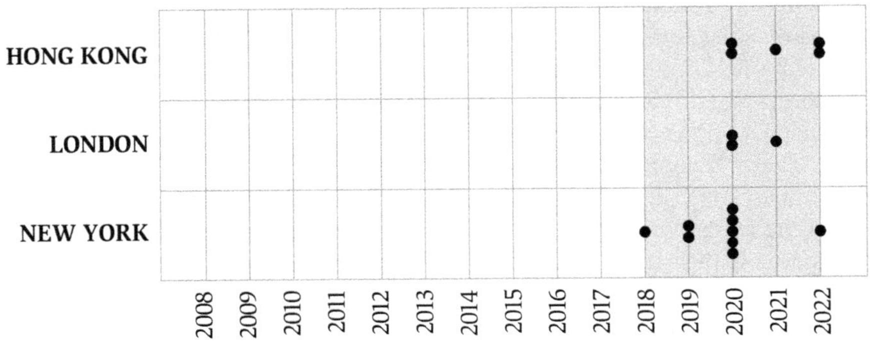

7.1.4.1 Converging Patterns

First, the Feedback analysis of the actions and behaviours directed by the concerned jurisdictions evidenced amendments to the regulatory frameworks formulated to govern DLT Offerings, while the regulatory approaches adopted remained largely the same, with a few exceptions. Notably, the analysis evidenced, in accordance with Figure 7.4, that the amendments effected by the concerned jurisdictions fell into one of two categories, including: (i) those effected to close existing regulatory gaps through the extension of the existing regulatory framework to unregulated DLT Offerings; and (ii) those effected to enhance the efficiency of regulatory processes associated with the existing regulatory framework. To this end, there was a noticeable emphasis on regulating stablecoins. In HK, the SFC expanded the virtual asset trading platform regime to include all virtual asset trading, including those not constituting 'securities'. The FSTB also proposed new regulatory regimes for firms operating virtual asset exchanges, and for stablecoins. In proposing these amendments, the SFC and the HKMA applied the 'same business, same risks, same rules' principle, in accordance with its non-legislative approach. The underlying purpose of these extensions was to provide enhanced investor protections and to fulfil the HK Government's international AML and CFT commitments. To this end, the review of the regulatory regime for virtual assets introduced in 2018 was conducted to ascertain whether it was still 'fit for purpose, and whether any modifications are required'. In the UK, the HM Treasury transposed the 5AMLD domestically through the amendment of the Money Laundering Regulations, aimed to tackle illicit use cases of cryptoassets through its application to firms engaged in one of the indicated specified cryptoasset business activities. The HM Treasury also proposed to extend the financial promotions rules to unregulated cryptoassets, to provide greater consumer protection and promote responsible innovation. Finally, the HM Treasury proposed to create a regulatory regime for stablecoins by extending the regulatory perimeter to include issuing or facilitating stablecoin use as a means of payment, in accordance with the 'same risk, same regulatory outcome' principle. In NY, the NYDFS announced its review of the BitLicense virtual currency regime introduced in 2015, resulting in several policy and regulatory initiatives including: (i) the establishment of a new adoption and listing coin regime; (ii) new practices aiming to support efficiency and transparency of the BitLicense application review process; (iii) a new conditional licensing framework; (iv) issuance of guidance on the prevention of market manipulation and other wrongful activity. The underlying purpose of the review was stated as ensuring that NY, as the centre of both consumer protection and innovation, adapted to the rapid pace of development of its dynamic financial services industry, and speedily delivered services to the market.

Second, the analysis evidenced, in accordance with Figure 7.4, converging regulatory responses to formulating a regulatory regime for stablecoins, in accordance with the view that the Feedback analysis aimed to close existing regulatory framework gaps. In the case of HK and London specifically, these actions and behaviours directed at formulating a regulatory framework for stablecoins illustrated a pattern of 'step-wise' or parallel movement. In particular, this is evidenced through the policy and regulatory initiatives implemented, as illustrated in Figure 7.4 above, with reference specifically to both the HK and UK Governments' publishing their proposed regulatory responses to stablecoins in January 2021 and January 2020, respectively. To this end, both the HK and UK Governments proposed regulatory responses to stablecoins were underlined by the same regulatory principle of ensuring that financial regulatory authorities use their 'agile' powers in formulating the regulatory rules governing DLT Offerings. The HK Government indicated that this agile approach should be used together with risk-based and proportionate regulation as guiding principles to establish a regulatory regime for stablecoins in HK.[1103] Once again, the actions and behaviours of the HK Government accorded with the UK Government's 'watch and learn' regulatory approach, characterised by its staged and proportionate nature, allowing it to monitor market developments, and respond accordingly when needed.

Further, both Primary Actors utilised similar regulatory principles, largely of the same import, to extend their existing regulatory framework to unregulated DLT Offerings, such as stablecoins. In HK this included the 'same business, same risks, same rules' principle, and in the UK this included the 'same risk, same regulatory outcome'. Once again, through the use of these similar underlying principles, the actions and behaviours directed by the HK and UK Governments illustrated a pattern of 'step-wise' or parallel movement to formulating appropriate regulatory responses. Figure 7.4 illustrates the NYDFS considered its own position on stablecoins during the time period 2021-2022, as with the HK and UK Governments, by publishing guidance on the issuance of US dollar-backed stablecoins.

Third, the analysis evidenced that competition policy considerations influenced the amendments effected to the regulatory framework developed for governing DLT Offerings. In HK, the SFC highlighted that HK was one of the first major jurisdictions to

1103. HKMA, 'Discussion Paper on Cryptoassets and Stablecoins' (January 2022), para. 5.2(ii).

develop a comprehensive regulatory framework for virtual asset trading platforms based on international standards recommended by standard-setting organisations. Notably, the FSTB indicated that there was wide-ranging support for the HK Government to reinforce HK's AML/CFT in alignment with international standards, thus maintaining and strengthening HK's reputation as a leading international financial centre. In the case of London, the FCA expressed its concern regarding the global nature of permissionless DLT systems, ripe for potential regulatory arbitrage, unbounded by geographical limitations, prompting it to collaborate with the FATF to address this issue. Notably, the HM Treasury indicated that the UK Government's regulatory approach fosters stablecoin industry growth, in accordance with the policy objective of placing the UK financial services industry 'at the forefront of cryptoasset technology and innovation'.[1104] In NY, the NYDFS indicated that its review of the BitLicense virtual currency regime aimed to foster innovation, advance NY's economy, and facilitate NY in continuing 'to blaze a trail in the virtual currency marketplace'.[1105]

7.1.4.2 Diverging Patterns

While the governmental actions and behaviours directed by the concerned jurisdictions in formulating their regulatory frameworks to governing DLT Offerings resulted in converging patterns, the initial regulatory responses themselves varied among the Concerned Jurisdictions. The HK Government applied largely the same regulatory approach; however, it undertook to consult more with the financial services industry in proposing legislative and regulatory amendments. In the case of London, the UK Government departed from its non-legislative approach through legislative measures and proposals thereof. This approach was evidenced primarily through the domestic transposition of the 5AMLD, and the proposed extension of the financial promotions regime to unregulated cryptoassets. In NY, the initial regulatory approach formulated to govern DLT Offerings remained largely unchanged. The review of its BitLicense virtual currency regime accorded with the NY Government's continuous fact-finding enquiry through accelerated policy and regulatory initiatives considering market developments, and through engagement with the financial services industry. To this end, the NYDFS focussed on regulatory initiatives aimed to enhance the efficiency of its BitLicense virtual currency regime. Notably, the NYDFS reinforced its position on the importance of AML standards and consumer protection, most notably through its guidance reminding virtual currency firms to be vigilant of market manipulation and to establish processes to detect, prevent and respond to fraud.

1104. HM Treasury, 'UK Regulatory Approach to Cryptoassets, Stablecoins, and Distributed Ledger Technology in Financial Markets. Response to the Consultation and Call for Evidence' (April 2022) 3.

1105. NYDFS, 'Superintendent Lacewell Launches Series of Virtual Currencies Initiatives' (24 June 2020).

7.2 DID HONG KONG, LONDON, AND NEW YORK ENGAGE IN REGULATORY COMPETITION WITH EACH OTHER?

The regulatory competition analysis undertaken in this book is examined within the International Regulatory Competition Environmental Context between HK, London, and NY. The actions and behaviours of the governments of these leading international financial centres are set within the perimeter of the respective systems of government and domestic legal systems. The systems of government include an autonomous SAR (HK), a parliamentary constitutional monarchy (UK, London), and a representative democracy and republic (US, NY). Accordingly, the direction of the regulatory competition examined in this book is the horizontal dimension between similar functional units of governments, i.e., cities forming part of sovereign-nation states. The Primary Actors whose actions and behaviours have been examined as part of the analysis include: (i) in HK, the LegCo, HKMA, SFC, and the FSDC; (ii) in London, the HM Treasury, FCA, PRA, and the DTI; and (iii) in NY, the NYDFS and the NY State Legislature. Together, these elements comprise the essential elements of regulatory competition based on the framework developed in this book (*see* Table 7.1 below).

With this in mind, the institutional theme analysis set out above can be leveraged to determine whether HK, London, and NY were engaged in regulatory competition with each other through their development of rules to govern financial products and services underlined by DLT. In particular, the analysis, delineated by the four institutional themes, is examined below to illustrate: (i) the extent to which the concerned jurisdictions were influenced by regulatory competition, or the threat thereof, in their regulation of DLT Offerings; and (ii) how concerned legislative and regulatory texts and policy instruments issued in the jurisdictions were formulated according to the influence of regulatory competition, or the threat thereof. This examination revealed that regulatory competition between HK, London, and NY was evidenced, but only to a limited extent. On this limited basis:

> First, the analysis evidenced that HK, London, and NY were influenced by regulatory competition concerns, or the threat thereof, as evidenced primarily through the policy goal of maintaining their respective reputations as leading international financial centres. However, this influence did not extend to the creation of lax or stricter regulatory rules to govern DLT Offerings for the purpose of engaging in regulatory competition.
>
> Second, the analysis evidenced that while regulatory competition influenced HK, London, and NY's 'competitive appetites' in formulating regulatory responses and developing regulatory rules to govern DLT Offerings, this influence only extended to how they viewed their positions as individual competitors generally, and not how these positions could be harnessed to engage in regulatory competition with each other.
>
> Third, in place of the operation of directed rules-based competition in which HK, London, and NY developed regulatory frameworks containing distinct legal and regulatory rules meant to lure Secondary Actors to their jurisdictions, and thus away from competing jurisdictions, the cities focussed instead

on developing regulatory frameworks characterised by similar regulatory features and underlined by similar foundational regulatory strategies.
Finally, despite the absence of rules-based competition, in developing their regulatory frameworks to govern financial products and services underlined by DLT, HK, London, and NY chose instead to promote other regulatory and policy features to attract actors to their jurisdictions (i.e., competitive advantages), but without any direct intention to lure those actors away from each other's locales.

These conclusions, which have been reached through an examination of the analysis of the four institutional lens themes, are discussed in further detail below.

7.2.1 The Significance of Competition Policy Agenda

The analysis supports the view that the governments of HK, London, and NY took account of regulatory competition concerns, or the threat thereof, in formulating their regulatory responses and in developing the regulatory rules to govern financial products and services underlined by DLT (*see* institutional lenses: Input, Process, and Output analyses above). The influence of regulatory competition can be seen clearly in the actions and behaviours of the concerned jurisdictions directed to achieving the policy goals of: (i) maintaining their reputations as leading international financial centres (IFC Policy Goal); and (ii) establishing their jurisdictions as 'FinTech Hubs' (HK and London, in particular). These policy goals were set with the purpose of securing relevant regulatory competition Drivers, notably foreign and regional capital and investment for the purposes of advancing economic growth. The Driver of attracting highly skilled labour was also indicated in the case of HK (*see* Table 7.1 below). Overall, the significance attached to achieving the IFC Policy Goal, and the related Fintech policy aims, provides strong support for the deduction that each jurisdiction formed a position on: (i) how they would market and promote themselves to attract Secondary Actors; and (ii) the particular legal and regulatory rules and initiatives which would be used to attract these actors (i.e., the Means).

The actions and behaviours directed by the HK government operated to progress the underlying policy goal of maintaining and strengthening HK as a leading international financial services centre (executed principally through the work of the LegCo, the HKMA, and the FSDC). This was supplemented by the government's Fintech policy goal of developing HK into a Fintech hub. These policy goals were aimed primarily at the regulatory competition Drivers of attracting and retaining international and regional capital, financial products, financial institutions, and highly skilled labour. To attract and retain these Drivers, the government made use of various Means, including formulating regulatory rules to govern DLT Offerings, targeted at Secondary Actors, including international and Mainland Chinese firms. The government also promoted HK's rule of law, freedom of information, and its ties to the international community as a means of promoting itself to Secondary Actors.

In the case of London, the actions and behaviours undertaken by the government operated to advance the underlying policy goal of strengthening the UK's economy, and London's position as a leading international financial centre. This policy aim was executed primarily through the work of the DTI, FCA, and the UKTI, as buttressed by its Fintech policy goals of growing the UK's Fintech sector and developing London into the 'FinTech capital of the world'. Together, these policy goals were directed principally to secure the regulatory competition Driver of attracting high-quality foreign inward investment. To this end, the government placed a premium on developing 'pro-innovation' laws and regulatory rules. This intention, however, did not extend to developing bespoke 'pro-innovation' rules for the governance of DLT Offerings. Instead, the regulatory competition Means used by the UK Government including extending existing regulatory frameworks to govern specific financial products and services underlined by DLT. These means were targeted primarily at Secondary Actors, including foreign and institutional investors, and Fintech start-ups. The government also promoted the UK as 'a springboard for growth', which could provide an attractive environment to start, finance, and grow a business, as a means of attracting Secondary Actors to the city.

In NY, the actions and behaviours advanced by the government operated to achieve the underlying policy goal of stimulating economic growth and maintaining NY as the world's financial capital. The 2008 GFC directed the NYDFS to focus on stimulating economic growth and job creation through various policy and regulatory initiatives. At the same time, this focus was directed together with the policy aim of maintaining NY's role as an international hub for financial services. As such, these overarching policy goals were aimed at spurring economic growth, thus forming the relevant regulatory competition Driver. Accordingly, the NYDFS employed regulatory competition Means in the form of developing a bespoke licensing and regulatory regime for virtual currency business activity in NY. On the basis of maintaining NY as the world's financial capital, these Means were targeted at Secondary Actors, including international and regional virtual currency business firms, and start-ups. The government also promoted the NYDFS' goal of modernising financial regulation through proactivity as a means of attracting economic activity to NY.

As such, the actions and behaviours of the governments of all three jurisdictions evidenced an appetite to develop and execute competition policy and regulatory initiatives with the purpose of executing their jurisdiction's specific IFC Policy Goal. This competitive appetite was evidenced to varying degrees, with HK and London displaying the highest degree of consideration for competition policy. While NY also displayed an interest in executing its IFC Policy Goal, greater emphasis was placed on economic recovery based on the fallout of the 2008 GFC. The consideration given to competition policy concerns, as evidenced by the competitive appetites, also impacted the manner in which the jurisdictions would later develop regulatory responses to the emergence of DLT Offerings, and the accompanying Fintech policy goals, particularly in HK and London.

Accordingly, the analysis supports the view that a causal connection was evidenced between: (i) the IFC Policy Goal transmitted in each of the concerned jurisdictions; and (ii) the importance of Fintech, and DLT Offerings, as a significant medium for achieving this policy goal, and for spurring economic growth generally. Through the prism of this causal connection, the analysis evidenced that HK, London, and NY were influenced by regulatory competition concerns, or the threat thereof, as illustrated through their varying competitive appetites. However, there is very little evidence to support the view that this influence extended to the creation of lax or stricter regulatory rules to govern DLT Offerings for the purpose of engaging in regulatory competition, specifically with each other. Instead, the influence of regulatory competition extended only to how they viewed themselves as individual competitors more generally, and not how their positions could be harnessed to engage directly in rules-based regulatory competition. The approach taken by the concerned jurisdictions to develop regulatory rules for DLT Offerings, in lieu of directed rules-based competition, is discussed in the next section.

7.2.2 Analogous Regulatory Treatment of DLT Offerings

The analysis supports the view that the governments of HK, London, and NY, while fully cognisant of regulatory competition concerns, or the threat thereof, developed regulatory frameworks to govern DLT Offerings incorporating similar hallmark features and foundational regulatory strategies (*see* institutional lenses: Process, Output, and Feedback). This approach was taken by the concerned jurisdictions as opposed to imposing relaxed or stricter regulatory rules with the purpose of directly engaging in rules-based regulatory competition with each other. The enforcement of analogous regulatory rules, based primarily on existing regulatory frameworks, as the regulatory competition Means, acted to cement minimum standards for the governance of DLT Offerings. This was evidenced in the analyses, most commonly, through the mandate balancing exercise conducted by the financial regulatory authorities of each of the concerned jurisdictions, which placed significant emphasis on protecting consumer interests and curbing money laundering activities.

With respect to the hallmark regulatory features, the financial regulatory authorities in the concerned jurisdictions endeavoured to balance their mandate of protecting consumer interests with the policy goal of promoting innovation and competition. For example, the HK Government sought to balance the development of the Fintech sector with consumers' need to be protected from the risks presented by new financial products and services. In the UK, this balancing exercise was performed by the FCA through its mandate to protect consumer interests and the corresponding goal of fostering innovation for their benefit. Finally, the NYDFS also performed a similar exercise by balancing the development of regulation (which did not stifle innovation) with preventing the illicit use of virtual currency. While innovation was promoted through several heterogeneous initiatives in each of the cities, the policy goal of protecting consumer interests appeared to be of paramount importance.

The enforcement of AML standards also formed a hallmark feature of the regulatory frameworks developed by the concerned jurisdictions to govern DLT Offerings. In HK, the government enforced AML standards with respect to virtual currency firms through the Guideline on AML and Counter-Financing of Terrorism. In the case of London, the UK Government transposed the 5AMLD into domestic law through the Money Laundering Regulations. In NY, the NYDFS incorporated AML requirements into the provisions of the BitLicense Regulations, including the obligation on licensees to establish and implement an AML programme, and to provide consumers with necessary written disclosures.

With respect to foundational regulatory strategies, the financial regulatory authorities in each of the concerned jurisdictions conducted fact-finding enquiries into DLT before developing their regulatory approaches and regulatory frameworks to govern financial products and services underlined by it. These investigations into understanding the purpose of the technology, and the uses to which it could be put in the financial services industry, formed a significant regulatory strategy for all three jurisdictions. Various policy and regulatory initiatives were implemented through governmental actions and behaviours, including establishing government taskforces, research initiatives, public consultations, subpoenas and public calls for information.

Further, the financial regulatory authorities in HK and London adopted analogous foundational regulatory strategies, as witnessed through the 'step-wise' or parallel movement of their actions and behaviours responding to the emergence of DLT Offerings. For example, the rapidly developing DLT sector influenced the regulatory approaches adopted, resulting in the financial regulatory authorities in both HK and the UK continuously monitoring the market, and responding appropriately using their 'agile powers'. At the time, this strategy was adopted largely as both governments viewed DLT Offerings as posing no systemic risk based on its low use and adoption rates. The financial regulatory authorities in both jurisdictions also chose to apply existing frameworks to DLT Offerings on the basis of the 'same business, same risks, same rules' and 'same risk, same regulatory outcome' principles, respectively. These principles are largely of the same import and provide credence to the non-legislative approaches adopted in both jurisdictions.

In respect to NY, no 'step-wise' or parallel movement of governmental actions and behaviours in alignment with HK and London was evidenced. This can be explained largely on the basis of timing, as the NYDFS developed its BitLicense Framework much earlier than HK and London's initial response to the emergence of DLT Offerings. However, while the NYDFS developed a new and bespoke framework for virtual currencies, this regime was based largely on existing banking laws and regulations. As such, the adoption of foundational regulatory strategies in relation to the formulation of regulatory frameworks is also evidenced, though partially, through the actions and behaviours of the NY Government.

Overall, therefore, in place of directed rules-based competition in which HK, London, and NY developed regulatory frameworks containing distinct legal and regulatory rules meant to lure Secondary Actors to their jurisdictions, the jurisdictions focussed on developing and enforcing regulatory frameworks characterised by largely similar regulatory features and underlined by largely similar foundational regulatory strategies. However, while regulatory competition did not operate between HK, London, and NY on the basis of enforcing lax or stricter regulatory rules, each jurisdiction made use of specific promotional measures to attract Secondary Actors to their respective locales. These measures are elaborated upon in the next section.

7.2.3 Setting Themselves Apart: Competitive Advantage

The analysis supports the view, that while the evidenced competitive appetites did not extend to the rules-based regulatory competition between each other, the governments of HK, London, and NY, adopted other measures to attract Secondary Actors to their locales, in relation to those offerings. These measures extend principally to competitive advantage and to the manner in which regulatory frameworks were delivered. These measures were used by the concerned jurisdictions to position themselves as competitors more generally but were not introduced in direct response to any external competitive pressures. Overall, these competitive advantages acted to delineate distinguishing features of the concerned jurisdictions' governance of DLT Offerings (*see* institutional lenses: Output and Feedback).

With respect to competitive advantage, the concerned jurisdictions used these means by incorporating flexible measures into the regulatory frameworks developed to govern DLT Offerings. In HK, these competitive advantages took the form of the flexibility with which the SFC applied its rules providing for a voluntary opt-in regime for virtual asset trading platforms trading at least one virtual asset constituting a security under the SFO. Further, the terms and conditions developed by the SFC for firms engaged in virtual asset activities are designed based on the requirements of the specific firm, thus providing an approach to regulation which is both flexible and more nuanced. In the case of London, competitive advantage took the form of the support provided by the FCA through the UK Government's flagship technology-driven platform, Project Innovate.

Further, in both HK and London, competitive advantage also took the form of established regulatory sandboxes which provide market participants with the opportunity to test their proposed DLT Offerings in a controlled environment with the support of the relevant regulatory authority before they are offered to consumers. Finally, in NY, the competitive advantage took the form of the NYDFS' Conditional BitLicense virtual currency regime which allowed start-ups and small businesses unable to fully comply with the regulations to continue business activity under a conditional licence. Specific regulatory initiatives were also adopted to enhance the efficiency of this regime, including improvements to the application process.

With respect to the manner in which regulatory frameworks were delivered, the concerned jurisdictions took varying approaches, despite their development of regulatory frameworks based primarily on existing rules. For example, in the case of HK and London, while there is evidence to support the existence of a 'step-wise' or parallel movement of the actions and behaviours to a certain extent, the mode of delivery of the applicable frameworks differed. Whereas both opted to extend existing regulatory frameworks as the basis for the rules governing DLT Offerings, the HK Government executed more robust actions and behaviours through the development of formalised regulatory rules. This approach would remain largely the same, save for later consulting with the financial services industry in proposing legislative and regulatory amendments. Whereas in the case of London, the UK Government executed actions and behaviours of a 'light touch' nature, at least initially, which culminated in the issuance of minimal regulatory guidance which considered whether DLT Offerings could be placed within the existing regulatory perimeter. At a later stage, however, the UK Government departed from its non-legislative approach by introducing legislative proposals and measures (*see* institutional lens theme Feedback). In contrast to HK and London, the NY Government opted to formulate the bespoke BitLicense virtual currency regime (albeit on the basis of existing banking laws and regulations). This approach too largely remained unchanged, with the NYDFS later directing its focus to regulatory initiatives aimed to enhance the efficiency of its BitLicense virtual currency regime (*see* institutional lens theme: Feedback).

While regulatory competition concerns, or the threat thereof, influenced the concerned jurisdictions in the development of their approaches to the emergence of DLT, and the regulatory frameworks developed for financial products and services underlined thereby, it is important to note that several external factors, not related to regulatory competition, also influenced the actions and behaviours of the respective governments. These external factors include, for example: (i) the prevalence of the use and adoption of DLT Offerings; (ii) the systemic risks posed by DLT Offerings; (iii) concerns raised by the financial services industry; and (iv) the use of DLT Offerings for illicit purposes. Further, and given the specific time period within which this book is framed, the fallout of the 2008 GFC significantly impacted the approach to the governance of DLT Offerings taken by the NY Government. Accordingly, the regulatory approaches and frameworks formulated to govern DLT Offerings in the concerned jurisdictions were influenced by these jurisdictional-specific attributes, resulting in both analogous and diverging actions and behaviours.

Overall, however, while HK, London, and NY did not engage in rules-based competition against each other in developing their regulatory frameworks to govern financial products and services underlined by DLT, the analysis supports the view that they chose instead to promote other regulatory and policy features to attract Secondary Actors to their jurisdictions, but absent any direct intention to lure those actors away from each other's locales.

Table 7.1 Regulatory Competition Framework Applied to RC Hypothesis Analysis

	RC Essential Element	*HK*	*London*	*NY*
1.	**Environmental Context**	International RC between HK, London and NY as cities within sovereign nation-states whose actions and behaviours are constrained by the separate legal systems in force domestically		
2.	**Direction**	Horizontal dimension of RC between similar or analogous functional units of government as cities within different sovereign nation-states		
3.	**Systems of Government**	Autonomous SAR of the People's Republic of China	Parliamentary Constitutional Monarchy	Representative Democracy and a Republic

	RC Essential Element	*HK*	*London*	*NY*
4.	**Actors**	**Primary:** HK Government represented by the LegCo, HKMA, SFC, and the FSDC	**Primary:** UK Government represented by HM Treasury, FCA, PRA, and the DTI	**Primary:** NY Government represented by NYDFS and NY State Legislature
		Secondary: International and Mainland Chinese firms, and highly skilled workers	**Secondary:** Foreign and institutional investors, and Fintech start-ups	**Secondary:** International and regional virtual currency business firms
5.	**Means**	**Regulatory:** Existing regulatory regime, with robust regulatory rules, and no legislative intervention Enforced rules on consumer protection and AML	**Regulatory:** Existing regulatory regime, with minimal guidance and minimal legislative intervention Enforced rules on consumer protection and AML	**Regulatory:** Bespoke regulatory regime Enforced rules on consumer protection and AML
		Policy: Rule of law, freedom of information, and its ties to the international community	**Policy:** UK 'springboard for growth' an attractive environment to start, finance and grow a business	**Policy:** Modernising financial regulation through proactivity and a 'first mover' advantage
		Competitive advantage: SFC regulatory rule flexibility	**Competitive advantage:** FCA support through Project Innovate	**Competitive advantage:** Conditional BitLicense

	RC Essential Element	HK	London	NY
6.	**Drivers**	**Drivers:** International and regional capital, financial products, financial institutions and highly skilled labour	**Drivers:** High-quality foreign inward investments	**Drivers:** Economic growth and job creation
		Underlying policy goal: Maintaining and strengthening leading international financial centre status, for financial services	**Underlying policy goal:** Strengthening the UK's economy, and London's position as a leading international financial centre	**Underlying policy goal:** Economic growth and maintaining NY as the world's financial capital
		Fintech policy goal: Developing HK into a Fintech hub	**Fintech policy goal:** Growing the UK's Fintech sector to develop London into the 'FinTech capital of the world'	**Fintech policy goal:** N/A
		External factors: Strategic economic partnership with Mainland China	**External factors:** Brexit (5AMLD)	**External factors:** 2008 GFC and use of DLT for criminal and elicit purposes

7.3 LESSONS DISTILLED: A VIEW TO THE FUTURE

On the basis of the conclusions drawn from the analysis set out above, it is possible to distil specific lessons regarding how novel technologies may potentially be regulated in the future. As international financial centres play an important role in the global financial system,[1106] the conclusions reached in this book may be applied more

1106. For the importance of international financial centres *see* Pamela Pogliani, Goetz von Peter & Philip Wooldridge, 'The Outsize Role of Cross-Border Financial Centres' BIS Quarterly Review (13 June 2022) and Irina Solovjova, Ramona Rupeika-Apoga & Inna Romanova, 'Competitiveness Enhancement of International Financial Centres' (2018) XXI(1) European Research Studies Journal 5 https://doi.org/10.35808/ersj/925.

generally as they may influence the actions and behaviours of other jurisdictions. To this end, a set of lessons distilled from the analysis is provided below.

7.3.1 The Role of Competition Policy: Bark Worse than Its Bite

A primary conclusion drawn by this book's analysis is that regulatory competition operated between HK, London, and NY, but only to a limited extent based on the policy goal of maintaining their jurisdictions as leading international financial centres. To this end, it can be deduced that, while regulatory competition may impact policy underlining the rules governing novel technologies, the influence of regulatory competition, or the threat thereof, may not be sufficient to persuade governments to amend or draft laws and regulations in response thereto. On this basis, competition policy may be viewed as no more than a marketing or promotional tool which is leveraged by jurisdictions to advertise their legal and regulatory environments to potential actors. While in the past jurisdictions were constrained by geographical borders, with the advent of the Internet and the rapid advancement of technology, governments are now able to promote their jurisdictions without being constrained by the need for businesses to relocate physically to their jurisdictions. Entrepreneurs are now able to provide their products and services on a cross-border basis, such as through establishing satellite offices or branches, or simply through operating a business by purchasing a registered address (a service available in both HK, London, and NY). Despite this expanded scope for regulatory competition, its influence appears to be minimal.

One reason which may explain this limited influence is the decentralised nature of competition policy, which is ordinarily transmitted through multiple arms of an individual government. In the UK, for example, competition policy is generally transmitted through the roles undertaken by various governmental arms, including the FCA and UKDIT, and even to some extent through the annual royal family speeches. As the analysis evidenced in this book, the absence of a centrally coordinated strategy on competition policy transmission could potentially result in a disconnect between policy aims and its eventual outcome. In the UK the government marketed its business and legal environment as being 'pro-innovation', whereas in reality the decision was made to simply apply the existing regulatory framework to DLT Offerings, in place of developing a technology-forward bespoke framework which is not based entirely on existing rules. This disconnect may have resulted in a failure to meet the market's expectation that the government would provide a 'pro-innovation' legal and regulatory environment, apt for business growth. The expectation of the market in this regard is reflected through the various responses to the UK government's proposed regulation of financial products and services underlined by DLT. For example, in response to the government's stablecoin regulatory regime, industry participants highlighted the need for the government to prioritise innovation and competition with the purpose of attracting firms to the UK, particularly in light of Brexit. The responses also stated that the UK government should ensure that its regulation of cryptoasset activities is 'not more onerous than that' of the regulation in other jurisdictions.[1107] These responses highlight the expectation that the UK government would value a pro-innovation approach, which ultimately considers regulatory competition.

The disconnect between policy aims and eventual outcomes highlights the limited ability of regulatory competition to influence the formulation of the rules which govern novel technologies. As government agendas adjust owing to a multiplicity of factors, such as changes in government and the occurrence of economic and social crises, this disconnect may appear to be an ordinary feature of how modern governments operate. Nevertheless, it should be borne in mind that in the absence of a centrally coordinated strategy on competition policy, it would be challenging for regulatory competition to operate fully, and thus for its influence to be extended more widely. However, in some cases, governments have managed to successfully connect underlying policy's aims and eventual outcomes. In NY, for example, the NYDFS successfully connected its policy aim of modernising financial regulation with the eventual outcome of introducing the world's first bespoke licensing framework for virtual currencies. To this end, the influence of regulatory competition can be clearly evidenced through the NYDFS' actions and behaviours. However, this influence is slightly diluted bearing in mind the NYDFS' primary focus on stimulating economic recovery based on the fallout of the GFC 2008. Accordingly, even where policy aims to connect clearly with eventual outcomes, competition policy forms but one aspect of the broader considerations taken into account by governments based on their varying agendas. Further, while the UK's stance on regulating novel technologies may not be consistently illustrative of a 'pro-innovation' approach, in the past the FCA has chosen to designate new Fintech Offerings as a specific 'regulated activity' under the RAO. This was the case in April 2014 when P2P lending (i.e., crowdfunding) became a regulated activity under the auspices of Article 36H of the RAO.

Accordingly, the lesson to be drawn is that the extent of the influence of regulatory competition on the formulation of rules governing novel technologies will, at times, be dependent on the consistent application of competition policy. However, as the successful transmission of competition policy is based on a myriad of factors, it is doubtful whether rule-based regulatory competition will have a significant impact on how governments formulate rules for financial products and services underlined by novel technologies. In the future, regulators will be faced with having to formulate rules for increasingly complex Fintech Offerings, also requiring consumers to be more sophisticated and knowledgeable. These challenges will be presented by, for example, the proliferation of AI and machine learning, the growth of DeFI, and the further integration of blockchain technology in the financial services sector, which will require proactive responses and regulatory certainty. To this end, a cohesive and centrally coordinated strategy on competition policy transmission would be required should jurisdictions wish to achieve the aims of regulatory competition more broadly on the basis of their regulation of financial products and services underlined by novel

1107. HM Treasury, 'UK Regulatory Approach to Cryptoassets, Stablecoins, and Distributed Ledger Technology in Financial Markets. Response to the Consultation and Call for Evidence' (April 2022), para. 2.22.

technologies. Such a strategy, coordinated by a centralised governmental body, should set out relevant policy goals clearly by identifying potential competing jurisdictions, the means to be used to secure the necessary underlining policy aims (i.e., laws, regulations, and tax incentives), and the market actors and participants (i.e., target audience) to whom the means are directed to.

Utilised this way, and without the need to engage in potential welfare-reducing rules-based regulatory competition, a cohesive and centrally coordinated strategy on competition policy transmission will ensure consistency between policy aims and their eventual outcomes. This will provide market actors and participants deciding where to direct their economic activities with clear and consistent messaging, thus enabling the formulation of regulatory frameworks for Fintech Offerings underlined by cohesive policy aims. In some cases, however, governments may, inadvertently, prefer the decentralised nature of competition policy transmission as it may provide more flexibility and agility, providing better adaptation to unexpected circumstances and events. To this end, some jurisdictions have expressed a preference for flexibility and agility, such as the regulators in HK and the UK who have highlighted their 'agile' powers in formulating regulatory rules to govern Fintech Offerings. However, the application of an 'agile' approach to regulation can be built within a cohesive and centrally coordinated strategy on competition policy transmission. For example, with respect to its proposed stablecoin regime, the UK government indicated that an 'agile' approach would enable regulators to adjust to market developments, based on rules appropriate for consumers and market actors.[1108] At the same time, however, HM Treasury also acknowledged that legislative change could be effected to 'deliver a world-leading' stablecoin regulatory regime, which would promote competition.[1109]

7.3.2 Competitive Advantage: The Last Holdout?

While the primary conclusion drawn by this book's analysis, is that the regulatory competition which operated between HK, London, and NY operated on a limited basis and did not extend to rules-based competition, the jurisdictions made use of competitive advantages to set themselves apart from potential competitors. The term 'competitive advantage' was coined by Michael Porter who proposed that firms should pursue strategies directed at selling high-quality goods at high prices by focussing on value chain activities as the root of competitive advantage.[1110] In the academic literature on business strategy, the term has taken on a more generalised meaning used principally to describe a business strategy which highlights improving a firm's products and

1108. HM Treasury, 'UK Regulatory Approach to Cryptoassets, Stablecoins, and Distributed Ledger Technology in Financial Markets. Response to the Consultation and Call for Evidence' (April 2022), para. 2.25.
1109. HM Treasury, 'UK Regulatory Approach to Cryptoassets, Stablecoins, and Distributed Ledger Technology in Financial Markets. Response to the Consultation and Call for Evidence' (April 2022) 3 and para. 1.14.
1110. Michael E Porter, *The Competitive Advantage: Creating and Sustaining Superior Performance* (NY: Free Press 1986).

services in a specific industry.[1111] This book borrows characteristics of both of the aforementioned uses to characterise competitive advantage as unique or distinguishing features of the regulatory frameworks governing financial products and services underlined by DLT which are used by jurisdictions as the Means to attract (and retain) foreign capital and highly skilled labour. On the basis of this study, the primary competitive advantages used by the concerned jurisdictions can be grouped as distinct: (i) policy features, including the 'first mover advantage'; and (ii) regulatory features, including flexible frameworks and regulatory processes.

The first-mover competitive advantage can simply be described as a firm being in a better off position than its competitors based on it being first to introduce a new product or service to a specific market.[1112] In the context of this study, this principle is applied to the actions and behaviours of governments and focusses on how governments leverage their status in this regard in the operation of regulatory competition. The paradigmatic instance of first-mover advantage in this book is NY, more specifically the NYDFS' introduction of the first bespoke licensing regime and regulatory framework for virtual currencies. The BitLicense regime was introduced at a time when virtual currencies had not yet entered the mainstream. Instead, it was introduced primarily as a response to high-profile cases dealing with illicit uses of virtual currencies (such as the dark web 'SilkRoad' website), and as a result of the economic fallout of the GFC 2008. Nevertheless, its introduction accorded with the NYDFS' policy aims to modernise financial regulation in NY and maintain NY as the world's financial capital. In doing so, it provided the benefit of regulatory certainty to market actors and participants as a result of the coherency created through establishing specific regulatory rules which also considered the technology aspects of the products and services being regulated. However, establishing a regulatory framework and mandatory licensing regime of this nature leaves less room for innovation to thrive, possibly representing a drawback for some market actors.

Further, a first-mover advantage may not always provide the reputation gains and policy outcomes which governments had originally intended. This may occur in particular where the introduction of a product or service to the market is premature or unfounded. Finland, for example, is touted as being the first country in the world to introduce a retail CBDC in the form of its 'Avant Smart Card' system.[1113] This system consisted of the use of smart cards which were preloaded with Finnish markka and functioned in a similar manner as debit and credit cards. However, the smart card system was discontinued in 2006 as it became more expensive to use than simple debit cards on the basis of fees which were later added to enable its use. Avant's downfall also represents a disconnect between policy aims and their eventual outcomes as the

1111. *See*, for example, Fernando Sanchez-Henriquez & Ignacio Pavez, 'The Effect of Open Innovation on Eco-Innovation Performance: The Role of Market Knowledge Sources' (2021) 13(7) Sustainability 3890 https://doi.org/10.3390/su13073890.
1112. *See* Fernando F Suarez & Gianvito Lanzolla, 'The Half-Truth of First-Mover Advantage', (Harvard Business Review, April 2005).
1113. *See* Aleski Grym, 'Lessons Learned from the World's First CBDC' (2020) 8 Bank of Finland Economic Review 2, https://publications.bof.fi/bitstream/handle/10024/43587/BoFER_8_2020.pdf.

smart card was originally introduced with the purpose of reducing consumer costs. An additional example of first-mover advantage going awry, and thus failing to meet its intended policy aims, is the Bahamas' introduction of its regulatory framework for digital assets. According to the Bahamas Financial Services Board, the Bahamas is 'one of the very first jurisdictions in the world to regulate digital assets through a comprehensive body of law'.[1114] On the basis of the first-mover advantage, businesses, including the high-profile digital asset exchange and hedge fund FTX Trading Ltd, moved to the Bahamas to take advantage of the regulatory framework which had been developed to govern digital assets. Former CEO Sam Bankman-Friedman reportedly indicated that he was drawn to the regulatory regime which allowed it to trade options which were riskier and not legal in the US.[1115] Bearing in mind the Securities and Exchanges Commission of Bahamas' objective for its digital asset framework to manage risks, especially systematic and contagion risks,[1116] FTX's subsequent collapse in November 2022, partially caused by a lack of regulatory oversight,[1117] is particularly ironic. The fallout which occurred subsequent to FTX's bankruptcy has since prompted the Bahamian government to tighten its digital assets business regulation through its Digital Assets and Registered Exchanges (DARE) Bill 2024.[1118]

Accordingly, the lesson to be drawn is that while a first-mover advantage can be implemented as a beneficial competitive advantage, particularly through the introduction of bespoke frameworks to regulate financial products and services underlined by novel technologies, taking this approach does invite scrutiny and criticism on an international basis. As such, this competitive advantage should be used with caution and should be developed as part of a centrally coordinated strategy on competition policy transmission which justifies the existence of taking this approach, and which avoids the pitfalls of welfare-reducing regulatory races and the effects of regulatory arbitrage.

Competitive advantage may also take the form of introducing distinct regulatory features, such as adopting a flexible approach to regulatory and licensing conditions or introducing measures which allow for the efficient execution of licensing application procedures. In October 2021, the NYDFS approved PayPal as the first approved entity

1114. Bahamas Financial Services Board, 'The Bahamas: A Complete And Compelling Choice' (2023) 2, https://bfsb-bahamas.com/wp-content/uploads/2023/12/BahamasMini-Edition4Report2023.pdf.
1115. David Yaffe-Bellany, 'How Sam Bankman-Fried's Crypto Empire Collapsed' (The New York Times, 14 November 2022), https://www.nytimes.com/2022/11/14/technology/ftx-sam-bankman-fried-crypto-bankruptcy.html.
1116. Securities and Exchanges Commission of Bahamas, 'The Bahamas Approach to the Regulation of Digital Asset Businesses' (21 September 2022), https://www.scb.gov.bs/wp-content/uploads/2023/04/The-Bahamas-Approach-to-the-Regulation-of-Digital-Asset-Businesses.pdf.
1117. *See* Thomas Conlon, Shaen Corbet & Yang Hu, 'The Collapse of the FTX Exchange: The End of Cryptocurrency's Age of Innocence' (The British Accounting Review, 11 November 2023) https://doi.org/10.2139/ssrn.4283333.
1118. Natario McKenzie, 'New Legislation Tabled in Parliament to Repeal DARE Act and Regulate the Digital Asset Market' (Eye Witness News, 16 May 2024), https://ewnews.com/new-legislation-tabled-in-parliament-to-repeal-dare-act-and-regulate-the-digital-asset-market.

for the conditional BitLicense.[1119] In approving the conditional BitLicense, the NYDFS superintendent expressed that such licences were intended 'to encourage, promote, and assist interested institutions to have a well-regulated way to access the New York virtual currency marketplace in a way that is both timely and protective of New York consumers, through partnerships with New York authorized virtual currency firms'. The superintendent also indicated that the NYDFS 'will continue to encourage and support financial service providers to operate, grow, remain and expand in New York and work with innovators to enable them to germinate and test their ideas, for a dynamic and forward-looking financial services sector'. Overall, therefore, the conditional BitLicense reduces the entry barriers into NY's virtual currency market and encourages market actors to direct their business activities to the city. Further, in 2018, HK's SFC introduced an opt-in regime for virtual asset platforms to voluntarily be included within its regulatory remit through trading at least one securities token. Accordingly, the SFC's requirements relating to AML, cybersecurity, internal audit and controls, private key management, and the safe custody of assets would also apply to such platforms. The advantage provided to virtual asset platforms as a result of this inclusion includes the regulatory certainty and reputational benefits of being regulated by one of the world's leading financial centre regulators. The intended benefits of this regime, however, have not been harnessed by many businesses, as only two virtual asset platforms have been licensed by the SFC under this opt-in regime, as of June 2023.[1120]

In the operation of regulatory competition, and through the transmission of competition policy, these distinct regulatory features provide governments and regulators with a safer approach to attracting market actors to their jurisdictions. In an international regulatory environment where regulatory rules for financial products and services underlined by novel technologies are increasingly being formulated on the basis of analogous principles, standards, and approaches, competitive advantage represents an opportunity for jurisdictions to set themselves apart from other jurisdictions, in place of resorting to welfare reducing rules-based regulatory competition. The adoption of competitive advantages may thus represent the last holdout for the successful influence of regulatory competition on the governance of Fintech Offerings.

7.3.3 Quick to React, Slow to Legislate: Technology Neutrality

On the basis of the analysis set out in this book, the operation of regulatory competition, particularly rules-based competition, is constrained by the widespread adoption of converging international regulatory principles used to govern financial products and

1119. NYDFS, 'Superintendent Linda A. Lacewell Announces PayPal To Be the First Approved Entity for DFS Conditional Bitlicense' (21 October 2021), https://www.dfs.ny.gov/reports_and_publications/press_releases/pr202010211?source = email.

1120. SFC, 'Keynote Speech at Executive Dinner Organised by the Hong Kong Economic and Trade Office in Bangkok, Office for Attracting Strategic Enterprises and InvestHK' (13 June 2023), https://www.sfc.hk/-/media/EN/files/COM/Speech/Bangkok-VA-speech_Eng_20230613.pdf?rev = 60238fdded9242bd8ab42ac483bfd2bc&hash = EADB3B3E5F30C3AED9B207C213008553.

services. These converging regulatory principles act to homogenise legal and regulatory rules which leave little scope for the rule variation required for rules-based competition to operate between jurisdictions successfully.

This appears to be the case largely with the internationally accepted 'technology neutral' principle for regulating financial services. In general, the principle provides that regulatory rules should govern the activities which the specific technology facilitates and the firms engaging in those activities, instead of regulating specific types of technology.[1121] The financial regulatory authorities of several major jurisdictions and quasi-federations, including Australia,[1122] the EU,[1123] Hong Kong, Singapore,[1124] and the UK currently adhere to the technology-neutral principle. It has also been endorsed by several multilateral organisations, including the FSB.[1125] In the EU, technology neutrality has been defined as neither imposing nor discriminating in favour of the use of any type of technology, but rather embracing proportionate steps for promoting specific services, where justified.[1126] This particular reasoning is often justified in tandem with the concept of 'same risk, same regulatory outcome'. According to the EU Parliament, this concept ensures that 'the same activities and services and associated risks are subject to the same rules'.[1127] This concept has also been adopted in several jurisdictions, including both HK and the UK, albeit under differently worded formulations.

The widespread adoption of these regulatory principles highlights the unwillingness of governments worldwide to develop new regulatory rules to govern financial products and services underlined by novel technologies, at least initially. As evidenced in this book, the decisional architecture, which sets out the sequence in which these principles have manifested more broadly, can be viewed through the actions and behaviours of governments, in at least three principle steps. First, an unregulated financial product or service underlined by a novel technology is introduced to the market. In most instances, the public's accelerated use of the relevant financial product or service draws the attention of governments and regulators, particularly where the product or service poses a threat to consumer interests and, at a more advanced stage,

1121. FCA, 'Discussion Paper on Distributed Ledger Technology' (DP17/3) (April 2017), 7, https://www.fca.org.uk/publication/discussion/dp17-03.pdf.
1122. Department of the Treasury (Cth), 'Token Mapping Consultation Paper' (February 2023) 8, https://treasury.gov.au/consultation/c2023-341659 and Stan Wallis et al., *Financial System Enquiry* (Final Report, March 1997), https://treasury.gov.au/publication/p1996-fsi-fr.
1123. Commission of The European Communities Proposal for a European Parliament and Council directive on the taking up, the pursuit and the prudential supervision of the business of electronic money institutions (September 1998) http://aei.pitt.edu/10704/l/.
1124. Monetary Authority of Singapore, 'Reply to Parliamentary Question to Regulation of NFT Activities' (15 February 2023), https://www.mas.gov.sg/news/parliamentary-replies/2022/reply-to-parliamentary-question-on-regulation-of-nft-activities.
1125. FSB, 'FSB Statement on International Regulation and Supervision of Crypto-asset Activities' (11 July 2022), https://www.fsb.org/2022/07/fsb-issues-statement-on-the-international-regulation-and-supervision-of-crypto-asset-activities/.
1126. Directive 2002/21 on a common regulatory framework for electronic communications networks and services [2002] OJL 108/33, recital 18.
1127. European Parliament, 'Markets in Crypto-Assets' (Briefing EU Legislation in Progress, November 2022) 3, https://www.europarl.europa.eu/RegData/etudes/BRIE/2022/739221/EPRS_BRI(2022)739221_EN.pdf.

financial stability. In these circumstances, financial regulatory authorities are prompted to respond appropriately on the basis of their regulatory mandate, in most instances through their mandate to protect consumer interests. Resultantly, and as an initial step, the relevant regulator issues a warning to the public informing them of the unregulated nature of the product or service, and cautioning them against its risky nature for investment purposes. This occurred in several jurisdictions, including both HK and the UK, where the SFC and the FCA, respectively, issued regulatory warnings to the public apprising consumers of the unregulated nature of virtual currencies and cautioning them of the risks associated therewith. Similar warnings have also been issued in relation to ICOs.

Second, as the unregulated product or service underlined by a novel technology gains further traction with the public through its accelerated adoption and use, governments and regulators are compelled to provide a more robust response. In these circumstances, regulators respond comprehensively to the emergence of an unregulated product or service by ensuring that it falls within the perimeter of its regulatory frameworks, where possible. This regulatory response is largely effected by the mechanisms of the technology-neutral principle and the 'same risk, same regulatory outcome' concept. At this point, the novel technology is still emerging, and its use cases still being developed, albeit at quite an advanced pace. Governments and regulators therefore endeavour to understand the novel technology through research initiatives into its benefits and risks. The regulatory response therefore appears to be measured and pragmatic and provides governments and regulators with a shield to justify any regulatory or legislative lag. On this basis, therefore, the two regulatory principles can be harnessed by governments as tools to delay their legal and regulatory responses to the rapid advancement of technology and the emergence of new products and services through the formulation of new rules, such as developing bespoke regulatory frameworks. The use of these tools may be particularly apt where governments and regulators lack the necessary expertise to understand how novel technologies work, and their likely impact based on their benefits and risks to the public at large.[1128]

However, governments and regulators should be cautioned on applying the technology-neutral principle and the 'same risk, same regulatory outcome' concept in too strict of a manner. In some instances, they may need to consider whether technology-specific regulation is actually needed, such as whether technical elements should be accounted for to guard any the existence of any new risks created by the specific technology. While this may not be very common, it is not an entirely new approach as governments have in the past developed rules which incorporate technological requirements. For example, in the UK amendments were effected to the regulatory framework to encompass 'new market and technological paradigms' which resulted from the move from paper-based to dematerialised securities.[1129] Accordingly,

1128. *See* Ross P Buckley, Douglas W Arner & Dirk A Zetzsche, *FinTech: Finance, Technology and Regulation* (Cambridge University Press 2023). *See also* Ross P Buckley et al., 'Building FinTech and Innovation Systems' (2024) 54 CapCo Institute Journal of Financial Transformation 50.

1129. Financial Conduct Authority, 'Discussion Paper on Distributed Ledger Technology' (DP17/3) (April 2017), 23, https://www.fca.org.uk/publication/discussion/dp17-03.pdf.

governments and regulators should survey whether applying these regulatory approaches is particularly apt for their jurisdictions, in place of a wholesale transplant. At a minimum, they should provide clear and consistent messaging on the adoption of these approaches to instil confidence in market actors to provide the necessary regulatory certainty required. In some jurisdictions these regulatory approaches have been applied to proposed regulation of Fintech Offerings in an inconsistent manner, creating doubt as to the manner in which they apply. In Australia, for example, while the Treasury's Proposal Paper on Regulating Digital Asset Platforms endorsed the application of the technology-neutral principle, its proposed rules appeared to account for the specific technical aspects of token-based systems which permit it to carry out the associated functions.[1130] On this basis, governments should ensure that regulatory approaches are adopted with specific intent and understanding to avoid confusion which may impact the rule-making process and the market's understanding of the rules which apply to them.

Third, once governments and regulators have had an opportunity to survey the regulatory landscape and the potential impact of novel technologies thereon, they ordinarily make the decision to introduce new legislation or formulate bespoke regulatory frameworks. However, in most cases, this rule-making action and behaviour is constrained by the need to close gaps within existing legal and regulatory frameworks, rather than to implement entirely new legal and regulatory frameworks. This has occurred in several jurisdictions in relation to developing frameworks to govern regulated activities associated with stablecoins. It is perhaps within these areas that rule-based competition has the most potential to impact the manner in which rules are formulated. In some instances, however, high-profile cases in the media exposing the illicit uses of unregulated products or services underlined by novel technologies may catalyse a more immediate government and regulatory response. This is precisely what occurred in NY on the basis of the development of the BitLicense regulatory framework. In such an instance, in place of applying the 'same risk, same regulatory outcome' concept, regulators decide to formulate news rules through bespoke regulatory frameworks which account for technology-specific requirements. To this end, the former NYDFS Superintendent Lawsky has expressed in the past that the established approach of categorising novel technologies into existing regulatory boxes may not always be the most sensible approach and that regulators should, where appropriate, draft regulation from a creative perspective.[1131] This view, however, may represent an outlier perspective based on the present adoption of converging regulatory principles on an international basis.

Accordingly, the lesson to be drawn is that in the future governments and regulators should decide on whether the internationally accepted regulatory principles apply appropriately, in place of applying a 'one size, fits all' solution which does not

1130. Australian Government: The Treasury, 'Regulating Digital Asset Platforms: Proposal Paper' (October 2023), https://treasury.gov.au/consultation/c2023-427004.

1131. New York Department of Financial Services, 'NYDFS Announces Final BitLicense Framework for Regulating Digital Firms' (Speech of Benjamin M Lawsky, Superintendent of the New York Department of Financial Services, 3 June 2015), http://business.cch.com/srd/NYDFSAnnouncesFinalBitlicenseFramework.pdf.

account appropriately for specific jurisdictional contexts. Such an approach may also assist governments and regulators in avoiding the 'step-wise' movement approach described in this book which may appear to be imitative in the absence of specific considerations offered for the approaches taken. Governments should also gain the required expertise and technology know-how to fully comprehend the novel technologies underlining new financial products and services. Regulators must, in particular, develop deep expertise, skills, and knowledge to enable them to decide appropriately on the manner in which financial products and services underlined by novel technologies should be regulated. On this basis, more scope may be provided for the operation of healthy regulatory competition which influences rule-making processes on a larger scale but avoids welfare-reducing regulatory races. Regulatory competition of this nature may therefore contribute to economic growth and to the creation of additional socio-economic opportunities within the Fintech sector.

CHAPTER 8
Conclusion

This chapter provides a conclusion to this book by setting out its principal aims and conclusions reached. It makes a pointed call for future research and sets out specific suggestions in respect thereto.

This book is concerned primarily with examining the extent to which regulatory competition influences the manner in which jurisdictions formulate rules governing financial products and services underlined by novel technologies. This particular enquiry was examined through the question: to what extent were HK, London, and NY engaged in regulatory competition with each other regarding their governance of financial products and services underlined by DLT during the period 2008-2022? Before embarking on this investigation, this book provided a bird's eye view of the technology forming its subject matter through a consideration of its core technical features, a sample of the types of DLT which exist, and their corresponding applications and use cases. To provide a theoretical foundation for the analyses conducted, a cohesive framework for understanding regulatory competition was conceived by parsing apart its essential elements based on the prevailing academic literature. With these two establishing prongs in mind, the regulatory competition analysis was conducted in respect of each of the concerned jurisdictions through the institutional lenses: Input, Process, Output, and Feedback. These lenses allowed for a methodical and thorough analysis of the actions and behaviours of the governments and regulators of HK, London, and NY to determine whether they were engaged in regulation competition with each other.

The book reached the conclusion that the jurisdictions focussed on developing and enforcing regulatory frameworks characterised by largely similar regulatory features and underlined by largely similar foundational regulatory strategies. As such, while HK, London, and NY were not engaged in rules-based regulatory competition, the analysis highlighted that the jurisdictions did in fact consider regulatory competition in formulating their respective responses to financial products and services underlined by novel technologies. The influence of regulatory competition was seen principally through the actions and behaviours of the jurisdictions to maintain their cities as leading international financial centres and to develop their cities into Fintech hubs. While regulatory competition did not operate between HK, London, and NY on the basis of enforcing lax or stricter regulatory rules, each jurisdiction, however, made use of specific promotional measures to attract foreign capital and highly skilled labour to their respective locales. These measures took the form of competitive advantages and the manner in which regulatory frameworks were delivered.

Most significantly, the conclusions reached by this book distilled three important lessons which provide a view of how regulators may formulate rules for financial products and services underlined by novel technologies in the future. The first lesson set out that, while regulatory competition may impact the policy underlining the rules governing novel technologies, the influence of regulatory competition may not be sufficient to persuade governments to amend or draft laws and regulations in response thereto. To this end, it was intimated that the extent of the influence of regulatory competition on the formulation of these rules will, at times, be dependent on the consistent application of competition policy. As such, to achieve the proper ends of regulatory competition, whose operation may be impacted adversely by the decentralised nature of policy, a cohesive and centrally coordinated strategy on competition policy transmission may be required. The second lesson provided that while jurisdictions may be less inclined to engage in rules-based competition, they may still make use of competitive advantages to set themselves apart from potential competitors. Some of the drawbacks of using these competitive advantages were also discussed. The final lesson considered that the operation of regulatory competition, particularly rules-based competition, will be constrained by the widespread adoption of converging international regulatory principles used to govern financial products and services. To this end, a warning was offered to governments and regulators to fully consider the suitability of applying international regulatory principles to their specific jurisdictions to ensure that it is fit for purpose within their unique contexts.

The author wishes that this book will provide the catalyst for further studies into this area of research, particularly bearing in mind the potential socio-economic impact of regulatory competition, and competition policy more broadly. As such, while this book focussed on the governmental action and behaviour of the governments and regulators of wealthy leading international financial centres, future research should be directed to the actions and behaviours of the governments and regulators within different socio-economic contexts. For example, such research should focus on examining the extent of regulatory competition between different Primary Actors in developing economies. This research focus would facilitate a more nuanced understanding of and provide additional insights into the operation of regulatory competition at an international level, but stratified at distinguishing economic levels. While this book focussed specifically on the case study of the regulation of DLT Offerings within the financial services industry, future research should be conducted on the operation of regulatory competition in different areas of law, or disciplines, through the use of different technologies, products, or services. Overall, this book intends to encourage future discussions on the value, or lack thereof, of the regulatory competition hypothesis among government officials, legislators, regulators, academics and practitioners, from a legal, socio-economic and political perspective. It is hoped that it will provide the foundation upon which future research into regulatory competition could be expanded and honed more deliberately, thus broadening the scope of this area of study.

Bibliography

A. Articles

Abbas SMA & Klemm A, 'A Partial Race to the Bottom: Corporate Tax Developments in Emerging and Developing Economies' (2013) 20 International Tax Public Finance 596.

Alhassan AL & Ohene-Asare K, 'Competition and Bank Efficiency in Emerging Markets: Empirical Evidence from Ghana' (2016) 7(2) African Journal of Economic and Management Studies' 268.

Ali R, 'Innovations in Payments Technologies and the Emergence of Digital Currencies' (2014) Quarterly Bulletin Q3 262.

Ammous S, 'Blockchain Technology: What Is It Good For?' (2019) 34(2) Banking and Finance Law Review 239.

Armour, J, 'Who Should Make Corporate Law? EC Legislation Versus Regulatory Competition' (2005) 58(1) Current Legal Problems 369.

Arner DW, Barberis JN & Buckley RP, 'Fintech, Regtech and the Reconceptualisation of Financial Technology' (2016) Northwestern Journal of International Law and Business 371.

Arner DW, Barberis JN & Buckley RP, 'The Evolution of FinTech: A New Post-Crisis Paradigm?' (2016) 47 Georgetown Journal of International Law 1271.

Barkin JS, 'Racing All Over the Place: A Dispersion Model of international Regulatory Competition' (2015) 21(1) European Journal of International Relations 171.

Barnard C, 'Social Dumping and the Race to the Bottom: Some Lessons for the European Union from Delaware?' (2000) 25 European Law Review 57.

Barzuza M & Smith DC, 'What Happens In Nevada? Self-Selecting into Lax Law' (2004) 27(21) Review of Financial Studies 3593.

Baum I, 'Innovative Regulation Through Competition: A Responsive to Rapidly Evolving Markets' (2016) 49(2) Israel Law Review 197.

Bebchuk L & Hamdani A, 'Vigorous Race or Leisurely Walk: Reconsidering the Competition Over Corporate Charters' (2002) 112 Yale Law Journal 553.

Becht MM, Meyer C & Wagner H, 'Where Do Firms Incorporate? Deregulation and the Cost of Entry' (2008) 14 Journal of Corporate Finance 241.

Berry WD, Fording RC & Hanson RL, 'Reassessing the "Race to the Bottom" in State Welfare Policy' (2003) 65(2) The Journal of Politics 327.

Bhat PI, 'Comparative Method of Legal Research: Nature, Process and Potentiality' (2015) 57(2) Journal of the Indian Law Institute 147.

Böhme R et al., 'Bitcoin: Economics, Technology, and Governance' (2015) 29(2) Journal of Economic Perspectives 213.

Bott J & Milkau U, 'Towards a Framework for the Evaluation and Design of Distributed Ledger Technologies in Banking and Payments' (2016) 10(2) Journal of Payments Strategy and Systems 153.

Brogan J, Baskaran I & Ramachandran N, 'Authenticating Health Activity using Distributed Ledger Technologies' (2018) 16 Computational and Structural Biotechnology Journal 257.

Brueckner JK, 'Welfare Reform and the Race to the Bottom: Theory and Evidence' (2000) 66(3) Southern Economic Journal 505.

Buckley RP & Malady L, 'The New Regulatory Frontier: Building Consumer Demand for Digital Financial Services' (2015) 132(1) The Banking Law Journal 35.

Buitenhek M, 'Understanding and Applying Blockchain Technology in Banking: Evolution or revolutIon?' (2016) 1(2) Journal of Digital Banking 111.

Bu M & Wagner M, 'Racing to the Bottom and Racing to the Top: The Crucial Role of Firm Characteristics in Foreign Direct Investment Choice' (2016) 47 Journal of International Business Studies 1032.

Carney WJ, 'The Political Economy of Competition for Corporate Charters' (1997) 26(1) Journal of Legal Studies 303.

Carruthers BG & Lamoreaux NR, 'Regulatory Races: The Effects of Jurisdictional Competition' (2016) 54(1) Journal of Economic Literature 52.

Cary WL 'Federalism and Corporate Law: Reflections upon Delaware,' (1974) Yale Law Journal 83(4) 663.

Chouinard S, 'The EU and Federalism' (2014) 24(1) Polities and Policies Compared, Regional and Federal Studies 125.

Church A, 'The Rise-and-Fall of Leading International Financial Centers: Factors and Applications' (2018) 7(2) Michigan Business and Entrepreneurial Law Review 299.

Coffee, JC 'Racing Towards the Top?: The Impact of Cross-Listings and Stock Market Competition on International Corporate Governance' (2002) 102(7) Columbia Law Review 1757.

Collins H, 'Methods and Aims of Comparative Contract Law' (1991) 11(3) Oxford Journal of Legal Studies 396.

Collins PA & Hayes MV, 'The Role of Urban Municipal Governments in Reducing Health Inequalities: A Meta-Narrative Mapping Analysis' (2010) 9 International Journal of Equity Health 3.

Costa-Font J, De-Albuquerque F & Doucouliagos H, 'Does Inter-jurisdictional Competition Engender a "Race-to-the-Bottom"? A Meta-Regression Analysis' (2015) 27 Journal of Economics and Politics 488.

Daines R, 'The Incorporation Choices of IPO Firms' (2002) 77(6) New York University Law Review 1559-1611.

Deakin S, 'Two Types of Regulatory Competition: Competitive Federalism Versus Reflexive Harmonisation. A Law and Economics Perspective on Centros' (1999) 2 Cambridge Yearbook of European Legal Studies 231.

Deakin S, 'Legal Diversity and Regulatory Competition' (2006) 12(4) European Law Journal 440.

Des Places SB, 'Taking Legal Rules into Consideration: EU Asylum Policy and Regulatory Competition' (2004) 24 Journal of Public Policy 75.

Dodd P & Leftwich, R 'The Market for Corporate Charters: 'Unhealthy Competition' Versus Federal Regulation' (1980) 53(3) Journal of Business 259-283.

Duanmu J, 'A Race to Lower Standards? Labor Standards and Location Choice of Outward FDI from the BRIC countries' (2014) 23(3) International Business Review 620.

Dong B, Dong J & Zhao X, 'FDI and Environmental Regulation: Pollution Haven or a Race to the Top?' (2012) 41 Journal of Regulatory Economics 233.

Easterbrook FH, 'Antitrust and the Economics of Federalism' (1983) 26 Journal of Law and Economics 29.

Easterbrook FH, 'The Race for the Bottom in Corporate Governance' (2009) 95 Virginia Law Review 685.

Eckhardt M & Kerber W, 'Developing Two-tiered Regulatory Competition in EU Corporate Law: Assessing the Impact of the Societas Privata Europaea' (2014) 41(1) Journal of Law and Society 152.

Eidenmuller H, 'The Transnational Law Market, Regulatory Competition, and Transnational Corporations,' (2011) 18(2) Indiana Journal of Global Legal Studies 707.

Enderwick P & Nagar S, 'The Competitive Challenge of Emerging Markets: The Case of Medical Tourism' (2011) 6(4) International Journal of Emerging Markets 329.

Godfrey N, 'Why is Competition important for Growth and Poverty Reduction' (2008) Paper Presented at the OECD Global Forum on International Investment, Session 1.3.: Competition policy, 27-28 March 2008.

Engel KH, 'State Environmental Standard-setting: Is There a "Race" and Is It "to the Bottom"?' (1997) 48 Hastings Law Journal 271.

Epstein L & King G, 'Empirical Research and the Goals of Legal Scholarship: The Rules of Inference' (2002) 69(1) University of Chicago Law Review 1.

Farber DA & Frickey PP, 'The Jurisprudence of Public Choice' (1987) 65 Texas Law Review 873.

Fenwick M, Kaal WA & Vermeulen EPM, 'Legal Education in the Blockchain Revolution' (2017) 20 V and. J Ent & Tech L 351.

Fischel DR, 'The "Race to the Bottom" Revisited: Reflections on Recent, and Developments in Delaware's Corporation Law' (1981) 76 Northwestern University Law Review 913.

Fleischer V, 'Regulatory Arbitrage' (2010) 89 Texas Law Review 229.

Fombad CM, 'Comparative Research in Contemporary African Legal Studies' (2018) 67(4) Journal of Legal Education 984.

Fowler MR & Bunck JM, 'What Constitutes the Sovereign State?' (1996) 22(4) Review of International Studies 381.

Frantz P & Instefjord N, 'Regulatory Competition and Rules/Principles-Based Regulation' (2018) 45 Journal of Business Financial Accounting 819.

Genschel P & Plumper T, 'Regulatory Competition and International Co-operation' (1997) 4(4) Journal of European Public Policy 626.

Goetz SJ et al., 'Sharing the Gains of Local Economic Growth: Race-to-the-Top Versus Race-to-the-Bottom Economic Development' (2011) 29(3) Environment and Planning C: Government and Policy 428.

Govea R et al., 'Emerging Technologies and Ethics: A Race-to-the-Bottom or the Top' (2012) 109 Journal of Business Ethics 553.

Gupta A & Gupta S, 'Blockchain Technology: Application in Indian Banking Sector' (2019) 19(2) Delhi Business Review 74.

Haddad C & Hornuf L, 'The Emergence of the Global Fintech Market: Economic and Technological Determinants' (2019) 53 Small Bus Econ 81.

Hecock RD & Jepsen EM, 'Should Countries Engage in a Race to the Bottom? The Effect of Social Spending FDI' (2013) 44 World Development 156.

Heyvaert V, 'Regulatory Competition: Accounting for the Transnational Dimension of Environmental Regulation' (2012) 25(1) Journal of Environmental Law 7.

Hollander R & Thornthwaite L, 'Competitive Federalism and Workers' Compensation: Do States Race to the Bottom?' (2018) 53(3) Australian Journal of Political Science 336.

Holman FE, 'Forms of Government' (1946) 32(4) American Bar Association Journal 190.

Holmes OW, 'The Path of the Law' (1897) 10(8) Harvard Law Review 457.

Holzinger K & Sommerer T, '"Race to the Bottom" or "Race to Brussels"? Environmental Competition in Europe' (2011) 49(2) Journal of Common Market Studies 322.

Hornuf L & Linder J, 'End of Regulatory Competition in European Company Law' (2014) Andrássy Working Paper Series No. 33, 6.

Jagannathan M & Pritchard AC, 'Do Delaware CEOs Get Fired?' (2017) 74 Journal of Banking and Finance 85.

Jepkemei B & Kipkebut A, 'Blockchain: A Disruptive Technology in Financial Assets' (2019) 2(9) IRE Journals 38.

Kahan M & Kamar E, 'The Myth of State Competition in Corporate Law' (2002) 55 Stanford Law Review 679.

Kelemen DR, 'The Structure and Dynamics of EU Federalism' (2003) 36(1-2) Comparative Political Studies (2003) 184.

Kerner A, 'Can Foreign Stock Influence Policymaking' (2015) 48(1) Comparative Political Studies 35.

Kim J & Wilson JD, 'Capital Mobility and Environmental Standards: Racing to the Bottom with Multiple Tax Instruments' (1997) 9 Japan and the World Economy 537.

Klöhn L, 'Supranationale Rechtsformen im Europäischen Gesellschaftsrecht' (2012) 76 RabelsZ 300.

Konisky DM, 'Regulatory Attitudes and the Environmental Race to the Bottom Argument' (2007) 18 Journal of Public Administration Research and Theory 321.

Law J, 'How Can We Define Federalism' (2013) 5(3) Perspectives on Federalism 91.

Lucier CA & Gareau BJ, 'From Waste to Resources? Interrogating Race to the Bottom in the Global Environmental Governance of the Hazardous Waste Trade' (2015) 25(2) Journal of World Systems Research 495.

Macey J, 'Delaware: Home of the World's Most Expensive Raincoat' (2005) 33(4) Hofstra Law Review 1131.

Majid MZA & Sufian F, 'Market Structure and Competition in Emerging Market: Evidence from Malaysian Islamic Banking Industry' (2007) 28(2) Journal of Economic Cooperation 99.

Norberg HC, 'Unblocking the Bottlenecks and Making the Global Supply Chain Transparent: How Blockchain Technology Can Update Global Trade' (2019) 12(9) Canadian Affairs Global Institute 4.

Oates WE & Schwab RM, 'Economic Competition Among Jurisdictions: Efficiency Enhancing or Distortion Inducing?' (1988) 35 Journal of Public Economics 333.

Olney WW, 'A Race to the Bottom? Employment Protection and Foreign Direct Investment' (2013) 91(2) Journal of International Economics 191.

Pavelin S & Porter LA, 'Race-to-the-Bottom or -Top at Home or Abroad: Health and Safety Standards and the Multinational Firm' (2011) 42(3) The Economic and Social Review 290.

Pérez-Solà C et al., 'Double-Spending Prevention Fort Bitcoin Zero-Confirmation Transactions' (2019) 18 International Journal of Information Security 451.

Phelan C & Rustichini A, 'Pareto Efficiency and Identity' (2018) 13 Theoretical Economics 979.

Pillania RK, 'Competitiveness and Emerging Markets' (2009) 10(2) Business Strategy Series 90.

Podobnik B et al., 'The Competitiveness Versus the Wealth of a Country' (2012) 678 Science Reports 1.

Polk D, 'New York's Final "BitLicense Rule": Overview and Changes from July 2014 Proposal' (5 June 2015).

Porter G, 'Trade Competition and Pollution Standards: "Race to the Bottom" or "Stuck at the Bottom"?' (1999) 8(2) Journal of Environmental and Development 133.

Radaelli CM, 'The Puzzle of Regulatory Competition' (2014) 24 Journal of Public Policy 1.

Reitz JC, 'How to Do Comparative Law' (1998) 46(4) The American Journal of Comparative Law 617.

Revesz RL, 'Rehabilitating Interstate Competition: Rethinking the Race-to-the-Bottom Rationale for Federal Environmental Regulation' (1992) 67 New York University Law Review 1210.

Ringe WG, 'Corporate Mobility in the European Union: A Flash in the Plan' (2013) 10 European Company and Financial Law Review 230.

Roe MJ, 'Delaware's Competition' (2003) 117 Harvard Law Review 588.

Romano R, 'Law as a Product: Some Pieces of the Incorporation Puzzle' (1985) 1(2) Journal of Law, Economics, & Organization 225.

Romano R, 'Competition for Corporate Charters and the Lesson of Takeover Statutes' (1993) 61(4) Fordham Law Review 843.

Romano R, 'Empowering Investors: A Market Approach to Securities Regulation' (1998) 107 Yale Law Journal 2361.

Sandstrom G, 'Is Blockchain an "Evolutionary" or "Revolutionary" Technology, and So What If It Is?: Digitally Extending Satoshi Nakamoto's Distributed Ledger Innovation' (2019) 8(3) Social Epistemology Review and Reply Collective 17.

Schueffel P, 'Taming the Beast: A Scientific Definition of Fintech' (2016) 32 Journal of Innovation Management 32.

Sinn HW, 'The Selection Principle and Market Failure in Systems Competition' (1997) 66 Journal of Public Economics 247.

Snidal D, 'Coordination Versus Prisoners' Dilemma: Implications for International Cooperation and Regimes' (1985) 79 American Political Science Review 923.

Subramanian G, 'The Disappearing Delaware Effect' (2004) 20(1) Journal of Law, Economics, and Organization 32.

Swire PP, 'The Race to Laxity and the Race to Undesirability: Explaining Failures in Competition Among Jurisdictions in Environmental Law' (1996) 14(2) Yale Law and Policy Review 87.

Tiebout C, 'A Pure Theory of Local Expenditures' (1956) 64(5) Journal of Political economy 416.

Trachtman JP, 'International Regulatory Competition, Externalization and Jurisdiction' (1993) 34(1) Harvard International Law Journal 47.

Van Loo R, 'Making Innovation More Competitive: The Case of Fintech' (2018) 65 UCLA Law Review 232.

Vezina PL, 'Race-to-the-Bottom Tariff Cutting' (2014) 22(3) Review of International Economics 444.

Whitfield E, 'China and the Great Doubling: Racing to the Top or Bottom of Global Labour Standards?' (2016) 7 Global Policy 37.

Willborn SL, 'Labor Law and the Race to the Bottom' (2014) 65(2) Mercer Law Review 369.

Winter RK, 'State Law, Shareholder Protection, and the Theory of the Corporation' (1977) 6 Journal of Legal Studies 251.

Yu PM, 'To Form a More Perfect Union? Federalism and Informal Interstate Cooperation' (1989) 102 Harvard Law Review 842.

B. Books

Armour J et al., *Principles of Financial Regulation* (OUP 2016).

Arner DW, *Financial Stability, Economic Development and the Role of Law* (New York: Cambridge University Press 2017).

Arner DW et al., 'Policy and Regulatory Challenges of Distributed Ledger Technologies and Digital Assets in Asia' in Chris Brummer (ed.), *Cryptoassets* (OUP USA 2019).

Babbie ER, *The Practice of Social Research* (12th edn, Belmont, CA: Wadsworth Cengage 2010).

Baldwin R & Cave M, *Understanding Regulation: Theory, Strategy and Practice* (OUP 1999).

Barnard C, 'Regulating Competitive Federalism in the European Union? The Case of EU Social Policy' in Jo Shaw (ed.), *Social Law and Policy in an Evolving European Union* (Hart Publishing 2000).

Bloom BS, *Taxonomy of Educational Objectives: The Classification of Educational Goals* (New York: Longmans, Green 1956).

Bradney A, 'The Place of Empirical Legal Research in the Law School Curriculum' in Peter Cane and Herbert Kritzer (eds), *The Oxford Handbook of Empirical Legal Research*, (OUP 2010).

Bratton W & McCahery J, 'Fiscal Federalism, Jurisdictional Competition, and Tax Coordination: Translating Theory to Policy in the European Union' in Daniel C Esty & Damien Geradin (eds), *Regulatory Competition and Economic Integration* (OUP 2001).

Bulner M, *Law and Society* (London: Routledge and Kegan 1974).

Burgess M, *Federalism and European Union: The Building of Europe, 1950-2000* (Routledge, London 2000).

Burton M, 'Doing Empirical Research: Exploring the Decision-Making of Magistrates and Juries' in Dawn Watkins & Mandy Burton (eds), *Research Methods in Law* (Routledge 2017).

Dionne AM & Macey JR, 'Offshore Finance and Onshore Market: Racing to the Bottom or Moving Toward Efficient?' in Andrew P Morriss et al. (eds), *Offshore Financial Centers and Regulatory Competition* (AEI Press 2010).

Cammiss S & Watkins D, 'Legal Research in the Humanities' in Dawn Watkins & Mandy Burton (eds), *Research Methods in Law* (2nd edn, London Routledge 2018).

Cane P & Kritzer H, *The Oxford Handbook of Empirical Legal Research* (OUP USA 2010).

Cryer R, Hervey T & Sokhi-Bulley B, *Research Methodologies in EU and International Law* (Hart 2011).

Denzin NK & Lincoln YS, 'Introduction: The Discipline and Practice of Qualitative Research' in Norman K Denzin & Yvonna S Lincoln (eds), *The Sage Handbook of Qualitative Research* (Sage 2005).

De Filippi P & Wright A, *Blockchain and the Law* (Harvard University Press 2018).

Dobson I & Johns F, 'Legal Research as Qualitative Research' in Mike McConville (ed.), *Research Methods for Law* (2nd edn, Edinburgh University Press 2007).

Esty DC & Geradin D, 'Regulatory Co-opetition' in Daniel C Esty & Damien Geradin (eds), *Regulatory Competition and Economic Integration* (OUP 2001).

Golding L, *Local Government* (Leonard Cutts ed., 3rd edn, The English Universities Press Ltd 1964).

Hage J, 'Comparative Law as Method and the Method of Comparative Law' in Maurice Adams & Dirk Heirbaut (eds), *The Method and Culture of Comparative Law* (Hart, Oxford 2014).

Henn M, Weinstein M & Foard N, *A Critical Introduction to Social Research* (2nd edn, Sage 2006).

Hensler DR, *Designing Empirical Legal Research* (5th edn, 2018).

Hertig G, 'Regulatory Competition for EU Financial Services' in Daniel C Esty & Damien Geradin (eds), *Regulatory Competition and Economic Integration* (OUP 2001).

Hirschman A, *Exit, Voice, and Loyalty: Responses to Decline in Firms, Organizations, and State* (Harvard University Press 1970).

Hutchinson T, 'Doctrinal Research: Researching the Jury' in Dawn Watkins & Mandy Burton (eds), *Research Methods in Law* (Routledge 2017).

Künnapas K, 'From Bitcoin to Smart Contracts: Legal Revolution or Evolution from the Perspective of De Lege Ferenda?' in T Kerikmäe T & Rull A (eds), *The Future of Law and eTechnologies* (Springer 2016).

Mark R, *Minority Verdict* (London: BBC Publications 1972).

McConville M & Chui WH, *Research Methods for Law* (2nd edn, Edinburgh University Press 2007).

Mills D et al., 'Distributed Ledger Technology in Payments, Clearing, and Settlement' (2016) Finance and Economics Discussion Series 095.

Milward A, *The European Rescue of the Nation-State* (Routledge 1992).

Mol APJ, 'Ecological Modernization: Industrial Transformations and Environmental Reform' in Redclift & Woodgate (eds), *The International Handbook of Environmental Sociology* (Elgar Publishing 1997).

Moravcsik A, 'European Federalism: Rhetoric and Reality' in Nicolaidis Kalypso & Howse Robert (eds), *The Federal Vision: Legitimacy and Levels of Governance in the United States and the European Union* (OUP 2001).

Morriss AP, 'The Role of Offshore Financial Centers in Regulatory Competition' in Andrew P Morriss et al. (eds), *Offshore Financial Centers and Regulatory Competition* (AEI Press 2010).

Muijs D, *Doing Quantitative Research in Education with SPSS* (2nd edn, London: Sage Publications 2010).

Murphy DE, *The Structure of Regulatory Competition: Corporations and Public Policies in a Global Economy* (OUP 2004).

O'Hara EA & Ribstein LE, *The Law Market* (OUP 2009).

Paris ML, 'The Comparative Method in Legal Research: The Art of Justifying Choices' in Laura Cahillane & Jennifer Sweppe (eds), *Legal Research Methods: Principles and Practicalities* (Clarus Press 2016).

Parker I, 'Qualitative Research' in Peter Banister et al. (eds), *Qualitative Methods in Psychology: A Research Guide* (OUP 1994).

Pendleton M, 'Rejecting the Dominance of Empirical Legal Scholarship: A Better Way of Choosing, Researching and Writing a Scholarly Article' in Mike McConville & Wing Hong Chui (eds), *Research Methods for Law* (2nd edn, Edinburgh University Press 2007).

Riker W, 'Federalism' in Greenstein Fred & Polsby Nelson (eds), *Handbook of Political Science* (Addison-Wesley 1975).

Salter M & Mason J, *Writing Law Dissertations: An Introduction and Guide to the Conduct of Legal Research* (Pearson 2007).

Sancton A, 'Canadian Cities in Transition: The Twenty-First Century' in Trudy Bunting & Pierre Filion (eds), *The Municipal Role in the Governance of Canadian Cities* (OUP 2000).

Schmitter P, 'Some Alternative Futures for the European Polity and Their Implications for European Public Policy' in Yves Mény, Pierre Muller & Jean-Louis Quermonne (eds), *Adjusting to Europe: the Impact of the European Union on National Institutions and Policies* (Routledge 1996).

Sinn HW, 'The New Systems Competition' Yrjö Jahnsson lectures (Blackwell Publishing Ltd UK 2003).

Van Boom WH, Desmet P & Mascini P, 'Empirical Legal Research: Chartering the Terrain' in Willem H van Boom, Pieter Desmet & Peter Mascini (eds), *Empirical legal research in action: Reflections on methods and their application* (Edward Elgar Publishing Limited 2018).

Vietor RHK, *How Countries Compete: Strategy, Structure, and Government in the Global Economy* (Harvard Business School Press 2007).

Vogel D, *Trading Up: Consumer and Environmental Regulation in a Global Economy* (Harvard University Press 1995).

Watkins D & Burton M, *Research Methods in Law* (2nd edn, London Routledge 2018).

Webley L, 'Qualitative Approaches to Empirical Legal Research' in Peter Cane & Herbert M Kritzer (eds), *The Oxford handbook of empirical legal research* (OUP 2010).

Wheare K, *Federal Government* (OUP 1946).

Wilson J, 'Capital Mobility and Environmental Standards: Is There a Theoretical Basis for a Race to the Bottom?' in J Bhagwati & R Hudec (eds), *Fair trade and harmonization: Prerequisites for free trade*? (Cambridge: MIT Press 1996).

Index

A

Agile powers, 163, 166, 207, 213, 220
American Institute of Certified Public Accounts, 191
Anti-money laundering (AML), 43, 48, 124–129, 131, 132, 145, 155, 159–161, 166, 177, 179, 180, 184, 186, 204, 206, 208, 212, 213, 223
Artificial Intelligence (AI), 219
ARPANET, The, 31
Avant smart card, 221

B

Bahamas Financial Services Board, 222
Benjamin Lawsky, 178
Binance, 48, 49
BitLicense, 184, 189–190
Brexit, 55, 218
Buterin, Vitalik, 30

C

Central bank digital currencies (CBDC), 2, 24, 42, 113, 130, 221
Chicago Mercantile Exchange, 119
Coin-listing, New York, 188, 189, 192
Competitive advantages, 17, 204, 214–217, 220–223, 230
Competitive appetites, 13, 15, 107, 143, 174, 209, 211, 212, 214
Competitive federalism, 60, 65, 68, 87, 91
Conditional BitLicense, 186, 189–190, 204, 214, 223
Constitution, United States, 170
Contracts-for-difference (CFDs), 120, 149, 154
'Controlled investments', 161, 162
Counter-Financing of Terrorism (CFT), 126, 127, 204, 206, 208, 212
Cryptoasset, 155–158, 161–163
Cryptoasset Taskforce, 150, 154, 161, 200
Cryptocurrency
  Bitcoin, 9, 17, 20, 21, 25, 26, 33, 34, 37, 39, 44–50, 52, 53, 109, 116, 119, 120, 145, 176, 180, 183, 202
  Ethereum, 9, 30, 39, 45, 51
  Mastercoin, 50
  Tether, 9
Cryptocurrency exchanges
  Bitstamp, 49
  Coinbase, 49
  FTX Trading Ltd, 222
  Mt. Gox, 48, 176, 183
  OKEx, 49
  UEEx, 49
  Zedcex Exchange, 49
Crypto-winter, 46
Cyber libertarianism, 20–22
Cyber security, 5, 51, 147, 174, 176, 179, 180, 184

D

Decentralised Finance (DeFI), 9, 219
Delaware, 7, 17, 80, 87, 90
Dematerialised securities, 225
Digicash, 21
Distributed ledger technologies (DLT)
- altcoins, 45
- asset-agnostic, 26, 27
- Blockchain technology, 38–39
- Cryptography, 36–37
- decentralisation, 30
- Directed Acyclic Graph (DAG), 39–40
- distributed database, 29–31
- general purpose technology, 5, 25, 26, 42
- Hashgraph, 39
- Holochain, 40–41
- Mining, 22, 32, 38, 40
- nodes, 22, 26, 28, 29, 31–42
- payment rail, 52–54, 145
- permissioned ledgers, 29
- peer-to-peer (P2P), 31-32
- Practical Byzantine Fault Tolerance (pBFT), 35–36
- prove-of-stake, 34–35
- prove-of-work, 33–34
- public ledgers, 41–42
- smart contracts, 43
- Tempo (Radix), 41–42
- tokenisation, 43

Double-spending problem, 21, 22, 44

F

Faster Payment Services, 54
Federal Deposit Insurance Corporation, 191
'Financial instrument', 149, 156, 158, 204
Financial Crimes Enforcement Network (FinCEN), 177–178
Fintech Advisory Group, 106, 110
Fintech Career Accelerator Scheme 2.0, 114, 116
Fintech Contact Point, 106, 109, 110
Fintech Facilitation Office, 106, 109, 110
Fintech Supervisory Sandbox, 106, 114, 116
First mover advantage, 171, 176, 183, 186, 198, 202, 221, 222
Fourth Industrial Revolution, The, 13, 22, 23
Fund distribution, 118–119, 130
Futures contracts, 119–123, 125

G

Global Financial Crisis (GFC), 2008, 135, 137, 138, 172, 173, 175, 184, 199, 202, 211, 215, 219, 221
Global FinTech Rankings, 4, 99, 134, 170
Greenlisting coins, 189, 192

H

Headquarters economy, 107

I

Incentives-based competition, 79, 81
Initial Coin Offering (ICO), 49–51
International Organization of Securities Commissions (IOSCO), 128, 132
Internet of Things, The, 24
Intra-national regulatory competition
- government departments, 68–69
- local governments, 66–67
- national governments, 69–70

International regulatory competition
- Sovereign nation-states, 70–71

Institutional lens theme
- Feedback, 205–208
- Input, 196–199
- Output, 203–205
- Process, 199–202

L

Lagarde, Christine, 2, 56
Local governments, 57, 65–67, 70, 85
London-Hong Kong Financial Services Forum, 106
London Stock Exchange (LSE), 138

M

Machine learning, 219
Market manipulation, 187, 192, 193, 207, 208
McKinsey Global Institute, 4
Monetary Authority of Singapore, 114
Mortgage crisis, 172, 175

N

Nakamoto, Satoshi, 20, 21, 25, 44
NY State Empire State Development Corporation (NYESD), 172
New York Stock Exchange (NYSE), 170

P

Pareto-efficiency, 85
PayPal, 52, 222
Ponzi scheme, 176
Porter, Michael, 220
Prisoner's dilemma, 88, 89
Pro-active approach, 177, 178, 182, 183, 186, 193, 202
Pro-innovation, 140, 145, 211, 218, 219
Proportionate regulation, 129, 145, 155, 165, 207

R

Race to the bottom
  Corporate charter competition, 89
  EU corporate charter competition, 90
  Delaware effect, 87–88
  Siège reel doctrine, 90
Race to the top
  California effect, 92–94
Real-time gross settlement (RTGS), 147
Regional government, 59, 68
Regulatory arbitrage, 7, 129, 131, 146, 154, 160–161, 167, 208, 222
Regulatory sandbox, 3, 109, 114, 141, 144, 146, 198, 214
Reflexive harmonisation, 91
Risk-based approach, 125, 205
Rules-based competition, 14, 58, 79, 80, 209–210, 212, 213, 215, 220, 223, 224, 230

S

Same business, same risks, same rules principle, 131, 206, 207
Same risk, same regulatory outcome approach, 164, 166
'Securities', 5, 7, 21, 23, 30, 39, 42, 50, 52, 54, 61, 89, 100–102, 113, 117–128, 131, 147, 149, 151, 152, 158, 162–164, 174, 176, 179, 180, 184, 203, 204, 206, 214, 222, 223, 225
Securities and Exchanges Commission of Bahamas, 222
Security token offerings (STO), 118, 125
Security tokens, 50, 118, 123, 152, 162–164
Schueffel, Patrick, 3, 4
Silk Road, The, 11, 176, 177, 183
Small and medium-sized enterprises (SMEs), 50–51
'Specified investment', 148, 150, 156–158, 204
Stablecoin, 129, 163–165, 190–192
Standard Chartered Bank, 174
Step-wise' or parallel movement, 17, 198, 207, 213, 214, 227
Systems of government
  autocracy, 64, 65
  constitutional monarchy, 64, 134, 209
  democracy, 134, 170, 209
  federalism, 60
  quasi-federalism, 60

republic, 64, 170, 209
SWIFT, 21, 53

T

Technology neutral, 109, 111, 114–116, 146, 147, 154, 201, 202, 223–227
Tiebout, Charles
Perfect mobility, 86
Tiebout's equilibrium, 185–187
Tiebout's model, 57, 62, 65, 74, 78, 85
Trading platforms, 123–124, 127–128

U

United Nations
Human Development Index, 99, 133, 170
Sustainable Development Goals, 4, 11
Unregulated cryptoassets, 151, 152, 160–163, 166, 206, 208

V

Virtual assets, 128–129
Virtual currency, 179, 180, 183, 184, 187, 189, 192, 193, 200, 202, 204, 208, 212, 223
Virtual currency firms, 179, 180, 183, 184, 187, 189, 192, 193, 200, 202, 204, 208, 212, 223

W

Watch and learn approach, 153, 154, 202
Winklevoss twins, 178
World cities, 138
World Competitive Ranking, 133–134, 170
World Justice Project Rule of Law Index, 133, 170

INTERNATIONAL BANKING AND FINANCE LAW SERIES

1. Jan Job de Vries Robbe, *Innovations in Securitisation. Yearbook 2006*, 2006 (ISBN 90-11-2533-7).
2. Jim Bartos, *United States Securities Law: A Practical Guide*, Third edition, 2006 (ISBN 90-411-2362-8).
3. Hui Huang, *International Securities Markets: Insider Trading Law in China*, 2006 (ISBN 90-411-2557-4).
4. Barth et al., *Financial Restructuring and Reform in Post-WTO China*, 2007 (ISBN 90-411-2573-6).
5. Zhongfei Zhou, *Banking Laws in China*, 2007 (ISBN 978-90-411-2519-4).
6. Jan Job de Vries Robbe & Paul Ali, *Expansion and Diversification in Securitization Yearbook 2007*, 2007 (ISBN 978-90-411-2661-0).
7. Ross Buckley, *International Financial System. Policy and Regulation*, 2008 (ISBN 978-90-411-2746-4).
8. Jan Job de Vries Robbe, *Securitization Law and Practice: In the Face of the Credit Crunch*, 2008 (ISBN 978-90-411-2715-0).
9. Phoebus Athanassiou, *Hedge Fund Regulation in the European Union: Current Trends and Future Prospects*, 2009 (ISBN 978-90-411-2856-0).
10. Jan Job de Vries Robbe, *Structured Finance: On from the Credit Crunch: The Road to Recovery*, 2009 (ISBN 978-90-411-2787-7).
11. Gaetane Schaeken Willemaers, *The EU Issuer-Disclosure Regime: Objectives and Proposals for Reform*, 2011 (ISBN 978-90-411-3394-6).
12. Panagiotis Delimatsis & Nils Herger (eds), *Financial Regulation at the Crossroads: Implications for Supervision, Institutional Design and Trade*, 2011 (ISBN 978-90-411-3355-7).
13. Raffaele Scalcione, *The Derivatives Revolution: A Trapped Innovation and a Blueprint for Regulatory Reform*, 2011 (ISBN 978-90-411-3430-1).
14. Douglas Arner & Ross Buckley, *From Crisis to Crisis: The Global Financial System and Regulatory Failure*, 2011 (ISBN 978-90-411-3354-0).
15. Anton P. Trichardt, *Letters of Comfort: A Trans-Systemic Analysis*, 2012 (ISBN 978-90-411-3600-8).
16. Eddy Wymeersch, *Alternative Investment Fund Regulation*, 2012 (ISBN 978-90-411-3690-9).
17. Asif H. Qureshi & Xuan Gao (eds), *International Economic Organizations and Law: The Perspective and Role of the Legal Counsel*, 2012 (ISBN 97890-411-3427-1).
18. Rhys Bollen, *The Law and Regulation of Payment Services: A Comparative Study*, 2012 (ISBN 978-90-411-3818-7).
19. Ramandeep Kaur Chhina, *Standby Letters of Credit in International Trade*, 2012 (ISBN 978-90-411-4560-4).

20. Dirk Zetzsche (ed.), *The Alternative Investment Fund Managers Directive*, Third Edition, 2020 (ISBN 978-94-035-0910-5).
21. Lorenzo Sasso, *Capital Structure and Corporate Governance: The Role of Hybrid Financial Instruments*, 2013 (ISBN 978-90-411-4843-8).
22. Pablo Iglesias-Rodríguez, *The Accountability of Financial Regulators: A European and International Perspective*, 2013 (ISBN 978-90-411-3874-3).
23. Seraina Neva Grünewald, *The Resolution of Cross-Border Banking Crises in the European Union: A Legal Study from the Perspective of Burden Sharing*, 2014 (ISBN 978-90-411-4909-1).
24. Megan Bowman, *Banking on Climate Change: How Finance Actors and Transnational Regulatory Regimes are Responding*, 2015 (ISBN 978-90-411-5223-7).
25. Jin Sheng, *China's Listed Companies: Conflicts, Governance and Regulation*, 2015 (ISBN 978-90-411-5925-0).
26. Sven Schelo, *Bank Recovery and Resolution*, Second Edition, 2020 (ISBN 978-94-035-1881-7).
27. Luis M. Hinojosa–Martínez & José María Beneyto (eds), *European Banking Union: The New Regime*, 2015 (ISBN 978-90-411-5263-3).
28. Gill North, *Effective Company Disclosure in the Digital Age*, 2015 (ISBN 978-90-411-3815-6).
29. Hanneke Wegman, *Investor Protection: Towards Additional EU Regulation of Investment Funds?*, 2016 (ISBN 978-90-411-5252-7).
30. Ruth Plato-Shinar, *Banking Regulation in Israel: Prudential Regulation versus Consumer Protection*, 2016 (ISBN 978-90-411-6791-0).
31. Bader Alkhaldi, *Saudi Capital Market: Developments and Challenges*, 2017 (ISBN 978-90-411-8351-4).
32. Yves Mauchle, *Bail-In and Total Loss-Absorbing Capacity (TLAC): Legal and Economic Perspectives on Bank Resolution with Functional Comparisons of Swiss and EU Law*, 2017 (ISBN 978-90-411-8998-1).
33. Uzma Ashraf Barton, *Rethinking Regulation of International Finance: Law, Policy and Institutions*, 2018 (ISBN 978-90-411-8838-0).
34. Phoebus L. Athanassiou, *Digital Innovation in Financial Services: Legal Challenges and Regulatory Policy Issues*, 2018 (ISBN 978-90-411-8781-9).
35. Gu Bin, *The Law and Governance of the Asian Infrastructure Investment Bank*, 2019 (ISBN 978-94-035-0631-9).
36. Gerald Nels Olson, *Money, Morality and Law: A Case for Financial Crisis Accountability*, 2019 (ISBN 978-94-035-0941-9).
37. Scott Farrell, *Banking on Data: Evaluating Open Banking and Data Rights in Banking Law*, 2023 (ISBN 978-94-035-3116-8).
38. Jan Meyers, *A European Central Bank Standing Guard over a European Currency Union*, 2024 (ISBN 978-94-035-2148-0).
39. Lucien J. van Romburg, *Digital Finance and Regulatory Competition: Regulating Distributed Ledger Technology-Based Financial Products and Services*, 2025 (ISBN 978-94-035-4518-9).

www.ingramcontent.com/pod-product-compliance
Lightning Source LLC
Chambersburg PA
CBHW071330230926
51849CB00002B/359

* 9 7 8 9 4 0 3 5 4 5 1 8 9 *